D1231927

VISUAL INFORMATION
PROCESSING

CONTRIBUTORS

John D. Bransford
Patricia A. Carpenter
William G. Chase
Herbert H. Clark
Lynn A. Cooper
John R. Hayes
Marcia K. Johnson

Marcel Adam Just
David Klahr
Allen Newell
Michael I. Posner
Roger N. Shepard
Herbert A. Simon
Tom Trabasso

ACADEMIC PRESS RAPID MANUSCRIPT REPRODUCTION

VISUAL INFORMATION PROCESSING

Edited by

WILLIAM G. CHASE

Department of Psychology
Carnegie–Mellon University
Pittsburgh, Pennsylvania

Proceedings of the Eighth Annual Carnegie Symposium
on Cognition, Held at the Carnegie-Mellon University
Pittsburgh, Pennsylvania, May 19, 1972

ACADEMIC PRESS New York and London 1973

A Subsidiary of Harcourt Brace Jovanovich, Publishers

COPYRIGHT © 1973, BY ACADEMIC PRESS, INC.
ALL RIGHTS RESERVED.
NO PART OF THIS PUBLICATION MAY BE REPRODUCED OR
TRANSMITTED IN ANY FORM OR BY ANY MEANS, ELECTRONIC
OR MECHANICAL, INCLUDING PHOTOCOPY, RECORDING, OR ANY
INFORMATION STORAGE AND RETRIEVAL SYSTEM, WITHOUT
PERMISSION IN WRITING FROM THE PUBLISHER.

ACADEMIC PRESS, INC.
111 Fifth Avenue, New York, New York 10003

United Kingdom Edition published by
ACADEMIC PRESS, INC. (LONDON) LTD.
24/28 Oval Road, London NW1

Library of Congress Cataloging in Publication Data

Symposium on Cognition, 8th, Carnegie-Mellon
University, 1972.
   Visual information processing; proceedings.

   1. Human information processing–Congresses.
2. Imagery (Psychology)–Congresses. 3. Visual
perception–Congresses. I. Chase, William G., ed.
II. Carnegie-Mellon University. III. Title.
BF455.S94 1972   150.1'4   72-9989
ISBN 0-12-170150-6

PRINTED IN THE UNITED STATES OF AMERICA

NMU LIBRARY

TO MOM, DAD, AND MICKI

CONTENTS

CONTRIBUTORS   xi
PREFACE   xiii

Part I. Visual Processes in Cognition

Chapter 1. Quantification Processes   3
David Klahr

Quantification Operators   4
Experiment I   10
Experiment II   14
Experiment III   19
Quantification Models   20
Summary and Conclusion   31

Chapter 2. Coordination of Internal Codes   35
Michael I. Posner

Encoding   37
Search of Active Memory   42
Rehearsal and Translation   51
Visual and Kinesthetic (Haptic) Codes   62
Conclusions   66

Chapter 3. Chronometric Studies of the Rotation of Mental Images . .   75
Lynn A. Cooper and Roger N. Shepard

Introduction and Background.   75
Review of Preceding Reaction-Time Studies of
    Mental Rotation   85
Experiment I: Determination of the Times Required
    to Prepare for and to Respond to a Rotated Stimulus . .   92
Experiment II: Demonstration of a Correspondence
    between an Imagined and an Actual Rotation   140
Conclusions   162

CONTENTS

Chapter 4. On the Function of Visual Imagery in Elementary
Mathematics   177
John R. Hayes

Study 1   179
Study 2   189
Study 3   194
Study 4   199
Studies 5 and 6   202
Study 7   207
Study 8   209
Conclusions   211

Chapter 5. The Mind's Eye in Chess   215
William G. Chase and Herbert A. Simon

Experiments on Chess Perception   215
An Information Processing Theory   244
Further Experiments on Chess Skill   252
Cognitive Processes in Chess   267
Conclusion   278

Chapter 6. You Can't Play 20 Questions with Nature and Win:
Projective Comments on the Papers of this Symposium . .   283
Allen Newell

Detection   284
Diagnosis   293
Prognosis   300
Conclusion   305

Part II. Visual Processes in Linguistic Comprehension

Chapter 7. On the Meeting of Semantics and Perception   311
*Herbert H. Clark, Patricia A. Carpenter,
and Marcel Adam Just*

Three Hypotheses   315
Negatives   317
Locatives   328
Comparatives   335
Spatial Adjectives   350
Concluding Remarks   376

CONTENTS

Chapter 8. Considerations of Some Problems of Comprehension . . 383
John D. Bransford and Marcia K. Johnson

Comprehension as a Process of Creating Semantic
    Products 384
Semantic Prerequisites for Comprehension 392
Alternative Contexts 415
Towards a Schematic Characterization of the
    Problem of Comprehension 420
Concluding Comments. 434

Chapter 9. Discussion of the Papers by Bransford and Johnson;
and Clark, Carpenter, and Just: Language and Cognition . 439
Tom Trabasso

Clark, Carpenter, and Just 441
Bransford and Johnson 448
Cognitive Strategies. 454

Part III. Information Processing Models

Chapter 10. Production Systems: Models of Control Structures . . . 463
Allen Newell

PSG: A Particular Production System 465
The Sternberg Paradigm 472
The Decoding Hypothesis. 496
Applications of the Theory 506
Conclusion 515

Chapter 11. A Production System for Counting, Subitizing,
and Adding 527
David Klahr

Productions Systems: A Theory and Language for
    Process Models 528
Subitizing 533
Addition 537
Counting 538
Conclusion 544

AUTHOR INDEX 547
SUBJECT INDEX 553

CONTRIBUTORS

Numbers in parentheses indicate pages on which the author's contributions begin.

John D. Bransford (383), Department of Psychology, State University of New York at Stony Brook, Stony Brook, New York 11790

Patricia A. Carpenter (311), Department of Psychology, Stanford University, Stanford, California 94305

William G. Chase (215), Department of Psychology, Carnegie-Mellon University, Pittsburgh, Pennsylvania 15213

Herbert H. Clark (311), Department of Psychology, Stanford University, Stanford, California 94305

Lynn A. Cooper (75), Department of Psychology, Stanford University, Stanford, California 94305

John R. Hayes (177), Department of Psychology, Carnegie-Mellon University, Pittsburgh, Pennsylvania 15213

Marcia K. Johnson (383), Department of Psychology, State University of New York at Stony Brook, Stony Brook, New York 11790

Marcel Adam Just (311), Department of Psychology, Stanford University, Stanford, California 94305

David Klahr (3, 527), Department of Psychology, Carnegie-Mellon University, Pittsburgh, Pennsylvania 15213

Allen Newell (283, 463), Computer Science Department, Carnegie-Mellon University, Pittsburgh, Pennsylvania 15213

Michael I. Posner (35), Department of Psychology, University of Oregon, Eugene, Oregon 97403

Roger N. Shepard (75), Department of Psychology, Stanford University, Stanford, California 94305

CONTRIBUTORS

Herbert A. Simon (215), Department of Psychology, Carnegie-Mellon University, Pittsburgh, Pennsylvania 15213

Tom Trabasso (439), Department of Psychology, Princeton University, Princeton, New Jersey 08540

PREFACE

Visual information processing was the topic of the Eighth Carnegie Symposium on Cognition (May 18 and 19, 1972). Each year, the symposium centers on a topic of current interest in cognition, and the aim of the series is to provide an outlet for the latest results from various research laboratories on the topic of interest. The motivation underlying the organization of this book is the growing interest in the role of visual imagery and visual processes in cognition, and this year it seemed appropriate to invite psychologists working on visual processes in thought.

The particular papers were solicited with several criteria in mind. First, all the papers represent work that seems important and exciting to me. Also, in each case, the work represents the latest results from ongoing, programmatic research projects from laboratories that ultimately aim to develop information processing models of cognition. The authors were directed to present their papers with two goals in mind. First, they were asked to update their research programs with new material, representing their latest work. And second, they were asked to evaluate the significance of their overall research programs. Within these guidelines, the authors were allowed the freedom to tell their story as they saw fit without the usual tight constraints imposed by page-starved journals. The value of this style of presentation is to give a better overall perspective of the topic—in this case, visual information processing. The book should therefore be understandable to advanced undergraduate and graduate students, as well as of value to professional workers in the area of cognition.

Part I of the book contains papers on the role of visual processes in cognition. These papers are arranged in order roughly from the simplest to most complicated tasks. The first paper, by Klahr, shows that quantifying the number of objects in the visual field depends in part on visual processes (e.g., grouping) and in part on elementary cognitive processes such as scanning memory, counting, and adding. Posner outlines the latest evidence showing that the external world is coded in terms of multiple representations (visual, auditory, kinesthetic), and that much of our immediate processing is based on these multiple codes. The paper by Cooper and Shepard presents convincing evidence that the mental rotation of objects in a visual image involves some continuous analog process, and the use of visual images as mnemonic devices in mental arithmetic is demonstrated by Hayes. The paper by Chase and Simon presents evidence for the importance of pattern recognition processes underlying skilled chess. One important generalization to be observed in these papers, taken collectively, is that visual-perceptual processes play a central role in thought.

Part II of the book is organized around the role of visual processes in language comprehension. Two important ideas originate from this section. First, our language structures reflect the way we perceive our world, and second, our understanding of language depends upon our knowledge of the world. Clark, Carpenter, and Just show that spatial terms in our language are designed to communicate how we perceive the three-dimensional world, and these in turn are probably structured by constraints arising from our perceptual apparatus and from the physical world. The paper by Bransford and Johnson demonstrates the importance of context—including visual context—in language comprehension. It is clear from their paper that thought processes—including visual thinking—are an integral part of language comprehension, and further, that language comprehension cannot be understood by analyzing only the processing of isolated sentences. Trabasso's discussion of these papers involves a new look at the old Whorfian hypothesis—that our particular language structures can determine how we perceive the world—and an analysis of the role of perception in language and cognition.

Part III of the book, on information processing models, is a direct outgrowth of Newell's discussion of papers in Part I. In this delightful paper, Newell engages in a little good-natured "hand-wringing" over the current status of psychological theorizing. But Newell practices what he preaches by presenting, in his paper in Part III, an explicit computer simulation of Sternberg's memory-scanning task, as well as other immediate processing tasks. Klahr's paper contains an explicit computer simulation of the processes underlying subitizing, adding, and counting that arose from his experimental investigations in Chapter 1. Both models are based on a new, more psychologically relevant, approach to simulation—that of production systems.

If there is a single organizing theme for this book, it is the mind's eye, or the contents of the mind's eye—images. Such a generalization is oversimplifying, however, since each paper addresses itself to many issues of importance to its particular research program. Thus, each paper, in its own right, is a tutorial for those readers interested in the work coming out of the various laboratories.

I am indebted to many people for their aid in organizing the symposium. I thank Betty Boal, who coordinated the whole thing, and Neil Charness, Micki Chi, Mrs. Yu-Tung Chi, Sylvia Farnham-Diggory, Lee Gregg, Larry Macupa, Herb Simon, and Richard Young, who helped out in various ways. I am particularly indebted to Lou Beckstrom, who typed much of the manuscript. And I am obviously grateful to Carnegie-Mellon University, and the office of Dean Schatz, for providing the funds.

VISUAL INFORMATION
PROCESSING

PART I

VISUAL PROCESSES IN COGNITION

QUANTIFICATION PROCESSES

David Klahr
Carnegie-Mellon University

The goal of the research to be described in this
paper is the formulation of an information processing
model of cognitive development. For several years
now, Iain Wallace and I have been engaged in this
pursuit, and last year, in the 7th Carnegie Cognition
Symposium, we reported upon some aspects of our work
(Klahr and Wallace, 1972). The focus then was upon
the analysis of the classic Class Inclusion (CI)
problem, first used by Piaget to assess one of the
components of the stage of concrete operations
(Piaget, 1952). In the CI task the child is shown a
collection of, say, 10 red objects, 7 of which are
square and 3 of which are round, and he is asked,
"Are there more red things or more round things?"
In general, children below age four fail this task,
and children above age 7 pass it. We formulated an
information processing model, cast in the form of a
production system, that could be used to explain
different patterns of success and failure and the
effects of training. At the heart of the production
system were some things we called *quantification
operators*. These quantification operators were nice
examples of what Walter Reitman meant when he once
characterized the information processing approach as
a way to "invent what you need to know" (Reitman,
1967). They were essential to the logic of our model,
and so we postulated their existence. We have since
been engaged in extending our knowledge about quantification operators in two related directions. One is
a theory about the relationship of such operators and
their development to a wider range of Genevan tasks,

3

in particular, conservation of quantity and transitivity (Klahr and Wallace, 1973). The other is an empirical study of quantification in adults, and that is the topic of this paper.

Our overall research strategy is to formulate models of performance of the developing organism at two different points in time, and then to formulate a model for the transition or developmental mechanisms. The research to be reported and reviewed here focuses almost entirely upon adult performance, and thus, represents only one aspect of this three-pronged approach.

Quantification Operators

A quantification operator is an organized collection of elementary processes that takes as input the stimulus to be quantified (e.g., a collection of blocks) as well as specified constraints (e.g., red only) and produces as output a quantitative symbol. Quantitative symbols are labeled internal representations (e.g., two, long, tiny) that can be used in quantitative comparisons. Given two such symbols, the system can determine their relative magnitudes; whereas given two non-quantitative symbols, it can only determine sameness or difference.

There is a compelling logical necessity for the existence of quantification operators in a wide variety of tasks, including those central to the paradigms of developmental psychology. In class inclusion, in transitivity, and in conservation tasks, the child is asked to compare the amount of two or more collections. In order to make the comparison, he must have some quantitative symbols to compare; and in order to generate such symbols from the stimulus, he must have some quantification operators.

For normal adults, all of the above-mentioned tasks are easy. Thus, we would expect to find the underlying quantification operators in their most stable and fully developed form in adults, and it is to an analysis of quantification operators in adults that this paper is primarily addressed. However, we shall return to the developmental problem after presenting the main results of investigations using adult subjects, both from our own laboratory and from the work of others.

There seem to be three quantification operators that are used by adults: subitizing, counting, and estimation. These are venerable topics in psychology. Some of the phenomena with which they deal have been studied in terms of "immediate apprehension" for over a century (Jevons, 1871) and the invention of the term "subitizing," as well as a comparison of the three processes, resulted from investigations in the late forties by Kaufman, Lord, Reese, and Volkmann (1949). Thus, there is a strong flavor of new wine in old bottles, with the new contents for the old labels having three characteristics. First, they are based upon a process analysis of the fine structure of the observable phenomena; second, these subprocesses are related to recent advances in our knowledge about the parameters of some of the central mechanisms, such as short-term memory; and finally, the analysis is ultimately devoted to the end of accounting for the development of the processes and the relationship between that development and more complex conceptual activity.

Subitizing

The early studies of what came to be called subitizing were centered upon the existence and extent of "immediate apprehension." The empirical question was whether the time required to quantify a collection of n items presented to view was independent of n, and if so, for what values of n. Figure 1(a) shows the hypothetical results from such a model. Initially, the answer seemed to support such a model, with an upper value of n approximately equal to 6 or 7 (e.g., Jevons, 1871). Von Szeliski (1924) discovered

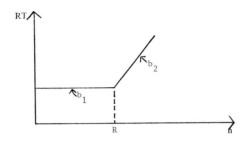

a) $b_1 = 0$

$R \sim 7$

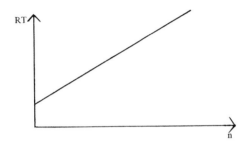

b) $b_1 = b_2$

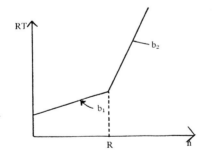

c) $b_1 < b_2$

$R \sim 5$

Fig. 1. Predicted reaction time as a function of n for three models of "immediate apprehension."

a continuous curve, arguing for Model b. During the late forties a brief series of papers presented evidence supporting or refuting Models a or b (Jenson, Reese, & Reese, 1950; Kaufman, *et al*, 1949; Saltzman and Garner, 1948). The final outcome of that exchange, reviewed by Woodworth and Schlosberg (1954) and further supported by the experiments reported below, is that Model 1c seems to be correct.

When we first began to attempt to determine the effect of different quantification processes upon children's performance on logical tasks, we found that for all its familiarity as a phenomenon, subitizing was essentially unexplained (and a bit unloved). For example, Beckwith and Restle (1966) find it

> "...amazing that although everyone knows
> that objects are enumerated by counting,
> most studies of enumeration or the judgment
> of number have attempted to rule out counting
> and ensure that only the primitive method of
> guessing is employed."

However, after an empirical study of counting, they conclude that simple enumeration is inadequate to account for the fact that "assemblies of discrete objects are perceived in groups," and they retain the term "subitizing" for the "somewhat mysterious but very rapid and accurate perceptual method" of quantification.

Two different procedures have been used for investigating subitizing. In both procedures, a collection of n items (usually a random dot pattern) is presented to view and subjects are told to respond by indicating (usually verbally) the number of items in the collection. In the *threshold* procedure, the items are exposed to view for brief periods and the subject's task is to respond as accurately as possible. The usual result of interest is the functional relation between exposure duration and the error rate for different values of n (e.g., Averbach, 1963).

7

In the *latency* procedure, the display remains visible
until the subject responds, and the subject is
instructed either for speed or for accuracy. The
important result from this procedure is the functional
relation between n and reaction time (e.g., Figure 1).
Another measure that has been used in both procedures
is the subject's report of his confidence in his own
judgment (Kaufman, *et al.*, 1949).

In almost every study of quantification in the
range $1 \leq n \leq 30$, striking discontinuities occur in
the region of $n = 6 \pm 1$. This is true for plots of
confidence vs n, reaction time vs n, and error rate
vs n. These discontinuities define subitizing: it
is the process that produces the results up to the
point of discontinuity. After that point another
process, here simply called "counting" (and described
below), is in operation.

Two parameters define subitizing:

(i) R, the maximum value of n or the upper
limit of the range for which the subitizing process operated, and

(ii) B, the slope of least squares linear
regression line of reaction time as a
function of n, for $1 \leq n \leq R$.

As mentioned above, the early studies of span of
apprehension sought to determine the value of R for
which B was zero. Even when it became apparent that
B was non-zero, the focus was still upon the existence
or nonexistence of a discontinuity in slope. None of
the existing studies report B, and one must extract
it from the tables and figures of the early papers.[1]

---

[1]The following sources were used to derive the
slopes given in the next paragraph: Table 3 from
Jensen, Reese, and Reese (1950, p. 376); Table III
from Kaufman, Lord, Reese and Volkmann (1949, p. 512);
Figure 5 from Saltzman and Garner (1948, p. 236). The

The values of R and B have had varied estimates.
Woodworth and Schlosberg (1954) estimate R to be 8,
while Jensen *et al*. (1950) estimate R ~ 5 - 6.   B has
been found to be ~ 50 msec. by Saltzman and Garner
(1948), 120 msec. by Kaufman *et al*. (1949), and 130
msec. by Jensen *et al*. (1950).   The discrepant findings may be due to both procedural variations (e.g.,
speed vs accuracy instructions, different visual
angles subtended by displays) and analytic variations
(reports of means vs medians, inclusion or exclusion
of error trials).

Furthermore, for any collection of data, B is a
function of the choice of R.   Thus, it is important
to specify a procedure for unambiguously determining
R before one attempts to precisely measure B.   Beyond
R, in the "counting" range of approximately $7 < n < 30$,
the slope has been found to be ~ 350 msec. by both
Jensen *et al*. (1950) and Beckwith and Restle (1966).

In order to further refine these parameters and
to determine the effects of certain stimulus variables upon the subitizing operator, we ran a series of
experiments.   The first experiment was designed to
determine whether or not the 50 msec. and 300 msec.
slopes that can be teased out of the old data would
be replicable.   A secondary purpose was to determine
the value of R and the effects of visual angle and
pattern density.   The experiment is described in
detail elsewhere (Klahr, Wallace and Chi, 1973); here
I will summarize the important features and results.

---

best-known result from Saltzman and Garner is probably
their Figure 4, which is included in Woodworth and
Schlosberg (1954, p. 97).   However, Figure 4, which
gives no clear indication of a slope discontinuity,
is based upon stimuli consisting of concentric circles, not dots.   Although Saltzman and Garner argue
that the curves in Figure 5 are no different from
those in Figure 4, we suggest that the interested
reader refer to the Saltzman and Garner paper and
draw his own conclusions.

Experiment I

Subjects, Materials and Apparatus

Three adult male subjects from the psychology department volunteered for the experiment. The materials consisted of patterns of from 1 to 20 dots randomly generated (according to a scheme described below) on a standard video monitor controlled by a computer. Subjects' responses triggered a voice-actuated relay which was sensed by the computer, yielding latency measurements, accurate to the nearest msec., from the time the pattern appeared on the screen until the relay was actuated.

Dot patterns were generated by locating dots along the borders of a set of concentric squares formed by the perimeters of m x m grids (m=3,5,7,9). The grid lines were about .5 in. apart. Up to 5 dots were distributed randomly among the p possible locations on an m x m perimeter [the number of possible dot locations, p on an m x m perimeter p=4(m-1)]. In the Inner condition, for a given value of n, the first 5 dots were located on the innermost square, the next 5 dots on the immediately surrounding square, etc., until n dots were distributed. In the Outer condition, dots were distributed from the outside (9 x 9) square inward, 5 to a perimeter, until all n dots were distributed. Figure 2 shows the grid scheme and a few typical patterns in the Inner and Outer conditions. The Inner grid subtends a visual angle of about 2.2°, while the Outer grid subtends about 8.5°.

Procedure and Design

Subjects were seated about 2 ft. in front of the video monitor, placed at eye level. At the start of each trial the word "READY" was displayed in the center of the screen. The subject pressed the response button and the dot pattern appeared on the

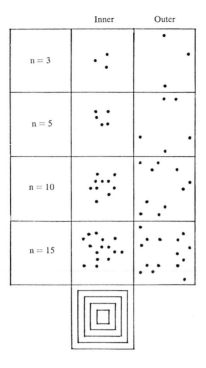

Fig. 2. Grid scheme and some typical patterns.

screen. The subject then responded by saying the number of dots he saw. This actuated the relay and removed the pattern from the screen. The response was then entered through a keyboard connected to the computer. Then the next trial began. For each value of n there were eight patterns generated in the Inner condition and eight in the Outer. For each subject, there was a total of 320 trials.

Results

The response latencies for errorless trials, averaged over 3 subjects and Inner/Outer conditions, are plotted in Figure 3. There appears to be a slope discontinuity in the region of $n=5$. The slope of the

11

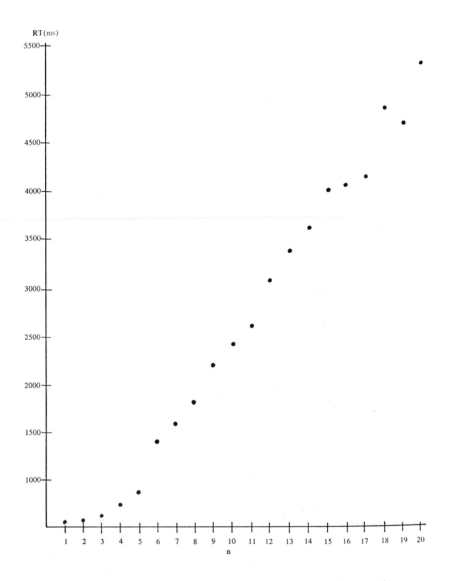

Fig. 3. Mean RT for 3 subjects with n = (1-20).

regression line for n=1-4 is 57 msec. and for n=5-20
it is about 300 msec. If n=5 is included in the
lower regression, the slope is about 77 msec.

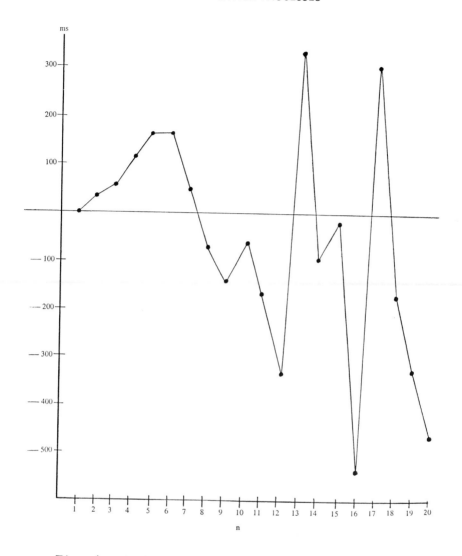

Fig. 4. Difference between means for Outer and Inner conditions.

The effect of Inner/Outer display interacts with n as indicated in Figure 4. For $n \leq 6$, the difference between the Outer and Inner condition systematically increases with n, but above that no consistent relationship emerges. As Figure 2 indicates, there is a complex interaction between visual angle, pattern density, and n. For low n, the consistently greater latencies for the Outer patterns could be the result of either additional eye movements, or more non-foveal processing.

Experiment I indicated that indeed two processes are operating when subjects perform this task. The slope of the lower line (77 msec.) and the point of slope discontinuity ($n=5$) are similar to the scanning rate and capacity of short-term memory (STM), and they suggested to us that there might be a relationship between scanning STM and subitizing. This hunch led us first to explore the reliability of the empirical findings and their invariance over such perceptual factors as visual angle and eye movement, and cognitive factors such as the subjects' awareness of the range of n. Finally, we were led to develop models of the subitizing process in terms of a STM scanning process.

Experiment II

In the next experiment in the series, we investigated the effect of varying the range of n and informing the subject of this range. We also wanted to get a larger group of subjects and further explore the effect of visual angle.

Subjects, Materials, Procedure and Design

Twelve subjects, students and faculty from the psychology department, served as volunteers. The same computer controlled apparatus was used. Three ranges of n were used: 1-5, 1-10, and 10-20. For each range, the same Inner/Outer display condition was used. However, the subjects were about 60 inches from the display, so that the Inner patterns for $n < 10$ were entirely within foveal view. The visual angles were $1.8°$ and $3.5°$ for the Inner and Outer grids, respectively. For each of the three ranges of

n there were 16 trials of each value of n, appropri·
ately randomized. At the start of a block of trials
for a given range of n, the subject was told what
that range would be.

The same general procedure was followed as in
Experiment I. The subject was instructed to fixate
the "A" in "READY" before pressing the response
button. After a delay of 1.5 sec., the dot pattern
was displayed.

Results

The main result is shown in Fig. 5, a plot of
mean RT against n for the three ranges of n. The
slope of RT vs n for $n \leq 5$ is around 70 msec. and for
$n > 5$ it is about 300 msec. However, this requires
closer analysis. We are attempting to determine the
rate of two different processes as well as which process is operating. Thus, we did some curve fitting
for different subranges of the range actually used.
In particular, we systematically included or excluded
the point $n=5$ in the linear regressions. The results
are shown in the top half of Table I. When only
points 1-4 are considered (lines 2 and 3), we get
slopes of 66 and 72 msec. for ranges of $n=1-5$ and
$n=1-10$ respectively. These are not significantly
different. When point 5 is included, the slope goes
down to 58 msec. for $n=1-5$ and up to 110 msec. for
$n=1-10$. Our explanation is that in the case of $n=1-10$
we are observing the effects of averaging trials
and/or subjects for which $n=5$ is sometimes subitized
and sometimes counted. In the case of $n=1-5$ we are
observing an "end error." Once he determines that n
is not 1, 2, 3, or 4, the subject responds "5" by
default. If the time to make this decision were less
than the subitizing rate, this would lower the
regression slope.

If we look at the results for a single subject,
in order to eliminate the inter-subject averaging, we
still find the same effect. Figure 6 shows the

15

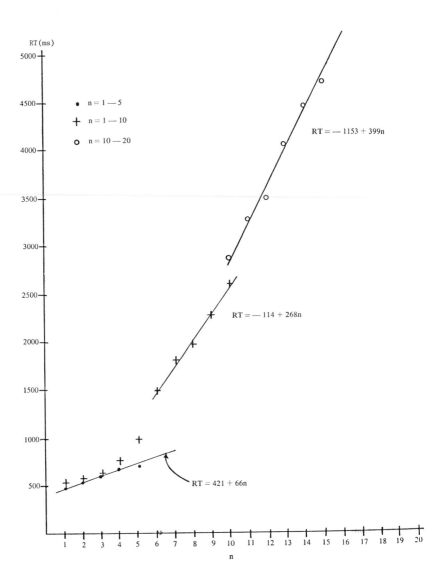

Fig. 5. Mean RT for 12 subjects in each range condition.

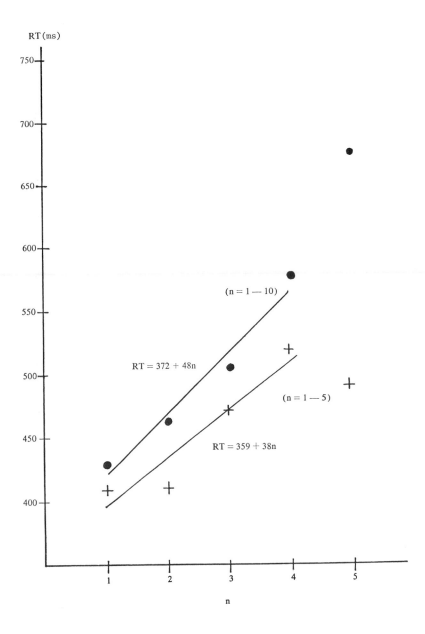

Fig. 6. Mean RT for single subject with n=1-4 in conditions n=1-5 and n=1-10.

Table I

Results of Linear Regression for Experiments II and III

	Subjects	Stimulus Range	Analysis Range	Intercept (msec)	Slope (msec/dot)	R^2	RMSD[*] (msec)
1		1-5	1-5	436	58	97.6	12.7
2			1-4	421	66	99.0	7.2
3	Group	1-10	1-4	451	72	91.6	24.3
4	of 12		1-5	375	110	87.0	57.9
5	(Exp.II)		6-10	-114	268	99.4	30.3
6			1-10	10	247	95.5	153.7
7		10-20	10-20	-1153	399	98.9	134.0
8	(Exp.II)	1-10	1-4	372	48	97.0	9.7
9	Individual	1-5	1-4	359	38	89.0	14.9
	W.C.						
10	(Exp.III)	1-5	1-4**	324	25	97.9	4.1
11			1-4***	308	60	90.1	22.2

    *   Root Mean Squared Deviation

    **   no eye movements

   ***   more than one fixation

results for a single subject over the range n=1-5 in the conditions with n=1-5 and n=1-10 with the regression line for the first four points. This is typical of the analysis of individual subjects. Note that this subject responds more rapidly for n=5 than for n=4, indicating that some process other than subitizing is operating.

Experiment III

Although the arrangement of the dot patterns within foveal view controls for the *necessity* of eye movements, it does not directly control eye movements. In the third experiment in the series, Michelene Chi decided to use eye movement recording apparatus. This enabled us to analyze only those trials on which no eye movements occurred, thus giving a subitizing rate uncontaminated by eye movement reaction times.

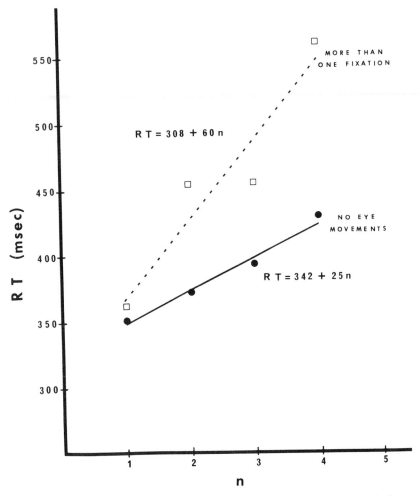

Fig. 7. Mean RT of a single subject on trials with and without eye movements (n=1-5).

19

This procedure provided an extremely reliable estimate of the subitizing parameters. Stimuli in the range n=1-5 were used in essentially the same configuration as in the earlier experiments. Some changes in procedure were necessitated by the eye-movement recording equipment (Chi, 1973), and subjects who had served in the previous two experiments were used. A videotape was made of a superimposed image of the stimulus field and the subject's fixations within the field using equipment designed by John Gould (cf. Gould & Peoples, 1972). An analysis of the tapes allowed us to detect those trials on which no eye movements occurred and to treat them separately in the analysis.

In the Inner condition eye movements occurred on less than 10% of the trials, while in the Outer condition they occurred on about 45% of the trials. If we include only those trials with a single fixation, we get the results shown in Figure 7. These results are also presented at the bottom of Table I, along with the other slopes for this same subject. The uncontaminated slope for subitizing is 25 msec. per item.

Quantification Models

Subitizing

As a first approximation we propose the following model for subitizing (see Model A in Figure 8). Subitizing involves a serial self-terminating scan of STM for a match between the encoded stimulus and a short ordered list of quantitative symbols. We assume that adults have, stored in LTM, a subitizing list consisting of an ordered set of quantitative symbols representing the first 5 (+1) cardinal values. When the subitizing operator is first invoked, the subitizing list is transferred from LTM to STM, where it is scanned at about 40 msec. per symbol.

Sternberg's (1967) studies of STM report both "length functions"--RT as a function of the length of the list being scanned, and serial position functions --RT as a function of the location of the target item in the list. Since the postulated subitizing list is of fixed length in any individual, the 40 msec. slope we observe in our studies is due to the serial position of the symbol corresponding to the encoded target. For context recognition tasks (subjects report whether or not two probe items are in the same order in the STM list), Sternberg reports individual subject mean serial position function slopes ranging from 22 to 240 msec. Ellis and Chase (1971) report a 40 msec. mean slope for the serial position function in item recognition (subjects report whether or not the probe item is in the STM list). This slope is consistent with the slopes on Sternberg's length functions, usually taken as *the* STM scanning rate.

If the encoded stimulus does not match any of the symbols in STM (and hence on the subitizing list) then subitizing cannot produce a final output for the quantification task. However, this is not a "no information" situation since the system knows that the quantitative value was at least greater than R, the value of the last symbol on the subitizing list. In the discussion of the "end effect" for $n=5$, we noted the effects of such a situation, and we shall return below to the way that this information can be used by another operator.

The model shown at the top of Figure 8 makes assumptions about the seriality, independence and linearity of its component processes. It separates perceptual processes from memory processes by having the encoding box sit outside the scanning loop. Although this is a fairly reasonable assumption for many models of cognition, it is a bit tenuous with processes that sit so close to the "perceptual-cognitive interface." Some support for this separation comes from Sternberg's experiments with degraded visual images of relatively complex stimuli like

21

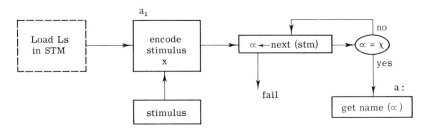

model A

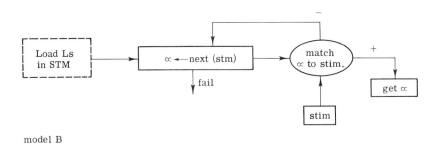

model B

Fig. 8. Two models for subitizing.

numbers and letters; degrading the image affected the
encoding time but not the memory scanning time. However, we are still engaged in a direct test of this
through the use of similar paradigms using our random
dot patterns. There is some evidence that is at variance with an encoding process whose time is independent of n. For example, Averbach (1963), using the
threshold procedure, exposed dot patterns in the range
of interest here for from 40 to 600 msec., followed
by an erasing field. He found almost 100% accuracy
for 4 dots at 150 msec.; but with a 40 msec. exposure
no more than 2 dots could be detected accurately on
more than 50% of the trials, and 4 dots were reported

correctly less than 20% of the time. Thus, the
encoding process seems to be dependent upon n.

If this evidence is further supported in our own
studies, we will have to revise Model A to account for
the fact that the time needed to encode the stimulus
is dependent upon the number of dots. From Averbach's
data it appears to be around 10 msec. per dot. But if
the encoding rate turns out to be around 40 msec.,
then what happens to the STM scanning model? An
equally plausible model would attribute all the slopes
to encoding, followed by direct access to the name of
the encoded symbol.

Model B in Fig. 8 is our proposed resolution for
this perceptual/cognitive conflict. The scan of the
subitizing symbols in STM remains, but the encoding
process has been eliminated as a primitive. In its
place is a more plausible "match" process in which the
STM symbol currently under consideration is matched
"directly" with the stimulus. Such a model is consistent both with Averbach's results and with our findings. The mysterious "encoding" process, which in
fact is not very satisfying at the center of a model
of subitizing--itself defined as an encoding process--
has been eliminated. Subitizing *is* the encoding
process.

Counting

Counting is defined as the process that generates
the steep slopes above $n=5$ in our experiments. Referring back to Fig. 5 we see slopes of 267 msec. for
$n=(6-10)$ in the (1-10) condition and 399 msec. for
$n=(10-20)$. This slightly positively accelerated function for RT vs n is consistent with some of the earlier
studies (Jensen, *et al.*, 1950; Von Szeliski, 1924).
However, it is most probably due to an increasing frequency of "restarts" with higher n, and we will assume
that the underlying process is linear. Counting requires the coordination of processes that notice each
item while generating the sequence of number names.
When there are no items remaining to be noticed, the

current name is assigned to the collection of items.

Counting thus requires two auxiliary structures in LTM: a finite ordered list of number names, together with rules for generating number names indefinitely, and rules to ensure that each item is noticed only once. There may be several different forms of such attention directing processes, ranging from motor routines that move or touch objects as they are noticed to well-defined eye-movement patterns.

More than half of the processing time per item appears to come from moving through the number-name list. Beckwith and Restle (1966) gave explicit instructions to "enumerate as quickly as possible." For random patterns of identical items they found average slopes of 350 msec. per item (579 msec. for children aged 7 to 9 years) in the range $n=(12, 15, 16, 18)$. In a task requiring subjects to implicitly recite the alphabet from an initial letter to a final letter, Olshavsky and Gregg (1970) found a processing rate of 150 msec. per item similar to the rate of implicit recitation found by Landauer (1962). When subjects were required to scan a specified number of letters, the rate increased to 260 msec. per item.

Thus the simple counting model (Model A) in Fig. 9 would seem to account for the data for item-by-item counting, with most of the time contributing to the slope being taken up by the first subprocess in the loop. The subprocess "mark" and "find" are not well defined, but they are intended as a surrogate for any strategies that might be used to direct attention to each item only once and to determine when the count is complete.

However, this model is quite at variance with the phenomenological experience of grouping and adding reported by most subjects. As noted earlier, Beckwith and Restle concluded that subjects deal with clusters of objects either by computing a running sum or by adding all the subtotals at the end. Model A also does not account for the fact that counting appears to start just above the subitizing range, rather than at zero.

24

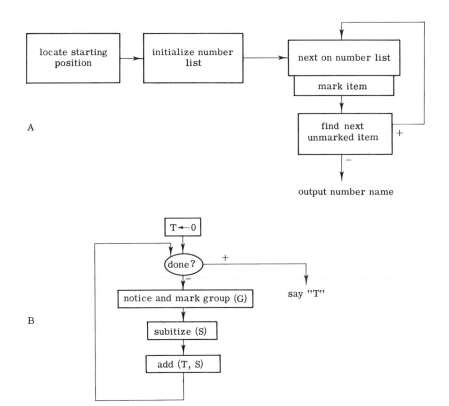

Fig. 9. Two models for counting.

Model B is an alternative to item-by-item count-ing. The counting sequence consists of several sub-processes which alternately subitize and add. The first subprocess segments the stimulus. Wertheimer's (1923) principles probably determine the grouping pro-cedure, since Beckwith and Restle found that "good" groups took less time to enumerate than random pat-terns. The next subprocess is subitizing; the groups are presumed to be within the subitizing range and once noticed, they are subitized. Next, the result from subitizing is added to a running total. Finally,

25

NMU LIBRARY

the group is "marked" and the model loops back to a
test for completion. If there are more objects to be
accounted for, the process is repeated.

From other studies we have estimates of the processing rates for subitizing and addition. Thus, we
can estimate the time required for the noticing and
marking operations. Assume that the average size of
the subgroup noticed is m. Then there will be approximately n/m passes (actually *int* [(n-1)/m] + 1) through
the loop to count n items.[2] Each pass involves the
time to notice and mark a subgroup of m items G(m),
plus the time to subitize them S(m), plus the time to
add the result to the total A(T,m). Thus the total
time for counting will be:

$$RT = C + \frac{n}{m} [G(m) + S(m) + A(T,m)].$$ (1)

From our own studies we have an estimate for subitizing of

$$S(m) = k_s + 40m$$ (2)

and from Groen and Parkman (1972) an addition model
that is a linear function of the minimum of the two
addends, $min(a_1, a_2)$, with a 20 msec. slope. In all
but the first time through, the minimum of T and m
will be m; thus we have:

$$A(T,m) = k_a + 20m.$$ (3)

Substituting Equations 2 and 3 into Equation 1, we get

$$RT = C + n \left[\frac{k_s + k_a}{m} + 60 + \frac{G(m)}{m} \right]$$ (4)

---

[2]Int(x) is the largest positive integer less than
or equal to x.

Differentiating with respect to n, we get an estimated slope for counting:

$$\frac{d(RT)}{dn} \cong 60 + G(m)/m + \frac{k_s + k_a}{m} \tag{5}$$

From the studies reviewed above, the slope of counting is approximately 350 ms; thus we get a final estimate:

$$G(m) \cong 290m - (k_s + k_a) \tag{6}$$

Note that k_s and k_a are not the intercepts from addition and subitizing experiments, but only a part thereof, since the intercepts include the time to vocalize the response given the internal symbol. Thus, it takes about 1/2-1 sec. to notice and mark a group of three to four objects.

This model for counting brings us back to the "failure" exit on the subitizing model. Since we have included the subitizing operator within the counting operator, we can treat the inability to subitize the entire group as an input back to the "notice and mark" process. Such information would be used to segment the current group into subgroups within the subitizing range, leaving the rest to be noticed on the next pass. The model is also consistent with the fact that subitizing always precedes counting (since counting slopes always have negative intercepts, counting one-by-one could not account for the entire range of stimuli). We need only assume that if n<m, the grouping process, since it involves no decisions, is essentially immediate and there is no addition needed. Thus, although the subject is "set" to count, if n is low, he subitizes "in spite" of himself.

Add to Count or Count to Add?

A high-speed addition process lies at the heart of the counting model proposed above. This process

(Groen & Parkman, 1972; Parkman & Groen, 1971) operates as a linear function of the min of the two
arguments. The finding of the min model as the best
fit to the reaction time data is similar to the findings of Groen (1967) on RT's of 5-year-old children
on simple addition. However, for children the slope
was on the order of 400 msec. Groen hypothesized that
a counting mechanism lay at the heart of the addition
process in children. Children set their "counter" to
the maximum of the two arguments and then count up the
minimum number of times, producing the sum. Thus, we
seem to have recursive paradox: a counting model that
has as a subprocess an addition model which has at *its*
center a counting model.

The problem can be disentangled by a careful look
at the differences in the subjects and the range of
variables. In Table II we have summarized the results
of the empirical studies mentioned above. The

Table II

Processing Rates for Different Tasks

	subjects	task	item	range	ms per item	reference
1	adults	addition[1]	integers	0-8	20	Parkman & Groen (1971)
2	adults	silent recitation[2]	syllables	10-50	110	Landauer (1962)
3	adults	count (quantify)[3]	random dots	6-20	350	Beckwith & Restle; Klahr
4	children (5 yrs.)	addition[1]	integers	0-4	400	Groen (1967)
5	children (8 yrs.)	count (quantify)[3]	random dots	10-20	580	Beckwith & Restle (1966)

1. The models for these operations are of the form RT = a + b min (x,y). The range
shown is for the min.

2. A linear regression of RT against the number of <u>syllables</u> in the Landauer tasks
yields the following equation:
$$RT = 330 + 110s \text{ (ms)}; R^2 = .95 \ .$$

3. The slopes for the Beckwith and Restle experiments are obtained from their conditions using random arrangements of identical items.

different slopes for children and adults in the addition tasks strongly suggest that two quite different processes are used. The rapid rate of adult addition and the limited range of variation studied are consistent with the notion that adult addition is a STM scanning process. If the symbol for each integer (in the range studied) has attached to it a short list of its neighbors and this list is loaded into STM and scanned for min (x,y) locations, then adult addition still retains its "counting-like" nature while being very fast. For children, these neighborhood lists do not yet exist and each number evokes only its successor, which must then be retrieved from LTM. Thus, children's addition *via* counting proceeds at a much slower rate.

In implicit recitation studies using adults, these slower rates also obtain, since the task requirement is not just to get from item x to item y, but to generate the full representation for each letter or number. This requires repeated LTM access. Furthermore, the implicit recitation tasks, if viewed as syllable string sequencing, involve a range in excess of STM capacity, requiring several LTM accesses per trial.

Thus, both the addition and the subitizing components of the adult counting model are comprised of high speed scanning in STM. Although counting-like in nature, the addition subprocess in the counting model is distinct from the count-to-add process used by children for addition.

Estimation

Quantitative symbols can be produced in situations involving great numbers, or limited exposure, or continuous quantity. Neither subitizing nor counting could function in such situations, and the need for an estimation process is clear. However, the determination of its nature is puzzling, because we are attempting to characterize a system that can encode continuous quantity and yet (if it is to be consistent with the body of literature on information processing models of cognition) must be composed of discontinuous data structures and processes. We do not have any good data on estimation, so here we offer only a few speculative comments on what an estimation model might look like.

Estimation is essentially measurement: repeated application of a "standard" unit to the stimulus to be quantified. As in the case of subitizing and counting, the determination of what constitutes a measurable item is controlled by an interaction between the sensory input and the goal of the quantification effort. In addition, the selection of the standard unit that will be used as the "measuring rod" is determined by previously acquired standards in LTM or by immediately prior stimuli (e.g., anchoring effects in psychophysics). In the case of the random dot stimuli we have used, the standard might be generated at "run time." The first 10 or 20 dots could be counted, and then certain characteristics of that group (density, area, etc.) are abstracted and utilized to count "by 20's" for the rest of the display.

A well-known result from a study of estimation by Kaufman et al (1949) is that with a 200 msec. exposure of from 1 to 200 dots, RT was constant above $n=6$. However, this is somewhat misleading, because associated with this constant RT was an increasing greater percentage error for increasing n. The error was all on the low side and, since there was no erasing field used in the experiment, it is possible that subjects simply processed as much of the visual image as they could before it disappeared, giving whatever amount they were up to when it was no longer available.

The estimation model we are considering here works in a similar fashion to the counting operator except that the "grouping" operation is replaced by the match between the current standard and part of the stimulus. The size of this standard could be a function of the size of the display. For example, if for $n \leq 50$ a 10-dot standard were used, for $50 < n \leq 200$ a 25-dot standard, etc., this would lead to RT slopes of $n/10$ for $n \leq 50$, $n/25$ for $50 < n \leq 200$, etc. Then we woulc get a shallow sawtooth in plotting RT vs n for individual subjects, and an essentially flat curve when averaging over subjects with different standards. A plot of some of the individual RT's from Kaufman's papeı makes such a model plausible, but no conclusions about estimation can be drawn yet.

Summary and Conclusion

The issues addressed in this paper are subordinate to the overall question about how the human information processing system develops. We have reviewed the adult evidence and postulated models for two of the three quantification operators and speculated on the third. In the course of this, we discussed a bit of evidence from children's performance on a task related to quantification. In this final section we offer a brief comment on the nature of the differences in the models suggested above in order to indicate the nature of developmental changes in information processing systems. [Recent views on this crucial issue are presented by Flavell (1971, 1973) and Newell (1972). An elaboration of some of the ideas here can be found in Klahr and Wallace (1972, 1973).]

Adopting an extreme engineering approach to the information processing system, we can view changes in terms of four major classes of variables: programs, data structures, capacities, and rates. Changes in the first two result from "software" variation; changes in the last two result from "hardware" variation. Newell (1972) has indicated the inherent ambiguity of the distinction between process and structure in a developing information processing system. The issue is evidenced here by the fact that this paper could have been called "Quantification Structures" as appropriately as "Quantification Processes." The difference between the two addition subprocesses are dependent upon the differences in the data structures they operat upon, and the development of counting appears to depend

upon internal representations of quantity. There is
an implicit assumption here that major differences in
processing rates also reflect changes in representation
rather than in hardware. It is not yet clear whether
similar increases in capacity (e.g., STM) can be
entirely attributed to such representational changes
or whether, as some believe (e.g., Pascual-Leone, 1970),
there is a "hardware" increase in STM.

It will be difficult to be very precise about
these issues as long as the models retain their current
lack of specificity. In a subsequent paper (Chapter
11), we have attempted to further explicate the subitizing and counting models presented above by writing
them as running production systems. Although the
overall strategies are unchanged, these models yield
a view of processes such as "STM scanning" and "marking"
that is rather different from the "black box" approach
taken in this paper. The advantage of such an approach
to modeling lies in the ability to create models that
are consistent with the empirical results while meeting
the constraints imposed by the production system interpreter (Newell, 1972). Any models functioning within
this system are task-specific variants of a general
theory of human problem solving (Newell & Simon, 1972).
Adherence to the underlying psychological assumptions
in such a model makes the problems facing the developmental theorist somewhat more tractable because of the
demonstrated generality and power of the adult version
of the problem solving system.

References

Averbach, E. The span of apprehension as a function of
exposure duration. *Journal of Verbal Learning and
Verbal Behavior*, 1963, 2, 60-64.
Beckwith, M., & Restle, F. Process of enumeration.
Psychological Review, 1966, 73, 437-444.
Chi, M. T. H. Subitizing without eye movements.
Paper presented at the 81st Annual Convention,
APA, Division 3, Montreal, August 1973.
Ellis, S. H., & Chase, W. G. Parallel processing in
item recognition. *Perception and Psychophysics*,
1971, 10, 379-384.

Flavell, J. H. Stage-related properties of cognitive development. *Cognitive Psychology*, 1971, 2, 421–453.

Flavell, J. H. An analysis of cognitive developmental sequences. *Genetic Psychology Monographs*, 1973, in press.

Gould, J., & Peoples, D. R. Eye movements during visual search and discrimination of meaningless symbol and object patterns. *Journal of Experimental Psychology*, 1972, in press.

Groen, G. J. An investigation of some counting algorithms for simple addition problems. Technical Report No. 118, Stanford, California: Stanford University Institute for Mathematical Studies in the Social Sciences, 1967.

Groen, G. J., & Parkman, J. M. A chronometric analysis of simple addition. *Psychological Review*, 1972, 79, 329–343.

Jensen, E. M., Reese, E. P., & Reese, T. W. The subitizing and counting of visually presented fields of dots. *Journal of Psychology*, 1950, 30, 363–392.

Jevons, W. S. The power of numerical discrimination. *Nature*, 1871, 3, 281–282.

Kaufman, E. L., Lord, M. W., Reese, T. W., & Volkmann, J. The discrimination of visual number. *American Journal of Psychology*, 1949, 62, 498–525.

Klahr, D., & Wallace, J. G. Class inclusion processes. In S. Farnham-Diggory (Ed.), *Information processing in children*. New York: Academic Press, 1972.

Klahr, D., & Wallace, J. G. The role of quantification operators in the development of conservation of quantity. *Cognitive Psychology*, 1973, in press.

Klahr, D., Wallace, J. G., & Chi, M. T. H. Subitizing and short-term memory, 1973 (in preparation).

Landauer, T. Rate of implicit speech. *Perceptual and Motor Skills*, 1962, 15, 646.

Newell, A. A note on the process-structure distinctions in developmental psychology. In S. Farnham-Diggory (Ed.), *Information processing in children*. New York: Academic Press, 1972.

Newell, A. A theoretical exploration of mechanisms for coding the stimulus. In A. W. Melton & E. Martin (Eds.), *Coding processes in human memory*. Washington, D. C.: Winston, 1972.

Newell, A., & Simon, H. A. *Human problem solving*. Englewood Cliffs, N. J.: Prentice-Hall, 1972.

Olshavsky, R. W., & Gregg, L. W. Information processing rates and task complexity. *Journal of Experimental Psychology*, 1970, 83, 131-135.

Parkman, J. M., & Groen, G. J. Temporal aspects of simple addition and comparison. *Journal of Experimental Psychology*, 1971, 89, 335-342.

Pascual-Leone, J. A mathematical model for the transition rule in Piaget's developmental stages. *Acta Psychologica*, 1970, 63, 301-345.

Piaget, J. *The child's conception of number*. New York: Humanities Press, 1952.

Reitman, W. Computer simulation models: How to invent what you need to know. Paper presented at Seminar on Behavioral Science Research, University of Chicago Graduate School of Business, April 1967.

Saltzman, I. J., & Garner, W. R. Reaction time as a measure of span of attention. *The Journal of Psychology*, 1948, 25, 227-241.

Sternberg, S. Retrieval of contextual information from memory. *Psychonomic Science*, 1967, 8, 55-56.

Von Szeliski, V. Relation between the quantity perceived and the time of perception. *Journal of Experimental Psychology*, 1924, 7, 135-147.

Wertheimer, M. Untersuchungen zur Lehre von der Gestalt: II. *Psychologische Forschung*, 1923, 4, 301-350.

Woodworth, R. W., & Schlosberg, H. *Experimental Psychology* (revised). New York: Holt, 1954.

Acknowledgments

This work is an extension of joint work with J. G. Wallace (Klahr & Wallace, 1972, 1973). The experiments were run by Michelene Chi. We are indebted to John Gould for his assistance in the use of his eye movement recording laboratory.

COORDINATION OF INTERNAL CODES

Michael I. Posner
University of Oregon

An important aspect of thought is the ability to represent information in the absence of external stimulation. It has been common for theories of thought to take one form of representation as basic. Prior to this century the visual image was often considered to be the crucial element of thought and it is still viewed as central for some types of thinking (Arnheim, 1969). More frequently, language is taken as the main vehicle for thought (Whorf, 1956). Another view has been to conceive of thought as a complex skill (Bartlett, 1958), for which an internal motor program serves as the form of representation. The problem of representation remains, even if one defines a "concept" as the basis for thought. A concept can be viewed as a complex network of interrelated words (Collins and Quillian, 1969; Freijda, 1972; Norman, 1970), a composite picture (Galton, 1907; Posner & Keele, 1968) or as an internalized rule which allows one to perform the skill of classification (Bourne, 1966).

It is possible to develop a theory of thought at a level of representation common to all codes. For example, the list language of Newell and Simon (1972) can be used to represent any code. However, there are reasons to believe that the efficiency of solving a problem may depend critically upon the form of representation. For example, the ability to solve a problem represented spatially is reduced by a simultaneous spatial task while verbal representation is affected more by a verbal task (Brooks, 1968). A subject who reports himself as good in visual imagery has an advantage in solving problems which involve

35

manipulating internal visual symbols (Snyder, 1972). Functional fixity which serves to block the ability of a subject to associate the visual form of an object with a particular use, may leave intact the object name-to-use association and the reverse (Glucksburg & Danks, 1968; Glucksburg & Weisberg, 1966). These are examples of why it might prove useful for a theory of thought to preserve the distinction between modes of representation.

Developmental psychologists (Bruner, 1966; Piaget & Inhelder, 1969) have emphasized the multiple bases upon which the same external situation may be represented. For example, Bruner views the child as shifting from a primary reliance upon enactive (motor) codes first to iconic (visual) and finally symbolic (e.g., language) representation.

Experimental psychologists working with adult subjects have also been studying the different forms of representation of information in perceptual and learning tasks (Bower, 1972; Paivio, 1970; Posner, Lewis & Conrad, 1972; Posner & Warren, 1972). The present paper takes as a starting point four conclusions resulting from these studies. First is the existence of objective techniques to demonstrate the reality of visual, verbal and motor codes (Bower, 1972; Paivio, 1971). Second is that these forms of representation are enduring and not merely rapidly decaying residues of stimulation (Posner & Warren, 1972). Third, individuals differ in their propensity for forming and using different representations (Neisser, 1967; Paivio, 1971). Finally, different representations of the same stimulus may serve as isolable subsystems in the sense that it is possible to manipulate experimentally the availability of one code without affecting other codes of the same stimulus (Posner, Lewis & Conrad, 1972).

Despite these experimental results there has been a strong desire to view complex tasks as involving only a single form of coding. The exact form has often been a matter of dispute. Currently, the issue is sharpest in studies of three term series problems. According to Clark (1969) these problems are solved by processes which are close to the operations of language. On the other hand, Huttenlocker (1968) and DeSoto (1965) have argued that visual representations constructed from the propositions are important elements in the problem solving process. It is certain that linguistic processing must be involved in comprehending the propositions which are presented to subjects. There is also little reason to doubt that subjects sometimes construct spatial representations of the problems as well. What we do not know is whether both codes have an effect on problem solution and if so, how they are related.

The controversy between single and multiple code theories has also been present in studies of much simpler conceptual and memory tasks. In this paper I have tried to outline three places in which there has been controversy between single and multiple coding views. Although the evidence favors multiple codes, the main interest of the paper is in attempting to discern how information from these codes is coordinated. The three areas which I have selected to review are encoding, search of active memory and conscious rehearsal.

Encoding

Suppose a subject is presented with a brief visual flash consisting of many items. One widely accepted view of this process is that a visual code of the letters is represented for a very brief time followed by a representation of the letter names (Neisser, 1967; Sperling, 1963). This view suggests that only a single code of a letter is represented in the nervous system at any one time. Elsewhere I tried to present evidence for a rather different view of this process at least for single letters and small arrays (Posner, Lewis & Conrad, 1972). According to this view both a visual and a name representation of the items are built up and coexist as separable codes.

Coltheart (1972) has presented a more detailed model of the growth of these codes with large arrays. He suggests that subjects are able to build a visual code which is not subject to masking. This code is developed at the rate of about 10 msec. per letter and has a maximum capacity of four letters. At the same time they develop a representation of the letter names at the rate of 100 msec. per letter. These two representations coexist for a time. The evidence for this view comes from a variety of studies in which a visual mask is superimposed upon parts of the array at varying intervals following stimulation.

An interesting feature of the Coltheart view is that the visual code tends to select letters from the two ends of the display while the name code proceeds from left to right. This feature postulates a great deal of independence between the processes which underlie the development of the two codes. It hardly seems likely that subject would have a conscious strategy to sort or select information in this way or that he would be able to carry it out if he did. Indeed, it is an increasingly common view that the processes of input coding are not much subject to the attentional control of the subject (Keele, 1972; Posner & Boies, 1971; Shiffrin & Gardner, 1972).

At this level of processing it is often more difficult to avoid the occurrence of a highly over-learned association than it is to achieve it. We have abundant evidence that the nervous system activates the name of visually presented words (e.g., Stroop effect) and frequent association (Warren, 1972) even when it is to subjects' interest to avoid doing so. These findings run directly counter to the views that subjects select from the stimulus distinctive features which control from the very start the way that stimulus is handled by the nervous system (Gibson, 1971). Rather, he has great difficulty in avoiding the activation of habitual associations to a given item.

Visual Search

There are other demonstrations of the multiplicity of codes activated by a given input letter. In the early work on visual search (Neisser, 1967) there was emphasis upon the development of low level analyzers which could screen visual information at an early stage. The basic idea was that the input items in the scanned array made no contact with the associations stored in long-term memory, but were shunted aside if they failed to meet low level feature tests defined by the target set.

Although there are data which seem to argue for the visual character of such search tasks (Gibson & Yonas, 1966) there is now abundant evidence which suggests that even in this task, information which subjects have in long-term memory is involved in the selection process. For example, Brand (1971) has shown that subjects can search for all the digits in a field of letters about as rapidly as any individual digit even without extensive practice. This suggests that they can use the letter-digit distinction as a means of separating target from non-target. Of course, it is possible to argue that a set of visual features specific to the digits is constructed immediately in this task but it seems more reasonable to propose, as Brand (1971) has, that the input items make contact with the well learned classification and that subjects simply respond on the basis of whether their internal representation of the digit set becomes activated. Krueger (1970) has shown that subjects are faster in searching through letter groups that make meaningful words or prose passages than they are for pseudo-words or nonsense materials. These findings suggest very strongly that visual scanning is not a task which is isolated from well learned classifications stored in long-term memory.

A direct demonstration of the effect of both visual and name processes in a scanning task is found in a study by Turnbull (1971). She had subjects

search a list of 300 items for either one visual form
(e.g., an upper case letter), two forms which had the
same name (e.g., A and a), two forms with separate
names, or four forms with two names. The subjects
were run at a relatively low level of practice. The
search list was a mixture of upper and lower case
letters equated for size.

Her results are shown in Table 1. Both the
number of forms and the number of names affect the
rate of search. These results indicate that the

Table 1. Search Rates (msec per letter) as a Function of Target Type

No. of Forms	No. of Names	No Interference	Audio Interference
1	1	130	133
2	1	140	151
2	2	148	163
4	2	176	181

search rate depends on both physical and name factors. However, when Turnbull manipulated the acoustic background, she found no significant interference
of the acoustic background with any of the conditions.
Thus, while on the one hand her data indicate that
both physical and name factors are involved in target identification, they do not suggest specific
interference from auditory items. In that sense they
are in agreement with the empirical data upon which
Gibson & Yonas (1966) based their argument for visual
processing in this task, but not with the interpretation.

Does evidence that names or categories affect
the rate of visual search imply that the task of re-
jecting a letter involves the conscious control by
subject over the task? I think not.

One of the striking reasons for Neisser's proposal that the search task involves "pre-attentive"
processes was that the target letter appeared to leap
out at subjects while the subjects seemed not to be
conscious of the existence of non-target letters.
This is a vague but compelling phenomenological experience in Neisser's task. Neisser tended to identify evidence for "pre-attentive" processes with low
level visual analysis. Recently, Cavanagh and Chase
(1971) have shown that very complex processes may
occur prior to this phenomenological indicant. They
presented subjects with a positive array of one to
six letters followed by a pair of letters. The subject's task was to indicate which of the pair was a
member of the positive set. Since a new array was
presented on each trial it was clearly necessary to
use memory to arrive at a decision. It was found, in
agreement with work by Sternberg (1966), that reaction
time in this task was a linear function of the number
of stored items with the slope of 40.4 msec. per item.
Despite this evidence for a memory search process
underlying the response, the subjects reported that
the target letter seemed to leap out at them and the
other item did not. The data suggest that both the
target and non-target items are subject to a memory
search process but only the target item gives rise to
the phenomenological experience of jumping out at the
subject. Thus, this phenomenological experience
occurs rather late in the sequence of processing as a
result of memory search and its occurrence in
Neisser's task cannot be used to infer that rejection
of a letter is a low level visual process.
    I think these results change the conception of
the human nervous system which prevailed in the 1950's
and 1960's. We must not think of a limited capacity
system as restricting the range of associations which
can be activated by input, provided that these associations are habitual. Indeed, it might require more
effort to inhibit such associations than to produce
them. Rather, we must understand the widespread
parallel effects which a given item causes. The

41

problem, then, becomes one of selection and coordination of these habitual associations in guiding their use during the performance of tasks.

Search of Active Memory

In 1966 Sternberg reported that the time to respond whether an item was a member of a positive set was linearly related to the number of items in the set. What kind of code underlies this match? Sternberg has argued that subjects match the input against a visual representation of the previously presented letters. In favor of that view was his finding that non-linguistic visual material gave similar functions and that the rate of search was affected at least initially by stimulus degradation. On the other hand, Wattenbarger (1970) concluded that arrays are encoded in terms of the letter names. The main evidence for his view came from a condition in which subjects received an array of mixed upper and lower case letters. They were instructed to respond "yes" to the probe only when it was physically identical to one of the array letters (physical match). He compared this task with conditions where subjects received both upper and lower case forms of each letter (name match) and where only one case was used for each array (control). The first condition was markedly more difficult than either of the other two, which in turn differed slightly (the last being somewhat superior). If subjects had only a visual representation of the letters, one would have expected the condition with both upper and lower case shown to be quite difficult, and the first condition to differ only slightly from the last condition. Thus, Wattenbarger concludes that subjects probably had only letter names available. He felt that the first condition was difficult because the more complex names were required to make a distinction between upper and lower case.

Multiple Codes

It is fairly easy to show that multiple codes *can* be available in tasks of this type. In one study the subjects were presented with an array of one to four letters which were either all upper or all lower case. Each letter was present for .5 sec. and the array was followed after .5 sec. by a single visual probe letter which either matched the array physically (.33), in name only (.33), or did not match (.33). The results are shown in Fig. 1. These data are better fit by a logarithmic rather than a linear

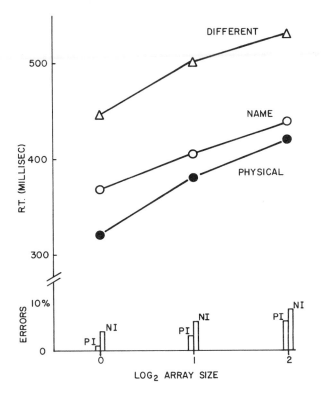

Fig. 1. Reaction times and errors for physical and name "same" responses and for "different" responses as a function of array size.

43

function which probably reflects the marked recency
function obtained when the probe follows closely after
the array. The functions differ significantly in both
intercept and slope. Moreover, in the four-item
arrays the physical and name matches differ for each
serial position (Fig. 2). It is also of interest that
the recency effect appears for both physical and name
matches.

We have since replicated these functions in
situations where the letter array is a mixture of
upper and lower case letters. However, the serial
position curves in this study do not give as clear
results as in Fig. 2.

Although our curves are well described by a
logarithmic function, the increase in RT between two
and four items is similar to values reported by
Sternberg. This suggests that the overall process in
our study is not markedly different than in other
experiments using this technique.

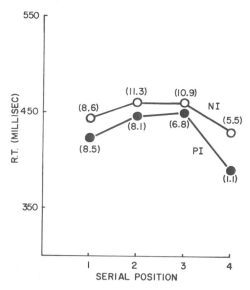

Fig. 2. Serial position curves for physical and
name "same" responses.

Our results fit quite well with a view that
subjects have represented both the physical form of a
letter and the letter name. Suppose they had represented the arrays only by letter name. In that case
there is no reason that physical matches should be
faster than name matches. Suppose they had only a
visual representation. In that case the name level
RTs should have reflected the time to transform each
stored visual item into its name. Previous work has
shown that this process would take something like 80
msec. per stored item (Beller, 1970; Eichelman, 1970).
It appears unlikely that the effects in this study
are sufficient for such a process. Moreover, it would
be difficult to square a theory which involved only
storing the visual form with the Wattenbarger data in
which physical matches were extremely difficult when
some of the array letters matched the probe name.
On the other hand, a dual coding theory fits
Wattenbarger's findings quite well. The long time for
physical matching in his data would be due to conflict
arising from the fact that some of the letters to
which the subject must say "no" do match one of the
two codes he has in the array.

More evidence for multiple codes of the same
items comes from recent experiments by Lively and
Sanford (1972). In this study the array was either
all digits or all consonants. Probe items could
either match an array item, be different and from the
same category, or be different both in item and category. The results showed that different responses
which matched in category were slower than those which
did not match in category. Thus the matching appeared
to involve elements of both the name of the item and
the category.

One difficulty with positing a visual and name
code is that Burrows (1972) found little evidence for
a visual code of previous letter arrays. He compared
all combinations of visual and auditory arrays and
probes. He found that physical correspondence between
array and probe only improved performance when both
were auditory. He concluded that only auditory codes

and abstract representations (logogens) of the previous list are present in memory. Although his conclusions agree with the idea of multiple coding between auditory and abstract codes, the failure to obtain evidence for it with visual presentation is clearly at odds with the ideas presented in this section. The reason for this difference may lie in the use of auditory probes in these experiments. Perhaps the fact that visual information was not a reliable cue to making the match inclines subjects to rehearse array names in all conditions. The relatively long times obtained in their study may be evidence of this. As we shall see, while data favor the simultaneous registration and retention of multiple codes of the same event, rehearsal does tend to be code-specific and thus to select out one of the codes for dominance.

Code Coordination

Our previous work using single letters and letter pairs has supported the idea that the physical and name codes of the letter could be manipulated separately (Posner, Lewis & Conrad, 1972) and that retrieval of the two codes went on in parallel (Posner, 1969; Cohen, 1969). We hoped to be able to find similar evidence when multi-letter arrays were being searched. We decided to start out with a situation where we could be sure that the arrays in the two codes were separate. To do this we presented subjects with a task in which the arrays consisted of one, two or four items. In the visual condition the items were all Gibson forms presented on a scope display. In the auditory condition they were all letter names presented from a tape recorder. In the mixed conditions the items were pairs of simultaneous Gibson forms and letters. The probe was always presented visually and was either a letter or Gibson form. The conditions were mixed so that subjects never knew whether the probe would be a Gibson form or a letter. The search functions are shown in Fig. 3.

46

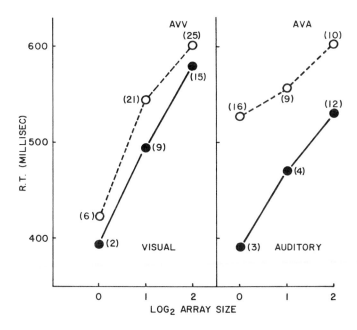

Fig. 3. RTs and errors ( ) for pure visual arrays, pure auditory arrays and simultaneous visual and auditory arrays as a function of array size. Visual stimuli are Gibson forms and auditory letter names.

The data are fit by logarithmic functions. As we hoped, the time to match in the visual code was not much affected by the presence of letter names. However, there was a very large affect of Gibson forms on name matching. Indeed, the time for letter matching is increased about as much by adding Gibson forms as by adding additional letters. In order to see if this effect was due primarily to memory strength, we studied a condition in which the probe item was delayed 2 sec. after the array. The results were virtually identical to those found in Fig. 3.

It seemed to us that the asymmetry between the codes
was probably introduced by the great difficulty in
dealing with the unfamiliar Gibson forms.

In order to eliminate this difficulty and to
determine what would happen when the subjects could
not tell which code to search from the class of the
probe, we replaced the Gibson figures with visual
letters. The visual letters came from the same set
of 12 as the letter names, but no repeats between the
two codes were presented on any trial.

The results of this study are rather interesting.
Figure 4 illustrates the functions relating RT to the
number of single letter (A and V) or letter pairs
(AVV, AVA) presented. In agreement with Burrows
(1972), there is little difference between auditory
and visual presentation with one letter. However,
with four-letter arrays the visual arrays were clearly
and significantly superior in both the V and AVV
conditions. This difference is particularly clear in
the last two serial positions. This result suggests
that the presence of a visual code becomes apparent
in conditions where it is most doubtful that subjects
have time to rehearse the letter names.

We had hoped that the visually and aurally
presented items would have sufficiently separate
codes that the time for search would be faster when a
given number of items were in two codes than when
they were all in the same code. That is, we hoped
that search of the visual and auditory codes would
overlap in time making it more efficient to search
separate codes. Figure 5 indicates that this was not
the case. A single function fits all the data
reasonably well regardless of the array condition.
This suggests that, as far as overall search time
goes, the code makes relatively little difference and
provides no evidence that search of separate codes
proceeds differently from search of one code, at
least under our conditions.

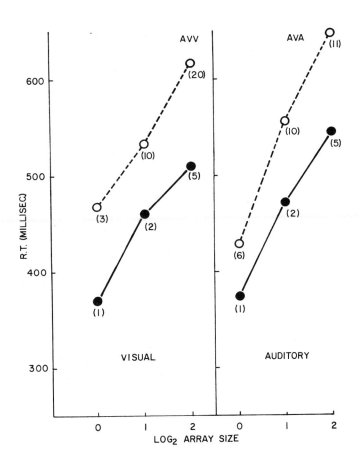

Fig. 4. RTs and errors ( ) for pure visual, pure auditory and simultaneous visual and auditory arrays as a function of array size. Visual stimuli are letter and auditory stimuli letter names.

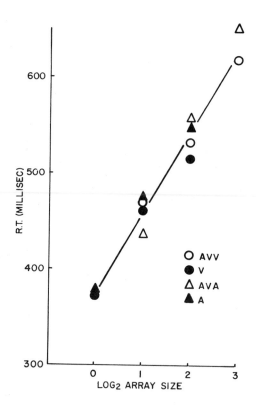

Fig. 5. RTs as a function of the log of the array size, collapsed over all type of arrays.

Summary

The data from encoding and memory search favor a multiple coding view. A given item activates a wide variety of codes and appears to do so in parallel. When multiple codes of the same item are activated there is facilitation of matching a new input item. When distinct items are present in the two codes, the subject gives evidence of being able to confine his tests to one code in the case of a visual match, but the presence of Gibson figures in memory gives rather marked interference in matching a visual letter against its auditory name. Whether this interference is in the search task itself or in the clarity of the memory trace is not determined. When the two codes have items which are not redundant but come from the same category (e.g., visual and auditory letters) there is as much interference in search as though the items were in the same code. These results do not provide a simple picture of the coordination of internal codes. They suggest that the subject often has difficulty in confining his search to a given class of items. Attempting to make a visual match in the presence of contradictory name information (Wattenbarger, 1970) is one example of this difficulty. Subjects do not have much control over the information which is contacted by the probe item, but must act to resolve conflict at a cost of time and errors. In the next section we turn to the use of conscious rehearsal as a means of selecting among the codes created by a given input item.

Rehearsal and Translation

What are the range of codes which are activated by a stimulus and how does the subject select among these codes? Does rehearsing a stimulus involve the simultaneous selection of all codes of that event? Does attending to one code leave other codes unchanged or does it suppress rival codes? What about codes which are not directly presented in the stimulus, but which, like the name of a letter, are habitual associations to the stimulus?

These questions are essential in understanding the role of memory codes in thought. The simplest situations in which to study them are ones in which a given stimulus event can be represented in different codes and the subject is given some opportunity to rehearse, translate or organize that event. Two situations in which these requirements are met are in the study of retaining the physical and name characteristics of letters, words, faces or pictures and the memory for

51

visual and kinesthetic (haptic) codes of either
voluntary movements or forms exposed to view and/or
touch.

Visual and Name Codes

Rivalry. When subjects are presented with a
visual letter and required to retain it there is
strong evidence for rivalry among different codes. In
the presence of competing visual letters, errors are
related to acoustic (articulatory) confusions (Conrad,
1964). Under the influence of a single code theory,
this finding was sometimes interpreted as meaning that
this was the only code possible. Recently, it has been
shown that in the presence of auditory shadowing subjects appear to attend to the visual code of the letters
and preserve them in that form (Parkinson, 1972). Taken
together, these findings are in accord with the multiple
code view of this paper and indicate how the code
selected reflects aspects of the task configuration.

Tversky (1969) found that subjects who are shown
either a schematic face or its name attended to the
name when a second matching event was most likely to
be a name and to the face when the match is most likely
to be a face. It may be that in some conditions both
codes are activated but only the expected one is kept
at the highest level of readiness.

Another manipulation which has been shown to affect
the code chosen by the subject is whether he is
instructed to recognize or recall. In a matching
situation, at least with short intervals, Smith and
Nielson (1970) found that subjects preserve the face in
a code which resembles a visual template. The speed of
responding "same" did not vary with the number of
relevant dimensions. However, with recall instructions
the code resembled a list in being sensitive to the
size of the stored array. Frost (1972) has also shown
that recognition versus recall instructions will alter
the relative salience of the visual code of pictures.
When the subjects thought they had to recall, clustering
by semantic categories dominated the order of their

output. However, when they expected to recognize, clustering involved a combination of visual shape and semantic content.

These experiments certainly suggest that the subject's attention to one code tends to bias his later performance in favor of that code. This means that rehearsal is code specific. The experiments also suggest some things which affect the direction of the bias. These include sources of interference, type of reinstatement task and probably habits and preferences which reflect a particular culture's or individual's learned experiences.

The fact that the subject attends to one particular code of a stimulus probably does not suppress the retention of other codes of that stimulus more than would be the case if he attended to irrelevant items. In one experiment Eichelman (1970) had subjects name successive letters as quickly as possible. On a small proportion of the trials the successive letters were physically identical (e.g., AA) and on other trials they had only the same name (e.g., Aa). His data show a highly significant advantage to physical over name matches of about the same magnitude as found when the subject's attention is specifically on the physical code. Thus, at least for a time, multiple codes may exist even when, as in many problem solving tasks, attention is directed to a particular code.

In two recent studies (Cruse & Clifton, 1973; Swanson, Johnsen, & Briggs, 1972), subjects were presented with an array consisting in the first named study of binary and octal digits and in the second of complex visual forms and two digit numbers. The array material could be probed either by a stimulus in the same code or by a probe which had a learned relationship to the array. In the case of the binary arrays, the probes could be the corresponding octal number and in the case of the visual forms a two-digit number which the subject has learned as the name of the form. In both studies the slopes of the function relating RT to array size increased when the probe was in a different code. Both authors interpret their data by suggesting that subjects

hold the array in the original code and translate it
only if the probe format requires them to do so. This
view accounts for the obtained slope differences.
According to this view, subjects have available only
one code at a time.

Another possibility is that both the original and
translated codes are present, but that their strengths
and thus their search rates differ. There is reason
to suppose that the translation of the stimulus would
not obliterate the original code. The crux of the
problem, however, is to determine the extent to which
the translation process is a voluntary act which can be
withheld versus an automatic look-up which takes place
when the relevant array item is presented. The next
sections consider some of the factors which may be
involved in the automatic character of translation.

Generation. Several years ago I reported (Posner
et al., 1969) that subjects could generate the visual
representation of a letter after being presented with
its name. The evidence for this was quite objective.
It involved finding that the time for matching a visual
stimulus following its aurally presented name declined
over a .5-1 sec. interval until it became as fast as
for same case matching of visual letters and much faster
than visual matches which involved switching cases.
However, there was a serious problem in this work. The
time for physical matches always increased with delay
so that the generated match was never as fast as could
be obtained when two physically identical letters were
matched at short delays.

Stephen Boies (1969, 1971) performed a series of
experiments which explored this problem and revealed
some important new points. At the time, we thought
that physical matches increased over a 1-sec. interval
because the visual code was reduced in availability
or clarity. He eliminated this possibility by leaving
the first letter present in the visual field until the
second letter appeared. In one study the first letter
could be either upper or lower case and was present for
500, 1000 or 1500 msec. The second letter could match

physically, only in name, or be different. The results of his study showed that physical match RTs increased about 30 msec. over the interval. At 500 msec. physical and name matches differed significantly (83 msec.) while after a 1500 msec. delay they did not differ significantly (15 msec.). While it appeared that generation had occurred, Boies had failed to prevent an increase in the time for physical matches, even when the first letter remained present in the visual field.

There might have been several explanations for the upswing in physical match times, but Boies chose what seemed at first a curious hypothesis. He felt that the time for physical matches increased because as the opposite case was placed in a visual code the subject had a positive set of two through which to scan. This meant, according to the Sternberg theory, that it should take him about 30 msec. longer to make his match. To explore this view Boies set up three different conditions. In one condition the subject had a first letter which was always upper case followed by a second letter which was always upper case (pure physical match). Boies reasoned that in this situation no generation was needed and there should be no tendency for physical matches to increase with exposure duration. The mixed condition was identical to the previous experiment. Finally, in a pure generation condition the second letter was always opposite in case to the first. The predictions were that the pure physical match condition should decline more slowly to the same level. In both these conditions the subject ends with a positive set of one visual item, although in one case it was physically in his visual field and in the other generated from the opposite case. The mixed condition should show an increase for physical matches and a decrease for name matches. With long intervals these two values should be equal and about 30 msec. longer than for the pure conditions. This is because the subject has a positive set of two. All these expectations were met (see Fig. 6).

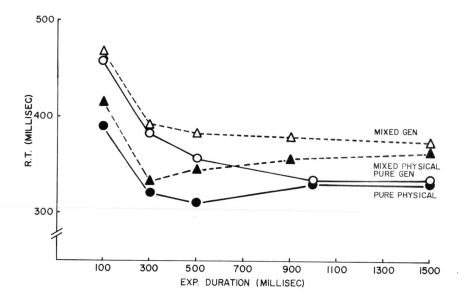

Fig. 6. RTs for "same" responses as a function of condition; pure generation, pure physical, and mixed, for various exposure durations of the first letter. After Boies (1971).

Boies also compared a condition where the subject was presented with upper and lower cases of the same letters to his generation condition. The data indicated that the dual case condition RTs initially lay between the physical and name match times for the single letter and as exposure duration increased, all three conditions converged to a common value.

Immediately after presentation, physical match times are identical whether the subject knows that all matches are physical or whether he sometimes has opposite case matches. Thus, having to deal simultaneously with the two codes does not affect RT according to Boies's data. It is only when the subject generates the opposite case and produces a positive set of two within the visual code that his time for physical matches increases to that of dual presentation. This

56

same result has now been obtained by Elias and Kinsbourne (1972) using non-verbal stimuli in which matching can be made by physical identity or a learned classification. Unfortunately, we were not able to find this degree of separability between codes for multi-item arrays as reported in Experiment III on search.

Boies's results give a strong sense of reality to the operation of generation. The end result of generation appears to be a visual code much like that retained from a just-presented visual stimulus.

Boies's results led us to another conclusion, however, which may not be correct. Recall that when a single letter is presented and removed subjects do not tend to generate the opposite case. Rather, the time for physical matches increases rapidly while name matches remain constant. In Boies's data, where the first letter is present in the field, subjects appear to generate the opposite case. These two findings led us to suppose that generation was both optional and difficult. Thus, we thought of generation as a voluntary attention-demanding translation much like recoding binary to octal digits. This seemed to square with the relatively long times required before generation is complete.

Attention demands of generation. The question of the difficulty of generation is really quite important because it bears upon the range of codes which might be available in the nervous system from which the subject selects. Our view was that presentation of a visual letter led automatically to activation of the letter name, but that the reverse was an optional process which required an attentional effort by the subject. This view has been challenged by results of studies which have involved matching of visual faces to their names.

Tversky (1969) found in her study of name-face matching that the match made was in the code of the second stimulus even when that stimulus was unexpected. This indicates that subjects find it easier to generate

57

a picture when he receives an unexpected picture than
to abstract the name of the second stimulus and match
on the basis of the name. This result seemed surprising to us because of the presumed attentional demands
of generation.

Tversky's data involved only a single ISI (1 sec.)
and no direct comparison between face-face and name-
face matching. Thus, Miriam Rogers (1972) sought to
replicate the Tversky result and see whether generation
occurred as measured by the criterion of a convergence
of RT between physical and name matches. Rogers used
exposure durations of .4 and 2 sec. and compared face-
face and name-face trials. As shown in Fig. 7, there
was a clear convergence of same RTs. For the long
delay there were no significant differences between
face-face and name-face trials. At the short delay
physical and name matches differed by about 70 msec.
By this criterion, generation seemed to take between
400 and 2000 msec. However, a finer analysis of the
results indicated that at both intervals the match was
based upon a visual face code. That is, in both cases,
subjects based the match on a visual representation of

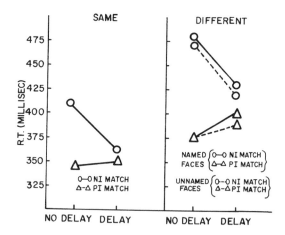

Fig. 7. RTs for face-face and name-face matching
as a function of delay. After Rogers (1972).

the first stimulus and not upon a name derived from the second stimulus. This was shown both by the fact that faces which had been given no name during learning were just as easy to classify as those to which the subject had learned names and by a detailed comparison of individual features for the face-face and name-face trials. In the case of short delay, generation appeared to follow the second stimulus, while in the long intervals it was complete when the second stimulus was presented. These results agree with Tversky's finding that subjects prefer to transform the memorial stimulus rather than abstract the name of the second stimulus. This finding also agrees with the result from the memory search data that subjects translate the array into the format of the probe rather than the reverse, even when the array size is large (Cruse & Clifton, 1973; Swanson, Johnsen & Briggs, 1972).

I will try to hazard a guess as to the meaning of these results. My guess is that the activation pattern of a given input item is mainly influenced by the strength of past associations and that the direction of these associations (i.e., abstraction vs. generation) matters little. When the subject is presented with a list of visual letters, the names are also activated though they may not be conscious. Similarly, when the subject hears a list of letter names the visual code is increased in availability. Indeed, Warren (1972) has shown this rather directly. Boies's data on generation may be rather special because they depend upon one case of a letter (e.g., A) activating another case (e.g., a). This association may be rather weaker than the link between either of these visual forms and the letter name. This view suggests that the subject's nervous system automatically activates a wide range of associations; however, unless they have been rehearsed deliberately their availability in matching tasks might not be very high. This would account for the higher slopes obtained on translated material. If these speculations are correct, the degree of automaticity of an association would depend more upon the strength of the association than upon either its direction or whether it is within or between modalities. The importance of this problem certainly warrants further analysis.

Generation and perception. There are many means of assessing the ability of the subject to generate a visual image. The most common are subjective reports of imagery ability. In recent years these have been joined by a variety of objective behavioral tests. It would seem important to know the degree of relationship among different tasks which are said to require imagery, and how closely related imagery is to perception. This second issue has been in considerable dispute. For example, Konorski (1967) argues that the same gnostic units which act to perceive input serve also as the basis of imagery. The Boies result seems to lend some support to this position. On the other hand, Piaget relates imagery to internalization of motor activity and not to a stage of visual perception. Charles Snyder (1972) began a systematic attack on these two questions through the study of individual differences.

He used three classes of activity. First was self report imagery scales. Second was the ability of subjects to solve problems based upon the manipulation of blocks. Third was the speed with which subjects are able to rotate two complex block patterns to state whether or not they are congruent (Shepard & Metzler, 1971). He found small but significant correlations between these three tasks. Subjects who reported themselves to be good in manipulating their images also solved the block problems more quickly and showed lower slopes relating RT to degree of rotation in the Shepard task (Fig. 8).

These findings were quite pleasing because the block task is very much a problem solving situation while the Shepard rotation task is much closer to perception. Indeed, I have argued elsewhere (Posner, 1969) that the ability to equate two visual items as being identical when they differ in size or rotation (analog matches) is the same skill which is involved in pattern recognition when the subject has to normalize the input

60

in order to match it against his stored representation. Thus it seemed that the correlation between the mental rotation task and self report imagery must mean that the ability to image is closely related to one component of the ability to see--namely, the speed at which one can compare input and internal code.

The idea that poor imagery meant poor perception (in this one sense) was surprising. To test this idea, Snyder chose high and low imagers and began to explore their threshold for various letter identification tasks. In the meantime a paper appeared (Paivio & Ernest, 1971) showing that poor imagers do have higher thresholds for reporting the identity of pictures and forms. Snyder has confirmed this effect for some aspects of letter identification. While Paivio's and Snyder's data raise a number of difficult questions, they seem to me to confirm the important link between imagery and perception and to argue for the cogency of Konorski's formulation.

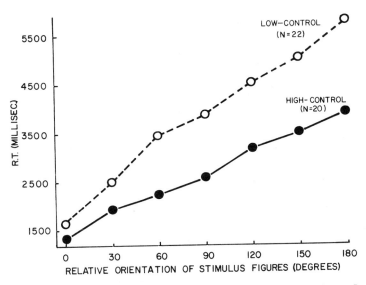

Fig. 8. RTs for equating pairs of complex forms as "same" as a function of the difference in orientation for low and high imagers. After Snyder (1972).

Visual and Kinesthetic (Haptic) Codes

Another area in which the same stimulus event gives rise to multiple codes is in the study of simple movements which may be visually guided or blind and forms which can be both seen and felt. A traditional developmental view has been that kinesthesis serves to control the development of vision (Berkeley, 1709, Piaget & Inhelder, 1969). In recent years, however, work in perception with adult subjects has emphasized that vision dominates when it conflicts with kinesthesis (Rock & Harris, 1967). There is little doubt, however, that both kinesthetic and visual cues can be maintained in memory. Evidence indicates that their retention characteristics differ. Thus, it may be instructive to compare this paradigm with the material which has just been reviewed on visual and name cues of letters and faces.

A number of years ago, I performed a series of experiments which taken together appeared to me to have some powerful implications. I compared retention of a blind motor movement with one which was visually guided (Posner & Konick, 1966; Posner, 1967). The blind movement, particularly when it required the reproduction of movement distance, showed a steady loss in accuracy over an unfilled interval of 30 sec. On the other hand, when the movement and its reproduction was visually guided, and especially when the subject could perform the task by retaining a position in space, the task showed no decline in performance over an unfilled interval and, unlike the kinesthetic distance task, was greatly affected by interpolated tasks which controlled the subject's ability to concentrate upon or rehearse the criterion stimulus. In the five years which have intervened since those studies, my results have sometimes been replicated (Adams, 1972; Bruchon, 1970; Stelmach & Wilson, 1970; Williams, Beaver, Spence & Rundell, 1969), often been refuted (Keele & Ells, 1972; Pepper & Herman, 1970), occasionally been clarified (Laabs, 1971; Posner & Keele, 1969), and in some cases extended in a way relevant to the coordination of internal codes

(Connolly & Jones, 1970; Goodnow, 1971; Jones & Connolly, 1970; Millar, 1971).

There are clearly many complexities in the area which have not been resolved. My generalization about kinesthetic memory may not apply to all the different cues which can be retained from a blind movement. Keele and I have shown that long movements are more apt to show the kinesthetic code results than short ones (Posner & Keele, 1969). Moreover, Laabs (1971) confirmed my earlier finding that location in space, even when arising from kinesthetic cues, behaves more like a visual code. Shagan (1970) found that blind subjects behaved more like normal sighted subjects than like blindfolded ones, suggesting that the results depended upon our habitual use of the cues rather than upon the basic organization of the sensory system. Laabs (1971) found that a minority of subjects will code a blind motor movement in terms of execution time and rate of movement by counting while they move. These subjects appear to obey somewhat different laws than those who do not observe this strategy. His results point out again the obstinate ability of subjects to create new codes of a given performance. Having made these qualifications, I still believe the basic difference between visual and kinesthetic codes has held up reasonably well where it has been carefully investigated. This asymmetry reflects the relative dominance of visual cues for the subjects' attention and the difficulty of rehearsing many of the cues which arise directly from kinesthesis. With this bias in mind, I will try to review a few studies which have tried to compare how subjects attempt to preserve information arising from visual and kinesthetic experience.

Retention

Laabs (1971) studied blind movements which required subjects to retain a position in space and those which required him to reproduce a distance. He was careful to separate from his results a minority of subjects who counted during the movement and stored a rate and time.

He found that accuracy of location was not much affected by a delay of 12 sec. but that retention of distance was. Moreover, he also showed that retention of location was greatly affected by having subjects count backward during the retention interval while distance reproduction was not at all affected. So great was this effect, that retention of location after counting backward was worse than retention of distance. Thus, Laabs found the same asymmetry in retention between location and distance of blind movements which I had reported previously for sighted versus blind movements. One reason for this similarity could be that spatial location is referred to a visual code (Attneave & Benson, 1969).

What is of interest for our purpose is that when both vision and kinesthesis are available for reproduction, the retention follows the rules of the visual code. When location and distance are confounded, retention resembles location.

This view leads to an interesting paradox. If subjects choose to use the visual cue and if interpolated tasks affect visual codes more than kinesthetic, it would follow that a blind movement could be reproduced better than the same movement when visually guided. Indeed, there is some marginal evidence of this. In one study (Posner, 1967) it was found that a visually guided movement following an interpolated classification task showed larger mean errors than the same movement which was executed without vision. Further evidence on this point is needed.

Recently, Goodnow (1971) compared retention of haptic and visual information about complex letter-like forms. The forms could either be seen or be felt. She used all four possible combinations of exposure and recognition (VV, KK, VK, KV). She varied the complexity of the task by requiring her subjects to pick out the form from either one, three, or five comparison forms. For intramodality matching, vision was superior and showed no decline with complexity, while haptic matching deteriorated markedly with complexity. For intermodality matching there was no difference between a visual and haptic standard with the simplest task (one comparison), but vision was greatly superior with three comparisons. If the complexity of the recognition task is viewed as an increased delay in memory, this pattern conforms to the asymmetry between visual and kinesthetic codes found in the movement reproduction.

Millar (1971) confirmed and extended some of Goodnow's findings. She showed that visual matching was superior to haptic for children of three and four years. However, she did not find a great difference between V-H and H-V as would be expected by a retention account. The addition of visual cues to the haptic matching task greatly improved performance of the four-year-olds; however, haptic cues added to a visual matching task had no effect. Once more, and even with quite young children, who might be thought to be "motoric" in orientation, one finds that visual cues dominate.

Translation

Connolly and Jones (1970) studied four conditions for reproducing or recognizing line length. The standard could be either visual or kinesthetic and the retention test could be either visual (recognition) or kinesthetic (reproduction). They found that for the VV condition there was no forgetting over an unfilled interval and a large effect of an interpolated naming task. The KK condition showed forgetting in about equal amounts with or without an interpolated task. The mixed conditions were more interesting. The VK condition resembled KK while the KV condition resembled VV. The authors argue that subjects translate the code into the modality of reproduction at the start of the interval. Unfortunately, we have no independent way of knowing that translation has occurred except by inference from the forgetting functions. It would be interesting to know whether, as the authors suggest, the modality of input would be maintained when subjects did not know which will be the comparison modality.

Summary

The experiments on visual and kinesthetic codes
suggest that the two codes may be isolable subsystems
which are selected and rehearsed independently. The
visual codes appear to dominate, although the reasons
may have more to do with experience than necessity.
The techniques available to separate and study the codes
in isolation are less direct than for verbal information. Nonetheless, the experiments on visual and kinesthetic codes paint much the same picture as the earlier
review of visual and name codes. The nervous system
portrays an experience in the form of distinct codes,
which have their individual advantages both in terms of
what they preserve and how they are retained. Some of
these codes are directly implicit in the stimulus and
some are habitual translations which may occur either
automatically or only where attention is available to
give to them. The information which the subject rehearses seems to be quite specific to one of these
codes. He has considerable option, but if more than
one code of the same stimulus is like more than one
item, it reduces available capacity. It seems most
likely that the choice of a given code to rehearse has
no direct effect upon the likelihood that other codes
will be preserved. That will depend upon the decay
characteristic of that code in the absence of rehearsal.
However, even if multiple codes are present in the nervous system it may depend upon the memory task whether
they will be used. For example, recognition tasks may
activate all relevant codes above a given strength
while a recall task inclines the subject to reproduce
only the codes he has chosen to attend during the
interval.

Conclusions

I believe that the data in this paper support the
reality of multiple codes. They are created and maintained in parallel. The range of codes which can be
elicited by a given input are not confined to physical

aspects of the signal but include habitual associations
which may be abstracted from it (e.g., a visual letter's
name) or generated from it (e.g., a name's visual form).
On the other hand, different codes tend to compete for
the subject's conscious attention. This rivalry makes
retention of an item in a highly activated form quite
code specific.

These results do no more than suggest a few of the
possible ways in which coding might affect thought. We
have emerged from a period in which almost all emphasis
in theories of thought has been upon verbal or linguistic processes (Whorf, 1956). Probably changes in our
general culture more than experimental results have led
to increased sympathy for non-verbal processes in
thought. However, this trend is in accord with experimental results such as those of Furth (1966) with the
deaf and of Paivio (1971) on the role of imagery in
learning. We need to do much more to understand the
contributions of different memory codes, their virtues
and pitfalls. In particular, we need more concentra-
tion on the coordination of these codes in our experience and behavior.

References

Adams, J. A., Marshall, P. H., & Goetz, E. T. Response
feedback and short-term motor retention. *Journal
of Experimental Psychology*, 1972, 92, 92-95.
Arnheim, R. *Visual thinking*. Berkeley & Los Angeles:
University of California Press, 1969.
Attneave, F., & Benson, B. Spatial coding of tactile
stimulation. *Journal of Experimental Psychology*,
1969, 81, 216-222.
Bartlett, F. C. *Thinking*. New York: Basic Books, 1958.
Beller, H. K. Parallel and serial stages in matching.
Journal of Experimental Psychology, 1970, 84,
213-219.
Berkeley, G. An essay toward a new theory of vision
(1709). In A. A. Luce & T. E. Jessup (Eds.)
Works of George Berkeley. London: Nelson, 1949,
159-239.

Boies, S. J. Retention of visual information from a single letter. Unpublished M.A. Thesis, University of Oregon, 1969.

Boies, S. J. Memory codes in a speeded classification task. Unpublished Doctoral Dissertation, University of Oregon, 1971

Bourne, L. *Human conceptual behavior*. Boston: Allyn & Bacon, 1966.

Bower, G. H. Mental imagery and associative learning. In L. W. Gregg (Ed.), *Cognition in learning and memory*. New York: Wiley, 1972.

Brand, J. Classification without identification in visual search. *Quarterly Journal of Experimental Psychology*, 1971, 23, 171-186.

Brooks, L. R. Spatial and verbal components of the act of recall. *Canadian Journal of Psychology*, 1968, 22, 349-368.

Bruchon, M., & Hay, L. Information visuelle, information proprioceptive et controle des positions du corps propre. *Psychologie Francaise*, 1970, 15, 205-212.

Bruner, J. S., Oliver, R. R., & Greenfield, P. M. *Studies in cognitive growth*. New York: Wiley, 1966.

Burrows, D. Modality effects in retrieval of information from STM. *Perception and Psychophysics*, 1972, 11, 365-372.

Cavanagh, J. P., & Chase, W. G. The equivalence of target and nontarget processing in visual search. *Perception and Psychophysics*, 1971, 9, 493-495.

Collins, A. M., & Quillian, M. R. Retrieval time from semantic memory. *Journal of Verbal Learning and Verbal Behavior*, 1969, 8, 240-247.

Cohen, G. Some evidence for parallel comparisons in a letter recognition task. *Quarterly Journal of Experimental Psychology*, 1969, 21, 272-279.

Coltheart, M. Visual information processing. In P. C. Dodwell (Ed.), *Psychology*. London: Penguin Books, 1972, in press.

Connolly, K., & Jones, B. A developmental study of afferent-reafferent integration. *British Journal of Psychology*, 1970, 61, 250-266.

Conrad, R. Acoustic confusions in immediate memory. *British Journal of Psychology*, 1964, 55, 75–83.

Cruse, D., & Clifton, C. Jr. Recoding strategies and the retrieval of information from memory. *Cognitive Psychology*, 1973, 4, 157–193.

DeSoto, C. B., London, M., & Handel, S. Social reasoning and spatial paralogic. *Journal of Personality and Social Psychology*, 1965, 2, 513–521.

Eichelman, W. H. Familiarity effects in the simultaneous matching task. *Journal of Experimental Psychology*, 1970, 86, 275–282.

Elias, M. F., & Kinsbourne, M. Time course of identity and category matching by spatial orientation. *Journal of Experimental Psychology*, 1972, 95, 177–183.

Furth, H. G. *Thinking without language*. New York: Free Press, 1966.

Frijda, N. Simulation of human long-term memory. *Psychological Bulletin*, 1972, 77, 1–30.

Frost, N. H. Encoding and retrieval in a visual memory task. *Journal of Experimental Psychology*, 1972, 95, 317–326.

Galton F. *Inquiries into human facility and its development*. London: J. M. Dent, 1907.

Gibson, E. J. Perceptual learning and the theory of word perception. *Cognitive Psychology*, 1971, 2, 351–368.

Gibson, E. J., & Yonas, A. A developmental study of the effects of visual and auditory interference on a visual scanning task. *Psychonomic Science*, 1966, 5, 163–164.

Glucksberg, S., & Danks, J. H. Effects of discriminative labels and of nonsense labels upon availability of a novel function. *Journal of Verbal Learning and Verbal Behavior*, 1968, 7, 72–76.

Glucksberg, S., & Weisberg, R. W. Verbal behavior and problem solving: Some effects of labeling in a function fixedness problem. *Journal of Experimental Psychology*, 1966, 71, 659–664.

Goodnow, J. J. Eye and hand: Differential memory and its effect on matching. *Neuropsychologica*, 1971, 9, 89-95.

Huttenlocher, J. Constructing spatial images: A strategy in reasoning. *Psychological Review*, 1968, 75, 550-560.

Jones, B., & Connolly, K. Memory effects in cross-modal matching. *British Journal of Psychology*, 1970, 61, 267-270.

Keele, S. W. Attention demands of memory retrieval. *Journal of Experimental Psychology*, 1972, 93, 245-248.

Keele, S. W., & Ells, J. G. Memory characteristics of kinesthetic information. *Journal of Motor Behavior*, 1972, 4, 127-134.

Konorski, J. *Integrative activity of the brain.* Chicago: The Chicago University Press, 1967.

Krueger, L. Search time in a redundant visual display. *Journal of Experimental Psychology*, 1970, 83, 391-399.

Laabs, G. J. Cue effect in motor short-term memory. Unpublished Doctoral Dissertation, University of Oregon, 1971.

Lively, B., & Sanford, B. J. The use of category information in a memory-search task. *Journal of Experimental Psychology*, 1972, 93, 379-385.

Millar, S. Visual and haptic cue utilization by pre-school children. *Journal of Experimental Child Psychology*, 1971, 12, 88-94.

Neisser, U. *Cognitive psychology.* New York: Appleton-Century-Croft, 1967.

Newell, A., & Simon, H. A. *Human problem solving.* Englewood Cliffs, N. J.: Prentice-Hall, 1972.

Norman, D. A. Comments on the information structure of memory. *Acta Psychologica*, 1970, 33, 293-303.

Paivio, A. *Imagery and verbal processes.* New York: Holt, 1971.

Paivio, A., & Ernest, C. H. Imagery ability and visual perception of verbal and nonverbal stimuli. *Perception and Psychophysics*, 1971, 10, 429-432.

Parkinson, S. R. Short-term memory while shadowing: Multiple-items of visually and of aurally presented letters. *Journal of Experimental Psychology*, 1972, 92, 256-265.

Pepper, R. L., & Herman, L. M. Decay and interference effects in short-term retention of a discrete motor act. *Journal of Experimental Psychology Monograph*, 1970, 83, No. 2, Part 2.

Piaget, J., & Inhelder, B. *The psychology of the child.* New York: Basic Books, 1969.

Posner, M. I. Characteristics of visual and kinesthetic memory codes. *Journal of Experimental Psychology*, 1967, 75, 103-107.

Posner, M. I. Abstraction and the process of recognition. In G. Bower and J. T. Spence (Eds.), *Advances in learning and motivation.* Vol. III., New York: Academic Press, 1969.

Posner, M. I., Boies, S. J., Eichelman, W., & Taylor, R. L. Retention of visual and name codes of single letters. *Journal of Experimental Psychology Monograph*, 1969, 79, 1-16.

Posner, M. I. & Boies, S. J. Components of attention. *Psychological Review*, 1971, 78, 391-408.

Posner, M. I., & Keele, S. W. On the genesis of abstract ideas. *Journal of Experimental Psychology*, 1968, 77, 353-363.

Posner, M. I., & Keele, S. W. Attention demands of movements. Proceedings of the 17th Congress of Applied Psychology, Amsterdam, Zeitlinger, 1969.

Posner, M. I., & Konick, A. F. Short-term retention of visual and kinesthetic information. *Organization Behavior and Human Performance*, 1966, 1, 71-86.

Posner, M. I., Lewis, J., & Conrad, C. Component processes in reading: a performance analysis. In J. F. Kavanaugh and I. Mattingly (Eds.), *Language by ear and by eye.* M.I.T. Press, 1972.

Posner, M. I., & Rossman, E. The size and location of information reducing transforms upon short-term retention. *Journal of Experimental Psychology*, 1965, 70, 496-505.

Posner, M. I., & Warren, R. Traces, concepts and conscious constructions. In A. W. Melton and E. Martin (Eds.), *Coding in learning and memory*. New York: Winston, 1972.

Rock, I., & Harris, C. S. Vision and touch. *Scientific American*, 1967, 216, 96–107.

Rogers, M. Visual generation in the recognition task. Unpublished M.A. Thesis, University of Oregon, 1972.

Shagan, J. Kinesthetic memory comparing the blind and sighted. Unpublished Doctoral Dissertation, George Washington University, 1970.

Shepard, R., & Metzler, J. Mental rotation of three dimensional objects. *Science*, 1971, 171, 77–110.

Shriffrin, R. M., & Gardner, J. T. Visual processing capacity and attentional control. *Journal of Experimental Psychology*, 1972, 93, 72–82.

Smith, E. E., & Nielsen, G. D. Representation and retrieval processes in short term memory recognition and recall of faces. *Journal of Experimental Psychology*, 1970, 85, 397–405.

Snyder, C. R. R. Individual differences in imagery and thought. Unpublished Doctoral Dissertation, University of Oregon, 1972.

Sperling, G. A. A model for visual memory tasks. *Human Factors*, 1963, 5, 19–31.

Stelmach, G. E., & Wilson, M. Kinesthetic retention, movement extent, and information processing. *Journal of Experimental Psychology*, 1970, 85, 425–430.

Sternberg, S. High speed scanning in human memory. *Science*, 1966, 153, 652–654.

Swanson, J. M., Johnsen, A. M., & Briggs, G. E. Recoding in a memory search task. *Journal of Experimental Psychology*, 1972, 93, 1–9.

Turnbull, E. Visual and name processes in a visual search task. Unpublished M.A. Thesis, University of Oregon, 1972.

Tversky, B. Pictorial and verbal encoding in a short-term memory task. *Perception and Psychophysics*, 1969, 4, 225–233.

Warren, R. Stimulus encoding and memory. *Journal of Experimental Psychology*, 1972, 94, 90-100.

Wattenbarger, B. The representation of the stimulus in character classification. Unpublished Doctoral Dissertation, University of Michigan, 1970.

Whorf, B. L. *Language, thought and reality*. Cambridge M.I.T. Press, 1956.

Williams, H. L., Beaver, W. S., Spence, M. T., & Rundell, O. H. Digital and kinesthetic memory with interpolated information processing. *Journal of Experimental Psychology*, 1969, 80, 537-541.

Acknowledgements

The project presented or reported herein was performed pursuant to a grant from the U.S. Office of Education, OEG-0-72-0717, Department of Health, Education, and Welfare. The opinions expressed herein, however, do not necessarily reflect the position or policy of the U. S. Office of Education, and no official endorsement by the U.S. Office of Education should be inferred.

I appreciate very much permission to quote from unpublished theses by Stephen Boies, Gerald Laabs, Miriam Rogers, Charles Snyder and Elaine Turnbull.

CHRONOMETRIC STUDIES OF THE
ROTATION OF MENTAL IMAGES

Lynn A. Cooper* and Roger N. Shepard
Stanford University

Introduction and Background

Following a long period of behaviorist-induced
skepticism regarding the possibility of a scientific
study of mental events, increasing experimental and
theoretical effort is now being directed toward an
understanding of the internal states and processes by
means of which we represent objects and events in the
external world. Two interrelated considerations have
undoubtedly encouraged a revival of interest in the
study of mental events. The first is that the richness and structure of human behavior can never be
fully and parsimoniously understood without reference
to those inner states and processes that we all recognize within ourselves but can never directly observe in others. The second is that these same
states and processes are amenable to empirical investigation by reference to orderly patterns in the externally observable behaviors that are presumably
mediated by these internal states and processes. In
particular, much of the recent research on mental images and mental transformations with which we shall
bê concerned here can be viewed as a search for experimental paradigms that yield behavioral evidence
to confirm and to elaborate the models for mental
processes that are suggested by introspection. In
this way, introspective reports concerning such
things as the vividness and controllability of mental
images (Richardson, 1969) need no longer constitute
the primary source of data for the study of internal

---

*Now at The University of California at San Diego.

events. Rather, self-report data can be reassigned
to a more appropriate role as just one among several
types of behavioral indicators of mental states and
processes.

Nature versus Function of Mental Images

Current experimental approaches to the study of
mental imagery appear to be addressed to two distin-
guishable, though interrelated problems. The distinction, long ago noted by Bartlett (1932), is
between questions concerning the *function* or behavioral consequences of mental images and questions
concerning the *nature* or internal structure of the
mental images themselves. With the exception of the
theoretical speculations of the Gestalt psychologists
(Koffka, 1935; Köhler, 1947), previous writings have
tended to focus almost exclusively on the former,
functional questions. For example, discussions of
one prominent kind of imagery, namely dreaming--
whether primarily concerned with manifest content
(Hall & Van de Castle, 1966) or latent significance
(Freud, 1900)--have concentrated upon the functional
role that dream images play in the ongoing life and
psychodynamics of the individual rather than upon the
fundamental nature and constitution of those images.
Much recent experimental work continues to pursue
these primarily functional questions. This is true,
for example, of the demonstrations of marked improvement in complex motor skills as a result of purely
mental practice (e.g., Rawlings, Rawlings, Chen, &
Yilk, 1972; Richardson, 1969) and of the demonstrations of powerful effects on learning and recall of
verbal materials of differences among stimuli, instructions, or individual subjects with respect to
mental imagery (e.g., Bower, in press; Paivio, 1969;
1971).

In harmony with largely independent developments
is psychophysiology (e.g., Dement, 1965; West, 1962)
and in philosophical psychology (e.g., Armstrong,
1968; Smart, 1963), experimental psychology has re-

cently been showing some renewal of interest in questions of the other, more structural type that had earlier preoccupied the Gestalt psychologists. These questions ask about such things as (a) the extent to which the internal representational processes that we call mental images (whether memory images, imagination images, dreams, or hallucinations) have something in common with the internal representational processes that constitute our normal waking perceptions and (b) the extent to which internal representations of either of these two types correspond structurally to the external objects that they represent in the senses either of "first-order" or "second-order" isomorphism (Shepard & Chipman, 1970; Shepard, in press). Several experimental paradigms that have recently been introduced in efforts to determine the "modality," "coded form," or "structure" of internal representations bear rather directly on these questions.

*Experimental Paradigms for Investigating
the Nature of Mental Images*

Selective Interference

In one type of paradigm, measures of selective interference have provided strong indications as to the principal modality of an internally generated representation (*viz.*, whether visual, auditory or, sometimes, kinesthetic). Segal and her associates have found that, when a subject is following instructions to form visual images, his ability to detect externally presented visual signals is diminished (Segal & Gordon, 1969). Moreover this reduction is attributable to the interfering effect of the visual imagery *per se*, rather than to a general decrease in attention to any form of external stimulation. For, further work showed that the detection of visual signals was disrupted more while imagining pictures than while imagining sounds and, conversely, that the detection of acoustic signals was disturbed more during auditory than during visual imagery (Segal & Fusella, 1970).

Such studies of selective interference indicate that mental imagery does indeed make use of some of the same information processing machinery that is used in the normal perception of external stimuli. It is tempting to suppose that within each modality there is a limited capacity for information processing. Consequently, whenever the subject has preempted some of that capacity for purposes of forming or operating upon mental images, his processing capability is reduced for external signals presented in that particular modality--but not (or at least not to the same extent) for signals presented in another modality.

It is not entirely clear, however, that this division of information-processing capacity coincides strictly with divisions between the sensory modalities. Perhaps this is an appropriate division only when, as in the experiments by Segal *et al.*, the task requirement is one of simple sensory detection. When more complex, cognitive interpretation of the external stimuli is required, the more abstract structural form of the resulting internal representations, rather than simply the modality of initial input, may be of primary importance. For example, the internal representations corresponding to visually scanning and to kinesthetically tracing the shape of a letter (e.g., "A") have much in common, even though they are associated with different sensory modalities. And the same is true of the internal representations corresponding to passively hearing and to subvocally articulating the acoustic name of that letter (cf., Wickelgren, 1969). At the cognitive level, then, the most powerful determinant of selective interference may be such abstract (i.e., non-modality-specific) structural aspects of internal representations, such as the spatial properties of a certain shape (whether initially apprehended in visual or kinesthetic form) or the temporal pattern of its conventional name (whether expressed in an acoustic or articulatory manner).

A natural extension of these considerations, consonant with the notions emphasized by Brooks (Brooks, 1968; cf., also, Shepard, in press), is that the most important and general divisions in cognitive processes are between entire coherent systems--perhaps most clearly the spatial and the linguistic systems. While these two systems communicate most efficiently with the external world through different sensory modalities (*viz.*, the visual-kinesthetic on the one hand, and the auditory-articulatory on the other), it is nonetheless clear that both systems are capable of operating quite effectively through all of the same major modalities. For example, objects and events can be quite accurately localized in the same physical space whether they are only seen, touched, or heard; and sentences can result in the same understandings whether they are spoken, written or presented via braille. Regardless of the particular modality of communication with the outside world, then, we might expect more interference within than between these two general systems resulting from either (a) the greater structural similarities among the internal representations within each system, as suggested above, or (b) the apparently distinct anatomical localization of these two systems in the right and left hemispheres of the human brain (Gazzaniga, Bogen, & Sperry, 1965; Kinsbourne, 1971; Sperry & Levy, 1970).

Brooks (1968) has used the measurement of selective interference in his ingenious experimental discrimination between internal representations of a primarily verbal or spatial character. He demonstrated that the amount of time required to make a serial classification interacts strongly with the response mode that the subjects are required to use. Thus, subjects are slower in classifying successive words in a previously studied sentence as nouns or non-nouns when they must respond verbally, by saying the words "yes" or "no," than when they can express the same classification spatially, by pointing to the locations of appropriate visual symbols ("y" or "n")

on an answer sheet. Conversely, subjects are considerably slower in indicating whether successive corners around the edge of a previously studied form
(e.g., the block letter "F") are at the top or bottom
(as opposed to the interior of the figure) when they
must respond spatially, by pointing to the positions
of the "y" or "n" on the answer sheet, than when they
can respond verbally, by saying "yes" or "no." A
further finding--that selective interference still
occurs in the task requiring spatial imagery when the
responses are guided tactually, rather than visually
--again suggests that the critical factor is the abstract (linguistic versus spatial) structure rather
than the particular sensory modality of the internal
representations being manipulated.

Selective Reduction of Reaction Times

Results of the sort described above indicate
that covert mental imagery and overt perceptual-motor
performance tend to interfere with each other when
two conditions are fulfilled: (a) The overt performance and the covert imagery make demands upon the
same information processing systems (whether at the
sensory or cognitive levels) or, perhaps equiva-
lently, involve internal representations with similar
abstract cognitive structures. (b) These two (overt
and covert) activities--though made mutually inter-
dependent by the requirements of the task--are nevertheless incompatible in the sense that they cannot
effectively be carried on at the same time.
If the second condition for the occurrence of
interference is changed so that the covert process is
suitably compatible with the required overt process,
then mutual facilitation rather than mutual interference should result. Performance should then be best
when the imagery is in a form (modality, structure,
or system) that is most--not least--similar to the
form of the externally presented material. For example, the time required to respond discriminatively to
some aspect of an externally presented stimulus

should be shorter when the subject is more prepared
for that stimulus. Accumulating evidence indicates
that to be more prepared for a stimulus is to have,
in advance, a more appropriate mental image; i.e., an
image that is closer to the external stimulus in abstract internal structure, that is represented within
the proper cognitive system and, perhaps, that is
associated with the appropriate sensory modality.

Posner and his associates have recently developed very successful paradigms for determining the
form of the internal representation remaining from a
previously presented stimulus by measuring the time
subjects take to respond discriminatively to an ensuing, related stimulus (e.g., Posner, Boies,
Eichelman, & Taylor, 1969). They have shown that,
when subjects are instructed to indicate whether or
not the second of two successively presented letters
has the same name as the first, their response "same"
is approximately 80 to 100 msec. faster when the two
letters are physically identical ("R" and "R") than
when they are identical only in name ("R" and "r").
The notion here is that when the subject's internal
representation in short-term memory is of the most
appropriate form (i.e., a "visual code" of the same
internal structure as the ensuing visual stimulus) he
can respond very rapidly by matching this internal
representation against that ensuing stimulus by some
relatively direct, template-like process. When, however, his memory representation is of a less appropriate form (i.e., a visual code of a different
structure--lower as opposed to upper case--or an auditory-articulatory code of the name of that letter),
additional time is needed to access the name of the
ensuing stimulus and then to test for a match between
the two derived (but case-invariant) names.

Additional evidence that a visual representation
mediates physical-identity matching lies in the disappearance of the superiority of the physical-identity match when the interval between the two letters
reaches about 2 seconds. (Presumably the visual
representation of the first letter has faded during

81

intervals of this length.) Posner *et al.* (1969) also report that when subjects are motivated to attend specifically to the visual aspects of the first stimulus (i.e., when subjects always know what the case-- upper or lower--of the second stimulus will be), then the speed of the physical-identity match, relative to the name-identity only match, is maintained over longer interstimulus intervals. Finally, Posner and his associates have presented evidence that visual codes can be generated in the absence of an external visual stimulus. If subjects are given the name of the first letter in auditory form only, some 750 msec. prior to the onset of the second stimulus, and if the case of this second letter is known in advance, then reaction times are as fast as those obtained for visual-visual matches of physical identity. The approximately .75-sec. lead time that seems to be required for this is, presumably, the time it takes a subject to construct an internal visual representation of the named letter.

Mental Transformations

Reaction-time experiments of the sort reported by Posner and his associates appear to furnish rather strong evidence concerning the nature of particular internal representations--specifically whether they are principally visual or verbal in form. However, the question still remains as to whether these particular internal representations or "codes" are what we ordinarily refer to as mental images. The implied contrast, here, is with the possibility that the "visual code" postulated by Posner consists (as he himself has suggested) solely in the priming of certain relevant feature detectors in the sensory receptor system. The resulting state of heightened readiness of the receptor system for certain specific patterns could account for the demonstrated reduction in reaction times to just those patterns. However, this selective priming of lower-order feature detectors would not in itself constitute what we ordinarily refer to as a mental image. For, by hypothesis, the state of readiness would not have any cognitive consequences for the subject in the absence of the subsequent presentation of a related external stimulus. Consider, for example, that one's perceptual system is more tuned to register the appearance of a familiar than an unfamiliar word without one's in any sense having a prior mental image of the more familiar word. Presumably, to have a mental image, then, is to activate an internal representation that--in addition to preparing one for a specific external stimulus--can be used as a basis for further information processing even if the relevant stimulus is never actually presented. Such further information processing could include, for example, the generation of a verbal description of the mental image.

The experiments that we wish to describe here follow Posner in the use of the selective reduction of reaction times to an ensuing visual stimulus for purposes of demonstrating a structural correspondence between (a) the internal representation with which the subject attempts to prepare for an upcoming stimulus and (b) the external stimulus itself. In addition, we introduce the new requirement that, in order to be fully prepared for the anticipated stimulus, the subject must first perform a transformation upon the internal representation--specifically, a transformation that corresponds to a rigid rotation of the stimulus in space. This addition serves two purposes. First, by demonstrating that the subject can perform such a transformation upon his internal representation, we establish that this representation is accessible to the subject himself for further cognitive processing. The representation then satisfies the important condition just set forth for its classification as a true mental image. Second, by requiring a transformation that corresponds specifically to a spatial rotation, we provide further support for the claim that the representation or "image" is primarily visual or at least spatial in form.

Evidence that these internal representations are spatial in nature comes, also, from the post-experimental introspective reports. Our subjects typically claimed that, in preparing for the anticipated presentation of a rotated stimulus, they did in fact (a) form a mental picture of the anticipated stimulus and then (b) carry out a mental rotation of that picture into its anticipated orientation. Their tendency to generate such a verbal report is consistent with the supposition that the internal representation was accessible to introspection--as we should require of a mental image. However, to classify these representations as purely visual images would be misleading. We should rather refer to them, more abstractly, as spatial images since several subjects reported appreciable kinesthetic components in their subjective experience.

We should note, parenthetically, that the verbalization of introspections need not be confined to reporting merely the existence and principal modality of a mental image. Reports dependent upon specific structural features of internal representations are of greater evidential value. To illustrate, in an experiment by Shepard and Feng (see Shepard, in press) times were measured for subjects to report the identity of the letter that results when a specified spatial transformation is applied to a letter that is designated only by name. The subjects could readily report, for example, that the letter "N" turns into the letter "Z" when rotated 90°. Evidently, the internal representation with which they were operating had a definite internal structure that was analogous to the structure of the corresponding physical letter and that was internally available for further processing--including spatial transformation, visual analysis, and verbal report. Moreover, reaction times were consistently longer for more extensive transformations (e.g., longer for 180° than for 90° rotations), providing additional support for the notion that the images and operations were of a basically spatial character.

In the experiments that we shall be describing, mental transformations and the selective reduction of reaction times are used, jointly, to establish that the internal representations and mental operations upon these representations are to some degree analogous or structurally isomorphic to corresponding objects and spatial transformations in the external world. In all of these experiments, each spatial transformation consists simply of single rigid rotation of a visual object about a fixed axis. However, in related work reported elsewhere, reaction times have been measured for much more complex sequences of imagined operations in space--for example, the operations required to fold a flattened pattern of six squares up into a cube (Shepard, in press; Shepard & Feng, 1972).

Review of Preceding Reaction-Time Studies of Mental Rotation

Rotation of One Stimulus into Congruence with Another

In an initial experiment (Shepard & Metzler, 1971), subjects were required to determine whether pairs of perspective line drawings depected three-dimensional objects of the same or of different shapes. On a random half of the trials, the two objects differed with respect to shape--one object being the mirror image of the other--while on the other half of the trials the two objects were identical in three-dimensional shape. In addition, regardless of whether they were the same or different in shape, the objects generally differed either by a rigid rotation in the two-dimensional picture plane or else by a rigid rotation in depth (specifically, about a vertical axis in a three-dimensional space).

When the two pictured objects were of the same three-dimensional shape, the reaction times were found to increase with the angular difference between their portrayed orientations according to a strikingly linear function (from about 1 sec. at 0° to 4 or 5 sec.

at 180°). Moreover, the intercept and slope of this linear increase were essentially the same for the two types of rotation--even though the depth rotations corresponded to a much more complex relationship between the two two-dimensional pictures as such. These results corroborate the subjects' own claims (a) that in order to determine whether the two objects were identical or only mirror images, they first had to imagine one object of the pair rotated into congruence with the other; (b) that, in order to preserve the essential structure of the object's shape, they could carry out this imagined rotation at no faster than a certain limiting rate (evidently about 60° per second for those objects); and (c) that, since they perceived the stimuli as three-dimensional objects rather than merely as two-dimensional designs, they could imagine the rotation around whichever of the two spatial axes was required with equal ease.

The strong dependence of reaction time upon angular difference in portrayed orientation is inconsistent with some alternative explanations that do not involve mental rotation. Subjects who first generated some rotationally invariant structural description of each of the two objects separately and who then simply compared these two descriptions, would be expected to yield a reaction-time function that is perfectly flat (except, perhaps, for a drop at 0° owing to the possibility of a direct perceptual match between the two pictures in that case). Without invoking the concept of mental rotation, one might attempt to account for the very marked increase in reaction time with difference in orientation by supposing that, whatever process (e.g., of feature-by-feature comparison) is used, it will become more difficult as the two pictures become more different. However, the burden would seem to be on the author of such an account to explain (a) why the increase in reaction time is so precisely linear, (b) why the increase is no greater for the pairs that differ by a rotation in depth, and (c) why the subjects themselves persist in speaking of an imagined rotation.

If, as we are inclined to suppose, the subjects
did indeed carry on an internal process that is in
some sense an analog of the sort of continuous rigid
rotation that might be performed on the corresponding
external object, then it seems reasonable to suggest
that the thing they were rotating was a mental image.
This is not to imply that this image possessed anything like the subjective vividness, detail, or clarity of a direct perceptual image. On the contrary,
many subjects indicated that the thing that they were
mentally rotating was very schematic (and indeed, in
some cases, was experienced as much kinesthetically
as visually). Nevertheless, the structural information about the three-dimensional shape of the mentally rotated object evidently remained sufficient to
permit a successful test of congruence or noncongru-
ence with a grossly similar appearing second object.

We do not wish to claim, either, that the rotation of this internal representation (however schematic) was in any sense strictly continuous.
Although the introspective reports were not very
clear on this point, it may well be that the process
was carried out in a number of small, discrete steps
rather than continuously. And in either case, of
course, in speaking of a mental rotation we do not
mean to imply that there was anything actually rotating within any subject's physical brain (any more
than that the right-angled corners of the three-
dimensional object were represented by right-angled
corners in a subject's physical brain). The isomorphism is undoubtedly more abstract than this. Indeed,
in accordance with a principle of "second-order"
isomorphism (Shepard & Chipman, 1970), it would be
sufficient, to justify speaking of mental rotation,
if the internal process that we are calling a merely
imagined rotation has a functionally important component that is uniquely shared with the internal
process that takes place when the same subject is
actually perceiving an externally presented rotation
--*whatever* the detailed nature of this process may be
at the neurophysiological level. Nevertheless,

further consideration of the results on mental rotation suggests that, beyond this very abstract "second
-order" isomorphism, there very likely also exists
at least some degree of structural analogy or "first-
order" isomorphism between the internal representation of an object that is rotating in space and the
spatial structure of the object itself (Shepard, in
press).

*Rotation of a Presented Stimulus into Congruence with
a Stored Representation*

If subjects perform a mental rotation in order
to determine whether one externally presented stimulus matches another externally presented stimulus,
then the question arises as to whether they might
similarly rotate a single external stimulus in order
to determine whether it matches some internal representation stored (in a particular "orientation") in
long-term memory. We might expect such a process to
occur when the externally presented stimulus consists
of a well-learned pattern (such as a familiar letter
or numeral) that (a) has almost always been experienced in one conventional upright orientation but (b)
is now presented in some other rotated orientation.
Actually, such a mental rotation is probably
not necessary for merely identifying a rotated alphanumeric character. It is quite possible that subjects can make such identifications solely on the
basis of certain orientational invariant distinctive
features (such as the presence of curvature, an enclosed space, and two free ends in the case of the
letter "R")--especially in the context of other
external cues, such as a line of print or the edge
of the paper, which serve to define the local axis
of orientation of the character. The fact that recognition time has been found to be somewhat slower
for inverted letters (e.g., Kolers & Perkins, 1969)
might result from less efficient processing of features when presented in less familiar orientations,

rather than from a mental rotation. Certainly one's subjective impression, when presented with a severely tipped letter (e.g., "ᴚ"), is one of immediately seeing that it is that letter ("R") without being aware of carrying out any rotation of the letter as a whole.

In order to make the discrimination more demanding and, hence, to force subjects to carry out a mental rotation, Shepard and Klun (see Shepard, in press) adopted the technique (introduced by Shepard & Metzler, 1971) of requiring the subject to discriminate between a stimulus and its mirror image--not merely between one stimulus and an entirely different stimulus. Under these conditions, it is extremely difficult to make the discrimination on the basis of rotationally invariant features, for, clearly, both the normal and the reversed versions of the letter "ᴚ" possess the same features of curvature, enclosed space, and two free ends. Indeed, it did subjectively seem that, while one could immediately see that "ᴚ" was the letter "R", it took additional time and perhaps a mental rotation to determine that it was the normal letter "R" rather than its mirror image "Я".

In the actual experiment, subjects were presented, on each trial, with one of 12 (asymmetric) alphanumeric characters (F, G, J, R, e, j, k, m, 2, 5, 4, 7). The characters appeared in various tilted orientations from 0° through 180° and the subjects were required to determine whether the character in question was the *normal* (standard) or the *backward* (mirror image) version of that character as generally seen in printed form--regardless of its orientation in the picture plane. As before, reaction time constituted the dependent measure.

The principal outcomes of this experiment were (a) that reaction time was a monotonically (though nonlinearly) increasing function of angular departure of a character from the upright position; and (b) that the response "normal" was consistently faster than the response "backward." Introspective reports of the subjects in this experiment indicate that the task was usually performed by imagining the visually

presented character rotated into the familiar, upright orientation--especially on those trials in
which the stimulus was tilted quite a way from upright. Some possible reasons for the nonlinear
nature of the increasing function will be considered
in detail later.

Rotation of a Stored Representation into Congruence with an Anticipated Stimulus

We have been suggesting that subjects in the
preceding two experiments made the required "match-
mismatch" discrimination by rotating a mental image
of a presented stimulus into the same orientation as
a second visual stimulus, in the first experiment, or
a canonical representation stored in long-term memory, in the second. In both of these experiments,
however, the stimulus to which a subject was to respond was visually displayed during the entirety of
any given trial. Consequently, one might argue (a)
that the processes that mediated the subject's response consisted merely in an ongoing analysis of the
visually present stimulus, (b) that this analysis
took longer when the stimulus departed more from the
thing with which it was to be compared and, hence,
(c) that any evidence for the existence of a rotating
mental image, as distinct from a perceptual analysis
of the externally presented stimulus, is at best
extremely indirect.

In order to obtain more direct evidence for the
existence of the hypothesized mental image, Shepard
and Klun (see Shepard, in press) undertook a second
experiment in which the alleged rotation of the image
preceded the presentation of the relevant visual
stimulus. Again, subjects were required to classify
individually presented rotated characters (this time
six lower-case letters) as "normal" or "backward."
This time, however, conditions were introduced in
which subjects were supplied with information as to
the identity and/or orientation of the upcoming

character in advance of the presentation of the character itself.

The advance information was always presented in auditory form; thus, if the subject were in the "identity information" condition, he might be told at the beginning of a certain trial that the next letter to appear would be, say, the (lower case) letter "t." Similarly, in the "orientation information" condition the subject might be told that the upcoming stimulus would appear, say, in the "6 o'clock position" corresponding to a rotation of $180°$ from upright). In the "identity *and* orientation" condition, the subject was always provided with both sorts of information about the ensuing stimulus. Note that in this condition the only information that the subject was still lacking prior to the onset of the actual stimulus was the critical information concerning whether that stimulus was to appear in its normal or backward version. Again, what was recorded was the reaction time, starting with the onset of the visual stimulus and terminating with the subject's classification of that stimulus as "normal" or "backward."

The major results of this experiment were (a) that, as in the previous study, with no advance information reaction time was a monotonically increasing function of angle of rotation; (b) that, when either identity information or orientation information was provided alone, reaction time again increased with angular departure from upright in much the same way as when there was no advance information, and, finally, (c) that, when *both* identity and orientation information were provided in advance, the reaction-time function flattened considerably and, indeed, for some subjects became uniformly low and completely horizontal.

This finding of a flattened function relating reaction time to angular departure from upright lends considerable support to the claim that, when they are provided with both identity and orientation information in advance, subjects prepared for the anticipated stimulus by first generating a mental image of the announced letter from long-term memory, and by then mentally rotating this image into the indicated orientation. Again, introspective reports corroborated this account. Subjects who yielded virtually flat functions reported that they did mentally rotate a primarily visual (though schematic) mental picture of the named letter into the designated position and, then, rapidly performed a direct "match-mismatch" comparison between this rotated mental image and the ensuing visual stimulus. Those subjects who failed to achieve flat functions reported that they could not always form a sufficiently well-defined and suitably rotated visual image on the basis of the auditory information given in advance.

Also of interest is the finding that the group reaction-time functions were quite similar in shape for the conditions in which no advance information was supplied and in which only orientation information was supplied. The fact that advance information as to orientation led to a flattening of the function only when combined with information as to the concrete identity of the character suggests that subjects are more able to rotate a mental image of a particular, concrete object than to rotate a general, abstract frame of reference.

We turn now to the detailed presentation of two further reaction-time experiments that we believe provide more definitive evidence concerning the formation and rotation of mental images.

Experiment I: Determination of the Times Required to Prepare for and to Respond to a Rotated Stimulus

We have argued that, in the second experiment of Shepard and Klun, the subjects prepared for the presentation of a rotated alphanumeric character by using advance information as to identity and orientation to generate a mental image of the appropriate character and to rotate this imaginal representation into the appropriate orientation. Regardless of this orientation, then, the required discriminative response (as to whether the presented character was normal or backward) could be made with uniform rapidity simply by comparing the presented stimulus against the generated mental image--used essentially as a template.

In the experiment we wish to report now, we introduced the refinement of precisely controlling the time during which the advance information as to orientation was available to the subject prior to the presentation of the rotated test stimulus itself. If subjects do indeed carry out some sort of mental rotation in the process of preparing for a tilted stimulus, this process should require more time for its completion as the orientation indicated in the advance information departs by larger angles from the standard upright orientation. Moreover, failure to complete this process of preparation prior to the onset of the ensuing stimulus should result in an increase in the reaction time to that stimulus since, in this case, some further mental rotation will still have to be carried out *after* the onset of the tilted stimulus itself. Thus, by determining how reaction time depends both upon the angle of the tilted stimulus and upon the duration of the advance information as to that angle, we hoped (a) to obtain somewhat more direct evidence that the generation and rotation of a mental image is in fact a part of the process of preparation for a rotated stimulus, and (b) to determine something about the time required to carry out this preparatory mental rotation.

Method

Subjects

Eight subjects--seven Stanford students and the second author--were run under all experimental conditions. The first four subjects were run in the

93

complete factorial design, which required about 7
hours of participation from each subject. The second
four were run in a half-replicate design and served
for 3 to 4 hours each. Although five male and three
female subjects were included, no consistent differences were observed in the performances of the two
sexes.

Stimuli

As in the experiments of Shepard and Klun, the
stimuli were all asymmetrical alphanumeric characters
--in this case the three upper-case letters (R, J, G)
and the three arabic numerals (2,5,7) exhibited in
Fig. 1. Each of these six characters appeared in
each of six equally-spaced orientations around the
circle (in 60° steps starting from the standard upright position, 0°) as is illustrated for the letter
"R" in Fig. 2. Since subjects were familiarized with

Fig. 1. Normal and backward versions of the six
alphanumeric characters used as test stimuli in
Experiment I.

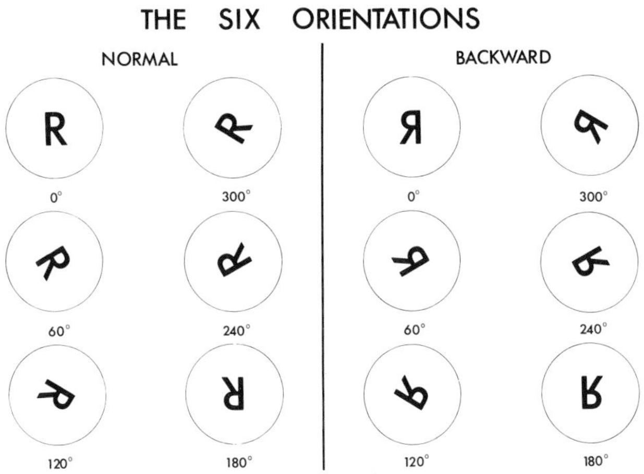

THE SIX ORIENTATIONS

Fig. 2. Normal and backward versions of one of the six characters, illustrating the six orientations in which it might appear as a test stimulus.

both the set of six characters and the set of six orientations, and since these all occurred equally often in the test stimuli, the informational uncertainties concerning identity and orientation were equivalent in the absence of advance information. As before, the subjects' task was simply to discriminate the normal versions of the characters (left-hand panels in Figs. 1 and 2) from the reflected or backward versions of those same characters (right-hand panels) regardless of their orientations within the picture plane (Fig. 2).

Following Shepard and Klun and, originally, Shepard and Metzler (1971), we hoped that, by requiring subjects to discriminate between mirror images of the same objects, we would prevent them from responding merely on the basis of some simple distinctive feature (such as the presence of an enclosed region in the case of the letter "R"), thereby forcing them to carry out a "mental rotation" in order to compare

a tilted character with the normal upright representation preserved in long-term memory. Notice, for
example, that any one of the characters displayed in
Fig. 2 can almost immediately be identified as *some*
version of the letter "R." In the cases in which that
character is markedly tipped, however, it seems to
take some additional time to determine whether that
letter is normal or backward. Typically, subjects
report that they do in fact imagine a markedly tilted
character rotated back into its upright orientation
to determine whether it is normal or backward, but
that this is unnecessary for merely determining its
identity. Indeed, we shall suggest that subjects may
have to identify a character before they can determine which is the top of the character and, hence,
can know how the character must be rotated to bring
it into its upright orientation.

In order to control precisely the duration of
the advance information, we abandoned the auditory
presentation of advance information used in the second experiment of Shepard and Klun in favor of exclusively visual presentation by means of a three-field
tachistoscope. The advance information cues, when
presented, appeared centered within the same circular
aperture as the subsequently ensuing test stimulus.
When presented, the identity cue was displayed in the
form of an outline drawing of the normal, upright
version of the upcoming test stimulus, and the orientation cue appeared as an arrow passing through the
center of the circular field and pointing in the
direction at which the top of the test stimulus would
appear. Figure 3, which shows the sequence of visual
displays that would appear within the circular aperture on an illustrative trial, provides a more concrete idea of the appearance of the identity and
orientation cues. The outline form of the identity
cue was chosen in order to minimize (a) possible confusions between advance information cues and the
actual test stimuli and (b) the persistence of visual
afterimages which might be expected following presentations of the more contrastive, solid characters.

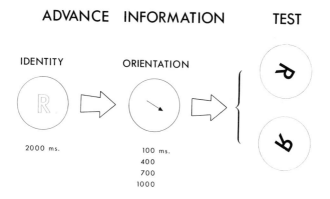

Fig. 3. Sequence of visual displays appearing within the circular aperture on a trial of type B, in which *both* identity and orientation information were presented in advance of the test stimulus (illustrated here at 120°).

The alphanumeric characters, which appeared both as test stimuli and as advanced information cues, subtended a visual angle of about 1-1/2°. The visual angle of the circular aperture within which these characters appeared was 4°, and the luminance levels of the two or three fields that succeeded each other within this aperture (depending upon the condition) were all in the vicinity of 20 foot-Lamberts.

Structure of Individual Trials

The subject sat in a dimly illuminated room with his head pressed against the shaped rubber light shield surrounding the viewing window of the tachistoscope. This permitted binocular viewing of all stimuli, but prevented physical rotation of the head. Following a warning signal at the beginning of each trial, the subject fixated the circular field where the test stimulus and the advance information cues (if any) were about to appear, and positioned his left and right thumbs on the two response buttons located on a box which he held in front of him. The subject always used the thumb of his preferred hand (i.e., the right hand except in the case of our one left-handed subject) to register his decision that the test stimulus was normal, and the thumb of his nonpreferred hand to signal that the stimulus was backward. The two cases, normal and backward, occurred equally often according to a random sequence. The test stimulus always remained on until after the subject made his response.

Each subject ran in eight different conditions of type and duration of advance information. Of central concern are the four variable time conditions (labeled "B" in Figs. 3 and 4) in which *both* identity and orientation information were supplied. On these trials the identity cue was displayed for 2000 msec., immediately followed by the orientation cue which persisted for 100, 400, 700, or 1000 msec. (depending upon which of the four conditions of type B was in effect). The orientation cue was then immediately replaced by the actual test stimulus. As is indicated in Fig. 3, even when the subject was provided with advance information as to both the identity and the orientation of the ensuing test stimulus, he still had to await the actual presentation of that stimulus in order to determine whether it was the normal or the backward version of that character at that orientation.

Figure 4 schematically illustrates the other four conditions, along with the conditions of type B (described above), for the case in which the test stimulus was to appear at 120°. The remaining four conditions were as follows: N, in which *no* advance information was provided (but only a 2000 msec. blank warning and adaptation field); I, in which only *identity* information was supplied; O, in which only *orientation* information was furnished; and, finally, C, in which the identity and orientation information were presented in a *combined* form followed by a 1000 msec. blank field before the onset of the test

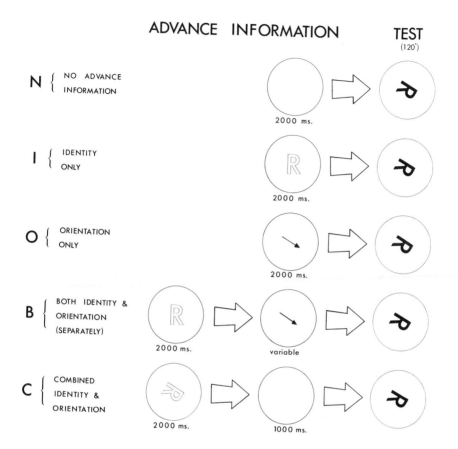

Fig. 4. Schematic illustration of the five basically different types of conditions, N, I, O, B, and C. (Since type B subsumes four conditions, with different durations of orientation information specified in Fig. 3, the total number of distinct conditions is eight.)

stimulus. The purpose of interposing the blank field in this last condition, C, was to ensure that the response to the test stimulus was based upon comparison with a representation in memory and not upon a purely sensory discrimination of continuity or change in the

outline of the external visual display (for normal or
backward test stimuli, respectively). For all conditions illustrated in Fig. 4, the large unfilled
arrows signify *immediate* replacement, upon the offset
of one visual display, of the display shown just to
its right (always within the same circular aperture).

Conditions I and C provided two reference points
with which to compare the four variable time Conditions B. At one extreme, when the duration of the
orientation information is made very short (as in the
B-Condition with only 100 msec.), we should expect
that the subjects' reaction times to the test stimuli
would approximate their reaction times to those same
test stimuli when no advance information as to orientation has been provided (as in the I-Condition). At
the other extreme, when the duration of the orientation information is made sufficiently long (as in the
B-Condition with 1000 msec.), subjects may have time
to generate an appropriate mental template of the
normal version of that character and to rotate it into
the designated orientation. If so, their reaction
times to the ensuing test stimulus should approximate
those obtained when such a rotated template is supplied visually (as in the C-Condition) and, hence,
does not have to be subjected to any mental rotation
before comparison.

Overall Experimental Design

Individual trials were blocked by condition,
with 12 trials to a block. At the beginning of each
such block the subject was given explicit instructions
as to the nature and duration of the advance information to be provided on all trials within that block,
and was then given practice trials of that type until
he felt ready to proceed with the actual trials of
the block. The order of trials within blocks was
randomized subject to the constraint that each of the
six orientations occurred twice within each block.
Hence, although the subject knew whether there would
be advance information and how long it would last,

until that advance information (if any) was actually presented on a given trial, he did not know which of the six characters would come up next or in which of the six orientations it would appear.

The complete factorial design (used for the first four subjects) required the completion of 576 trials per subject in order to obtain one observation for each cell of the design. Each of these subjects was run for six one-hour sessions consisting of eight blocks (one for each of the eight different conditions) of 12 trials each. The order of conditions was counterbalanced over sessions. Prior to these six sessions, each subject was given an initial practice session to familiarize him with the stimuli, the experimental procedure, and the various conditions of advance information.

After all data had been collected from the first four subjects, we found that the mean reaction times in which we were interested were virtually unchanged when we recomputed them on the basis of only half of the observations selected from the entire factorial design by means of a "checkerboard" half-replicate design. Accordingly, the remaining four subjects were run only on the trials specified by this half-replicate design. After the initial practice session, therefore, each of these subjects completed only three 1-hour sessions of 96 trials each, yielding a total of 288 observations per subject.

Subjects were instructed, for all conditions, to indicate whether the test stimulus was normal or backward (regardless of its orientation in the picture plane) as rapidly as they could, without making errors, by pressing the appropriate button on the response box. Although error rates for the different conditions and orientations were positively correlated with mean reaction times, error rates averaged over all conditions were uniformly quite low, ranging from 3.6% to 8.7% for individual subjects. Nevertheless, throughout the experiment all trials on which errors were made were later repeated until an errorless reaction time had been obtained from each

subject for each combination of character, orientation, version (normal or backward), and condition
called for by the factorial design (or its half-
replicate variant).

Reaction-Time Results

The Effect of Orientation of the Test Stimulus

First we consider the condition, N, in which the
subject was given no advance information concerning
the identity or orientation of the upcoming test
stimulus. The mean reaction times for this condition
(averaged over all correct responses to either the
normal or the backward version of the test stimulus)
are plotted as the uppermost curve in Fig. 5. The
independent variable, here, is the orientation of the
test stimulus as specified in degrees of clockwise
rotation from the standard upright orientation of the
character. (In this and subsequent plots of this
type, all points are independent except the points at
$360°$ which merely duplicate the points at $0°$.)
This curve is quite similar in shape to corresponding curves obtained in the earlier experiments of
Shepard and Klun (see Shepard, in press). In the
absence of any advance information concerning the upcoming stimulus, reaction time increases very markedly
as the orientation of that stimulus departs from its
standard upright orientation. Indeed, as we move
from $0°$ to $180°$ there is a roughly two-fold increase
in mean reaction time, from between 500 and 600 msec.
at the upright orientation to nearly 1100 msec. at
the completely inverted orientation. From the symmetry of the curve we see that the increase in reaction time resulting from a given angle of tilt is the
same for both clockwise and counterclockwise rotations. However, this increase is not strictly linear
but concave upward, with the sharpest increase occurring as we approach the completely inverted orientation of $180°$ from $60°$ away on either side (i.e., from
the orientations of either $120°$ or $240°$).

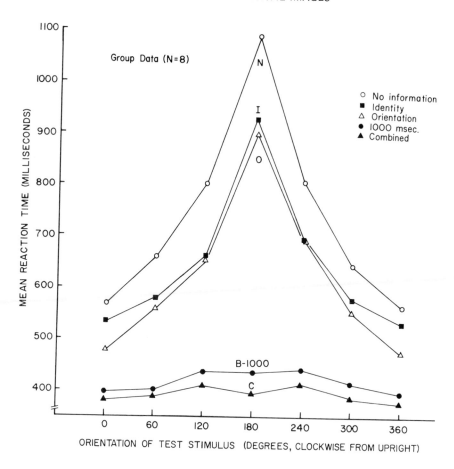

Fig. 5. Mean reaction time as a function of orientation of the test stimulus for those conditions in which advance information, if presented at all, persisted for the maximum duration.

The reliability of the shape of this curve is indicated (a) by its very close similarity to the curve obtained in the first experiment by Shepard and Klun (in which there were five equally spaced angles of departure from upright between 0° and 180°--rather than just the two sampled here), (b) by its remarkably

symmetric form, and (c) by the highly similar shapes
of the two reaction-time curves plotted in Fig. 5
just below this curve for Condition N (namely, the
curves for the Conditions I and O, in which the subjects were given either identity information or
orientation information only).

Despite the nonlinearity of these functions, we
take the very marked increase in reaction time with
departure of the test stimulus from its standard upright orientation to be supportive of the notion that
the subject carries out some sort of a mental rotation. In particular, we suggest (a) that, in order
to compare a markedly tilted character with the representation of the normal version of that character in
long-term memory, the subject must first imagine the
tilted character rotated into its upright orientation,
and (b) that the greater this tilt, the longer it will
take to complete the corrective rotation. Reasons for
the nonlinearity of the increase in reaction time that
are consistent with this notion of mental rotation
will be presented in the theoretical discussion.

*The Effect of Advance Information as to Identity
and/or Orientation*

We turn, now, to a comparison among all five
conditions in which the subjects were given adequate
time to take full advantage of whatever advance information (if any) was provided; namely, Conditions N, I,
O, C, and the one B-Condition in which the orientation cue persisted for the full 1000 msec. The five
different curves plotted in Fig. 5 exhibit the dependence of reaction time on orientation of the test
stimulus for these five conditions.

These results replicate the essential pattern
obtained in the second experiment by Shepard and Klun
(see Shepard, in press). First, they show that the
reaction-time curves for the two Conditions I and O
with advance information as to identity or orientation only--though somewhat lower than the corresponding curve for the Condition N with no advance infor-

mation--are nevertheless relatively close to it in height and, particularly, in overall shape. Second, and of central importance, they establish that the reaction-time curve for the Condition B, in which both identity and orientation information were separately presented, is dramatically lower than the other three curves and virtually flat.

A further aspect of the present results, which is not shown in Fig. 5, is also consonant with the earlier findings of Shepard and Klun. This is that the response used to signal that the test stimulus was the normal version of that character was consistently faster than the response used to signal that it was the backward version of that character--by a difference that was essentially constant over all conditions and orientations and that ranged from roughly 10 to 150 msec., depending on the particular subject. (Evidence for the statistical reliability of this and other differences in the data will be more explicitly considered later.) In this particular experiment it is not possible to partial out the contributions to this difference of the two confounded factors (a) of normal-versus-backward test stimulus and (b) of preferred-versus-nonpreferred response hand. However, on the basis of other experiments in which the functions of the two hands have been systematically interchanged, it appears that the factor of overriding importance is the subject's choice of what to test for first (in this case, normalness or backwardness), rather than the particular hand that is then set to register a positive outcome of that test (cf., Clark & Chase, 1972; Trabasso, Rollins, & Shaughnessy, 1971).

The present results also go beyond the earlier findings of Shepard and Klun in certain respects. First, they indicate more clearly than before that relative to the condition in which no advance information is provided (N), the conditions in which either identity or orientation information is supplied (I or O) tend to produce reaction times that are shorter by a constant amount (roughly 100 msec.), regardless of the orientation of the test stimulus. (The minor departure from virtually perfect parallelism of these three curves attributable to the one point for condition I at $0°$--and duplicated at $360°$--is not statistically reliable.) Second, the curve for the condition with both kinds of advance information presented separately (B) achieves an even closer approximation to a completely flat function than the corresponding curve obtained in the second experiment of Shepard and Klun. And third, by comparison with the new condition in which complete advance information was presented in combined form (C), we can now conclude that the internal representation that the subject constructs on the basis of separate information about identity and orientation (in Condition B) is just about as efficient a mental template as a memory image of the rotated character itself (in Condition C).

The Effect of Varying the Duration of the Orientation Information

We turn now to a consideration of the remaining three B-Conditions. In these conditions, the duration of the advance information as to orientation was reduced (from the full 1000 msec.) to values of only 700, 400, or 100 msec. The mean reaction times for these conditions (again averaged over all correct responses to both normal and backward stimuli) are plotted as a function of the orientation of the test stimulus in Fig. 6. For purposes of comparison, we also include the limiting reference or control conditions I and C already shown in Fig. 5. As before these group curves are highly reliable and representative of the curves for individual subjects.

Comparisons among these curves enable us, for the first time, to make some quantitative inferences concerning the time that it takes to prepare for a stimulus that is about to appear in some rotated orientation. From the flatness of the function for the 1000-msec. B-Condition, we know that this process of preparation can generally be completed within 1 second. However, when the duration of the orientation cue is reduced (by only 300 msec.) to 700 msec., a pronounced peak in the reaction-time function emerges at 180°, indicating that on the average the discriminative response to the ensuing test stimulus takes over 200 msec. longer whenever that test stimulus appears in an inverted position. When the duration of the orientation cue is further shortened (by another 300 msec.) to 400 msec.,

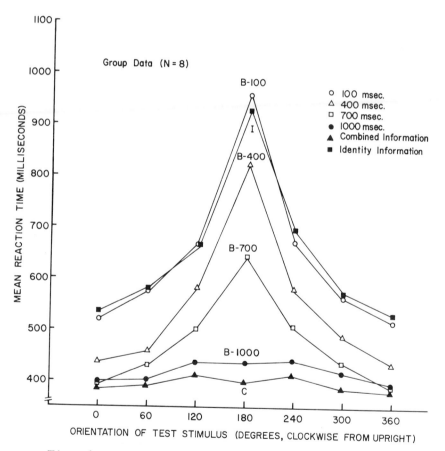

Fig. 6. Mean reaction time as a function of orientation of the test stimulus for those conditions in which identity information was provided.

the reaction times increase by another 200 msec. at 180°, and also by some 80 msec. at 60° on either side of 180°. Finally, when this duration is cut down (by still another 300 msec.) to only 100 msec., the reaction times are essentially identical, at all orientations, to the reaction times when only identity information is provided (Condition I).

Following the experiment, the subjects themselves offered explanations for their reaction times under these B-Conditions that ran along the following lines: When the duration of the orientation cue was reduced below a second (e.g., to 700 msec.), they were often unable to rotate their mental image of the anticipated stimulus around to 180° before that stimulus actually came on, although they usually were able to complete rotations of only 60° or even 120°. When the duration was further reduced (e.g., to 400 msec.), they were almost never able to get to 180° before the onset of the test stimulus and, now, often failed even to reach 120°. Finally, they reported that a duration of only 100 msec. was generally of no use at all; for, by the time they were able to interpret the orientation cue (i.e., to determine which way the arrow was pointing), they discovered that the test stimulus itself had already appeared.

Results for Individual Subjects

When we turn from the average reaction times for the group of eight subjects as a whole (Figs. 5 and 6) to the corresponding reaction times for individual subjects, we immediately discover that there were stable and very substantial differences among subjects in their mean reaction times. However, these differences were very pronounced only for those conditions that tended to produce long reaction times; they all but disappeared for the Conditions (B-1000 and C) in which complete advance information was furnished. Thus for the most difficult case in which no advance information preceded a completely inverted test stimulus (Condition N at 180°), the mean reaction times varied over a more than two-fold range, from just under 700 msec. for the fastest subject, to just over 1700 msec. for the slowest. At the same time, though, the reaction times for the 1000-msec. B-Condition (averaged over all orientations) ranged only from about 350 msec. to a little under 500 msec. for these same two subjects.

It appears that the average rate of mental rotation (which can be very roughly estimated as 180° divided by the difference between the reaction times a 0° and 180° under the N-Condition) varied from something like 800° per second for the fastest subject to something like 164° per second for the slowest. However, when subjects are already prepared with an appropriately oriented image of the upcoming stimulus (as in Conditions B-1000 and C), these very different individual rates of mental rotation are not involved. Consequently, in these conditions most subjects respond with approximately equal rapidity--within some 350 to 500 msec. The fact that both of the above estimated rates of rotation are much greater than the rates, of only about 60° per second, estimated by Shepard and Metzler (1971) for complex three-dimensional "nonsense" shapes is presumably attributable to the greater simplicity and familiarity of the alphanumeric characters used here.

If, now, we plot entire sets of reaction-time curves corresponding to those already displayed for the group of eight subjects as a whole (in Figs. 5 and 6), we find that despite these enormous individual differences in average reaction time, the shapes and relational pattern of the curves are strikingly constant from subject to subject. Although we have examined these curves for all eight subjects individually, it appears impractical to present them all here. Instead, we present complete sets of curves for just two representative subjects; namely, the one with the shortest and the one with the longest overall average reaction time. The patterns exhibited by these two appear to us to be typical of the patterns exhibited by the other, intermediate subjects.

The individual curves for these two extreme subjects are all displayed in Fig. 7. The plots on the left, which correspond to the earlier Fig. 5, are for the conditions in which the advance information (if any) persisted for its maximum duration. The plots on the right, which correspond to the earlier Fig. 6, are for all conditions in which identity information

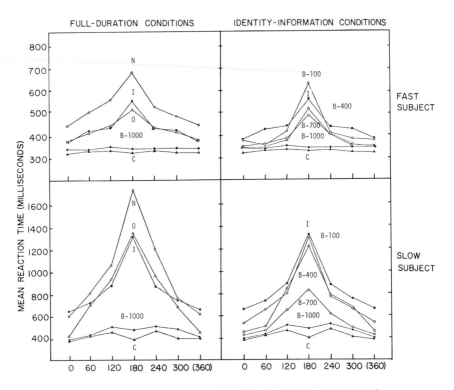

ORIENTATION OF TEST STIMULUS (DEGREES, CLOCKWISE FROM UPRIGHT)

Fig. 7. Mean reaction time as a function of orientation of the test stimulus for two individual subjects--the fastest subject (upper panels) and the slowest subject (lower panels). Left-hand panels correspond to the group functions displayed in Fig. 5, and right-hand panels correspond to the group functions displayed in Fig. 6.

was provided (including those in which the advance information as to orientation was reduced in duration). The two upper plots are for the subject whose responses were, on the average, the quickest. The two lower plots are for the subject whose responses were, on the average, the slowest. Owing to the fact that the longest mean reaction times for this second subject were over twice as long as the longest mean reaction times for the first subject, the vertical scales in the two lower plots have been linearly compressed with respect to the vertical scales in the upper plots.

Note, particularly, the extreme flatness of the curve produced by the faster subject under the B-1000 Condition. Perhaps the most atypical aspect of the curves for this subject (beyond the fact that, overall, their absolute height is quite low) is the relative lowness of the curves for the I and O Conditions relative to that for the N Condition. For the other subjects these three curves were generally closer to each other. The curves for the slower subject appear to be somewhat more variable. Even so, they seem quite orderly--particularly in view of the fact that this subject was run through only the half-replicate design and, so, contributed only half as many observations. It does seem, then, that the major features of the pattern observed in the group data (Figs. 5 and 6) are also found in the data of the individual subjects.

Statistical Reliability of the Principal Results

We attempted an initial assessment of the statistical reliability of the results for the four conditions of central interest--namely the B-Conditions with durations of 100, 400, 700, and 1000 msec.--by performing an analysis of variance on the group data (with the highest order or four-way interaction used as the error term). The main effects of all of the four factors in this analysis (subjects, durations, orientations, and normal-versus-backward versions) were highly significant ($p < .01$ in all cases). All two-way

interactions with the factor "subjects" were also
significant. The only other two-way interaction that
achieved statistical significance was between durations
and orientations ($p < .01$), which corresponds to the
theoretically important flattening of the reaction-
time function with increasing duration of the orientation cue. No three-way interactions were of even
marginal statistical significance.

Similar analyses of variance were done for each
of the eight subjects separately with regard to the
three remaining factors (durations, orientations, and
versions). The results of these individual analyses
can be summarized as follows: All eight of the subjects showed highly significant main effects of both
duration and orientation ($p < .01$ in all cases), while
five of the eight subjects showed a significant main
effect of version (with $p < .01$). Six of the eight
subjects showed a significant interaction between duration and orientation (with $p < .01$). But neither of
the remaining two-way interactions (both with the factor "version") approached statistical significance for
any subject.

The question remains as to the extent to which the
data for individual subjects under the four B-Conditions
can be explained solely in terms of the basic prediction (a) that reaction time should increase monotonically with departure of the test stimulus from upright
but (b) that this monotonic trend should diminish and
finally disappear with increasing duration of the
advance information. In order to enable a test that
was more specifically tuned to this prediction, we
constructed a set of orthogonal contrasts, of the sort
designed for the test of monotonic trends by Abelson
and Tukey (1963), that seemed to capture the essence
of the predicted joint effect of the two factors of
orientation and duration.

The outcome of the eight within-subject analyses
of variance, which used these contrasts to account
simultaneously for the main effects and the interaction
of the two principal factors of duration and orientation, were as follows: For all eight subjects, the

contrasts were overwhelmingly significant ($p < .001$).
For five of the eight subjects, moreover, the residual
term did not approach statistical significance, and
for a sixth the residual was of only marginal significance ($p < .05$). The lack of significance of the
residual allows us to say that, for these subjects
anyway, the chosen contrasts embody a hypothesis that
is a sufficient explanation of the data.

Questions can of course be raised concerning the
appropriateness of the analysis of variance model for
these data which (as is typical for reaction times) are
distributed with unequal variances and appreciable
skewness. However, an entirely different kind of
analysis, based solely upon the slopes of the mean
curves relating reaction time to departure from upright
for individual subjects, also showed that the predicted
interaction between orientation and duration held up
for every one of the eight subjects.

Additional statistical analyses are relevant to
certain more specific features of the data that appear
to be of special theoretical interest. First, the
question arises as to whether the reaction-time function
(B-1000, in Fig. 5), resulting when the preparatory
image must be mentally rotated by the subject himself,
shows any reliable departure in shape from flatness or,
more crucially, from (the virtually flat) shape of the
function (C), resulting when that image has already
been externally rotated for the subject. Two different
analyses failed to find any evidence of a reliable
difference in shape between these two curves: In an
analysis of variance for just the two Conditions C and
B-1000, the interaction between conditions and orientations was nonsignificant ($F < 1.0$); and in a further
analysis of the slopes of the functions relating reaction time to departure from upright (in *either* the
clockwise or counterclockwise direction), the difference
between the slopes for the two conditions was also
nonsignificant ($t = 1.02$, with 7 df).

There does appear to be a slight but consistent
elevation of the entire curve for Condition B-1000
relative to that for Condition C. This approximately

113

20-msec. mean difference may be attributable to a greater visual definition of the preparatory image under Condition C. Better definition in that condition might have resulted either from the fact that the image had not been subjected to a mental transformation or merely from the fact that the complete information as to identity *and* orientation had been available for processing for a total of 3 seconds prior to the onset of the test stimulus in Condition C, but only for 1 second in Condition B-1000. There also appears to be a very slight humping up of the curves for both C and B-1000 around 180°. Possibly this reflects a greater speed of comparison between two images (perceptual and memorial) that are in the upright orientation, as compared with two inverted images (cf., Egeth & Blecker, 1971).

A second question concerns the similarity in shape of the reaction-time functions for the three Conditions N, I, and 0. In an analysis of variance for just these three conditions, the interaction between conditions and orientations was found to be nonsignificant (F = 1.72, with 10 and 70 df). Even at 0° the mean reaction times for Conditions I and 0 do not differ significantly (t = .74 with 7 df). This is the basis for the earlier statement that the seeming departure from parallelism of the curve for the one Condition I at 0° is not statistically reliable. Despite the similarity in shape of these three curves, the overall elevation of the curve for Condition N is reliably different from that of either of the (lower) curves for I or for 0. (F is greater than 90 for either comparison and, with 1 and 35 df, p < .01 in both cases.) The overall mean reaction time for N is 100 msec. longer than for I and 122 msec. longer than for 0. (The 22-msec. difference between the elevations for I and for 0 is not significant: F = 4.0 with 1 and 35 df).

A third question has to do with the apparent nonlinearity of the relation between reaction time and departure from upright (whether clockwise or counterclockwise) in all conditions without complete advance information. While an analysis of the group data for

114

Conditions N, I, and O demonstrated significant linear trends ($p < .05$ for all conditions), the concave upward departure from linearity is apparently reliable also, since every one of the 24 individual functions for each of the eight subjects under each of these three conditions exhibits the same kind of nonlinear upswing as it approaches the point for 180°.

Distributions of Reaction Times under Different Conditions

So far we have been concerned with just the *means* of the distributions of reaction times for different conditions and orientations (whether for individual subjects or for the whole group). An examination of the entire distributions can provide additional information relevant to notions about what kinds of processes are going on within individual subjects. Although we have surveyed the computer-plotted distributions for all eight subjects, under all eight conditions, at each of the six orientations, it is clearly impractical to display all 384 of these individual distributions here.

Comparisons among the distributions obtained from different subjects indicated, however, that the eight subjects could be divided into a group of five subjects with relatively long reaction times and a group of three subjects with relatively short reaction times. Moreover, distributions plotted for either group as a whole then turned out to be reasonably representative of all subjects within that group (whereas this was not true for distributions plotted for the much more heterogeneous group consisting of *all* eight subjects). Among all 48 combinations of condition and orientation, the most informative cases appeared to be (a) those in which the test stimulus came on, essentially without advance information as to orientation, at each of the four degrees of departure from upright, 0°, 60°, 120°, and 180° (whether in the clockwise or counterclockwise direction); and (b) those in which the test stimulus came on at 180°, but following periods in which advance information as to this orientation had been presented for 100, 400, 700, or 1000 msec.

115

Distributions of the first sort are displayed in Fig. 8. In order to obtain relatively stable shapes, each curve is based on the pooled data for the two essentially equivalent Conditions I and B-100 and for

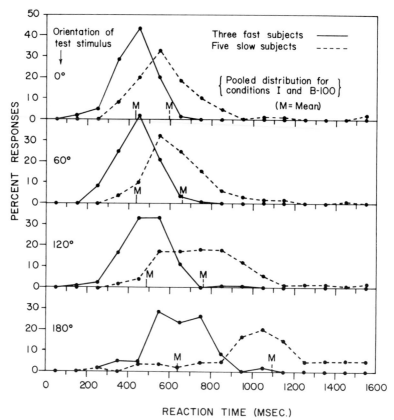

Fig. 8. Distributions of reaction times to test stimuli presented at 0°, 60°, 120°, and 180° angular departures from the upright orientation. Distributions are pooled over conditions in which, effectively, no orientation information was provided (Conditions I and B-100). Separate distributions are plotted for the three fast subjects (solid lines) and the five slow subjects (dashed lines).

all (three or five) subjects within the indicated
group (fast or slow). The distributions for the three
"fast" subjects (shown by solid lines) are relatively
compact and symmetrical. The distributions for the
five "slow" subjects (shown by dashed lines) tend to
be somewhat broader (particularly at $120°$). For both
groups of subjects, the distributions shift to the
right and become broader as the test stimulus departs
more and more from upright. This rightward shift is
considerably more marked for the five slower subjects.
Perhaps what most characterizes these slower subjects,
then, is a slower speed of mental rotation. The relatively compact, sharply peaked shapes of most of these
distributions is a consequence of the fact that the
subjects within either group were relatively homogeneous. Nevertheless there were still some variations
among subjects within either group and, so, these
pooled distributions tend to be somewhat broader than
those for most of the individual subjects.

The second set of distributions of interest
includes those for reaction time to a completely inverted test stimulus following various durations of advance
information as to the $180°$ orientation. These distributions are displayed in Fig. 9, for the three fast
subjects, and in Fig. 10, for the three slow subjects.
Again, these pooled distributions, though slightly
broader, appeared to be quite representative of the
distributions for individual subjects from each group.
At the top of these figures we see that, when the
orientation information was available for a full second
(B-1000), the reaction-time distribution was quite
compact, sharply peaked and, indeed, very similar in
shape to that obtained under Condition C (in which the
preparatory image had already been rotated for the
subject). At the bottom we see that, when the orientation information was available for only a tenth of
that time (B-100), the distribution was shifted
markedly to the right, spread out and similar in shape
to that obtained under Condition I (in which there was
no orientation information at all). As in the earlier
Fig. 8, this shift to the right was much greater for

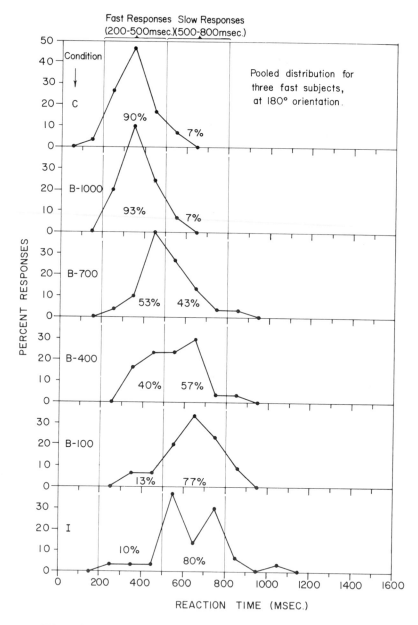

Fig. 9. Distributions of reaction times to test stimuli presented at 180° for the three fast subjects. Separate distributions are plotted for each condition in which identity information was provided.

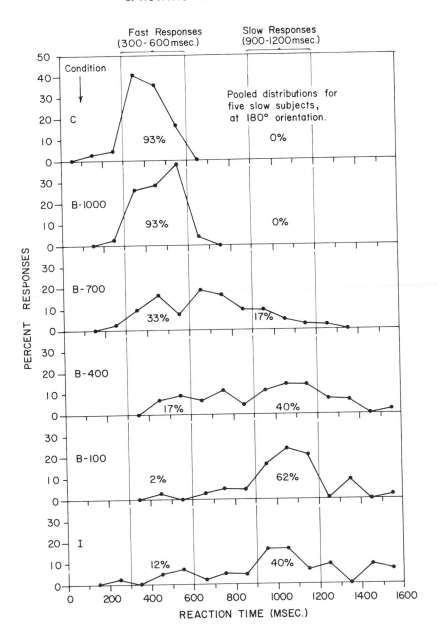

Fig. 10. Distributions of reaction times to test stimuli presented at 180° for the five slow subjects. Separate distributions are plotted for each condition in which identity information was provided.

the slower subjects--which we should expect if their longer reaction times were due primarily to a slower rate of mental rotation (in this case, of the preparatory image rather than of the test stimulus itself).

Here, however, the intermediate cases (B-400 and, for the five slow subjects, B-700 too) yield distributions that are more spread out than the distributions even for the extreme case B-100. We could explain this by supposing that the rate of preparatory rotation is somewhat variable from trial to trial, depending in part upon the particular character to be rotated. And, in fact, most subjects reported that some characters, e.g., R and 2, were generally easier than others, e.g., 7 and J. Under the extreme conditions we should expect that on virtually all trials the subjects either would be fully prepared (Condition B-1000) or would not be at all prepared (Condition B-100) for the inverted test stimulus. Consequently, their reaction times would be consistently short or long, respectively. Under the intermediate conditions, however, we should expect that on some proportion of the trials the subjects would be prepared and on some proportion they would not. When they were prepared, they would be able to respond rapidly (perhaps as rapidly as under Condition B-1000). When they were not prepared, though, their reaction times would be longer and more variable. In the latter case, they might drop their preparatory rotation and start all over with the test stimulus itself, in which case their reaction times would be comparable to their times under Condition B-100. Alternatively, they might continue their preparatory rotation into congruence with the test stimulus, in which case their reaction times could fall anywhere between their times for B-100 and for B-1000, depending upon how far along they were with their preparatory rotation before the onset of the test stimulus.

It appears, from Fig. 9, that a fast subject typically responds in 200 to 500 msec. when he is prepared for the inverted test stimulus and in 500 to 800 msec. when he is not; and, from Fig. 10, that a slow subject usually responds in 300 to 600 msec. when he is prepared and in 900 to 1200 msec. when he begins his rotation with the presentation of the test stimulus itself. These two cases, labeled "fast responses" and "slow responses" are indicated in Figs. 9 and 10 by the two vertical bands drawn in each figure. Numbers have also been included to indicate, for each distribution, the percentage of its total area that falls within each of these two vertical bands. These numbers thus provide a very rough estimate of the percent of trials of each type for which the subject was prepared for the inverted test stimulus either fully or not at all. For the five slow subjects, for example, we see that the estimate of the percent of trials on which the subjects were fully prepared systematically declines from 93%, when they had a full exposure to advance information as to orientation (in both Conditions C and B-1000), to only about 10% or less, when they had little or no chance to take advantage of that advance information (in Conditions B-100 and I, respectively). The intermediate responses, which were made in 600 to 900 msec. (e.g., in Condition B-700), may represent trials in which a subject, though not fully prepared at the onset of the test stimulus, was nevertheless able to continue with his preparatory rotation until he did achieve congruence. This would explain the reduction in overall processing time, as measured from the onset of the test stimulus.

Theoretical Discussion

The Nonlinear Effect of Orientation of the Test Stimulus

In the experiment by Shepard and Metzler (1971), the time subjects required to determine that two perspective pictures were of the same three-dimensional object increased in a remarkably linear manner with the angular difference in their portrayed orientations. This, together with the subjects' introspective reports, was taken to support the notion that they made each comparison by imagining one object rotated into

121

congruence with the other and that this "mental rotation" could successfully be carried out at no greater than a certain fixed rate (of about 60° per second for those objects). If we wish to invoke a similar notion of mental rotation to account for the marked increase in reaction time to rotated alphanumeric characters, we need to explain why the increase in reaction time (shown in Figs. 5 and 6) consistently departs from linearity. At least four explanations appear consistent with the data.

First, both theoretical and introspective considerations suggest that it is not always necessary to rotate a tipped character into its upright orientation to make the required normal-versus-backward discrimination. The representation or "template" for the normal, upright character in long-term memory may be so broadly tuned that this discrimination can often be made for characters tilted by 60° or even more without any need for mental rotation. Suppose that there were some critical angle, Θ, such that characters within Θ of upright could be discriminated immediately, while characters tipped beyond Θ would need to be rotated to within Θ of upright in order to make this discrimination. In this case the reaction-time function should be completely flat from 0° out to the critical angle Θ and then should climb linearly from that point on out to 180°. But if, as is more likely, this critical angle Θ were to vary from subject to subject, from character to character and, perhaps randomly, from trial to trial, the resulting average curve would become rounded and might resemble the concave upward functions obtained here (Figs. 5 and 6) and in the previous experiment by Shepard and Klun.

On this theory it might be considered surprising that the sharpest bend in the curve should occur nearer to 120° than to 60° from upright. However, the force of this possible objection is difficult to evaluate. The range of orientations that can be directly matched against the representation in long-term memory may be quite broad--owing, perhaps, to the considerable experience we have all had in reading words (such as the labels for the vertical axes in the present figures) that are rotated by as much as 90°.

A second explanation, which has some relation to the first, is based upon the dual notions (a) that the rate at which an object can be mentally rotated increases with the familiarity of that object, and (b) that letters and numbers are less familiar when viewed in more or less inverted orientations. The first notion seems plausible on subjective grounds and finds some objective support in the higher overall rates of mental rotation (of between 164 and 800 degrees per second) estimated here for familiar letters and numbers, as contrasted with the rates (of only about 60° per second) estimated for the much less familiar three-dimensional nonsense shapes used by Shepard and Metzler. The second notion also appears plausible on introspective grounds-- especially in view of the vastly greater exposure that we have had to upright as opposed to inverted charac- ters. Again, whether this explanation can account for the occurrence of the sharpest bend in the reaction-time function near 120° is not yet clear. To answer that question we would need to know more about the frequen- cies with which we process letters in different orien- tations, and about how speed of rotation depends upon such frequencies.

A third and quite different kind of explanation derives from the claim of a few subjects that they sometimes resorted to a different strategy when the test stimulus appeared in an inverted orientation. Speci- fically, some said that when the character was complete- ly upside down, instead of imagining it rotated into its upright orientation within its own picture plane, they sometimes would first imagine it flipped rightside up about its horizontal axis (lying within that plane). Then they either would imagine it flipped about its vertical axis (which is necessary to restore its original parity--normal or backward) or else would remember to reverse their response to the uprighted character (using the left thumb to indicate "normal" and the right thumb to indicate "backward"). An experi- ment by Shepard and Feng (see Shepard, in press) has shown that it does take longer to imagine a letter flipped first about a horizontal and then a vertical axis than to imagine that same letter rotated 180° in the picture plane--even though the two ways of transforming the image result in the same final state. Moreover in the first experiment by Shepard and Klun, a subject who emphasized that he used this alternative strategy showed an especially marked increase in reaction time at 180°. This explanation may account for some of the nonlinear upswing for some subjects and, certainly, could account for why the upswing is most pronounced in the vicinity of 180°. However, it does not seem to offer a plausible account of the results for most of the subjects, who claimed to use the same strategy (of rotation within the picture plane) throughout.

A fourth possibility is that the operations of determining the identity and/or the orientation of the test stimulus (which presumably must be completed before the rotation can even be started) may themselves increase nonlinearly as the test stimulus departs from upright. However, for reasons to be considered later (in support of a tentative information-processing model), we believe that any dependence of these non-rotational processing times upon orientation is negligible and, so, can not account for more than a very small part of the nonlinearity in question.

It is possible that any or all of the above explanations are to some degree correct for at least some subjects. Moreover, all four are specifically designed for the case of stimuli, such as alphanumeric characters, that have a well-defined standard or upright orientation. Hence, the fact that the reaction-time functions obtained by Shepard and Metzler were perfectly linear is compatible with these explanations; for, the three-dimensional nonsense shapes presented in that study had no uniquely established conventional or preferred orientation. We conclude, therefore, that the finding of a consistently nonlinear relation between reaction time and orientation of the test stimulus here does not weigh against the hypothesis that subjects

typically used mental rotation to determine whether
an inverted test stimulus was normal or backward.

*The Nonadditive Effects of Advance Information as to
Identity and Orientation*

A very central finding is that of a virtually flat
reaction-time function under the 1000-msec. B-Condition
(in which complete advance information is given, separately, for both identity and orientation). This finding
offers substantial support for the notion that, in
preparing for the presentation of a tilted stimulus, the
subject carries out a purely mental rotation of something that might be called a mental image of the anticipated stimulus. Further support comes from the
subjects themselves who, after completing the experiment, typically claimed that in this B-Condition--just
as much as in the C-Condition (in which the appropriate
visual image was supplied to the subject already rotated)--they were ready with what seemed, introspectively,
to be the same sort of mental image. Regardless of
whether the orientation of this internal representation
had been achieved by external, physical rotation
(Condition C) or by purely internal, mental rotation
(Condition B-1000), these subjects were equally ready
to use this "rotated" internal representation as a
template against which they could rapidly match the
visually presented test stimulus when it then appeared
in that same orientation.

What needs to be noted, however, is that such a
mental rotation evidently cannot be carried out on the
basis of just the orientation information alone. For,
the curve for Condition 0--far from being completely
flat--has the same steep slope as the curves for the
N, I, and 100-msec. B Conditions, in which subjects
were not given (or were not able to utilize) any
orientation information.

This might seem surprising. To the extent that
the subject has already been given information as to
the orientation of a stimulus, it is natural to suppose
that the redundant reappearance of that same information

in the actual test stimulus should then have little effect. And this is in fact what has happened in the 1000-msec. B-Condition. There, as a result of having provided advance access to the orientation variable, that variable no longer had any effect on the latency of the subsequent response to the stimulus itself. Why is it, then, that advance access to the orientation variable did not in any way diminish the effectiveness of that same variable when it reemerged in the test stimulus in Condition 0?

The answer seems to be that, under the conditions of this experiment, subjects can only rotate the mental representation of a specific, concrete object or character. They evidently are not able to rotate a general, abstract frame of reference--at least when their head orientation is fixed with respect to gravitational upright (cf. Attneave & Olson, 1967; Rock & Heimer, 1957). Both in this experiment and in the second experiment of Shepard and Klun, when subjects were informed of both the character (e.g., the letter "R") and its orientation (e.g., at "4 o'clock"), they were able to imagine that character rotated into that orientation in advance of its actual presentation. When, however, they were informed only that the character would appear in, say, the 4 o'clock position without being told *which* character would appear in that position, they could only wait until the actual presentation of the character itself and, then, had to imagine it rotated into the upright orientation in order to determine whether it was normal or backward.

A consequence is that the effects of identity information and orientation information, though possibly quite additive when the stimulus appears in its upright orientation, become increasingly nonadditive as the orientation departs from upright. As is evident in Fig. 5, each kind of information alone results in a roughly 100-msec. drop in the reaction-time function as a whole, without having any appreciable effect on the shape of the function. However, when both kinds of information are provided, the reaction-time function becomes so much lower and flatter that there is a drop of at least 600 msec. at 180°.

We are not saying that the advance presentation of orientation alone has no effect on subsequent reaction time--only that it has no effect on the way in which reaction time depends upon the orientation of the ensuing test stimulus. The advance presentation of either identity or orientation information alone does have an effect--indeed, approximately the *same* effect--as is evident from the 100-msec. decrease at all orientations. This is especially striking at $0°$ where the test stimulus appears in the standard upright position for all conditions. Consider, in particular, Conditions I and C at the $0°$ point. In both cases the subject sees essentially the same thing; namely, an upright outline of the appropriate character followed by the upright presentation of that same character (or its mirror image). And yet from Fig. 5 we see that, at $0°$, mean reaction time was over 100 msec. longer under Condition I than under Condition C; and this difference is statistically reliable ($t = 2.4$, $df = 7$; $p < .05$).

We do not think that the explanation for this difference lies in any difference in the physical displays under the two conditions. The fact that a 1-second blank field is interposed between the advance information and the test stimulus in Condition C could only account for a longer, not a shorter, reaction time under that condition. The explanation lies, rather, in the different interpretations that the subject has been instructed to place on the same advance information cue in the two types of trials. Under Condition C, the appearance of an upright outline of the letter "R," for example, informs the subject both that the test stimulus will be the letter "R" *and* that it will appear in the upright orientation. Under Condition I, however, the appearance of that very same cue informs the subject only that the test stimulus will be the letter "R;" he still has no basis for assuming anything about the orientation in which it will appear.

How, then, does advance information as to either identity or orientation alone have its effect upon reaction time? One hypothesis, which we now tend to reject, is that either type of advance information

127

cuts down on the set of alternatives through which the
subject scans in preparing for the upcoming test stimulus. According to this hypothesis, the subject with
advance information as to orientation, say, might mentally cycle through the six alternative characters that
could appear in the designated orientation. On one out
of six trials he would, by chance, be ready with the
right template and, so, would be able to respond rapidly.
(In the absence of any advance information, this could
happen on at most one out of 36 trials.) Clearly,
though, this hypothesis cannot explain either the marked
dependence of reaction time upon orientation of the test
stimulus, or the disappearance of this dependence when
advance information concerning *both* identity and orientation is presented for its maximum duration. There is,
moreover, no indication of the tendency toward bimodality
that this hypothesis might lead one to expect in the
distributions of reaction times for Conditions I, O, and
and N at 0°.

A tentative information-processing model that we
shall shortly propose is based upon a different hypothesis. We shall argue that the only effect of presenting advance information either as to identity or
as to orientation alone is merely to cut down, by a
constant amount of about 100 msec., the time that it
would otherwise take to determine the identity or
orientation of the test stimulus itself. When, however,
both kinds of advance information are furnished, the
subject is able to proceed with an entirely different
preparatory process of rotating a mental image of the
indicated character into the indicated orientation and,
thus, enables himself to respond with uniform rapidity
to the ensuing test stimulus.

*The Relationship between Pre-Stimulus and Post-Stimulus
Rotation*

The present experiment, unlike previously reported
experiments on mental rotation (including the two by
Shepard and Klun), permits us to estimate not only the
time required to respond to a rotated stimulus but also

the time required to *prepare* for a rotated stimulus.
We assume that both times include the time needed to
carry out the rotation of a mental image. However,
there are differences between the two cases.
    When (as in Condition I) the rotation is started
only after the onset of the test stimulus, we assume
that the mental image of the test stimulus is rotated
from the tipped orientation in which it has been presented back into the standard upright orientation in
which it can be compared with the normal representation
in long-term memory. When (as in Condition B-1000) the
rotation is completed prior to the onset of the test
stimulus, we assume that the mental image of the normal
version of the designated character is rotated from the
standard upright orientation in which its outline has
appeared as the identity cue into the tipped orientation
in which it is about to appear as the actual test stimulus. Moreover, the character that is being mentally
rotated is continuously present as a visual stimulus in
the first case, but is present, if at all, only as a
memory representation in the second. The question
naturally arises as to whether the mental images in
these two cases (which require rotation in opposite
directions and in the presence of different degrees of
external support) are nevertheless rotated at similar
rates.
    Now, whenever some portion of the required mental
rotation has been carried out in preparation for the
upcoming test stimulus, the subsequent reaction time
should depend less strongly upon the orientation of
that test stimulus. Condition B-1000 furnishes the
extreme example. Here, the entire rotation is completed
in advance and, so, results in a virtually flat reaction-
time function. In the case of Condition B-400, however,
the reaction-time function--though lower than the functions for Conditions I and B-100--does not differ from
either of them in shape (Fig. 6). (An analysis of
variance for Conditions I and B-400, in particular,
showed that the condition-by-orientation interaction
was non-significant; $F = .73$, with 5 and 35 df.) A very
similar picture emerges from the reaction-time distributions plotted in Figs. 9 and 10. Although the proportion

of "fast" responses does increase as we move from
Condition I to Condition B-400 (particularly for the
three "fast" subjects), the modal peak of the 180°
distribution shifts no more than 100 msec. for either
the "fast" or the "slow" subjects. A full 700-msec.
duration of the orientation cue is necessary for the
reaction-time function to flatten appreciably (Fig. 6)
and for the modal peak of the reaction-time distribution
to shift markedly to the left (Figs. 9 and 10). Apparently orientation information must be supplied for a
400-msec. period before there is a significant reduction
in the amount of post-stimulus rotation on most trials.

By analogy with the time apparently required to
determine orientation on the basis of the test stimulus
itself, we might have expected that the time required
to determine orientation on the basis of the advance
cue would also take about 100 msec. However, if 100
msec. sufficed to extract this information from the
inclined arrow in a fully usable form, then the curve
for Condition B-100 should have been displaced downward
by some 100 msec. from the curve for Condition I (in
which the orientation information had to be determined
after the presentation of the test stimulus). However,
there is no difference between the heights of the reaction-time curves for I and B-100, whereas the curve for
Condition B-400 *is* displaced downward from both of
these by about 100 msec. Accordingly, we tentatively
arrive at the unexpected conclusion that close to 400
msec. may be needed to complete the processing of the
orientation cue. In addition to the time needed merely
to determine the orientation of the tipped arrow, this
time may include times needed to convert this information into a form applicable to an ensuing alphanumeric
character and, possibly, to overcome any backward masking of the arrow or disruption of its interpretation
caused by the sudden onset of the test stimulus.

As a rough approximation, we suggest that, following
the onset of the orientation cue, (a) a period of about
400 msec. is usually required before the preparatory
rotation is effectively started and (b) a period
approaching 1000 msec. is needed to ensure that nearly

all of the subjects have completed a rotation of 180°.
By subtraction, we conclude that the time required to
complete a 180° preparatory rotation for one of these
stimuli is 600 msec.--or less, in view of the variability in the more directly estimated post-stimulus
rotation times (Fig. 8). For, if 600 msec. sufficies
to ensure completion of a 180° rotation on almost *all*
trials, then the time required to complete the preparatory rotation on an *average* trial is less than 600 msec.
--perhaps closer to 400 or 500 msec. This estimate
agrees well with the estimated time required to rotate
180° *after* the presentation of the test stimulus. For,
the differences between the mean reaction times for 0°
and 180° under all of the four Conditions N, I, O, and
B-100 (Figs. 5 and 6) range between roughly 400 and
500 msec.

Separate consideration of the "fast" and "slow"
subjects permits a further comparison of the pre-stumulus
and post-stimulus rotations. Notice in Fig. 8 that, as
we move from 0° to 180°, the mean reaction time under
conditions of post-stimulus rotation (I and B-100) shifts
about 200 msec. for the three fast subjects and about
500 msec. for the five slow subjects. Then notice in
Figs. 9 and 10 that, as we move from Condition B-400
to the condition of pre-stimulus rotation, B-1000, the
peak of the reaction-time distribution for a stimulus
at 180° correspondingly shifts about 300 msec. for the
three fast subjects and about 500 msec. for the five
slow subjects. Again, there is a reasonably good agreement between the pre-stimulus and post-stimulus cases
(except, possibly, for the 100-msec. discrepancy for
the smaller group of three fast subjects).

We have been focusing, here, on those conditions
in which a preparatory rotation either could be completed before stimulus onset (B-1000) or else could,
in most cases, not even be started (I, B-100, and B-400).
We turn now to a consideration of the relation between
pre-stimulus and post-stimulus rotation in the intermediate condition, B-700, in which the preparatory rotation is usually initiated but not completed prior to
the onset of the test stimulus. Again, it is best to
discuss the groups of fast and slow subjects separately.

131

In the case of the group of five slow subjects, the reaction-time distribution for Condition B-700 (Fig. 10) is quite widely spread out and contains the suggestion of three components--with modal peaks centered, respectively, in the 300-600 msec. fast range, in the 600-900 msec. intermediate range, and in the 900-1200 msec. slow range (as these three ranges are depicted by vertical bands in the figure). We could interpret the (33%) fast responses as resulting from trials in which the subject was able to complete the 180° rotation before stimulus onset, and the (17%) slow responses as resulting from trials in which the subject abandoned his incomplete preparatory rotation and started over with a (reverse) rotation of the test stimulus itself. If so, it is most natural to attribute the remaining intermediate responses to trials in which the subject continued a preparatory rotation (which had been started but not completed before stimulus onset) until it was completed *after* stimulus onset.

The quantitative values of the means and relevant modal points of the reaction-time distributions are in satisfactory agreement with this account in the case of the larger group of five "slow" subjects. Notice, again, that as we move from Condition B-400 to B-700 to B-1000 in Fig. 10, the modal point (and indeed the overall mean) shifts left by roughly 300 msec., each time, from the middle of the band of slow responses, to the middle of the band of intermediate responses, to the middle of the band of fast responses. In other words, each additional 300 msec. of time allowed for preparatory rotation cuts about 300 msec. off the time that the subject then requires to complete that rotation after the presentation of the actual stimulus.

This trade-off between pre- and post-stimulus rotation time does not emerge quite so clearly in the case of the smaller group of three "fast" subjects. In Fig. 9, the leftward shift of the mode of the reaction-time distribution from Condition B-400 (or B-100) to B-700 is closer to 200 msec. than to 300 msec., and the full 300-msec. shift is not achieved until Condition B-1000 when, according to our analysis, the subjects

have had at least 600 msec. in which to complete their
preparatory rotation. If the three fast subjects were
faster simply by virtue of faster mental rotation (as
their post-stimulus reaction-time distributions suggest
in Fig. 8), then we should expect that they would nearly
always be ready for the test stimulus in Condition B-700.
The distribution for B-700 would then be essentially
identical to that for B-1000, rather than displaced
100 msec. to the right--as it is in Fig. 9. (Possibly
there is a connection between this 100-msec. discrepancy
and the other 100-msec. discrepancy, noted earlier, for
these same three subjects.)

Indeed, several of the differences between the
results for these two internally homogeneous groups of
subjects suggest that the "fast" subjects may have used
a different method in addition to their postulated
greater rate of mental rotation. These differences
include (a) the two 100-msec. discrepancies that, as we
just noted, occurred only for the group of fast subjects,
(b) the more compact reaction-time distributions obtained
from this group (Figs. 8 and 9), and (c) the greater
tendency of the individual reaction-time functions
obtained for this group to bend sharply at about 60°
on either side of 180° (as is illustrated for one of
these subjects at the top of Fig. 7). Owing in part to
the small number of subjects in the "fast" group, we
do not feel prepared at this time to make a definite
claim concerning their method of processing.

Despite some uncertainty about these three subjects,
we believe that the data from all eight subjects support
our general conclusion that subjects carried out mental
rotations both to respond to a rotated stimulus in the
absence of advance information as to its orientation,
and to prepare for a rotated stimulus on the basis of
such advance information. Moreover, we believe that
the data from the majority of the subjects agree quite
well with our more specific conclusion that subjects
carried out such pre-stimulus and post-stimulus rotations at essentially the same rates.

A Tentative Information-Processing Model

Figure 11 schematically presents our first approximation to a model for what takes place within a typical subject on a trial (of type N) in which no advance information is provided as to the identity or orientation of the upcoming stimulus. The small empty squares represent events that are externally controlled or recorded, whereas the larger numbered rectangles represent component processes that, though not directly observed, are assumed to go on within the subject. We shall also consider how this model might be applied to trials in which advance information is supplied and how it may need to be refined or modified in certain respects.

Following the onset of the blank warning field (which initiates a trial under Condition N), there is an externally controlled 2-second period during which the subject presumably (a) adjusts his fixation and accommodation to the position and distance of the circular field within which the stimulus is about to appear and (b) readies his preferred hand. Thus, if he determines that the ensuing test stimulus is normal (as opposed to backward), he can execute the appropriate response as rapidly as possible. Although we have not directly measured the time required for this particular preparatory act (indicated in the rectangular box numbered 1), evidence to be considered below (in connection with Box 6) suggests that the readying of one hand as opposed to the other takes no more than about a tenth of a second.

The next significant external event consists of the simultaneous onset of the test stimulus and the reaction-time clock. As soon as the subject detects the appearance of a stimulus in the previously blank field, he presumably must perform two operations: He must determine which of the six alternative characters has appeared (Box 2), and he must determine in which of the six alternative orientations that character has appeared (Box 3). We claim that, if each of these operations takes a fixed time, then this time is

3. ROTATION OF MENTAL IMAGES

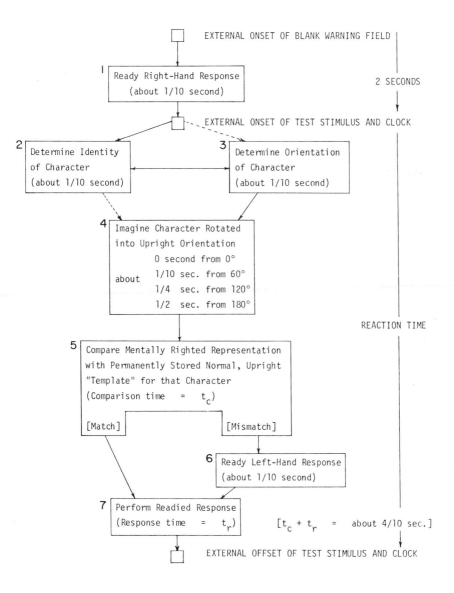

Fig. 11. An information-processing model to
account for the reaction times obtained in Experiment I.

135

approximately a tenth of a second. We base this claim on the findings (a) that, if either of these two pieces of information is presented in advance of the stimulus (as in Conditions I or O), the entire reaction-time function is lowered by about 100 msec., and (b) that, if both pieces of information are presented in advance (Condition B), the reaction-time to a stimulus at the $0°$ orientation is lowered by about 200 msec.

As a refinement of this model, one could also entertain the possibility that the times required to determine identity and/or orientation of a tilted stimulus are increasing functions of the departure of that stimulus from its normal upright orientation--as suggested by previously reported findings of increased recognition time for inverted letters (e.g., Kolers & Perkins, 1969). However, we have two reasons to believe that any such dependence of these two processing times upon orientation is negligible in our situation. First, any marked dependence of this sort in the present experiment should result in an appreciable departure from parallelism of the three curves for Conditions N, I, and O (Fig. 5). For, if the times required to determine identity and orientation both increase with departure from upright, then the curve for N (which includes the times for both processes) should be steeper than the curves for both I and O (each of which includes the time for only one of these two processes). Or, if the time for only one of these two processes increases with departure from upright, then the curve for the condition (I or O) in which that process is not required should be flatter than the other two. Although the curve I does appear slightly less steep near $0°$, it is quite similar to the other two in overall shape and, as we have already noted, the slight difference at $0°$ is not statistically significant. Second, and more conclusive, in a subsidiary experiment using the same six characters and same six orientations, one of us (LAC) found that the mean reaction time for orally reporting the identity of each character (regardless of orientation) was virtually constant (at about 550 msec.) over all six orientations.

Even if the times required for these two pre-rotational operations are essentially independent of orientation, a question remains as to whether one of these operations must be completed before the other is started or whether there can be some degree of time sharing between them. It may be that the determination of identity precedes the determination of orientation (as indicated by the solid, as opposed to the dashed, arrows in the figure). For, while the identity of a character can often be recognized on the basis of orientation-invariant features (e.g., curvature, enclosed space, two free ends, etc., for "R"), the orientation may be difficult to determine without knowing anything about the identity of the character and, hence, about which is the top end and which is the bottom end of that character. On the basis of the present data, we are justified in saying only that the approximate additivity of the additional times required to determine identity and orientation, when the B-1000 condition at the $0°$-orientation is taken as the baseline, indicates that these two operations are not carried out independently, in parallel.

Once the identity and the orientation of the presented character have been established, the subject can proceed to imagine that character rotated into its standard, upright orientation. For present purposes we need not commit ourselves to any one of the alternative explanations offered earlier for the nonlinear dependence of reaction time upon departure from upright. On the basis of the empirical data we can simply make the general statement (indicated in Box 4) that an additional rotation time of roughly 100, 250, or 500 msec. is required when the presented stimulus is tipped away from upright (in either direction) by 60, 120, or 180 degrees, respectively.

The mentally-righted image of the presented character is then compared (in Box 5) with the normal, upright representation of that character in long-term memory—as might be expected on the basis of the "congruence" principles of Clark (see Clark & Chase, 1972) or of Trabasso (see Trabasso, Rollins, &

137

Shaughnessy, 1971). If there is a match, the response
that has previously been readied (Box 1) is immediately
executed (Box 7) and, thereby, stops the reaction-time
clock. If there is a mismatch, however, the subject
must switch control to the other, nonpreferred hand
(Box 6) before executing the final response (Box 7).
The constant within-subject difference in reaction time
between the responses used to signal "normal" and
"backward" indicates that this extra operation requires
a constant additional time that, typically, is about a
tenth of a second (but that may be anywhere between 10
and 150 msec. for individual subjects). The times
required for comparison with the stored representation,
t_c, (Box 5) and execution of the final response, t_r,
(Box 7) cannot be separately estimated from our data.
Together, however, they evidently require a total of
some 400 msec.

In order to use this model to account for reaction
times on trials in which advance information is provided
as to identity, orientation, or both, we simply by-pass
those operations (Boxes 2, 3, or 4) that are rendered
superfluous by the particular information that has been
presented (for an adequate duration) in advance. Specifically, the route to Box 5 would be through Boxes 3 and
4 on a trial of type I or B-100; through Boxes 2 and 4
on a trial of type O; through Box 4, only, on a trial of
type B-400; and directly to Box 5 on a trial of type
B-1000 or C.

The only type of trial that is not explicitly
handled in this way is the type, B-700, in which the
mental rotation referred to in Box 4 is started but not
completed before the onset of the test stimulus. Owing
to variations in rate of rotation, the prediction of the
extent of the rotation remaining after stimulus onset
and, hence, the reaction time to that stimulus on a
particular trial of this type becomes hazardous. Moreover, the prediction of reaction times at the intermediate orientations (between $0°$ and $180°$) will depend,
in this case, on the relative contributions of the
various factors proposed earlier to account for the
nonlinear dependence of reaction time upon orientation.
Nevertheless, the "tradeoff" between preparation time
and reaction time noted in the preceding section indicates that, on the average, the reaction times under

Condition B-700 are consistent with the presently proposed model--especially for the orientations that were
specifically examined (*viz*., 0° and 180°) and for the
larger group of five "slow" subjects.

It would be premature to maintain that we now have
a complete understanding of the internal processes by
means of which subjects prepare for or respond to a
rotated stimulus. At this early stage in our investigations, our principal efforts have not been directed
toward the development and testing of models that precisely specify all the numerous subprocesses that
mediate between the various stimulus events and the
resulting response in this experiment--particularly
since many of these subprocesses are related only peri-
pherally to the formation and transformation of mental
images. Still, in order to support our claim that
subjects in this experiment did use a process of mental
rotation, it seemed desirable to show that at least one
plausible model in which a subprocess of mental rotation
plays a critical role is able to account for the principal features of the obtained data.

As we have noted, there is some uncertainty concerning the ability of the model schematized in Fig. 11
to account for certain 100-msec. discrepancies in the
data from the three "fast" subjects. Nevertheless, this
model does furnish a quantitatively satisfactory account
of the mean reaction-time functions plotted, for the
entire group of eight subjects, in Figs. 5 and 6, and a
qualitatively satisfactory account of the pooled reaction-time distributions plotted, for the larger subgroup
of five "slow" subjects, in Figs. 8 and 10. Until a
comparably plausible and explicit model that does not
incorporate any process of mental rotation has been
shown capable of providing an equally satisfactory
account of these data, we take the generally good fit
achieved here as supportive of our claim that the subjects did use a process of mental rotation. We leave
for the following experiment a clarification of the
sense in which something is actually rotating during
such a process of mental rotation.

Experiment II: Determination
of a Correspondence between
an Imagined and an Actual Rotation

Our purpose in undertaking this second experiment
was to obtain evidence bearing upon two notions that
have been implicit throughout our discussion of Experiment I but that could not be directly substantiated on
the basis of that experiment. One notion concerns the
nonlinearity of the obtained relationship between reaction time and orientation of test stimulus. Although
the original evidence for a process of mental rotation
was largely based upon the finding of a strongly linear
relationship (Shepard & Metzler, 1971), we have been
arguing that the relationship found in the present
Experiment I (and in the closely related experiments by
Shepard and Klun)--despite a consistent and marked non-
linearity--is also the result of an underlying process
of mental rotation. The other notion concerns the sense
in which this mental process is one specifically of
rotation. Since the term "rotation" is ordinarily
defined only in relation to an external physical process, our use of this term in connection with an internal
mental process implies that there is some sort of one-
to-one correspondence or isomorphism between mental and
physical processes of rotation.

It is possible that an internal process quite
different from rotation--such as visual search, feature
detection, verbal analysis, or some other "digital
computation"--might enable a subject to determine that
two objects (or images) are identical except for orientation. Such a process might even become more difficult
and protracted as the two objects differ more widely in
orientation. In order for an internal process to qualify as the kind of "analog process" that we would call a
mental rotation, however, intermediate stages of the
process must have a one-to-one correspondence to intermediate stages of an actual physical rotation of the
one object into congruence with the other in the external
world. Central to the concept of an analog process,
then, is the idea of the path or trajectory of the

140

process. Not only should the starting point and end point of such a process correspond to the two objects compared, if the internal process is one of rotation, but also any intermediate point on this trajectory should correspond to an external object in an intermediate orientation--even though such an external object may not be physically present.

But what does it mean to say that at a given point in time an internal process has a one-to-one correspondence to a particular external object that is not physically present? It does not necessarily mean that there is any concrete structural resemblance or "first-order" isomorphism between the pattern of activity in the subject's physical brain at that moment and the corresponding external object (if it were present). Nor does it mean that there has been anything actually rotating within the subject's physical brain. It means only that there is a one-to-one relation between the internal representation and the corresponding external object in the specific sense that the subject is especially disposed to respond to that particular object in that particular orientation at that particular moment --if it were actually to be presented (Shepard, in press).

To be literally "turning something over in one's mind," then, is to be passing through an ordered series of dispositional states. On the basis of introspective evidence and other considerations presented earlier, we are inclined to refer to these states as successive mental images of a rotating object. Although there are reasons to suppose that there may be some degree of abstract "first-order" isomorphism between such an internal process and a corresponding external rotation of the imagined object (Shepard, in press), all we require in order to speak of "mental rotation" is that the internal process produce the necessary series of dispositional states. This may be achieved by means of a "second-order" isomorphism (Shepard & Chipman, 1970) according to which the internal process--whatever its neurophysiological nature--has an important part in common with the internal process that goes on when one is actually *perceiving* such an external rotation.

In this second experiment, we have subjects imagine an alphanumeric character rotating at a certain (externally paced) rate within a blank circular field. At a random point during this purely mental process, we display a normal or backward version of the imagined character--either in the orientation that the subject should be imagining at that moment in his rotation or in some other orientation chosen at random. If the subject is actually carrying out a mental rotation, the speed with which he can discriminate whether this probe stimulus is normal or backward should be greatest when the probe appears in the orientation momentarily assumed by his mental image. For, only then, will he be able to make an immediate match between his internally rotating image or template and the externally presented test probe. Results of this sort should enable us to say that something is indeed rotating during this process; namely, the orientation at which the subject is most prepared for the external presentation of the corresponding physical stimulus.

With regard, next, to the matter of nonlinearity, all four of the alternative explanations that we offered for the concave upward shape of the reaction-time functions were based on two observations. The first was that the alphanumeric characters (unlike the stimuli used by Shepard and Metzler) have a uniquely defined and well-learned upright orientation. The second was that the hypothesized rotation was always between the orientation of the presented test stimulus and this unique upright--not (as in the experiment by Shepard and Metzler) between the two orientations within all possible pairs. If any or all of the four explanations that we offered for the obtained nonlinearity are correct, we should be able to counterbalance the asymmetrical effects of the unique upright orientation and, thus, be able to obtain a more nearly linear function. We merely need to ensure that any mental rotations that the subject must perform *after* the onset of the test probe have starting and stopping points that are *both* evenly distributed around the 360° circle.

The theoretically critical point, therefore, resides--not in the linearity itself--but in the indication that it can give us that the underlying process is composed of parts (corresponding to rotations through smaller angles) that are necessarily performed in sequential order and for which, consequently, the performance times are additive. Thus, no matter what the effective rotation times may be between particular adjacent points separated by 60° around the circle, if the time required to go from any one point to any other nonadjacent point is an additive combination of the component times to go between the intervening adjacent points, then the average time to go between the points in all pairs separated by n 60° steps should increase linearly with n. To show that the time to rotate from A to C is an additive combination of the times to rotate from A to B and from B to C is to furnish another kind of evidence that the process of rotating from A to C passes through a point, B, corresponding to an intermediate orientation. A finding of linearity would thus support, further, our claim that the process of mental rotation is an analog process.

In order to provide for a test of this predicted linearity, we depart from the previous procedure in which the presentation of the test stimulus was always in strict agreement with any advance information as to identity or orientation. This time, the test stimulus does not always appear in the orientation for which the subject is preparing at the given moment. On half of the trials it appears in each of the five other evenly spaced orientations with equal probability. In this way we are for the first time able to determine the relationship of reaction time to departure of the test probe--not only from upright--but also from the orientation in which that probe was expected. On the basis of our previous results, we might anticipate that any nonlinearity will be confined to the former relationship. If our explanations as to the source of this nonlinearity are correct, we should expect the latter relationship to approximate the linearity found by Shepard and Metzler (1971).

Method

Subjects

Eight subjects were individually run through the complete experimental design, requiring four hours of participation from each. Of these subjects, two were female and two others (one student and the second author) had previously participated in Experiment I. The results for the two females and for the two experienced subjects were all typical of those for the remaining four experimentally naive male students.

Stimuli

This time we used only two from the set of six asymmetric alphanumeric characters employed in Experiment I--the upper-case "R" and the numeral "2." As before, each of these characters could appear as a normal or backward test stimulus in any of the six orientations, spaced in equal 60° steps around the circle. And again, the subjects were instructed to determine, as rapidly as possible, whether each such test stimulus had appeared in its normal or in its backward version, regardless of its orientation within the two-dimensional test field (see Figs. 1 and 2). The tachistoscopic apparatus, the visual angles of the stimuli, and the right- and left-hand push button responses were all the same as described for Experiment I.

Structure of Individual Trials

All trials in this experiment were analogous to trials of type B in Experiment I in that cues as to both identity and orientation were available in advance of the onset of every test stimulus. However, there were three important changes from the procedure used in Experiment I: (a) As in the earlier experiment by Shepard and Klun, the advance cues were presented in auditory rather than in visual form. (b) While the cue as to identity again agreed with the identity of the ensuing test stimulus on all trials, the cue as to orientation this time agreed with the orientation of the test stimulus on half of the trials only. (c) The cue as to orientation, rather than being fixed in a single random orientation on each trial, indicated an orientation that was progressively moving in a clockwise direction throughout the course of any one trial.

During each trial, the subject sat fixating the blank circular field before him in the tachistoscope. To start a new trial, the experimenter orally announced which of the two characters, "R" or "2" (with which the subject had previously been visually familiarized), was scheduled to appear as the test stimulus on that trial. Then the experimenter started playing a magnetic tape on which the verbal commands "up," "tip," "tip," "down," "tip," "tip" had previously been recorded at a controlled rate of one command per half second. As a result of prior instructions and practice trials, the subject understood that he was to imagine the normal version of the announced character starting in its upright orientation and rotating clockwise at a rate of $60°$ per half second, in synchrony with the auditory commands. Thus the initial command "up" notified the subject that he should begin rotating his internally generated mental image from its initial upright orientation and, three commands later, the word "down" informed him that he should by then have this image rotated around into its $180°$ orientation. To assist the subject in keeping pace with the auditory commands, there were six small tick marks visible around the border of the circular field at $60°$ steps (starting at the center of the top).

Quickly following a randomly preselected one of these verbal commands, the probe stimulus appeared in one of the six equally spaced orientations within the circular field. Thereupon the subject was to actuate the right- or left-hand switch as rapidly as possible to indicate whether the visual probe was the normal or backward version of the character, respectively. (As in Experiment I, however, this response assignment was reversed for the one left-handed subject.) The auditory commands terminated with the onset of the visual test

stimulus, but the test stimulus remained on until
after the subject made his response. The interval from
the onset of the visual probe to the actuation of one
of the two response buttons was recorded as the reaction
time.

Overall Experimental Design

One half of the trials, determined according to
a random sequence, were "probe-expected" trials in which
the probe stimulus was presented in the orientation
designated by the current auditory command. The other
half of the trials were "probe-unexpected" trials in
which the probe appeared, with equal probability, in
any one of the five other possible orientations. As a
consequence there were five times as many probe-expected
observations as probe-unexpected observations at each
orientation. Within both the probe-expected and probe-
unexpected trials, one half of the probe stimuli were
presented in their normal and one half in their backward
versions, again according to a random sequence. This
entire set of observations was collected for both test
characters ("R" and "2"), yielding a total of 240
experimental trials per subject (following an initial
set of 48 practice trials). Order of trials was randomized anew for each subject, and there was no blocking
of trials by any experimental factor. Trials on which
errors were made were retaken, if possible within the
same session, and error rates were low (ranging from
10% to 2% for individual subjects).

Reaction-Time Results

The Effect of Absolute Orientation of an Expected Test Stimulus

"Probe-expected" trials, in which the visual probe
appeared in the orientation corresponding to the current
auditory command, could be considered analogous to
trials of type B-1000 in Experiment I. For, if the
subject were in fact rotating a mental image of the

146

designated character in time with the auditory commands, then he should be able to make a direct match of his current mental image against the visual probe when it suddenly appears. Thus, he should be able to determine whether that probe is normal or backward with great rapidity--whatever the currently designated orientation happens to be. Just as in the earlier Condition B-1000, then, the function relating reaction time to absolute orientation of the test stimulus should be relatively flat (cf. the earlier Figs. 5 and 6).

Mean reaction times for those trials in the present experiment in which the probe stimulus appeared in the expected orientation are plotted in Fig. 12 as a function of the angular departure of the (expected) probe from its standard upright orientation. These times are averaged over correct responses to both test characters for all eight subjects. However, they are plotted separately for trials in which the probe was normal or backward, as indicated in the figure.

In agreement with Experiment I, the earlier experiments by Shepard and Klun, and our proposed information-processing model, the responses to the backward probes were consistently longer than the responses to the normal probes--by an amount that was independent of departure from upright (and also independent of departure from expected orientation--as we shall soon see). In the present experiment, this difference in reaction time was on the order of 100 to 150 msec. The average difference is therefore some 50 msec. longer than the average difference between reaction times to normal and backward stimuli in Experiment I. We shall argue that this is the result of an additional operation that must be carried out in the present experiment. Since the test stimulus was always presented in the orientation indicated by any advance orientation cue in Experiment I, a mismatch with an already rotated preparatory image automatically ensured that the stimulus was backward. In the present case, however, the subject must make a further determination as to whether the mismatch was the result of the probe's being presented in its backward version *or* in an unexpected orientation.

147

For simplicity of presentation in this and the following figures, we have averaged the reaction times for the symmetrically related orientations of 60° and 300° and of 120° and 240°. Thus the independent variable is now departure from upright in either direction, rather than absolute orientation in a specifically

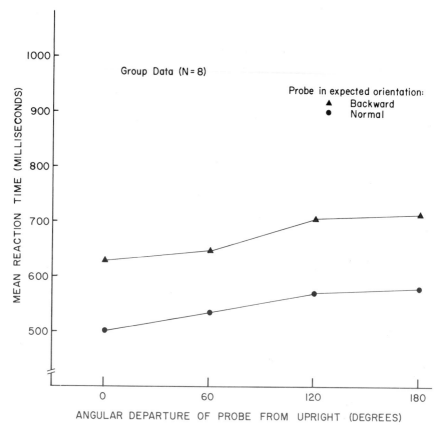

Fig. 12. Mean reaction time as a function of angular departure of the probe stimulus from the upright orientation for those trials on which the probe stimulus appeared in the expected orientation. Separate curves are plotted for reaction times to "normal" and "backward" test stimuli.

clockwise direction. As a consequence, the points plotted for 60° and 120° are based upon twice as many observations as the points plotted for 0° and 180°. However, if these reaction-time functions are "unfolded," so that all six orientations of the test stimulus are plotted separately, the functions become symmetrical about 180°--as in the earlier Figs. 5 and 6.

The results displayed in Fig. 12 are in good agreement with our expectations. The slight humping up near 180° in the previously obtained reaction-time functions for Conditions C and B-1000 reappears here as the small but consistent rise in reaction time from 0° to 180°. As we suggested before, subjects may simply require a little more time to compare two images when those images are both in a less familiar orientation. In any case, the average increase from 0° to 180° is only about 80 to 90 msec. If we contrast this with the 400 to 500 msec. increase in reaction time at 180° found (in the previous Conditions N or I) when no orientation information was provided, we see that the effect of the absolute orientation of an expected test stimulus is again very small.

The fact that subjects in the present experiment were able to classify a test stimulus as normal (as opposed to backward) in only 500 to 600 msec., as long as the orientation of that stimulus coincided with the rotating orientation expected, supports our claim that they arrived at their classification by matching the presented probe against a "rotating" mental image. However, as further support, we also need to show that subjects required appreciably more time whenever the probe appeared in an unexpected orientation.

The Effect of Angular Departure from Expected Orientation

In this experiment we can observe for the first time what happens when the test stimulus is presented in an orientation that departs from what the subject has been led to expect. Figure 13 illustrates the main result. Mean reaction time is plotted as a function of

149

the angular difference between the orientation of the visual probe and the orientation that the subject should have been expecting at that point in the sequence of auditory commands. As in the preceding figure, separate curves are presented for trials in which the probe was normal or backward and, again, responses to probes of the latter type were some 100 to 150 msec. slower. Also as before, the reaction times have been averaged over

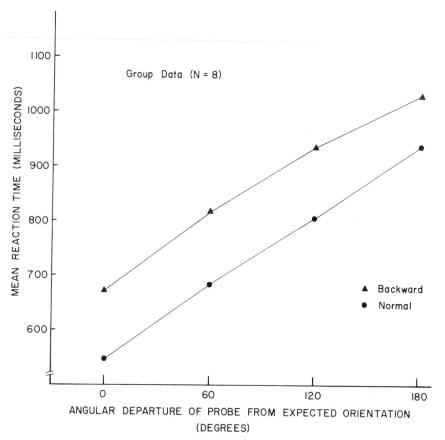

Fig. 13. Mean reaction time as a function of angular departure of the probe stimulus from the expected orientation. Separate curves are plotted for reaction times to "normal" and "backward" test stimuli.

corresponding clockwise and counterclockwise departures
at both 60° and 120°, over both test characters, and
over all eight subjects. In addition, for this figure
the reaction times have also been averaged over all
angular departures of the probe from upright.

As predicted, when the probe appeared in some
orientation other than the (rotating) orientation
expected, reaction time increased markedly with the
difference between the expected and the actually presented orientations. Indeed, the overall increase from
no departure to 180° departure is close to 400 msec.
This increase is some five times greater than the 80-
to 90-msec. increase shown in the preceding Fig. 12.
At the same time, it is quite comparable to the 400-
to 500-msec. increase observed in Experiment I for
departure from the orientation naturally expected when
there was no advance information as to orientation--
namely, the standard upright orientation.

Although the functions exhibited in Fig. 13 thus
agree with the functions displayed (in Figs. 5 and 6)
for the earlier Conditions N, I, O, and B-100 with
respect to overall slope, they differ markedly from
those earlier functions with respect to shape. For,
whereas the earlier functions were uniformly concave
upward, the functions shown in Fig. 13 are both
strikingly linear. But the linearity of these new
functions is just what we have predicted on the basis
of two assumptions. The first is that when the orientation of the probe fails to agree with the imagined
orientation, the subject must undertake an additional,
post-stimulus rotation in order to achieve a match
between that probe and the internal representation of
the corresponding normal character. The second assumption is that when the starting and ending points of the
required post-stimulus rotations are evenly distributed
around the circle, the biasing effects of the special
upright orientation should cancel out in such a way as
to reveal the linear and, hence, the underlying
sequential-additive nature of mental rotation.

The Joint Effects of Departures from Expected and Upright Orientations

We have argued that any nonlinearity in the present data should emerge when reaction time is plotted against departure from upright (as in Experiment I) rather than against departure from expected orientation (as in the preceding Fig. 13). Evidence supporting this argument is illustrated in Fig. 14. Here, the dependence of reaction time upon angular departure of the probe from upright is separately plotted for each value of angular departure of the probe from its expected orientation. The plotted means are averaged over subjects, characters and, this time, over both "normal" and "backward" responses as well. The lowest curve (for $0°$) is thus the average of the two curves displayed earlier in Fig. 12. Again, the flatness of this bottom-most function shows that when the probe appears in the expected orientation the absolute angle of this orientation has relatively little effect on reaction time. In this case we cannot expect to find any nonlinearity.

As the visual probe departs more and more from its expected orientation, however, three changes take place in the average data. The function relating reaction time to departure from upright (a) rises in overall height, (b) increases in positive slope, and (c) becomes increasingly concave upward. The first change--the increasing height of successive functions in Fig. 14-- is just the effect illustrated in Fig. 13. As we saw there, this increase is essentially linear with departure from expected orientation. The second and third changes--the increasing steepness and curvature of the successive functions--are to some extent analogous to the changes in the family of curves for the B-Conditions in Experiment I (Fig. 6). In both cases the relation of reaction time to departure from upright becomes stronger and more nonlinear as the advance information as to orientation is decreased in effectiveness--whether by a reduction in duration (Fig. 6) or in accuracy (Fig. 14).

The analogy between the family of curves in the present Fig. 14 and the B-family of curves in the earlier Fig. 6 should be advanced with caution. In view of the smaller number of observations contributing

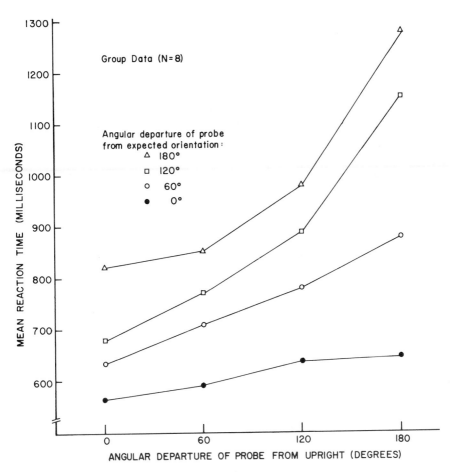

Fig. 14. Mean reaction time as a function of angular departure of the probe stimulus from the upright orientation, plotted separately for each of the four angular departures of the probe stimulus from the expected orientation. (Reaction times to "normal" and "backward" test stimuli are averaged together.)

to each of the points in the three upper "probe-unexpected" curves of Fig. 14 (particularly at $0°$ and $180°$),
the shapes of these upper curves vary considerably from
subject to subject. Thus the average pattern shown for
the group of eight subjects in Fig. 14 is not as representative of the corresponding patterns for individual
subjects as was the average pattern shown for the
earlier group of eight subjects in Fig. 6. (This fact
will also be apparent from the statistical analyses to
be considered shortly.) Moreover, the strong (and nonlinear) dependence of reaction time on departure from
upright in the "probe-unexpected" curves of Fig. 14 may
have two quite different sources--only one of which
relates directly to our earlier explanations for the
nonlinearity evident in Figs. 5 and 6.

Consider, first, the source that does have a direct
relation to those earlier explanations. In one of those
explanations, the mental rotation of a familiar character is assumed to be slower whenever that character is
an unfamiliar orientation (i.e., inverted). The rotation of the mental image into congruence with the probe
would then generally be slower (even for a given angle
of separation) when the probe is near $180°$. Such considerations (and similar considerations based upon the
other three proposed explanations for nonlinearity) help
to account for the upswing of the present "probe-
unexpected" curves as they approach $180°$.

However, an additional consideration, which does
not arise in connection with Experiment I, may come into
play in the present experiment. Consider trials represented by the left-most datum point of the highest curve
in Fig. 14. These are trials on which the subject has
presumably rotated a mental image of the designated
character into its upside-down position but on which
the test probe unexpectedly appears in its upright position. Some subjects reported that, when this happened,
they identified the upright test probe as normal or
backward without rotation--presumably by comparing it
against the normal upright representation in long-term
memory, rather than by continuing to rotate their short-
term image (which was then at $180°$) all the way back to

$0°$ for comparison with the upright probe. We would expect subjects who operated in this way to yield relatively short reaction times to probes that unexpectedly appear near $0°$. Such relatively rapid reaction times may contribute considerably to the slopes of the upper curves in Fig. 14.

A less contaminated comparison with the B-family of curves from Experiment I can be made by considering only those trials in the present experiment in which the probe appeared at $180°$. On these trials, the orientation of the unexpected probe is at least as close to that of the subject's "rotating" mental image as to that of the permanent (upright) representation in long-term memory. In this case the reaction time should reflect the time needed to rotate between the current orientation of the temporary mental image and the $180°$ orientation of the test probe. Differences between the mean reaction times obtained for pairs of such cases in which the probe was expected in orientations separated by $60°$ provide estimates of the time to rotate $60°$ in different absolute positions around the circle. These estimated $60°$ rotation times are about 140 msec. between $0°$ and $60°$, 260 msec. between $60°$ and $120°$, and 280 msec. between $120°$ and $180°$ from upright. Although these estimates are based on a rather small subset of the data and, so, are not very reliable, they do support our conjecture that mental rotation is slower between less familiar orientations.

Perhaps the most striking comparison illustrated in Fig. 14 is between the right-most point of the lowest curve and the left-most point of the highest curve. This comparison reveals that on the average subjects responded nearly 200 msec. faster to an expected test stimulus at $180°$ than to an unexpected test stimulus in the standard upright orientation. As a consequence of the relatively small number of observations contributing to the upper point, the numerical value of this difference is somewhat unreliable; however, the direction of this difference is the same for all eight subjects. This comparison therefore furnishes strong evidence that the internal representation that the subjects were "mentally rotating" in time with the auditory commands was more available for matching against the externally presented test stimulus than was the permanent representation of the normal upright character that the subjects presumably retain in long-term memory.

Results for Individual Subjects

As we have already mentioned, when we break the data down finely enough to reveal the effects of departures from the expected and upright orientations jointly (as in Fig. 14), the end points of the three upper curves are based on too few observations to be reliable for individual subjects. When we combine the data to show the effects of the two kinds of departure separately (as in Figs. 12 and 13), however, the resulting curves stabilize nicely even for individual subjects. In Fig. 15 we follow our earlier convention of presenting the curves for the two subjects that were most extreme with respect to overall reaction time.

The two panels on the left correspond to the earlier Fig. 12, while the two panels on the right correspond to the earlier Fig. 13. There is a considerable difference in overall height of the curves obtained for the "fast" subject (top panels) and the "slow" subject (bottom panels). (Note, incidentally, that the vertical scales for the "slow" subject have been linearly compressed with respect to the vertical scales for the "fast" subject.) Nevertheless, both subjects yielded functions that were essentially flat when the probe appeared in the expected orientation, and that increased monotonically and approximately linearly with departure of the probe from its expected orientation. Curves for all of the other subjects were similar in shape to these curves (and for some of the subjects the curves corresponding to those plotted on the right in Fig. 15 were even more linear).

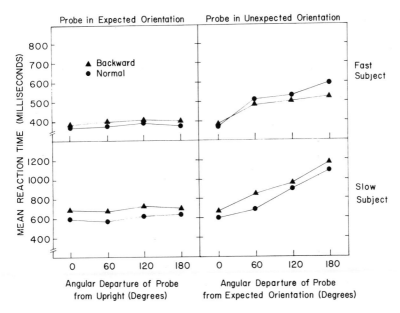

Fig. 15. Mean reaction-time functions for two individual subjects--the fastest subject (upper panels) and the slowest subject (lower panels). Left-hand panels correspond to the group functions displayed in Fig. 12, and right-hand panels correspond to the group functions displayed in Fig. 13.

Statistical Reliability of the Principal Results

Analyses of variance were performed for the group data and for the data of individual subjects. For the analysis of variance on the group data, the highest order or four-way interaction comprised the error term. The main effects of all four factors in this analysis (subjects, angular departure of the probe from the expected orientation, angular departure of the probe from upright, and normal-versus-backward versions) were highly significant ($p < .01$ in all cases). All two-way interactions with "subjects" as a factor were highly significant, and the only other significant two-way interaction--illustrated in Fig. 14--was between angular departure of the probe from the expected orientation and angular departure of the probe from upright. Neither of the remaining two-way interactions and none of the three-way interactions approached statistical significance.

Similar analyses of variance were performed on the three within-subject factors (angular departure of the probe from the expected orientation, angular departure of the probe from upright, and normal-versus-backward versions) for each subject separately. The results were as follows. For each of the eight subjects, the main effect of angular departure of the probe from the expected orientation was highly significant ($p < .01$ in all cases). For five of the eight subjects, the main effect of angular departure of the probe from upright was highly significant; and for four of the eight subjects, the main effect of version was highly significant ($p < .01$ in all cases). For only one of the eight subjects was the interaction between angular departure of the probe from the expected orientation and angular departure of the probe from upright significant ($p < .05$). Perhaps the failure to establish significance of this interaction in many of the individual subjects is a reflection of the small number of observations underlying certain of the points--as noted before. Neither of the remaining two-way interactions was statistically significant for any of the eight subjects.

General Discussion

The introspective reports that the subjects gave us following their participation in Experiment II are consonant with our interpretations of their reaction times. The subjects claimed that they were indeed able to imagine the normal version of the designated character rotating clockwise in time with the auditory commands. The subjects also indicated that they used this rotating mental image as a sort of template against which to compare the test stimulus when it suddenly appeared within the circular field. If a match was achieved, they immediately executed the readied (e.g., right-hand) response. If not, they then had to determine whether the mismatch resulted from the fact that the stimulus had been presented in its backward version or in an unexpected orientation.

If the subjects determined that the visual probe was backward (perhaps by performing an additional mental operation of reflection), they then switched control to the other hand before executing their response. The average additional time for a mismatch response in Experiment II was some 50 msec. longer than in Experiment I. This difference may be the time required for the additional operation (possibly of reflection) that was required only in Experiment II (in which, for the first time, the probe could differ from what was expected by a reflection *or* a rotation).

Concerning trials on which the visual probe differed from the subject's internal representation by a rotation, subjects reported two different strategies. When the probe departed markedly from upright, they tended to carry out a further (post-stimulus) rotation in order to bring their rotating mental image into congruence with the external probe and, then, proceeded as described above for the case in which no such further rotation was necessary. When the probe was close to upright while their mental image was far from upright, they tended to abandon their rotating mental image and to determine whether the probe was normal or backward directly--after imagining the probe itself rotated back to upright, if necessary.

With respect to the reaction-time results, we regard as especially significant (a) that reaction times were short and relatively independent of orientation whenever the probe appeared in the (rotating) orientation expected and (b) that these times increased as the probe departed from this expected orientation--even when this very departure brought the probe closer to its standard upright orientation. This conclusively demonstrates that, during the alleged process of mental rotation, something was indeed rotating--namely, the orientation in the external world at which the subject was most prepared for the presentation of the test stimulus. It also demonstrates that this process of mental rotation was an analog process at least to the extent that it went through intermediate states that had a one-to-one relation to intermediate orientations in the external world.

We are not claiming that the "mental rotation" was analogous to a corresponding physical rotation to the extent of being strictly continuous. Quite possibly the rotation was carried out as a sequence of discrete steps--each corresponding to a jump through an angle of some 60° or perhaps much less. Such a step would not itself be an analog process since, by hypothesis, inter-mediate stages of *its* process would not have the required one-to-one relation to external orientations. However the entire rotation, composed of several such steps, would still qualify as an analog process in the impor-tant sense that, again by hypothesis, it has interme-diate states (albeit only a finite number) that have the required one-to-one relationships.

Subjects found it hard to specify the extent to which a mental rotation consists of a sequence of such discrete jumps, as opposed to a smooth or continuous flow. To determine the angular sizes of such hypotheti-cal jumps by introspection appears, therefore, to be very difficult at best. Further experiments that we (and our colleagues) are undertaking, in which subjects are allowed to carry out rotations freely without exter-nal pacing or any discrete markers, may enable us to place some upper limits on the sizes of any irreducible component steps. We expect that the more valuable con-tribution of such experiments, however, will be the estimates that they provide concerning the rate at which such mental rotations are performed in the absence of the corresponding external stimulus.

We also are not claiming that the "mental image" that was being rotated (or, possibly, stepped around) possessed the concrete detail or vividness of a percep-tual image of an actually presented external stimulus (whether stationary or rotating). The introspections of the subjects suggest that the internal representa-tions with which they were operating, although highly abstract and schematic in comparison with a concrete

perceptual image of the external stimulus itself, embodied the essential structure of that stimulus with
enough fidelity to permit a quick and definitive comparison against the actual test stimulus when it
appeared. In order to obtain more objective evidence
concerning the fidelity of the rotating internal representation, in some further experiments we are planning
to introduce a variety of probe stimuli (in addition
to just the normal and backward versions used here).
Estimates of the time subjects require to discriminate
the normal version of the designated character from *any*
other probe (including ones that are similar to the
designated character in various of its distinctive
features) should provide a clearer indication of the
degree of completeness and specificity of the mental
image that is being rotated.

One possible hypothesis that we may then be in a
position to reject more conclusively than at present
is the hypothesis that subjects in the present experiment were merely tracking (around the tick-marked
circle) the expected position of some one distinctive
feature (such as the sharp angle or cusp that appears
at the lower left corner of the "2" when it is in its
normal upright position). Even now, however, such a
hypothesis faces difficulties. For example, the most
appropriate distinctive features are not located at
the center of the top of the character, as they would
need to be in order to be directly related both to the
verbal commands ("up," "tip," "tip," "down," "tip,"
"tip") and to the corresponding tick marks around the
edge of the circle. More importantly, knowledge merely
of the location of such a feature is not generally
enough to permit discrimination between the normal and
backward versions of the test probe. (The cusp of the
"2" may well appear near the 240° tick mark, as expected
on a particular trial; but this does not in itself
ensure that the presented character is the normal "2"
at 0°--it could also be the backward "2" tipped to 120°.)

In order to explain the speed and accuracy of the
subjects' discrimination between normal and backward
versions of the same probe, it appears necessary to

161

assume that any feature analyzers that the subjects were relying upon were specifically tuned to detect a spatial structure (a) that corresponds to a substantial portion of the test character, (b) that is localized in a systematically changing position, and, probably, (c) that is oriented in a systematically changing direction. But such an escalated assumption of feature detection begins to satisfy our conditions for speaking of the mental rotation of an internal representation. As the lowest curve in Fig. 12 shows, the subjects required an average of only 500 to 600 msec. to perceive the probe, to match it against the "mentally rotating" internal representation, and to make a correct response. This suggests that the representation was in a form that was particularly suitable for comparison with the visual stimulus. Although for several subjects there undoubtedly were kinesthetic concomitants, it is tempting to refer to this "rotating" internal representation as a visual image.

Conclusions

Empirical Findings

The stimuli used in both experiments were two-dimensional visual patterns (certain upper-case letters and numerals) that (a) are highly familiar, (b) are characteristically seen in a well-learned and uniquely defined upright orientation, and (c) are not symmetrical about any axis. On each trial one such stimulus or its mirror image was presented in some orientation within its two-dimensional plane. The subjects were instructed to actuate a right-hand or left-hand switch, as rapidly as possible after the onset of the stimulus, to indicate whether that stimulus was presented in its normal or backward version, respectively--regardless of its orientation within the picture plane. The principal findings concerning the measured reaction times can be summarized as follows:

1. Throughout, reaction times were consistently shorter to the normal stimuli than to their mirror images. The difference averaged about 100 msec. or somewhat less and was independent of orientation and several other experimental variables (Experiment I, and Figs. 12, 13). However, this difference varied somewhat from subject to subject, and it averaged some 50 msec. longer when the stimulus could depart from what was expected by a rotation as well as by a reflection (Figs. 12, 13).

2. When the stimulus appeared in an orientation for which the subject was not specifically prepared, reaction time increased monotonically with the departure of the stimulus from the natural upright orientation (Experiment I, Conditions N and I), or from the rotated orientation that the subject had been set to expect (Experiment II). For the maximum possible departure of 180°, the average increase in reaction time was on the order of 400 to 500 msec. (but, again, varied from subject to subject).

3. When the subject was not set to expect the stimulus in a particular (rotated) orientation, the increase in reaction time with departure from upright consistently conformed to a concave upward function (Fig. 5, Conditions N and I).

4. When the subject was set to expect a particular stimulus in a particular orientation, the increase in reaction time with departure from that expected orientation (when averaged over all such orientations) conformed to a remarkably linear function (Fig. 13)--reminiscent of the functions reported by Shepard and Metzler (1971) for rotated three-dimensional objects.

5. When the subject was given advance information only as to the identity of the stimulus or only

163

as to its orientation, reaction time was reduced by a constant amount of about 100 msec. in either case, regardless of the (nonconflicting) orientation of the ensuing stimulus (Fig. 5, Conditions I and O versus Condition N).

6. When the subject was given valid advance information as to both identity and orientation, reaction time to an upright stimulus was reduced by the sum of the reductions attributable to the two kinds of advance information provided separately; i.e., by a total of some 200 msec. (Figs. 5 and 6, Condition B-1000 at 0° or Condition B-400, as compared with Condition N).

7. When the subject was thus set for a specific stimulus in *any* specific orientation, reaction time to such a stimulus was consistently short (about 500 msec.) and remarkably independent of the angle of that expected orientation (Fig. 5, Condition B-1000, and Figs. 12 and 15). Consequently, when the expected orientation was other than upright, the reduction in reaction time resulting from the two kinds of advance information exceeded the sum of the reductions attributable to either kind alone. (For a stimulus at 180° from upright, the reduction averaged about 600 msec. rather than the 200 msec. prescribed by simple additivity.)

8. When a particular stimulus was expected in a particular rotated orientation, the reaction time to such a (rotated) stimulus was consistently shorter than the reaction time to that same stimulus presented in the standard upright orientation--in which it was then no longer expected (Fig. 14, second, third, and fourth points on the lowest curve versus the corresponding left-most points on the second, third, and fourth curves, above).

9. The time required to be fully prepared for presentation of a particular stimulus at a particular
orientation increased as the (validly) indicated
orientation departed from the standard upright
orientation. For an orientation of 0°, minimum
reaction times (of about 500 msec.) were achieved
if the orientation information had been available
400 msec. prior to stimulus onset. But for an
orientation of 180°, reaction times approaching
this minimum (500-msec.) level were not achieved
until the orientation information had persisted
for about 1000 msec. (Fig. 6, Conditions B-400
and B-1000).

10. Except, possibly, in the case of a few "fast"
subjects, there was an approximate trade-off
between preparation time and reaction time such
that each additional 300 msec. of orientation
information (beyond the 400 msec. needed for
optimum performance at 0°) reduced the subsequent
reaction time to a stimulus at 180° by another
300 msec. (Figs. 6, Conditions B-400, B-700, and
B-1000 at 180°; and Fig. 10).

11. Reaction times to an expected stimulus had approximately the same short (500 msec.) values whether
the advance information was presented (a) in the
form of a visual outline of the stimulus already
rotated to the orientation in which it was to
appear (Fig. 5, Condition C), (b) in the form of
a visual outline of that stimulus in its upright
orientation followed by a rotated arrow to indicate the orientation in which it was to appear
(Fig. 5, Condition B-1000), or (c) in a purely
auditory form (Fig. 12; and second experiment by
Shepard and Klun).

12. Subjects were able to maintain an optimal level
of readiness for the appearance of a visual stimulus in an orientation that was rotating clockwise
(in accordance with concurrent auditory cues) at

a rate of 120° per second (Fig. 12). (Higher rates may also be feasible for some subjects but have not yet been tried.)

Theoretical Interpretations

Nowhere in the preceding list of "empirical findings" did we speak of any such things as a mental image or a mental rotation. Our intention in preparing that list was to confine ourselves to objective and, we hope, reproducible patterns evident in the "hard data" of the recorded reaction times. We even avoided any mention of the subjects' post-experimental introspective reports. The list was thus put forward as a set of facts standing in need of a theory. It may be that someone will be able to formulate a theory that satisfyingly accounts for this particular set of facts without invoking any such concepts as mental imagery or mental rotation. Until this happens, however, we are inclined to favor a theory (a) that *has* now been formulated (at least in outline) and (b) that *is* consonant with the subjects' own introspective reports that they did indeed rotate mental images. Accordingly, the theoretical interpretations that we have been proposing to account for the empirical findings can be summarized as follows:

1. Subjects determine whether a familiar asymmetrical stimulus has been presented in its normal or in its backward (mirror-image) version by comparing the stimulus against an internal representation or mental image. Unless instructed otherwise (or unless presented in advance with the other version to be used as a model), subjects use the internal representation of the normal version for this purpose. (See Findings 1, 2, and 7, listed above.)

2. If the stimulus fails to match the image, the subject performs an additional operation (requiring 100 msec. or somewhat less) in

order to switch control to the alternative
response (Finding 1). If there is the possibility (as in Experiment II) that the mismatch
may result from a rotation rather than just from
a reflection, the subject may perform still
another operation (requiring perhaps 50 msec.
more) in order to verify that the mismatch was
the result specifically of a reflection (Finding 1).

3. If the stimulus appears in its familiar upright
   orientation and the subject is not specifically
   expecting it in that orientation, the internal
   representation used for comparison against the
   stimulus is the permanent representation of the
   normal upright version of that stimulus in
   long-term memory (Findings 2, 6, 8).

4. If the stimulus appears in some other orientation
   that departs markedly from any orientation that
   the subject may have been specifically expecting,
   a mental image of the presented stimulus is
   mentally rotated from the orientation in which
   the stimulus appeared back into its standard
   upright orientation for comparison with the
   upright representation in long-term memory
   (Findings 2, 8).

5. Before the subject can compare the stimulus
   against an internal representation or can begin
   to rotate a mental image of it into a particular
   orientation, he must know both the identity and
   the orientation of that stimulus. Either or
   both of these two pieces of information that he
   does not have in advance must be independently
   extracted from the stimulus itself at the cost
   of about 100 msec. for each piece--and, hence,
   of about 200 msec. for both (Findings 5, 6).

6. If information is provided sufficiently in
   advance as to both the identity and the orientation of the ensuing stimulus, a mental image of

the normal version of the designated stimulus is formed in its standard upright orientation (from the identity cue, in Experiment I; or from long-term memory, in Experiment II) and is mentally rotated into the designated orientation for rapid comparison with the stimulus when it appears (Findings 4, 7, 8, 10, 11).

7. If the stimulus appears in a rotated orientation different from the orientation of the preparatory mental image, the preparatory image is then rotated into the orientation of the stimulus for purposes of comparison. This is true whether the difference in orientation arises because the preparatory rotation has not been completed (Findings 9, 10), or because the orientation of the stimulus is different from what the subject has been set to expect (Findings 2, 4). In the former case, however, the preparatory rotation will not even be started unless the advance orientation information--when presented in the form of a rotated arrow--has been available for some 400 msec. (Findings 9, 10). When the duration of the orientation cue is too short, preparatory rotation is abandoned and an image of the stimulus itself is rotated back into upright --as described in Point 4, above.

8. Although the rate of mental rotation depends upon the individual subject (and, probably, upon the complexity and familiarity of the stimulus), on the average subjects can rotate a mental image of an alphanumeric character through 180° in some 500 msec. (Findings 2, 9, 12). Moreover the rate is about the same whether the rotation is carried out in the presence of the external stimulus, after it has appeared (Finding 2); or in the absence of that stimulus, in preparation for it (Finding 9)."

9. Subjects are only able to carry out the mental rotation of an internal representation of a

particular concrete object--not a general abstract
frame of reference. Thus, even though a subject
is given adequate advance information as to the
orientation of an upcoming stimulus, he is not
able to perform any preparatory rotation unless
he is also given advance information as to the
identity of that stimulus (Findings 5, 7).

In the case of stimuli (such as alphanumeric
characters) that have characteristically been
seen in (or close to) one particular orientation,
that familiar upright orientation plays a special
role in processes of rotation and/or matching.
Such processes are relatively slow when the mental
image being rotated or matched is in an unfamiliar
orientation and, especially so, when the image is
close to 180° from upright (Finding 3).

Mental rotation is an analog process with a serial
structure bearing a one-to-one relationship to the
corresponding physical rotation. The time required (mentally) to rotate from an orientation
A to an orientation C is just the sum of the times
required to rotate from A to some intermediate
orientation B, and to rotate from B to C (Finding
4). Moreover, in mentally rotating an object
between any two widely separated orientations,
A and C, the internal process passes through the
mental image corresponding to that same object
in some intermediate orientation, B (Finding 12).
Consequently, the orientation at which the subject
is most prepared for the appearance of that object
at each moment is actually rotating with respect
to the external world (Findings 7, 8, 12).

Even though the mental image may be internally
generated in the absence of the corresponding
visual stimulus (Finding 11), it nevertheless
possesses an internal structure that is at least
abstractly isomorphic to the structure of that
external visual stimulus. For, the image can be

169

transformed in a way that corresponds specifically to a rigid rotation of the external stimulus (Finding 12); and, even after such a transformation, the image can be matched against the subsequent presentation of the rotated visual stimulus with essentially the same speed and precision as if it were a straight memory image remaining from an immediately preceding presentation of the identical rotated stimulus (Findings 7, 11).

Final Remarks

We are not claiming that the many familiar objects that we all encounter in various positions in our everyday lives have to be mentally rotated into some canonical orientation before they can be recognized. Nor are we claiming that mental rotation is ordinarily performed in the reading of tilted letters or numbers. In the case of most objects and symbols with which we have to deal, there are sufficiently numerous, redundant, or orientationally invariant distinctive features that we may well achieve recognition directly--without need of a preliminary mental transformation. It is only under rather special circumstances, such as arise when an object must be discriminated from its mirror image, that the usual distinctive features no longer suffice for recognition and, hence, that a mental rotation may become necessary.

On the other hand we *are* claiming that a demonstration that human subjects are capable of mentally rotating spatially structured objects is of considerable importance--even if the demonstration requires such special circumstances and is based upon the use of alphanumeric characters. With respect to the selection of stimuli, it should be clear that our choice was not primarily motivated by an interest in the specific problem of how people read rotated letters, numbers, or text. Rather, the alphanumeric characters were chosen simply as a convenient example of spatially structured objects with the properties called for by the experimental tests; namely, the properties of (a) simplicity,

(b) familiarity, (c) asymmetry, and (d) possession of a well-defined natural upright orientation. With respect to the importance of demonstrating that human subjects have the capability of performing mental rotations, three points should be noted.

First, although mental rotation may not play any role in most ordinary processes of *recognition*, it may nevertheless play an indispensable role in certain other kinds of mental processes that are prominent in many familiar and sometimes very significant human activities. Consider, for example, such activities as the following: assembling the pieces of a jigsaw puzzle; rearranging furniture in a room; finding and fitting together the variously shaped parts of a complicated mechanical device; and (at a much more abstract, theoretical level) working out a creative solution to a problem in geometry, electrical engineering, stereochemistry, or theoretical physics. It seems doubtful that a person incapable of mental rotation would excel in these particular activities.

Second, mental rotation is just one of a large class of mental operations that may be carried out in a more or less analogical manner. Among the "similarity" transformations (translation, dilation, reflection, and rotation), rotation appeared to be particularly suitable for initial experimentation since the necessity of performing a mental transformation (as opposed to merely responding to distinctive features of the stimuli) seemed more likely in the case of rotation. Other kinds of spatial transformations may also play important roles in human thinking. These include, for example, nonrigid transformations and plastic deformations of the sorts involved in stretching and shrinking, bending and folding, choreography, gymnastics, modeling in clay, or solving problems in topology. If rotation is mentally performed in an analogical manner, then the imagining, understanding, and planning of many other kinds of operations in the physical world may also be accomplished in an analogical manner. Hence, the mere demonstration that humans solve some problems (however contrived) by means of a basically analog process has important implications for the nature of the human mind.

171

At the very least, it raises a question about the
advisability of formulating theories of human behavior
solely in terms of discrete processes of verbal mediation or symbol manipulation--as has been characteristic
in experimental psychology and in computer simulation,
respectively.

Third, even if an internal representation is subjected to mental rotation only rarely, the mere fact
that it can be operated upon by such an analog process
tells us something important about the nature of that
representation. It tells us that the representation
has an internal structure that is itself to some extent
analogically related to the structure of its corresponding external object. For, during the process of rotation, the parts and the relationships among the parts
must be transformed in very constrained ways in order
to enable the kind of rapid, template-like match against
an ensuing visual stimulus that we have demonstrated
here.

Clearly the internal representation cannot ade-
quately be regarded either as an undifferentiated neural
event (such as the activation of a particular neuron
or population of mutually interchangeable neurons) at
the neurophysiological level, or simply as an unanalyz-
able symbol at the information-processing level. In
further work it may be established that the rotational
process is essentially continuous (or at least carried
out in many small steps) and, also, that the internal
representation preserves the essential metric relationships within the object during such a process. If so,
it becomes doubtful that any fundamentally discrete,
categorical representation (such as the kinds of tree
structures that have mostly been proposed for computer
simulation) will prove satisfactory.

Evidently we still have a way to go before we
achieve an adequate characterization of mental images
and of mental operations upon mental images. At the
moment, though, we feel that we are on a promising
track.

References

Abelson, R. P., & Tukey, J. W.   Efficient utilization of non-numerical information in quantitative analysis: General theory and the case of simple order. *Annals of Mathematical Statistics*, 1963 34, 1347-1369.

Armstrong, D. M.   *A materialist theory of mind*.   New York: Humanities Press, 1968.

Attneave, F., & Olson, R. K.   Discriminability of stimuli varying in physical and retinal orientation. *Journal of Experimental Psychology*, 1967, 74, 149-157.

Bartlett, F. C.   *Remembering*.   Cambridge: Cambridge University Press, 1932.

Bower, G. H.   Mental imagery and associative learning. In L. Gregg (Ed.), *Cognition in learning and memory*.   New York: Wiley, in press.

Brooks, L. R.   Spatial and verbal components of the act of recall. *Canadian Journal of Psychology*, 1968, 22, 349-368.

Clark, H. H., & Chase, W. G.   On the process of comparing sentences against pictures. *Cognitive Psychology*, 1972, 3, 472-517.

Dement, W. C.   An essay on dreams: The role of physiology in understanding their nature.   In *New directions in psychology* II.   New York: Holt, Rinehart & Winston, 1965, 137-257.

Egeth, H., & Blecker, D.   Differential effects of familiarity on judgments of sameness and difference. *Perception & Psychophysics*, 1971, 9, 321-326.

Freud, S.   *The interpretation of dreams*.   New York: Basic Books, 1955.   (Originally published in 1900.)

Gazzaniga, M. S., Bogen, J. E., & Sperry, R. W.   Observations on visual perception after disconnection of the cerebral hemispheres in man. *Brain*, 1965, 88, 221-236.

Hall, C. S., & Van de Castle, R. L.   *The content analysis of dreams*.   New York: Appleton-Century-Crofts, 1966.

Kinsbourne, M. The control of attention by interaction between the cerebral hemispheres. Paper presented at the Fourth International Symposium on Attention and Psychology, Boulder, Colorado, August, 1971.

Koffka, K. *Principles of Gestalt psychology.* New York: Harcourt-Brace, 1935.

Köhler, W. *Gestalt psychology.* New York: Liveright, 1947. (Mentor Books MT644.)

Kolers, P. A., & Perkins, D. N. Orientation of letters and their speed of recognition. *Perception & Psychophysics*, 1969, 5, 275-280.

Paivio, A. Mental imagery in associative learning and memory. *Psychological Review*, 1969, 76, 3, 241-263.

Paivio, A. *Imagery and verbal processes.* New York: Holt, Rinehart & Winston, 1971.

Posner, M. I., Boies, S. J., Eichelman, W. H., & Taylor, R. Retention of visual and name codes of single letters. *Journal of Experimental Psychology Monographs*, 1969, 79, No. 1, Part 2.

Rawlings, E. I., Rawlings, I. L., Chen, S. S., & Yilk, M. D. The facilitating effects of mental rehearsal in the acquisition of rotary pursuit tracking. *Psychonomic Science*, 1972, 26, 71-73.

Richardson, A. *Mental imagery.* New York: Springer, 1969.

Rock, I., & Heimer, W. The effect of retinal and phenomenal orientation on the perception of form. *American Journal of Psychology*, 1957, 70, 493-511.

Segal, S. J., & Fusella, V. Influence of imaged pictures and sounds on detection of auditory and visual signals. *Journal of Experimental Psychology*, 1970, 83, 458-464.

Segal, S. J., & Gordon, P. E. The Perky effect revisited: Paradoxical thresholds or signal detection error? *Perceptual and Motor Skills*, 1969, 28, 791-797.

Shepard, R. N. Studies of the form, formation, and transformation of internal representations. In E. Galanter (Ed.), *Cognitive mechanisms.* Washington, D. C.: V. H. Winston & Sons, in press.

Shepard, R. N., & Chipman, S. Second-order isomorphism
of internal representations: Shapes of states.
Cognitive Psychology, 1970, 1, 1-17.
Shepard, R. N., & Feng, C. A chronometric study of
mental paper folding. *Cognitive Psychology*, 1972,
3, 228-243.
Shepard, R. N., & Metzler, J. Mental rotation of three-
dimensional objects. *Science,* 1971, 171, 701-703.
Smart, J. J. C. *Philosophy and scientific realism.*
New York: Routledge & Kegan Paul, 1963.
Sperry, R. W., & Levy, J. Mental capacities of the
disconnected minor hemisphere. Paper presented
at the meeting of the American Psychological
Association, September, 1970.
Trabasso, T., Rollins, H., & Shaughnessy, E. Storage
and verification stages in processing concepts.
Cognitive Psychology, 1971, 2, 239-289.
West, L. J. (Ed.) *Hallucinations.* New York: Grune
& Stratton, 1962.
Wickelgren, W. A. Auditory or articulatory coding in
verbal short-term memory. *Psychological Review*,
1969, 76, 232-235.

Acknowledgments

This work was supported by the National Science
Foundation through research grants GS-2283 and
GB-31971X to the second author. The present report
of this work was jointly prepared by the two authors
while the first author was on a National Science
Foundation Predoctoral Fellowship and while the second
author was a John Simon Guggenheim Fellow at the Center
for Advanced Study in the Behavioral Sciences, Stanford.
We are indebted to many colleagues for a variety of
important contributions to this work. Mr. Joseph Klun's
earlier work (in collaboration with the second author)
provided much parametric information that was extremely
useful to us in designing the present Experiment I.
Professor Ernest Hilgard generously permitted us to use
an Iconix three-field tachistoscope provided by his
NIMH grant No. 03859. Dean Lincoln Moses offered

valuable advice concerning the half-replicate design and the statistical analyses. Ms. Elizabeth Smith and Mr. James Cunningham assisted extensively in the running of the experiments. Finally, we owe a special debt of gratitude to Ms. Christine Feng for her unstinting and indispensable assistance throughout all phases of the work, from the preparation of the stimuli to the plotting of the data.

ON THE FUNCTION OF VISUAL IMAGERY
IN ELEMENTARY MATHEMATICS

John R. Hayes
Carnegie-Mellon University

For some time, I have been concerned with the problem of teaching mathematics to college students who are not mathematically inclined. Since my students often have difficulty in handling mathematical notations, I considered the possibility of trying to teach mathematics notation-free. Consulting both my colleagues and the literature, however, I found at least three lines of reasoning which suggested that the use of abstract notation, even if troublesome at first, was in the long run a valuable aid to problem solving. The first line is exemplified in Dantzig's assertion (1954) that abstract notations promote generalization. He argues, for example, that by the use of symbolic notation, we can represent expressions like $3X^2+5X-7$ and $6X^2-X+2$ by the abstract expression of aX^2+bX+c and hence can recognize and deal with all quadratic forms as a class.

The second line of reasoning is incorporated in Skemp's suggestion (1971) that mathematical notation provides "a verbal shorthand" which has the advantage of "any shorthand--a saving of time and trouble." For example, if we let N represent the number of cars produced in Detroit in 1972, clearly we achieve a considerable saving in effort each time we refer to N rather than to the phrase for which it stands.

In the same reference, Skemp also presents the third line of reasoning, namely that mathematical notations promote the use of visual imagery in problem solving. He points out that visual imagery is important not just in geometrical problems but in algebraic ones as well. Spatial symbolism, he says, "finds its way into every detail of the verbal-algebraic system." As examples, he cites the spatial arrangements of elements in a matrix and the positional information in the number system. For example, position in a division problem shows which number is to be divided by which, and the position in a multi-digit integer, say 271, indicates how each digit is to be interpreted; the 2 is worth 200 but the 7 only 70, etc.

The importance of verbal factors and of visual imagery is confirmed by Hadamard (1945) for professional mathematicians, by Ball (1956) for calculating prodigies, and for ordinary students by the Twenty-First Yearbook of the National Council of Teachers of Mathematics, where champions may be found both for the importance of verbal factors (Brune, 1953) and of visual imagery (Syer, 1953).

The support for these lines of reasoning, however, consists of little more than expert opinion backed by some subjective reports. Clearly, each line needs to be explored with more powerful experimental tools. In this paper, I have chosen to explore the third line--that is, to investigate the role of notation-related imagery in mathematical problem solving.

Our task is not to prove the existence of visual imagery. The cumulation of work by Shepard (1970, 1971, 1972), Posner (1967, 1969), Brooks (1967, 1968), and others has already accomplished this task in a convincing way. Rather, our task is to explore the extent to which visual imagery penetrates into the structure of the problem solving process.

The work I will report in this paper is a mixture of subjective and objective methodologies. The eight small empirical studies which I describe below constitute a tentative and incomplete exploration into the role of visual imagery in solving elementary mathematical problems.

The investigation began with a protocol study in which people were asked to report on their use of visual imagery in the solution of elementary mathematical problems. The following seven studies employed chronometric measures and were intended to provide "hard" evidence on points raised by or related to the first study. Study 2 proves the striking spatial integration of image with stimulus reported by subjects in Study 1. Studies 3 and 4 are concerned with the temporal duration of images; Studies 5 and 6 with the relation of generated images to memory for specific visual formats, and Studies 7 and 8 with further spatial properties of generated images.

Study 1

The stimulus materials used in Study 1 consisted of the 11 4"x11" cards illustrated in Figure 1. The subjects were 19 students and faculty members at

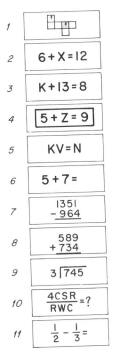

Fig. 1. Stimulus cards used in Study 1.

Carnegie-Mellon University. The interviews were conducted individually in a quiet office and transcribed (not tape-recorded) by the experimenter. The subject was informed that the purpose of the study was to investigate imagery in the solution of simple mathematical problems and was reassured that only elementary skills would be required of him. The first card, which presented a paper folding task borrowed from Shepard and Feng (1972), was included to give the subject some practice in reporting his imagery. After he had solved the problem, the subject was asked whether he had folded the cardboard toward or away from himself and whether any parts of the figure obscured any other parts as he solved the problem.

In the remainder of the problems, the subjects were given the general instruction to report on their imagery during the solution process. However, during the interviews I frequently asked the subjects to elaborate on a point they had discussed, e.g., to provide information on the location of an image, or to direct their attention to some aspect of the solution process which they had not discussed.

The results of the study show extreme diversity in the amount and kind of imagery reported both among subjects and among problems. Problem 6, the simple addition problem, is the prime example of a task which elicits few reports of imagery. Thirteen of the 19 subjects reported no imagery at all in solving it. In this respect, Problem 6 is quite atypical of the total problem set since most problems, as we shall see, elicited considerable imagery.

I will present the results of Study 1 in three sections:

1. Evidence of the interaction of generated images with the physical stimulus.

2. Evidence that generated images are used in the storage of the partial results of the solution process.

3. Evidence that images may be involved in the execution of elementary mathematical operations.

Interaction of Generated Images with the Physical Stimulus

By generated images, I mean perceived forms which the subject can produce or modify at will or by instruction. For example, I mean forms such as the subject will produce when we say to him, "Imagine a large capital 'A'. Now tilt it left." I want to distinguish such generated images from sensory images and after-images which are much more strongly controlled by the physical stimulus and much less under the subject's own control. We will take as evidence that a reported image is generated rather than sensory if by the subject's report it is (1) different in form from anything in the physical stimulus or (2) occupies a location different from similar forms in the physical stimulus. In Studies 5 and 6, we will provide solid experimental evidence for the distinction between generated images on the one hand and sensory images and after-images on the other.

For each of the 19 subjects, there was evidence that, at least in some of the problems, the subject perceived a spatial relation between the images which he generated and the physical stimulus provided by the problem card. In solving simple algebraic equations (Problems 2, 3, 4, and 5 in Figure 1), 14 of the 19 subjects reported movement of symbol images. Usually the image moved from one side of the equation to the other, either above or below the "equals" sign, *but in the plane of the stimulus card.* In some cases, the image was reported to move either forward or behind the plane of the card. For example, in solving Problem 2, Subject 8 reported that he "pulled the 12 and the 6 together" by imagining the card rolled in a circle in the horizontal plane so that the two numbers were located in space behind the "X".

For other subjects solving the algebraic equations, there was no perceived motion of the symbols. Rather, the symbols changed form without changing place. For example, in Subject 1's solution of Problem 2, the X disappeared and was replaced by a 6. Subjects who reported change of form rather than motion also reported that the "action" occurred at the position of the variable they were solving for. Subjects who reported motion of symbols, on the other hand, reported that the "action" was on the right side of the equation.

Problem 4 was included to dramatize the interaction of generated images with the physical stimulus. In fact, it didn't do this very well. Only three of the subjects experienced any difficulty which could be attributed to the unusual format. One subject said that he had to remove the bars in order to move the symbols and two others said that they felt constrained to move the symbols as if they were tiles in a frame. For example, Subject 10 said, "I don't swing things around because the bar doesn't let me. I shift the symbols horizontally."

Problem 8 troubled our subjects a good deal more. Twelve of the subjects reported at least some difficulty resulting from the low placement of the numbers on the card. A very common response, after an initial expression of annoyance, was to say, "I have no place to write the answer." Subject 8 reported that he resolved the difficulty as follows: "In my mind, I scotch-taped, not stapled, a piece of paper underneath to write the answer on." Two subjects who performed the addition without such an ingenious aid said that the lack of a uniform background made the images which they projected considerably less stable than they would otherwise have been. One of these subjects was driven to the desperate device of holding the images in place with his finger.

In the processes of division and of addition and subtraction of multidigit numbers, the spatial relation between generated images and the physical stimulus is especially obvious. The answer, when it was visualized (and sometimes even when it was not-- see below), was placed in a well-defined location with respect to the original problem. The digits of the answer were lined up with the columns of the problem card and placed immediately below them in the addition and subtraction problems and above them in the addition problem.

In solving the addition problem, one subject (Subject 11) computed the digits of the answer in the usual right to left order, but without visualizing them. Then, looking at each "place" of the answer in turn, that is, at each position where the numbers would have appeared had they been written, she recited the answer in the left to right order, but still without visualizing the digits. Thus, for this subject, the digits were located spatially even though their forms were not generated. In solving Problem 7, Subject 19 also reported that a digit which was not visualized had a spatial location with respect to the problem card.

While generated images were usually perceived as having a spatial relation to the problem card, this was not invariably the case. In several problems, Subject 5 reported that he projected images of symbols not onto the problem card but rather onto an imagined flat white surface about two feet in front of him. Similarly, Subject 15 reported images located "in space."

In sum, these examples clearly illustrate the fact that our subjects very often, but not always, perceived their generated images as being integrated into a spatial schema which includes the physical stimulus. When this integration occurs, we will speak of the generated image and the physical stimulus taken together as a "Hybrid Image."

Use of Generated Images in the Storage of the
Partial Results of the Solution Process

Many of our subjects reported imagery in association with the process of carrying. The images
varied somewhat with the type of problem. In addition
problems, the most common experience was to imagine
a mark, sometimes a "1", sometimes just a "blip,"
above the column to the left of the one being added.
Less commonly, it was reported that the top digit in
the next-left column had been changed to the next
higher digit. Subject 12 reported that in Problem 8,
the 8 changed into a 9 and the 5 into a 6.

In subtraction problems, the reported techniques
were somewhat different. Very often a borrowed digit
was visualized in the "tens" place in combination
with a real image in the "ones" place. For example,
in Problem 7, eight of the subjects reported that
they borrowed a 1 from the 5 and saw an 11 located
above the 4. (Notice that these hybrid two-place
integers, consisting of a generated digit and a digit
of the physical stimulus, illustrate in a very dramatic way the point we were making in the last section.)

In some cases, the borrowed-from column was
modified by reducing the minuend by one. For four of
the subjects, the 5 disappeared and was replaced by a
4. For two others, a slash appeared across the 5 and
a 4 appeared beside it. In other cases, the subtra-
hend was increased by one. For Subjects 9 and 12,
the 6 in the subtraction problem was changed to a 7.

In solving the cancellation problem (Problem 10),
most subjects reported generating either two or four
lines to mark the two R's and the two C's. Three of
the subjects (Subjects 9, 11, and 12) said that they
solved the problem by examining the hybrid image,
consisting of the original problem plus the generated
cancellation marks, and reading off the unmarked
letters.

The hybrid image in the cancellation problem
consisted of a generated slash superimposed on a real
digit. The hybrid image in the subtraction of frac-
tions problem (Problem 11) was more complex. Subject
3 described the solution process as follows: "I put

in three-sixths and two-sixths. I put the three-
sixths right over the one-half. The three-sixths was
nearer to me but in a lighter shade, sort of grayish.
The one-half was clearly visible through it." Four
other subjects described very similar phenomena in
which generated digits were overprinted on digits of
the stimulus card.

In the addition and subtraction problems
(Problems 7 and 8), most subjects worked from right
to left, processing each column in turn and storing
the result. The results were announced in the left
to right order. Thirteen of the subjects reported
that they stored the results of column processing in
images. Subject 3 said that the important thing
about generating "imaginary figures is that they stay
while you move to the left to do more calculation."
Many subjects described the experience of reading off
the answer from left to right. Three subjects volunteered that they had to read the answer quickly
because the image faded rapidly. Others said that
they went back to "refresh" the image of the partial
answer before proceeding with the remainder of the
calculations.

*Images May be Involved in the Execution of
Elementary Mathematical Processes*

In the previous section, we emphasized the role
of imagery in storing the partial results of arithmetic or algebraic processes. The fact that Problem
6 elicited very little imagery suggests that the
elementary arithmetic processes, such as adding and
subtracting one-digit numbers, may not involve imagery
in their execution. In this section we will present
evidence that visual imagery may in some cases play
an important role in elementary mathematical
processes.

First, I will discuss the phenomenon of counting
points which I discovered, much to my surprise, in
the course of interviews with two of the subjects.

Figure 2 shows the counting points for Subject 8.
They work as follows: Suppose that you are adding 7
and 3. Starting the count at 7, you look at the first
counting point on the number 3 and say 8. Then you
look at the second counting point and say 9, and
finally at the last counting point to announce the
answer, 10. For Subject 8, counting tends strongly
to occur on the (spatially) lower of the two digits.

As Figure 2 shows, each digit has its own unique
set of counting points which are related to the form
of the digit they are used to count. Subject 13
differs somewhat from Subject 8 in the exact positioning of the counting points and in the fact that he
assigns counting points to the digits 1 and 2 while
Subject 8 does not. However, the function of the
counting points is exactly the same for the two subjects. Since conducting this study, I have encoun-
tered four other individuals who report they make
similar use of counting points in doing arithmetic.

Two of our subjects report that in solving
Problem 3, which yields a negative solution, they

Fig. 2. Counting points for Subject 8.

used a sign-checking process which involved imagery. Subject 7 described it this way: First he substracted 8 from 13 to get 5. Then, to get the sign of this quantity, he visualized a vertical bar, representing 8, with its bottom resting on a horizontal zero line. He then placed a longer bar, representing 13, next to the first so that the tops of the two were aligned. Since the bottom of the longer bar projected below the zero line, he decided that the answer must be negative. Subject 8 reported a very similar sign-checking process employing a thermometer image.

Neither in the case of the counting points nor in the case of the sign-checking procedure do the data suggest that arithmetic processes are carried out entirely visually. For example, since counting points contain no representation of the succession of numbers, e.g., that 9 follows 8, they cannot be sufficient in themselves to account for addition. Counting points simply serve a placekeeping function to tell the subject when to stop counting, but they do not tell what number comes next.

In the cancellation problem which we described above, however, visual operations *may* be sufficient for solution. The sequence of operations might be as follows: (1) The identification of pairs of items to be cancelled is determined by visual search of the physical stimulus; (2) Cancellation marks are generated and stored in a hybrid image; (3) The answer is read from the hybrid image deleting the marked items.

To summarize our results in Study 1, we find:

1. That the subjects, as a group, reported a great deal of imagery in association with the solution of elementary mathematical problems and that there was considerable diversity both among subjects and among problems in the amount and kind of imagery reported.

2. That almost always the images which the subject generated were perceived as being integrated into

a spatial schema which included the problem card. We have called such integrations "hybrid images." Sometimes the integration is quite close, as in the case of the hybrid two-digit integers.

3. That generated images are often associated with the storage of partial results of a problem solving process.

4. That for some problems and for some subjects, images may be involved in the execution of some elementary arithmetic and algebraic processes.

It is appropriate to speculate a bit about the role of visual imagery in the sorts of problems we have been studying. First, we observe that complex arithmetic and algebraic problems are learned and, very frequently, performed with the aid of pencil and paper. In pencil and paper form, the solution of such problems clearly involves the integration of a sequence of internal computations with a sequence of perceptual and motor acts oriented to the external environment. Thus, the problem solver can generate and use external visual cues in the sequencing of operations, the interpretation of elements, and the storage of partial and final results. The important aspects of these external visual cues include not only the general form of the letters and digits involved but also their locations in a larger problem format which indicate whether the digit is part of the answer, a partial product, or a carry. Size may also be important since carries are frequently written small.

I speculate that visual imagery is important in mental mathematics because it acts as a surrogate for the external visual cues which the problem solver would generate if he had pencil and paper. Further I suggest that visual images have a special usefulness in this surrogate function not so much because it represents the identity of the digits—which auditory images can do as well or better—but rather because they are especially good for encoding the spatial properties and relations of digits, e.g., their locations and sizes.

Study 2

Our second study[1] was suggested by the observation that the two European-trained subjects had a peculiar sort of difficulty with the division problem in Study 1. The European subjects complained that the problem had been made unnecessarily difficult by placing the divisor on the left-hand side of the dividend. Further exploration with foreign-born faculty members revealed that those who learned elementary mathematics in continental Europe, e.g., France, Spain, Italy, Germany, and Latvia, are accustomed to using division formats which differ from the typical U. S./British pattern. While the European formats differ in some respects from one another, they are similar in requiring the divisor to be placed on the right, rather than the left, of the dividend. This reported dependence of problem difficulty on format suggested a way to test our hypotheses about hybrid images.

Let us consider two models of the solution process:

1. Assume that the subject solves the problem by:

   A. Generating an image in familiar format from the problem card, and then

   B. Solving the problem using the generated (but not hybrid) image by the usual manipulations of the familiar format.

If this model were the correct one, we would expect that an unfamiliar format on the problem card

---

[1] Conducted with Glenn Lea

would slow down stage A, but not stage B. Thus, an unfamiliar format would increase the time required to set the problem up for solution and therefore delay the appearance of the first digit of the solution, but it would not increase the time required to solve the problem once it was set up.

2. Assume that the subject solves the problem using a hybrid image which includes within itself whatever format is presented on the problem card. If this model were the correct one, we would expect that the effects of an unfamiliar format would be distributed through the solution process.

If the subject does not use imagery in the solution process, then we have no reason to expect that an unfamiliar format will make problem solution more difficult.

In designing this experiment, we have assumed that an unfamiliar format remains unfamiliar for more than a problem or two (in fact, for at least 24 problems). This assumption seemed very reasonable to us at first--in fact, trivial--since most of our European-trained subjects, even though they spoke fluent English and had lived for many years in the United States, did arithmetic only in their native language. These facts suggested to us that such early and well-learned habits were very resistant to change. When we found, however, that some of our European subjects were quite unaware that American division format differed from their own, we realized that there may be very little pressure on an adult to change such habits. Our assumption, then, is still an assumption, but not a trivial one.

In this experiment we used nine Americans and three Europeans as subjects. All problems were division problems involving a two-digit divisor and a three-digit dividend. One half of the problems were presented with the divisor on the left (American format), e.g., 24:731, and the remaining half were presented with the divisor on the right (European format), e.g., 731:24.

In the instruction period, subjects were told (1) that the purpose of the experiment was to study the effect of format in division; (2) that in all cases, the task would be to divide a two-digit number into a three-digit number; (3) that they should carry the answer out to three significant places; and (4) that they should announce each digit of the answer as soon as they found it. The subjects were shown examples of problems in each format.

The first two problems, one in each format, were solved with the aid of pencil and paper. These problems provided the subjects an opportunity to practice the procedures and provided the experimenter an opportunity to observe the division format which the subjects chose to employ.

The next 24 problems (really 12 problems presented once in each format) were solved mentally. Problems were presented in blocks of three, all problems in a block were of the same format, and the format was alternated from block to block. Each of the 12 problems was presented once before any problem was repeated. Each problem, typed on a 5"x8" card, was presented at a viewing distance of 18 inches in a polymetric tachistoscope. The problem card was continuously visible during the problem solving period. The problem solving sessions were tape recorded for later timing. At the end of the experimental session, the subject was interviewed concerning his use of imagery.

The difficulties of collecting data in this experiment proved to be considerable. Mentally dividing a three-digit number by a two-digit number is a very difficult task which some subjects could not do at all and which even the best subjects had difficulty performing accurately. It proved impractical to collect a large sample of subjects who could solve the problems with 90% accuracy, i.e., less than 10% of all digits in error. Our initial plan of analysis had been to match the solution times for each of the 12 problems solved in one format against the solution time for the same problem solved in the other format. Data for any pair of problems in which either member contained an error were to be dropped from the analysis. This plan was abandoned because of the high error rates. (Averaged over all subjects and all conditions, 30% of the digits were in error.) We observed, however, that results excluding pairs with errors were similar in all essential respects to results computed on the basis of all of the problems whether correctly solved or not.

Figure 3 shows the means of the subjects' median times to compute each of the three digits of the answer. For example, the results for the second digit are measures of the time interval between the first and second digits of the solution.

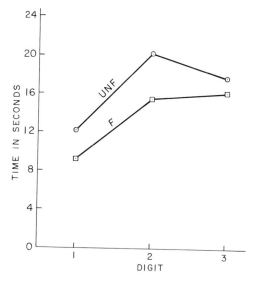

Fig. 3. Means of subjects' median times to compute successive digits in the answers of problems presented in familiar (F) and unfamiliar (UNF) division format.

The curves in Figure 3 show results for the ten subjects who reported that they visualized figures spatially related to the problem card while solving the problems. Two subjects, both Americans, who reported that they did not use such imagery, are not included. The curve labeled "F" is for familiar format--American format for Americans and European format for Europeans--and the one labeled "UNF" is for unfamiliar format.

For the ten "imagers," both the first and the second digits were computed significantly more rapidly in familiar format than in unfamiliar format ($p = .02$ by two-tailed sign test). The difference for the third digit was in the same direction as for the first two, but did not reach significance. The "imagers" were also more accurate on familiar format --73% vs. 63% correct--but the difference was not significant.

While the two non-imagers provide too little data to allow us to draw reliable conclusions, it is interesting to note that these subjects did *not* solve the problems faster in familiar format.

These data clearly support the hypothesis that subjects who report using hybrid imagery are in fact using hybrid imagery. Some of the post-experimental interviews were fairly specific in pinpointing the locus of the trouble which unfamiliar format caused in handling the hybrid image. One European subject listed the following steps in the solution of the problem shown in Figure 4.

$$67'3 : 15 = 4$$
$$73$$

Fig. 4. Imagery reported by a European subject during solution of the problem 673:15 =

1. She marked off the first two digits of the dividend by imagining a small mark as shown. (It seems reasonable to believe that there was a step prior to this one in which the subject examined the divisor. Otherwise, how would she know to mark off two places, rather than one or three?)

2. She divided 15 into 67 to get 4 as the first digit of the answer.

3. She subtracted 60 (= 4 x 15) from 67 and imagined the difference, 7, in the line below.

4. She brought down the 3 and imagined 73.

5. She then looked to the right of the dividend to examine the divisor. It was at such points, she said, that American format gave her trouble by violating her expectations about the location of the divisor.

While the solution time data and the post-experimental interviews are certainly consistent with the hybrid imagery model, we can hardly claim that they prove it. Indeed, while, as we said earlier, there is certainly strong reason to believe in visual imagery, such a model requires us to ascribe to images many properties, such as size and location with respect to external frameworks, which have not been experimentally established. The remaining six studies which I will describe below are all concerned with establishing relevant properties of the visual image.
The reader should note that all of the studies which follow employ but a single, albeit well trained and well motivated, subject, namely myself.

Study 3

Study 3 was originally concerned with two purposes in mind. The first purpose was to investigate the length of time over which spatial information could be retained in a visual image. Posner and Mitchell (1967) have clearly demonstrated the retention of visual form information in a recognition memory task. In many of the studies, evidence of retention was not obtained for retention intervals greater than 1.5 seconds. Other studies by Phillips and Baddeley (1971) and Parkinson (1972) have reported evidence of retention over longer intervals. The length of this retention interval is of some importance in the interpretation of our data. If our subjects in Study 1 were storing partial results in images (whether sensory or generated) as they said they were, then these images would either have to persist considerably longer than 1.5 seconds--in Problems 7 and 8, for example, they would have to last 10-15 seconds--or they would have to be regenerated.

Our second purpose in this study was to investigate the laterality phenomenon in recognition memory. In the context of the Posner and Mitchell task (1967), both Cohen (1972) and Ledlow, Swanson, and Carter (1972) have found strong evidence of laterality for simultaneously presented comparison stimuli. That is, they found that name matches were facilitated by presenting stimuli to the right visual field-left cerebral hemisphere, and physical identity matches were facilitated by presenting stimuli to the left visual field-right cerebral hemisphere. Such results are widely interpreted as indicating that the left cerebral hemisphere, specialized for handling language, has an advantage in handling names, while the right cerebral hemisphere has an advantage in processing visual images (see Gazzaniga, 1970, for example). We were interested in determining whether or not the same laterality effects for name and physical identity matching could be found if one of the two items to be compared, and therefore half of the relevant visual information, was stored in memory.

I should note at this point that Klatsky has found evidence of laterality in two studies (1970,

1971) employing a Sternberg task in which presentation of the memory set and the test probe were separated by more than 5 seconds. Under the circumstances of Klatsky's experiments, however, the subjects did not need to store visual information in order to perform the task, and indeed it appears to me very unlikely that they would have done so. I believe that Klatsky's positive laterality results depend on visual processing at the time the test probe was presented.

Study 3 was conducted in the Carnegie-Mellon computer-controlled psychology laboratory employing a program written by Dr. Allen Pinkus. Stimuli were presented to the subject on a C. R. T. screen at a viewing distance of 30 inches. The stimuli were chosen from one of the two following ten-item sets: The words, DOLLAR, STAR, CIRCLE, TRIANGLE, BAR, POUND, SLASH, PLUS, SQUARE, EQUALS, or the symbols, $, *, 0, △, —, #, /, +, ☐, =. On each trial, the subject was presented a memory set of four words or four symbols chosen at random without replacement from the set of ten. Whether a word or a symbol memory set was to be used on a given trial was determined randomly, the alternatives being equally probable.

A trial started with the appearance of the word, "Ready?" on the C. R. T. screen. The subject was provided with three response buttons--a "yes" button on the right, a "no" button on the left, and a central "home" button on which he rested his two thumbs. When the subject pressed the "home" button, the memory set appeared and remained visible while the subject memorized it. When the subject pressed the "home" button for the second time, the memory set disappeared and the screen remained blank for 4 seconds. A fixation figure then appeared in the center of the screen where it remained until the end of the trial. When the subject pressed the "home" button for the third time, the test figure appeared after a delay of 0.5 seconds, either 3° to the right or 3° to the left of the fixation figure. Three binary choices were made

concerning the test figure by the program which controlled the experiment. All of the alternatives were
equally probable.

1. The test figure either was or was not in
   the memory set.

2. The test figure was either a symbol or a
   word.

3. The test figure was presented either on
   the left or on the right of the fixation
   figure.

These three binary choices for the test figure,
together with the choice of memory set format (words
or symbols), combine to yield 16 experimental conditions.

The test figure was presented for 250 msec. The
subject responded "yes" if the test figure had the
same name as one of the items on the memory set, and
"no" otherwise. If the response was incorrect, the
word "WRONG" appeared in the center of the screen.
No signal was given for correct responses.

The subject was instructed that during the delay
period he should attempt to rehearse the images of
the memory set as it had been presented, that is, that
he should rehearse visual images of words if words
had been presented, and images of symbols if symbols
had been presented.

Five hundred practice trials were given before
data collection began. The subject reported that his
skill in rehearsing images increased markedly during
practice. At the beginning of practice, he reported
difficulty in rehearsing the four items once each in
the 4 seconds before the fixation figure appeared.
By the end of practice, he reported that he could
easily get through the list twice in the 4-second
delay period and that in many cases he would project
items in groups of two's and sometimes three's. In

the most typical situation, the items of the memory
set were rehearsed one at a time in order from the
top of the list to the bottom, the rehearsed images
being identical in format and located in approximately the same place on the screen as the corresponding
item on the memory set. Words, especially the long
words, were often rehearsed in two parts. For
example, "DOLLAR" was rehearsed as "DOL" and "LAR".
The simpler symbols like "_" and "/", if they were
adjacent in the memory set, might be rehearsed as a
group rather than singly.

The experiment consisted of ten daily experimental sessions of 300 trials each.

Median response times were calculated for each
of the 16 conditions for each experimental day. Response times for all incorrect responses were omit-
ted. Separate analyses of variance were performed on
these medians for the positive and the negative response conditions. Means of the daily medians are
shown in Table 1, together with a summary of the
results of the analyses of variance.

TABLE 1

Data from Study 3

		Memory set:symbols		Memory set: words	
Test probe		symbol	word	symbol	word
pos.	left	593.15	638.15	721.50	605.70
	right	597.65	631.95	718.30	597.95
neg.	left	825.80	757.15	935.75	760.40
	right	815.45	764.05	889.60	720.55

Significant effects within positives:
    Main effect for memory set $p=.001$
    Main effect for test probe $p=.001$
    Interaction between memory set and test probe $p=.001$

·Significant effects within negatives:
    Main effect for test probe $p=.001$
    Main effect for memory set $p=.001$
    Interaction between memory set and test probe $p=.001$
    Main effect for left-right $p=.05$

In the positive response condition, response times, averaged over both memory set formats, were 78.8 msec. faster when the memory set format matched the test probe format than when it did not--clearly showing that the subject was storing visual information about the memory set format during the delay interval. This result closely parallels similar results obtained by Chase and Calfee (1969), Swanson and Briggs (1972), and Cruse and Clifton (1971). Notice, however, that our result is not symmetrical over formats. While the physical matches were about equally fast in either format, the name matches were not. For word memory sets, the difference between response times for physical and name matches was about three times as great as the corresponding difference for symbol memory sets (118 vs 40 msec.). This asymmetry suggests that the name of an item was more easily retrieved when the test probe was a word image than when it was a symbol image.

In the negative response condition, response times were faster when the test probe was a word rather than a symbol, when the memory set consisted of symbols rather than words, and when the format of the memory set matched that of the test probe than when it did not. The presence of these significant effects in the negative condition indicates that we cannot account for our results with as simple a network model as Posner and Mitchell (1967) were able to use for their data. In the Posner and Mitchell model, response times were determined by the success or failure of two tests applied in sequence: a physical match test and then a name match test. In this model, there is nothing to distinguish among cases which fail both tests, that is, the negative response cases.

Study 4

To be sure that it was the imposed delay between memory set and test probe that was responsible for the absence of a laterality effect, Study 4 replicated Study 3 in all respects (including using the same subject) with the exception that the 4-second delay was reduced to an 0.1-second delay. This reduction, of course, had the concomitant effect of preventing the rehearsal of images. A minor difference was that Study 4 was run for seven rather than ten days.

Study 4 was analyzed in the same way as Study 3. See Table 2 for a summary of the results of Study 4. As in Study 3, response times were faster when the memory set format matched the test probe format than when it did not—again clearly showing that the subject was storing visual information about the memory set format during the delay interval. Also, as in Study 3, the result was not symmetrical over formats. Here again physical matches were about equally fast in either format, but the word test probe to a symbol memory set was much faster than a symbol test probe to a word memory set.

TABLE 2

Data from Study 4

		Memory set:symbols		Memory set:words	
Test probe		symbol	word	symbol	word
pos.	left	602.71	654.64	691.93	568.57
	right	594.79	605.43	665.57	597.07
neg.	left	799.00	763.00	912.29	755.86
	right	814.43	758.36	913.29	731.50

Significant effects within positives:
Main effect for test probe   p=.001
Interaction between memory set and test probe   p=.001
Test probe by memory set by left-right interaction   p=.05

Significant effects within negatives:
Main effect for memory set   p=.001
Main effect for test probe   p=.001
Interaction between memory set and test probe   p=.001

There was a laterality effect in Study 4. Unlike Study 3, name matches were relatively faster in
the right visual field (636 msec.) than in the left
visual field (673 msec.), and physical identity matches
were relatively faster (586 msec.) in the left visual
field than in the right (596 msec.).

Undoubtedly, there are many ways to account for
the relation we have observed between delay and
laterality. Perhaps the simplest and least interesting is to postulate that as a stimulus trace ages,
its laterality goes away. While our data would certainly support such a position, I would like to propose another possibility. My alternative hypothesis
is that during the process of rehearsal, the stimulus
trace actually fades out of existence and is replaced
by an internally generated image. The generated image preserves information about the visual format of
the stimulus (and thus mediates the interaction between memory set format and test probe format in
Study 3) but does not display laterality when compared
to a stimulus trace.

More specifically, I am proposing that two distinct entities are involved in the storage and
retrieval of visual information: the sensory trace
and the generated image. The properties of the sensory trace are:

1. It is initiated by an external stimulus.

2. It carries information about the visual
    format of the stimulus.

3. It fades rapidly (e.g., 1.5 sec.), and

4. It shows laterality when compared to
    another stimulus trace.

The properties of the generated image are:

1. It is initiated by the subject.

2. It carries information about the visual format either of the stimulus or of some stored "template," and

3. It does not show laterality when compared to a stimulus trace.

This alternative hypothesis has important implications for the use of imagery in problem solving. It implies that visual information in the stimulus trace must be regenerated if it is to be used over temporal intervals such as are typically required by arithmetic and algebraic problems. It is tempting to speculate that generated images fade in the same way as do stimulus traces and to conclude that all images must be regenerated. While some of the comments of subjects in Study 1 suggest that generated images do fade rapidly, at present we have no hard evidence on this point.

Studies 5 and 6

These next studies are concerned with the ability of generated images to carry information about specific visual formats. In particular, they test the notion that generated images can mediate the interaction of memory set format and test probe format which we observed in Study 3. Two studies in the literature are directly relevant to this issue. The first is by Tversky (1969) and the second by Posner, Boies, Eichelman, and Taylor (1969).

In Tversky's experiment, subjects were taught nonsense names for a set of schematic faces. Then, in a memory task using both visually presented names and faces as stimuli, subjects were asked to indicate as quickly as possible whether or not a second stimulus presented after a brief delay had the same name as the first stimulus. Tversky manipulated the subjects' expectation of the format of the second stimulus and found that response times were fastest when the format of the second stimulus matched the subjects' expectation, irrespective of the format of the first stimulus.

We take this result as strong evidence that her subjects were able to generate images specifically in the expected format.

The experiment of Posner *et al.*, however, had a very different outcome. In this experiment, the first stimulus was a letter name presented in auditory mode which the subject was instructed to interpret as a capital. The second stimulus was either an upper- or a lower-case letter presented visually. Under these circumstances, the subjects were able to identify matches as rapidly as if they had been comparing two physically identical visual stimuli. This fact strongly suggests that the subjects were generating visual representations. The puzzling result, however, is that the matches were equally fast for upper- and lower-case letters. The authors suggested two possibilities to account for this anomaly:

1. Despite instructions, the subjects actually generated *both* upper- and lower-case visual formats.

2. What the subjects generate is general enough to serve for matching either upper- or lower-case.

If either of these possibilities obtained under the conditions of our Study 3, generation could not account for the interaction of memory set format with test probe format, since the interaction depends on differentially facilitating *one or the other* of the two visual formats. Studies 5 and 6 were designed to clarify the issue.

Study 5 was a recognition memory study similar in most respects to Studies 3 and 4. The stimuli were typed on 5" x 8" cards and presented in a Polymetric Model V-0959 tachistoscope. The memory set consisted of four words chosen from the following list of eight:

STAR, BAR, PLUS, POUND, DOLLAR, CIRCLE, SLASH, EQUALS.
The memory set remained visible until the subject
signaled to the experimenter that he had memorized it.
The subject was then presented with a simple arithmetic equation which was either correct or incorrect,
e.g., 6 + 7 = 14. This arithmetic task was interpolated in an attempt to terminate the sensory image (See
Posner, Boies, Eichelman, & Taylor, 1969). The subject had three response buttons available to him,
placed left, center, and right. He was instructed to
respond to the equation as quickly as possible by
pressing the right button if it was correct and the
left button if it was not. When the subject responded
the equation disappeared and was replaced by a blank
field. The subject now rehearsed either the images
of the words on the memory set or the images of the
symbols corresponding to the words on the memory set.
On Days 1, 3, and 5 of the experiment, the subject
rehearsed word images on the first half of the trials
and symbol images on the second half. On Days 2 and
4, the order of rehearsal was reversed. When the
subject had rehearsed the appropriate images for about
5 seconds, he pressed the center button to obtain the
test probe. He then responded as rapidly as possible,
pressing the right button if the probe had the same
name as an item on the memory set and the left button
otherwise.

Each of the five daily sessions consisted of 64
trials. Half of the trials were positive (test probe
was on the memory set) and half were negative. Half
of the test probes were words and the other half were
symbols, and in half of the cases the test probe
matched the format of the rehearsed images.

The procedure for Study 6 was identical to that
in Study 5 with the exception that the memory set consisted of four symbols chosen from the following
eight: *, _, +, #, $, 0, /, =.

Median response times were computed for each of
the eight experimental conditions for each of the
five experimental days and for each of the studies.
The means of these median response times together with

a summary of the analysis of variance results are shown for the two studies in Table 3.

In both of the studies, the speed of recognition of words and symbols depended significantly on the format of the images which the subject generated. When the subject rehearsed symbols, symbols were recognized faster than words (563 vs. 651 msec. averaged over both studies). On the other hand, when he rehearsed words, words were recognized faster than symbols (533 vs. 811 msec. averaged over both studies). These relations hold irrespective of the format in

TABLE 3

Study 5 - Work stimuli presented

generated image	symbol		word	
test probe	symbol	word	symbol	word
positive	588.33	704.17	851.67	558.33
negative	799.17	811.67	1090.87	725.83

Significant main effects for:
  generated image, test probe, and positive-negative.
Signiticant interactions for:
  generated image X test probe, and
  test probe X positive-negative.

Study 6 - Symbol stimuli presented

generated image	symbol		word	
test probe	symbol	word	symbol	word
positive	537.50	598.75	770.00	506.25
negative	718.75	682.50	980.00	662.50

Significant main effects and interactions same as above.

which the memory set was presented. In both Studies 5 and 6, the magnitudes of the differences attributable to the format of the generated images were large enough to account for the differences observed in Study 3. In fact, the differences in response time between name and physical matches were more than twice as great in Studies 5 and 6 than in the corresponding differences in Studies 3 and 4. This fact suggests that in Studies 3 and 4 the format in which the memory set is presented has its effect on response times by influencing the format which the subject rehearses and that its influence on what is rehearsed is not as strong as the experimenter's specific instructions.

We conclude that, under the conditions of our studies, generated images can carry specific information about visual format and that in particular they can account for the interaction of memory set format and test probe format observed in Study 3. These results are entirely consonant with those of Tversky (1969) but they diverge from those of Posner *et al.* (1969).

Earlier we noted that the length of time over which an image persists is an important parameter in the process of solving problems like Problem 7 in Figure 1. Indeed, subjects' reports in Study 1 that the fading of images caused them to hurry the solution process suggest that this is so. However, the evidence provided by our Studies 5 and 6 and by Tversky's (1969) study clearly indicate that visual images can be generated, and consequently regenerated, from the images' name (or, one would suppose, from any other information sufficient to identify it). The possibility of regeneration means that an image generated during the solution process may not need to persist as an image for any extended period of time. Rather, its name or some other identifying information may be stored and used to regenerate the image when it is needed.

If we accept this regeneration view of the function of imagery in problem solution, then we are immediately faced with another question. If the

subject has information stored which is sufficient to
regenerate the image, why doesn't he just work with
that information in solving the problem and dispense
with the generation of images? A possible answer to
this question is that there may be some processing
and retrieval operations which are easier to perform
with the regenerated image than with the cues used to
regenerate that image. It seems reasonable to believe
that the generated image is especially useful for processing and retrieving spatial information in such
subtasks of arithmetic problems as identifying columns
of digits, indicating carries, interpreting positional
notation, and so on.

Studies 5 and 6 have shown that generated images
are useful in handling one kind of spatial informa-
tion--namely information about visual format. Studies
7 and 8 will explore the possibility that generated
images can contain two other types of spatial informa-
tion--namely the orientation and size of such formats.

Study 7

The apparatus for this study was the same as that
used in Studies 5 and 6. At the beginning of each
trial, the subject seated at the tachistoscope viewed
the fixation figure shown in Figure 5. He was

Fig. 5.   Fixation figure used in Study 7.

verbally instructed to visualize a specified capital
letter chosen from the following set of eight: A, B,
D, E, H, K, R, T. Further, he was to visualize the
letter at a specified tilt, either 30 degrees right or
30 degrees left. The fixation figure provided base-
lines for orienting the generated images appropriately.

When the subject was ready, he pressed the center
button. This caused the presentation of the test
probe--one of the eight capital letters oriented either
left or right--at the location of the fixation figure.
The subject's task was to press the right-hand button
if the test probe was the same letter as he had generated irrespective of its orientation, and the left-hand
button otherwise. The correct response was "right" in
half the cases and "left" in the other half. In half
of each of these subsets of trials, the orientation of
the test probe was the same as that of the generated
image. In the remainder of the trials, the orientation of the two was different. Each of the five daily
sessions consisted of 64 trials.

Table 4 shows the median response time for each
experimental condition on each day of the study.
Response times were faster in the positive condition

TABLE 4

Study 7 - Tilt

Day	Letter Tilt:	Same		Different	
		same	different	same	different
1		410	465	560	540
2		380	395	525	510
3		347	365	470	460
4		365	382	460	465
5		322	331	432	435
Mean		364.8	387.6	489.4	482.0

208

when the tilt of the test probe matched that of the generated image than when it did not (365 vs. 388 msec.). No such effect is found in the negative condition.

There are two points that we should make about this result. First, the effect gets smaller as we go from Day 1 to Day 5. The possibility that the effect will disappear with extended practice should be checked. Second, it appears likely that this effect is different from the one reported by Cooper and Shepard (this volume). If the average difference in response time, 22.8 msec., is interpreted as the time required to rotate the test figure through 60°, we would have to assume average rotation rates of 2630 degrees per second. This is entirely out of the range of values reported by Cooper and Shepard. It is possible that the practice effect and the small magnitude of the difference indicate that the subject is learning to prepare for both formats.

We can conclude, at least tentatively, from the data of Study 7, that generated images have tilt. However, Cooper and Shepard's data (this volume) provide a much more convincing demonstration of this same point.

Study 8

This study used the same equipment as Study 7. At the beginning of each trial, the subject viewed a fixation figure consisting of a vertical column of four dots, each dot separated from its neighbors by 0.5°. The subject was asked to visualize one of the eight capital letters used in Study 7 in an upright orientation but either "large," that is, fitting between the outer two of the four dots, or "small," that is, fitting between the inner two of the four dots.

When the subject was ready, he pressed the center button and one of the eight capital letters appeared in either "small" or "large" size in the position of the fixation figure. The subject's task was to press the right-hand button if the presented letter was the same (disregarding size) as the generated letter, and to press the left-hand button otherwise. The subject ran 64 trials on each of four successive days. On half of the trials, the presented letter matched the generated one in form. On the other half it did not match. In half of the cases, the size of the presented letter matched that of the generated one and on half of the trials it did not.

Table 5 shows the median response time for each of the eight experimental conditions for each of the four experimental days. Response time is on the average more than 60 msec. faster when the size of the presented letter matches the size of the generated letter than when it does not. The effect appears to be quite stable. No effect of size is observable when the letters do not match.

It seems quite clear that the generated image can carry size information.

TABLE 5

Study 8 - Size

Projected Image Size:	Same letter				Different letters			
	Small		Large		Small		Large	
Letter Size:	small	large	small	large	small	large	small	large
Day 1	336	385	450	330	460	450	440	445
2	322	375	360	300	425	425	380	410
3	315	345	355	300	400	395	395	430
4	325	340	395	275	415	415	420	430
Mean	324.5	361.2	390.0	301.2	425.0	421.2	408.7	428.7

Conclusions

While the nature and the amount of data available to us in this sequence of studies allows us to draw no more than tentative conclusions, all of our results are consistent in indicating an important function for notation-related imagery in the solution of elementary mathematical problems. I feel that two of the topics we have explored are of great potential usefulness for understanding this function. These are:

1. The capacity of generated images to carry spatial information about specific visual formats such as their shape, their orientation, and their size.

2. The ability of subjects to construct hybrid images by combining elements of the physical stimulus with generated images in a unified spatial schema and to use them in the solution of problems.

I am, at the time of writing, attempting a theoretical analysis of the role of imagery in problem solving, employing production systems in a manner modeled after Newell and Simon (1972) and Newell (in press). The most essential problems attacked in this analysis are:

1. The nature and specificity of spatial information stored in the image.

2. The spatial integration of images with external stimuli.

References

Ball, W. W. R. Calculating prodigies. In J. R. Newman (Ed.), *The world of mathematics*, Vol. I. New York: Simon and Schuster, 1956.

Brooks, L. R. The suppression of visualization by reading. *Quarterly Journal of Experimental Psychology*, 1967, 19, 289-299.

Brooks, L. R. Spatial and verbal components in the act of recall. *Canadian Journal of Psychology*, 1968, 22, 349-368.

Brune, K. H. Language in mathematics. *The learning of mathematics*. Twenty-First Yearbook. National Council of Teachers of Mathematics. New York: Bureau of Publications, Teachers College, Columbia University, 1953.

Chase, W. G., & Calfee, R. C. Modality and similarity effects in short-term recognition memory. *Journal of Experimental Psychology*, 1969, 81, 510-514.

Cohen, G. Hemispheric differences in a letter classification task. *Perception and Psychophysics*, 1972, Vol. 11, 139-142.

Cruse, D., & Clifton, C. Recoding strategies and the retrieval of information from memory. Report 71-1, Cognitive Processes Laboratory, Department of Psychology, University of Massachusetts, 1971.

Dantzig, T. *Number: The language of science* (4th ed.) New York: Macmillan, 1954.

Gazzaniga, M. S. *The bisected brain*. New York: Appleton-Century-Croft, 1970.

Hadamard, J. *The psychology of invention in the mathematical field*. Princeton: Princeton University Press, 1945.

Klatsky, R. L. Interhemispheric transfer of test stimulus representations in memory scanning. *Psychonomic Science*, 1970, 24, 201-203.

Klatsky, R. L. Specialization of the cerebral hemispheres in scanning for information in short-term memory. *Perception and Psychophysics*, 1971, 10, 335-338.

Ledlow, A., Swanson, J. M., & Carter, B. Specialization of the cerebral hemispheres for physical and associational memory comparisons. Paper presented at the Convention of the Midwestern Psychological Association, Cleveland, 1972.

Newell, A. A theoretical exploration of mechanisms for coding the stimulus. In A. W. Melton & E. Martin (Eds.), *Coding Processes in human memory*. Washington, D. C.: Winston, in press.

Newell, A., & Simon, H. A. *Human problem solving*. Englewood Cliffs: Prentice-Hall, 1972.

Parkinson, S. R. Short-term memory while shadowing: Multiple-item recall of visually and of aurally presented letters. *Journal of Experimental Psychology*, 1972, 92, 256-265.

Phillips, W. A., & Baddeley, A. D. Reaction time and short-term visual memory. *Psychonomic Science*, 1971, 22, 73-74.

Posner, M. I., & Mitchell, R. F. Chronometric analysis of classification. *Psychological Review*, 1967, 74, 392-409.

Posner, M. I., Boies, S. J., Eichelman, W. H., & Taylor, R. L. Retention of visual and name codes of single letters. *Journal of Experimental Psychology Monographs*, 1969, 79, No. 1, part 2.

Shepard, R. N., & Chipman, S. Second-order isomorphism of internal representations: Shapes of states. *Cognitive Psychology*, 1970, 1, 1-17.

Shepard, R. N. & Feng, Christine. A chronometric study of mental paper folding. *Cognitive Psychology*, 1972, 228-243.

Shepard, R. N., & Metzler, J. Mental rotation of three-dimensional objects. *Science*, 1971, 171, 701-703.

Skemp, R. R. *The psychology of learning mathematics*. Harmondsworth: Penguin, 1971.

Swanson, J. J., Johnsen, A. M., & Briggs, G. E. Recoding in a memory search task. *Journal of Experimental Psychology*, 1972, 93, 1-9.

THE MIND'S EYE IN CHESS

William G. Chase and Herbert A. Simon
Carnegie-Mellon University

In this paper, we would like to describe the progress we have made toward understanding chess skill. In the first section of the paper we will summarize our earlier work on perception in chess, adding some new analyses of the data. Next, we will give a simple theoretical formulation that we think begins to characterize how expert chess players perceive the chess board. Then we will describe some new tasks that also correlate well with chess skill, and finally we will give a more complete account of our current thinking about the cognitive processes of skilled chess players.

Experiments on Chess Perception

Chess is interesting to us because it is a very complicated thinking task that involves a great deal of visual-perceptual processing. Our earlier work (Chase & Simon, 1973), in conjunction with the pioneering work of de Groot, has led us to conclude that the most important processes underlying chess mastery are these immediate visual-perceptual processes rather than the subsequent logical-deductive thinking processes. The evidence for this conjecture is incomplete, but nevertheless quite compelling.

The early work on chess skill was done over 30 years ago by de Groot (cf. de Groot, 1965). He asked what it is that differentiates Master chess players from weaker players, and he studied some of the best chess players in the world at that time. What de Groot did was to show chess players an interesting

position, ask them to find the best move, and ask
them to talk aloud while thinking. From an analysis
of the verbal protocols, de Groot concluded that
there was nothing in the gross thought processes and
the search through possible moves that distinguished
Masters from weaker players. Masters search about
as deep as weaker players; if anything, Masters consider fewer alternatives than weaker players before
choosing a move. In a difficult position, a Master
might typically consider 30 to 50 moves, and search
to a depth of 2 or 3 moves.[1] It is quite unusual for
a Master to consider a continuation tree of more than
100 moves or to search deeper than 5 moves, and this
is true of weaker players also. One result of de
Groot's analysis, then, was to dispel the idea that
Masters typically "see" further ahead than weaker
players.[2]

In short, de Groot found that Masters and weaker
players have a great deal in common in the gross
structure of their thought processes, but he was
unable to discover any quantitative differences that
might underlie chess skill. And nothing has been
discovered in the past 30 years to change this basic
finding. Nevertheless, Masters invariably explore
strong moves, whereas weaker players spend considerable time analyzing the consequences of bad moves.

---

[1] A "move" sometimes refers to the move of a
single piece, and sometimes to the moves of White and
Black pieces in succession. We will use the term
"ply" to refer to the move of a single piece, and
"move" to refer to a pair of successive plies.
[2] There are occasional documented reports of
Masters seeing as far ahead as 10 or 15 moves (e.g.,
Alekhine, 1927, Game 43), but this is very rare, and
generally occurs under very special circumstances
when the branching of the search tree is very sparse
--as when a series of "forcing" moves is explored.

The best move, or at least a very good one, just seems to come to the top of the Master's list of plausible moves for analysis.

de Groot did, however, find an intriguing difference between Masters and weaker players in their ability to perform a task involving perceptual and short-term memory processes. Masters were able to reconstruct a chess position almost perfectly after viewing it for only 5 seconds or so. There was a sharp drop-off in this ability for players below the Master level. This result could not be attributed to a generally superior visual short-term memory capability of the Masters because, when the pieces were placed randomly on the board, recall was equally poor for Masters and weaker players. Masters are subject to the same limitations on short-term memory as everyone else.

To understand this feat of memory, therefore, we must ask what it is that the Master is perceiving during the brief exposure of a coherent position. It appears that the Master is perceiving familiar or meaningful constellations of pieces that are already structured for him in memory, so that all he has to do is store the label or internal name of each such structure in short-term memory. At recall, then, the Master simply uses the label to retrieve the structure from long-term memory. With a normal memory span of about 5 to 7 chunks (Miller, 1956), the Master must be perceiving about 4 or 5 pieces per chunk in order to recall about 25 pieces.

We believe that this interesting demonstration of de Groot's, far from being an incidental side effect of chess skill, actually reveals one of the most important processes that underlie chess skill: the ability to perceive familiar patterns of pieces. To understand the skilled process more fully, we must isolate and characterize these perceptual structures that the Master holds in memory. Our earlier work was aimed at developing a technique for isolating these structures; the basic idea was to use pauses in

217

the recall to define their temporal boundaries.

Isolating and Characterizing the Structures

In our first experiment we used two tasks. The *Memory* task was very similar to de Groot's task: chess players saw a position for 5 seconds and then attempted to recall it. Unlike de Groot, we used multiple trials--5 seconds of viewing followed by recall--until the position was recalled perfectly. For our purposes, however, we will mostly be interested in performance on the first trial. The second task, which we will call the *Perception* task for simplicity, involved showing chess players a position in plain view. Adjacent to this position was an empty board and some pieces, and the task was to reproduce the position on the empty board as quickly and accurately as possible. In both tasks, the behavior of the subjects was recorded on video tape.[3]

We used the pauses in the recall phase of the Memory task to segment the output into chunks, on the assumption that a pause will be associated with the retrieval of a new chunk from memory. And in the Perception task, we used the player's head movements, as he looked back at the position, to segment the output into chunks, on the assumption that when the player looks back at the position he will encode only a single chunk and place those pieces on the adjacent board before looking back again. We hoped that with these two tasks we could identify the perceptual structures.

We studied three chess players of varying strength in these experiments: a Master, a Class A player, and a beginner. The Master is currently one of the top 25 players in the country, and he has also won the World Correspondence Chess Championship. The

---

[3] For further descriptions of these experiments and their results, see Chase & Simon (1973).

Class A player ranks at about the eighty-fifth percentile of players rated by the United States Chess Federation. The beginner has never competed in any tournaments, and has played very little chess. The three players are otherwise roughly equated for intelligence: the Class A player has a Ph.D. and the Master and beginner are both candidates for the Ph.D. The probability that the Class A player could beat the Master, or the beginner could beat the Class A player, is extremely small--perhaps one in a thousand. By a rough estimate, the amount of time each player has spent playing chess, studying chess, and otherwise staring at chess positions is perhaps 10,000 to 50,000 hours for the Master; 1,000 to 5,000 hours for the Class A player; and less than 100 hours for the beginner.

In both tasks, players saw five middle game positions, five end game positions from games between advanced players and published in chess books and magazines, and four randomized positions--a total of 28 positions in all. Figure 1 shows examples of a middle game, an end game, and the corresponding randomized positions.

Figure 2 shows the accuracy data from the middle games, with results that verify de Groot's basic findings. The top part of the figure shows that the Master was placing about 16 pieces correctly on the first trial, the Class A player about 8 pieces, and the beginner about 4 pieces. On subsequent trials, the Master very quickly learned the positions, while the beginner typically took many more trials to learn and the Class A player was intermediate between the others. The bottom part of Figure 2 shows that, unlike the coherent positions, recall of the randomized positions was the same for everyone, and uniformly poor. Everyone placed only 2 or 3 pieces correctly on the first trial, which is even poorer than the beginner's first trial performance with coherent positions.

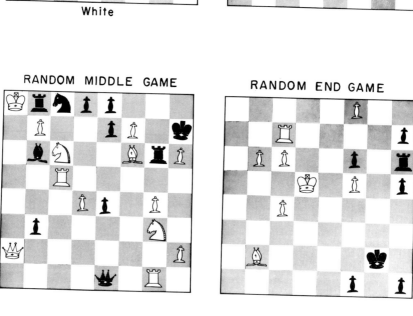

Fig. 1. Examples of a middle game, an end game, and their randomized counterparts.

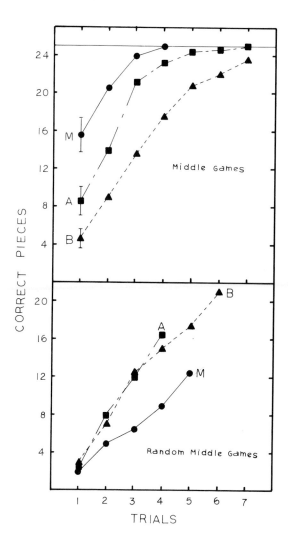

Fig. 2. Number of pieces correctly recalled for the Master (M), the Class A player (A), and beginner (B) over trials for the middle games (top) and their randomized counterparts (bottom). The brackets on Trial 1 represent one standard error, based on five positions.

221

Figure 3 shows pretty much the same story for
end games, although here there wasn't as big a difference between levels of chess skill as for the
middle games, presumably because there is less familiar
structure in the end games.

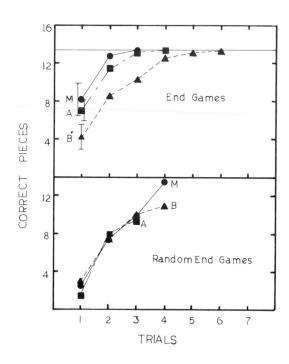

Fig. 3, Recall performance for end games (top)
and their randomized counterparts (bottom).

There were some quantitative differences between
our results and de Groot's. Our Master was only recalling about 16 pieces out of 24 or 25 pieces in the
middle games, whereas de Groot's Masters were getting
23 and 24 out of 25 pieces. The reason for this
difference seems to lie in the differences between
our positions and de Groot's. de Groot very carefully chose his positions so that they were quiet,

whereas our positions were chosen at some arbitrary point in the game. Several of our positions caught the game at a point where an exchange was in progress. The middle game shown in Figure 1 is a good example of this kind of position. In this case, there are both black and white pieces in the middle of an exchange. Our Master complained that he had trouble "getting the sense" of these positions.

Accordingly, we ran all three players for one trial on 9 new quiet positions taken from a book of chess puzzles from actual Master games (Reinfeld, 1945). Figure 4 shows an example of one of these positions. For these new positions, the Master, the Class A player, and the beginner averaged 81, 49, and 33 percent correct, respectively, as compared to 62, 34, and 19 percent, respectively, on the first trial of the previous positions. Taking these new results into account, then, our findings unequivocally replicate de Groot's important findings. One unexpected result we found is worth commenting on at this point.

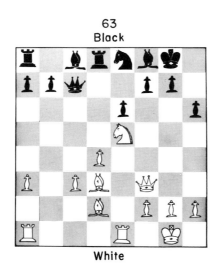

63
Black

White

Fig. 4. An example of a quiet position from Reinfeld (1945).

The Master recognized 4 of these 9 new positions--he was, for example, able to name the people who played the game--and always within the first second of exposure, yet his performance was virtually identical for recognized vs. unrecognized positions: 83 vs. 79 per cent, respectively. Also, for one of the previous middle games, the Master suddenly recognized the game after he had placed the pieces on Trial 1, but his discovery did not help him learn the position on subsequent trials.

We explored one further difference between our procedure and de Groot's. We asked for immediate recall from our players, whereas de Groot encouraged his players to "concentrate for some time (with eyes closed)..." to 'integrate' his data. The usual result of such delays, if anything, is to weaken the memory for material that has been most recently attended to (the recency portion of the serial position curve), presumably because this material is less well organized and therefore susceptible to retroactive interference. To investigate this possibility, the Class A player was shown 20 diagrams from Reinfeld's (1945) book for 5 seconds each; half the positions were recalled immediately and half were recalled after a 30-second delay. There was no significant difference in recall between these two procedures: 60% correct for immediate recall and 58% correct for delayed recall. We can therefore discount this minor difference in procedures.

One clue to the underlying representation is found in the kinds of errors that occur. Most errors are errors of omission, but there are some interesting aspects to the errors of commission. Given that a piece is incorrectly recalled, what kind of information is still present? We classified the misplaced pieces into four categories: (1) Translation errors: the right piece is misplaced by a square or two. (2) Wrong piece: a piece is placed on a square that requires a different piece of the same color. (3) Wrong color: the correct piece is placed on the correct

Table 1. Percentage of Various Types of Placement
Errors for Real and Random Positions

Errors	Real Positions	Random Positions
Translation	76.7	74.7
Wrong Piece	6.6	8.2
Wrong Color	1.6	3.5
Other	15.1	13.5

square, but it is the wrong color. (4) Other: errors
that can't be classified into the above three categories.

Table 1 shows the relative percentages of each
of the four types of errors for the 19 real positions
and 4 random positions. Since there weren't any
differences among the three players, the errors were
summed over the three levels of chess skill. These
percentages are based on 305 errors in the real positions and 170 errors in the random positions.

At least 85% of the placement errors still preserve some information about the location, identity,
and color of the pieces. Almost all the information-
preserving errors were translation errors, and there
were very few wrong-piece and wrong-color errors.
These translation errors often occurred as units (e.g.,
Pawn chains), so that several pieces were displaced
one or more squares, but the correct configuration of
pieces still remained intact. Another type of translation error occurred when pieces were displaced along
paths that they control, such as Bishops along diag-
onals or Rooks along ranks or files. This kind of
error still preserves an important function: the
control of squares within the scope of a piece. These
errors suggest that the absolute location of pieces
is not as important as their relative location--rela-
tive to other pieces in a configuration and relative
to squares under their control.

We asked next whether the pauses in recall would
segment the chunks for us. It is not an easy task to

look at the distribution of times between the placement of two pieces in the Memory task and infer two
underlying processes--slow times associated with retrieving a new chunk from memory, and fast times
associated with placing pieces from the same chunk.
We used the distribution of times from the Perception
task to help identify these two processes, specifically, the times associated with placing successive
pieces without looking back at the displayed position.

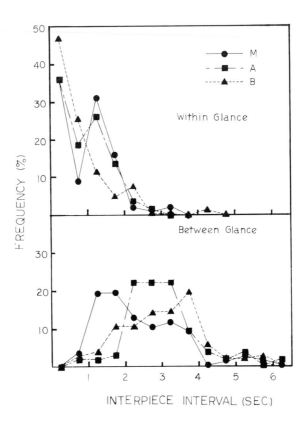

Fig. 5. The distribution of interpiece latencies within a single glance (top) and between glances
(bottom), for the Master (M), the Class A player (A),
and the beginner (B).

The top part of Figure 5 shows that almost all
of these times are less than 2 seconds, and the distributions look pretty much the same for everyone.[4]
We decided to use this 2-second time as the criterion
cutoff point in the Memory experiment. We hypothesized that a pause longer than 2 seconds is associated with the retrieval of a new structure from
short-term memory, whereas a pause less than 2 seconds
is associated with a succession of pieces drawn from
the same perceptual structure. This 2-second criterion is admittedly somewhat arbitrary, but our results
would not be seriously altered by lengthening or
shortening the interval a bit.

An interesting aspect of the between-glance
latencies, shown in the bottom of Figure 5, is that
the Master generally took only a second or two to
gather new information by looking back in the Perception experiment whereas the beginner's modal "look-
back" time was about 4 seconds. The Class A player's
times were generally intermediate between the Master
and the beginner. The speed with which players can
perceive information on the chess board depends, then,
upon their chess skill.

One fairly strong prediction of our chunking
hypothesis is that a chunk, defined by our 2-second
criterion, should have a tendency to remain a chunk
on subsequent trials. The tendency to recall pieces
in the same order from trial to trial did increase
over trials, but it is difficult to define chunks on
subsequent trials because as the position gets learned,
the interpiece latencies become shorter and more uniform. Also, chunk boundaries probably disappear as
new relations are learned.

---

[4] The second mode at around one second is an
artifact due to the extra time needed to find and pick
up additional pieces at the side of the Board. The
control for this artifact is described later in the
paper.

Since we have developed an objective criterion for chunk boundaries only for the first trial, we analyzed the first two trials of the middle and end games to see if the pieces within a chunk on the first trial, defined by the 2-second criterion, tended to be recalled together on the second trial. Since there were so few chunks involving two or more pieces for the beginner, we present data only for the Master and the Class A player.

As expected, there was a considerable tendency for chunks to remain intact on the second trial. A chunk was defined as intact on the second trial if at least two thirds of its pieces were recalled together. Some 65% of the Master's chunks and 96% of the Class A player's chunks remained intact on the second trial. It is interesting, however, that pieces were recalled *in the same order* for only about half of the intact chunks. A common example of this phenomenon is when a player recalls a Pawn chain in reverse order from the previous trial. We conclude from these data, therefore, that chunks, as we have defined them, show the necessary stability over trials, but that there is no stereotyped order of recall of pieces within a chunk.

We asked next whether the time between two successive pieces depends upon the chess relations between the two pieces. We expected that the shorter the time between two pieces, the more likely that the two pieces are closely related in some way. And if two pieces with short times are closely related, what is the relation?

We scored five relations between the two pieces: Do they attack each other (A); do they defend each other (D); are the pieces proximate, that is, is one of the pieces within one of the eight adjoining squares of the other (P); are they the same color (C); and are they the same type, for example, both Pawns (S). There are sixteen possible combinations of these five relations containing from 0 to 4 relations each. For example, a King and a Queen of the same color

228

placed next to each other on the board have three
relations between them (DPC), while two adjacent Pawns
in a Pawn chain have four relations between them
(DPCS).

Figure 6 shows quite conclusively that the
shorter the latency between the placing of two pieces,
the more likely they are to have many relations between them. These data are for recall on the first
trial only, and the function looks the same for all
three levels of chess skill.

On the basis of this evidence, taking the data
from the Memory experiment, we separated successively
placed pieces on the first trial into those that were
separated by at least 2 seconds and those separated
by less than 2 seconds, and then analyzed the structural relations between pieces placed within 2 seconds
of each other. We then compared these relations with
the relations one would expect if the two pieces were
simply picked at random.

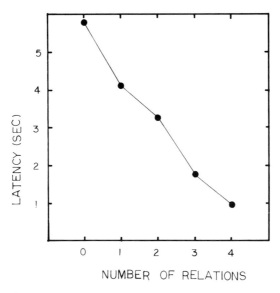

NUMBER OF RELATIONS

Fig. 6. Average latency between two pieces as a
function of the number of relations between them.

Table 2 shows the statistics (for all three players combined) for the sixteen possible combinations of chess relations. The statistics of most interest are the mean latencies, the observed probabilities (P_o), and the probabilities one would expect if the two pieces were randomly chosen (P_e). If there is no structure in the recall, then we would expect P_o and P_e to be the same. However, if there is structure in the output, then the important structural relations should occur with frequencies that are much greater than chance. These probabilities are compared in Table 2 with the aid of the z-distribution.

It can be seen from Table 2 that there is a great deal of non-randomness or structure between pieces placed within 2 seconds of each other, but the data are virtually random for successive pieces separated by at least 2 seconds.

We asked next whether these relations correspond to those noticed in the Perception experiment. If our assumption that the Perception and Memory tasks converge on the underlying perceptual structures-- i.e., that the within-glance latencies reveal the

Table 2. Chess Relations for the Memory Data
for Long and Short Interpiece Latencies

		Less Than 2 Sec.						Greater Than 2 Sec.				
Relations	N	$\overline{RT}$	$SE_{\overline{RT}}$	P_o	P_e	z	N	$\overline{RT}$	$SE_{\overline{RT}}$	P_o	P_e	z
--	15	1.75	.062	.031	.320	-36.4	99	6.42	.612	.258	.320	-2.8
A	5	1.50	.188	.010	.0201	-2.1	7	5.53	1.452	.018	.0201	-.3
P	2	1.75	.177	.004	.0057	-.5	4	4.45	1.073	.010	.0057	.9
C	43	1.48	.052	.089	.255	-12.7	86	5.54	.586	.224	.255	-1.5
S	14	1.23	.121	.029	.148	-15.5	27	5.43	.994	.070	.148	-6.0
AP	7	1.39	.168	.015	.0077	1.3	9	4.58	.670	.023	.0077	2.0
AS	5	1.44	.100	.010	.0025	1.7	3	3.00	.245	.008	.0025	1.2
DC	26	1.22	.082	.054	.0423	1.1	24	6.17	1.079	.063	.0423	1.6
PC	13	1.48	.114	.027	.0159	1.5	12	6.20	1.444	.031	.0159	1.7
PS	4	1.00	.300	.008	.0075	.2	1	7.20	--	.003	.0075	-1.9
CS	22	1.18	.120	.046	.0939	-5.1	18	5.10	1.096	.047	.0939	-4.4
APS	2	.50	0	.004	.0022	.7	0	--	--	0	.0022	--
DPC	95	1.28	.045	.198	.0469	8.3	73	4.28	.392	.190	.0469	7.2
DCS	38	.91	.071	.079	.0057	6.0	6	2.97	.259	.016	.0057	1.6
PCS	104	.57	.044	.216	.0105	11.0	5	4.58	1.564	.013	.0105	.4
DPCS	86	.68	.046	.179	.0162	9.3	10	3.34	.583	.026	.0162	1.2
		1.02						5.40				

within-chunk retrieval distribution and that when the
players look back at the board they are encoding a
new perceptual chunk--then there must be considerable
correspondence between the two tasks.

Table 3 shows that there is indeed a close similarity between the two tasks. This table shows the
correlations that exist between various conditions
across the sixteen observed probabilities. (We don't
include the data from the randomized boards in the
Memory experiment because there simply weren't enough
data from the first trial.) There are two clusters
of correlations in this table. First, the within-
glance relations for games from the Perception experiment correlate .89 with the short pauses (less than
2 seconds) from the Memory experiment. In other
words, the same structure exists for the short pauses
in the Memory experiment and the within-glance data
from the Perception experiment. Second, the probabilities estimated on the assumption of randomness,
the long pauses from the Memory experiment (greater
than 2 seconds), and the between-glance relations
from both structured and random games all correlate
about .90. In other words, pieces separated by long
pauses in the Memory experiment and pieces separated
by a glance back at the board in the Perception

Table 3. Intercorrelation Matrix for the Perceptual,
Memory, and Random Chess Relation Probabilities

Task	1	2	3	4	5	6	7
1 Within-Glance (Random)		.49	.59	.06	.02	.09	-.19
2 Within-Glance (Games)			.89	.06	.12	.18	-.04
3 Less Than 2 Sec.				.08	.10	.23	-.03
4 Between-Glance (Random)					.92	.93	.91
5 Between-Glance (Games)						.91	.81
6 Greater Than 2 Sec.							.87
7 Random							

experiment both look virtually random. Third, there was even a moderate correlation between pairs of pieces placed within a single glance from random boards in the Perception experiment and the highly structured pairs (the short pauses in the Memory experiment and the within-glance pairs from real games of the Perception experiment). It would seem that even in the randomized boards, players are noticing the same kinds of structures as those they perceive in the coherent positions, even though these structures occur rarely in the randomized boards.

Apparently, our technique really does segment the output in terms of the perceptual structures. What kind of structures are they? They are things like Pawn chains, and clusters of pieces of the same color that lie close together and usually also defend each other; the players see local clusters of pieces on the board. It is interesting to note that in addition to the chess relations such as defense and same piece (which is important for Pawn chains, and for Rook and Knight pairs), visual properties, such as color and spatial proximity, seem also to be important. Even the same-piece relation may represent visual properties because of the physical identity of the pieces.

We were a little surprised at the importance of these visual properties and, related to this, we were surprised that the players made so little use of the attack relation. Granted that in real game positions attacking relations are relatively rare, they are of great importance when they do occur and we would expect them to be noticed. However, the data clearly indicate that the attack relation was not often noticed. Finally, we were a little surprised that there were no differences in the kinds of relations noticed by different players. For example, we expected the Master to notice more attacks, but that was not the case. The only difference was that the structures were bigger for the better players.

When we took a more detailed look at the Master's chunks, we were able to classify 75% of them as highly stereotyped. Of the 77 cnunks that he gave us on the first trial of the Memory experiment, 47 were Pawn chains, sometimes with a nearby supporting or block-ading piece. Ten chunks were castled King positions --a very common defensive structure. Twenty-seven chunks were clusters of pieces of the same color (exclusive of castled King positions), and 19 of these were of familiar types: 9 chunks consisted of pieces on the back rank, often in their original undeveloped positions; and 9 chunks consisted of connected Rooks, or the Queen connected with one or two Rooks--a very powerful attacking structure. These categories are not mutually exclusive, but they give the flavor of the kind of chunks that the Master was recalling.

Table 4 gives an example of the recall protocol of the Master for one of the positions in the Memory

Table 4. A Sample of the Master's Recall of Pieces, Interpiece Latencies, and Chess Relations

Piece and Square	Time (sec.)	Relations
K_w at KR3		
K_b at KN1	1.3	S
	2.7	--
R_w at K5		
	2.7	DPC
P_w at KB4		
P_w at KN3	.3	DPCS
	3.4	S
P_b at KB4		
P_b at KN3	.2	DPCS
P_b at KR4	1.3	DPCS
P_w at KR4	.4	PS
	2.1	CS
*P_w at QR3		
P_b at QR2	1.5	S
P_b at QN3	.2	DPCS
	2.2	C
R_b at Q4		
R_b at Q1	1.2	DCS
Q_b at Q2	1.6	DPC
	2.1	--
R_w at K2		
Q_w at Q1	1.6	DPC

*Incorrect

experiment and Figure 7 illustrates the chunk-by-chunk recall of the position. In this position, the Master made only a single mistake, placing White's Pawn at Queen's Rook 3 rather than Queen's Rook 2. The notation in the first column of Table 4 refers to the placed piece (K=King, Q=Queen, R=Rook, P=Pawn), its color (w=White, b=Black), and the square where it was placed (e.g., KN1=King's Knight 1). The second and third columns give the inter-piece latencies and chess relations, respectively. This position contains instances of Pawn chains, Rook- and Queen-Rook connections, and some degenerate remnants of castled King positions. The recall protocol here is fairly typical of the kind of data we got from the Master, and many of the stereotyped structures appear as chunks in the recall. So it does appear that these perceptual structures are very stereotyped, and are seen every day when the Master looks at the chess board.

We carried out one further analysis of the Master's protocols to see if we could determine whether he was attending to attacks. Taking the five middle game and nine puzzle positions in the Memory experiment, we identified the pieces taking part in the strongest attacks. Of the 18 strong attacks we were able to identify, 11 were chunked in the Master's protocols in the sense that at least two of the attacking pieces appeared within the same chunk. Rarely did the attacked pieces also appear in the same chunk as the attackers. Of these 11 attacks, 6 consisted of Rook and Queen-Rook combinations--one chunk also contained a Pawn in combination with the Queen and Rook--and the other 5 chunks consisted of a Knight in combination with a Queen or Rook. In these chunks, no direct attack relation is scored.

We conclude from this analysis that two kinds of attacks are perceived. The first kind is a fortuitous attack characterized by an attack relation between two adjacent pieces (the AP relation was greater than chance). The second kind of attack is more abstract and involves combinations of pieces of the

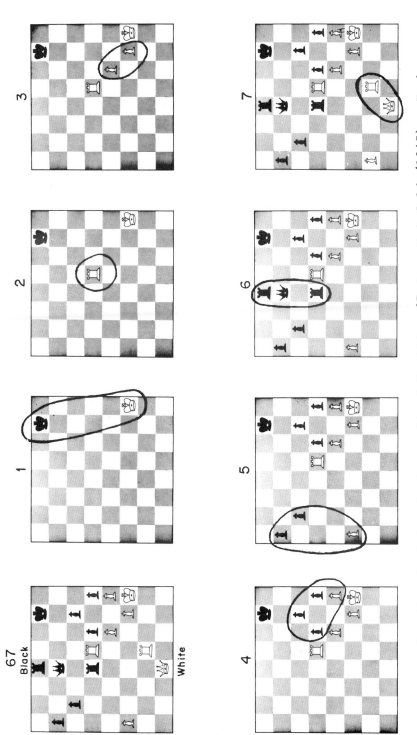

Fig. 7. The chunk-by-chunk recall of Position 67 from Reinfeld (1945). Each new chunk is circled.

same color converging, usually, on the opponent's King
position--classic maneuvers against a stereotyped
defensive position.

To sum up our progress so far, we have shown that
the amount of information extracted from a briefly
exposed chess position varies with playing strength,
thus confirming earlier experiments of de Groot. With
the aid of the Perception and Memory tasks, we have
analyzed the perceptual structures that chess players
see when they look briefly at chess positions. By
measuring the time intervals between placements of
successive pieces when the players attempted to reconstruct the positions, we were able to identify the
boundaries of perceptual chunks. And on the basis of
this technique, we characterized these structures as
local clusters of pieces of the same color that usually
defend each other. The evidence seems to suggest that
these structures are built around visual features, such
as color and spatial proximity, as well as chess functions, such as defense and identity of type of piece.

Memory Span for Chunks

Having segmented the recall protocols into chunks,
we need to address the question of how large the memory
span is for these chunks. This question is important
to us because we will later talk about a theoretical
account of the cognitive processes underlying chess
and these chess-like tasks which relies fairly heavily
upon a short-term memory of limited capacity for
chunks. We consider the hypotheses (1) that everyone
has about the same memory span for chunks, (2) that
this limit is about the same as the traditional limit
of short-term memory, 7 ± 2 chunks, and (3) that the
superior recall of skilled players is associated with
larger chunks.

Table 5 shows that two of the three hypotheses
are supported, and a third is not. First, for both
middle and end games, the average number of chunks
recalled is in the right range for the traditional
short-term memory capacity. Second, chunk size is

Table 5. Average Sizes of Successive Chunks on the First Trial
of the Middle Game and End Game Positions of the Memory Experiments
for the Master (M), Class A player (A), and Beginner (B)

| | | \multicolumn{8}{c|}{Successive Chunks} | Average Chunks Per Trial |
		1	2	3	4	5	6	7	8	
Middle Games	M	3.8	3.0	2.5	2.3	1.9	1.5	2.2	2.0	7.7
	A	2.6	2.5	1.8	1.6	1.7	1.7	2.1	2.5	5.7
	B	2.4	2.1	2.0	1.6	1.4	1.5	1.0	2.0	5.3
End Games	M	2.6	1.6	1.4	1.8	1.8	1.2	2.3	1.0	7.6
	A	2.4	1.4	2.0	2.0	1.0	1.0	1.0	1.0	6.4
	B	2.2	2.4	2.2	1.0	1.0	1.0	1.0	0	4.2

larger for better players. For example, the size of
the first chunk recalled for the middle game positions
averaged 3.8, 2.6, and 2.4 pieces per chunk for the
Master, Class A player, and beginner, respectively.
For the more skilled players, the size of these chunks
then gets progressively smaller for subsequent chunks
in recall and the difference in chunk size between the
players disappears. Also, for the end games, which are
less structured, there is less of a difference in size
as a function of chess skill, and again, the difference
disappears for the later chunks in the protocol.
Finally, the hypothesis that everyone has the same
memory span is disconfirmed. As can be seen from
Table 5, more chunks are recalled by the better players
for both middle and end game positions.

If we want to retain the concept of a limited
capacity short-term memory, then we must account for
the fact that the Master not only recalls larger
chunks, but recalls more chunks as well. If everyone
has the same memory capacity, then where do these extra
chunks come from? There are at least three possible
explanations.

The first possibility is that the difference is
due to a guessing artifact. The recall protocols
generally consist of two phases: an initial recall
phase where the players dump all they know from short-
term memory, and then a reconstruction phase where
players tend to guess or "problem-solve" where the rest

of the pieces ought to be. During the first phase,
recall is fast and the chunks tend to be large and
error-free, but during the second phase recall is
piece-by-piece with long pauses and many errors. This
second phase was more prominent in the Master's protocols than in the others. We tried to remove this
reconstruction phase from the data by eliminating the
portion of the protocol following a long pause (10
seconds or more) followed mostly by errors, or the
portion having a series of long pauses (5 seconds or
more) with errors. However, we may have been unsuccessful in eliminating the reconstruction phase
entirely, particularly if the Master is very good at
guessing. de Groot (1966), for example, has shown
that players can average better than 44% pieces correct
simply by putting down the most typical, or prototype,
position derived from Master games. And the Master
can undoubtedly reconstruct far better than 44%
accuracy when partial information is already
available.[5]

A second possibility is that the Master's long-
term memory is structured so that information associated with particular chunks serves as a cue to
retrieve other chunks from memory. Thus, whenever the
first member of such a pair of chunks is retrieved, the
retrieval of the second member is thereby cued. In
this way a single chunk in short-term memory could
permit the recall of several chunks from long-term
memory.

---

[5]The Pennies-Guessing Task is an interesting
demonstration of how easy it is to reconstruct a position from partial information. This task involves
selecting a quiet position from a Master game and replacing all the pieces with pennies. The player's
task is then to replace all the pennies with the
correct pieces. The Master is virtually perfect at
this task, and the Class A player also scores well
over 90% correct.

For example, a Pawn at KR2 defending a Pawn at KN3 (a chunk) might later evolve the overlapping pattern: a Pawn at KN3 defending a Pawn at KB4. Or, in Fig. 7, the long-term memory representation of the Rook-Queen-Rook configuration (the sixth chunk) might have contained the information that there was a target piece on Q1, leading to the retrieval of the next Queen-Rook chunk (the seventh chunk).

We have no direct evidence to support this explanation, but the Master did appear to find, in pieces already placed on the board, cues to additional chunks. Until we have additional data, the possibility remains speculative.

A third possibility, on which we will comment further below, is that a "chunk" is not a unit of quite uniform size. A highly overlearned structure of information may occupy only a little short-term memory (only its "name" need be held), while to hold a less well-learned structure of equal complexity may require several pieces of descriptive or relational information to be retained. For example, the Rook-Queen-Rook configuration in Fig. 7 (the sixth chunk) might be represented in long-term memory as a single chunk and only its name held in short-term memory. Or it might be a composite of two chunks from long-term memory (e.g., Rook-Queen and Queen-Rook) and the chunk might be structured in short-term memory as a proposition involving the names of the two chunks plus the relation that holds them together. In the limit, the poorer player might have to represent this configuration in terms of even more elementary propositions about the two defense relations, the location of pieces relative to each other, and the location of the total configuration on the board. Thus, the efficiency of the code for a chunk in short-term memory would depend upon how much structure is available in long-term memory to build upon. Then, in short-term memory of given size, more overlearned chunks could be held than chunks that required partial descriptions.

The additional assumption we need to make is that the speed of recall of pieces within a chunk is fast, regardless of whether the chunk is stored in long-term memory as a single unit or assembled hierarchically in short-term memory out of several chunks from long-term memory.[6] A chunk, according to this view, is a collection of pieces related in some way, regardless of whether or not the relations are overlearned in long-term memory.

All of these possibilities are quite plausible, they represent interesting processes in and of themselves, and there may be some truth to all three. However, the evidence is fairly strong in support of some kind of limited-capacity short-term memory where these structures or the internal names of familiar structures are stored.

Effect of Changing the Stimulus Notation

The first round of experiments supports the hypothesis that much of the skilled processing in chess occurs at the perceptual front end. We have conducted some experiments to test this perceptual hypothesis against one possible artifact, and we were further interested in seeing how robust the perceptual processing is when the stimuli are subjected to a degrading transformation.

One possible alternative to our perceptual hypothesis is that the structures we are isolating actually

---

[6]There are probably subtle differences in the speed of recall for these different chunks. For example, Pawn chains, double rooks, etc., are usually recalled very fast (less than 1/2 second per piece), so that chunks containing these sub-structures would probably be recalled with a slight pause (but still less than 2 seconds) between these sub-structures. Although there are some indications of this hierarchical organization in our data (e.g., in Castled King positions), we haven't studied this problem in any systematic way as yet.

arise from the organization of the output at recall
rather than from the perceptual process, and the
pauses really represent an artifact because players
need to pause in order to pick up a new set of pieces
before continuing their recall. This hypothesis has
trouble explaining why pieces recalled together in time
are also functionally related, but it is possible that
this organization is somehow imposed at recall rather
than at the time of perception.

We reasoned that if our perceptual hypothesis were
true, then we ought to be able to disrupt these perceptual processes by perturbing the stimuli in some way.
However, if the response organization hypothesis is
true, then the way to disrupt performance is by changing the response mode.

We presented the Class A player with 32 new positions taken from Reinfeld (1945), but half the positions
were presented as schematic diagrams in which a piece
is represented by the first letter of its name, and
black pieces are circled. Figure 8 shows an example
of such a letter diagram position. The other 16 positions were shown normally, as pieces on an actual board.

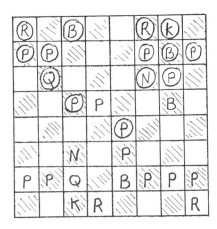

Fig. 8. Example of a letter diagram.

Also, half the positions were recalled normally by placing pieces on a board, and the other half were recalled by writing letter diagrams like Fig. 8. Thus, we have a 2 x 2 design with boards vs. letter diagrams as stimuli, and boards vs. letter diagrams as responses.

The results, shown in Table 6, are straightforward. Looking at the data on the first 16 trials, it didn't make any difference, in response, whether pieces were placed on a board or a schematic diagram was drawn. On the stimulus side, however, it made a big difference whether real boards or letter diagrams were presented. The Class A player was getting almost twice as many pieces correct when real boards were presented as when diagram stimuli were shown. This result was highly significant statistically ($p < 10^{-6}$), and neither the response mode nor the stimulus-response interaction was significant.

The advantage of boards over letter diagrams was due to more chunks being recalled for boards than for diagrams (7.5 vs. 4.0, respectively); the number of pieces per chunk was relatively constant for the different stimulus conditions (2.3 vs. 3.0, respectively).

Table 6. Percent Correct Recall
for Boards vs Diagrams as Stimuli and as Responses

Trials	Response	Stimulus		
		Written Diagram	Board	Average
1-16	Written Diagram	37	58	48
	Board	33	67	49
	Average	35	62	49
17-32	Written Diagram	50	46	48
	Board	48	55	51
	Average	49	50	50

242

It appears, therefore, that the schematic diagrams slow down the perceptual process, so that fewer perceptual structures are seen in the 5-second exposure.

However, this effect washes out very quickly with practice, so that after about an hour or so the Class A player was seeing these schematic diagrams about as well as real board positions. Neither the main effects nor the interaction was significant for the second block of 16 trials.

This experiment shows, first, that regardless of whether the player writes a letter diagram of the position or whether he picks up pieces at the side of the board and places them on the board, his performance is the same. This result eliminates the possibility that the pauses are artifacts due to picking up the pieces. Second, the fact that stimuli in the form of letter diagrams are initially disruptive suggests that performance in this task really depends upon perceptual rather than recall processes. The Class A player rapidly overcomes the difficulties of viewing the letter diagrams. Apparently some easy perceptual learning takes place so that the non-essential surface characteristics of the diagrams are ignored and the underlying invariant relations are perceived.

In a second experiment, we were interested in seeing how chess players of various strengths are affected by diagrams. In this experiment, we gave two Class A players and a beginner the same 5-second task, but this time we compared real board positions with printed (pictorial) diagrams from chess books. Figure 9 shows an example of these pictorial diagrams, selected from Reinfeld (1945), and in both cases real pieces were placed on a board at recall. Performance on pictorial diagrams is interesting because chess players spend a lot of time looking at diagrams like these when they read chess books and magazines.

Table 7 shows the basic results. Both Class A players did equally well for real boards and pictorial diagrams, but the beginner recalled real boards better than diagrams ($p < .001$). These limited data provide no evidence of a practice effect. These results

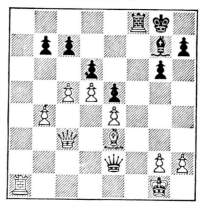

169

BLACK

WHITE

Black moves

Fig. 9. Example of a pictorial diagram (No. 169) taken from Reinfeld (1945).

presumably reflect the fact that the Class A players have had considerable experience with pictorial diagrams (but not with letter diagrams), whereas the beginner has had little or none.

An Information Processing Theory

In this section, we discuss a concrete theoretical formulation that we believe begins to characterize the perceptual processes we have described. The theory, developed by Simon & Gilmartin (1973), tries to capture the pattern recognition processes that underlie performance in de Groot's immediate memory task by postulating a few simple processes.[7] The basic idea is that

---

[7] For details of the theory, see Simon & Gilmartin (1973).

Table 7. Percent Correct Recall of Boards
and Diagrams for two Class A Players and a Beginner

| | | Stimuli | |
Player		Boards	Diagrams
1. Class A		61	60
2. Class A		56	58
3. Beginner		35	24

a large repertoire of patterns is stored in long-term
memory and there is some mechanism that accesses these
patterns: a discrimination net (EPAM net). In addition, a short-term memory of limited capacity stores
the labels (names) of the patterns.

Another important component of the system is a
process that makes a preliminary scan of the board to
detect salient pieces. It is assumed that the same
relations among pieces that account for chunking will
cause a piece having many such relations to be perceptually salient. This idea is derived from PERCEIVER,
an earlier simulation of the elementary processes that
determine eye movements over a chess board. Simon &
Barenfeld (1969) showed that PERCEIVER could produce
a good simulation of the initial (5 seconds) eye movements of a skilled chess player scanning a chess position. The saliency score of a piece depends not only
on the relations it has with other pieces, but also on
its intrinsic importance, which, in turn, is correlated
with its physical size (Kings and Queens largest, Pawns
smallest).

The EPAM discrimination net itself is organized
as a tree structure, with each node of the net representing a test for a piece on a certain square. Suppose, for example, that the King on KN1 were the
salient piece. The next test then might ask for the
piece in front of the King--on KN2. At this node the
tree might have, say, three branches corresponding to

a Pawn, a Bishop, or an empty square. The next node on the branch containing the Bishop might ask for the piece on KR2, and so on. The net, then, amounts to a set of instructions to the perceptual system for scanning the board systematically for prescribed patterns of pieces. Each path through the tree represents a different pattern of pieces on the board. Finally, at the end of each path is stored the internal name or label representing the pattern that was discovered or perceived by following that path. It is this label that is stored in short-term memory for later use at recall.

The theory, then, is very simple. The salient piece detector first derives a list of salient pieces rank-ordered from highest down.[8] Each salient piece is sorted in turn through the EPAM net and the label of the pattern that is recognized is stored in short-term memory. This label can be thought of as representing both (internally) a path through the EPAM net and (externally) a cluster of pieces about the salient piece. This recognition process continues until attention has been directed to all the salient pieces or short-term memory is filled with labels.[9] Finally, in recall, the labels from short-term memory are used

---

[8] In the present program all salient pieces are detected before the patterns surrounding them are recognized. A more plausible, detailed simulation would interleaf the processes of detecting salient pieces and recognizing patterns.

[9] The control processes of short-term memory are greatly oversimplified--there is no rehearsal, organization or forgetting in the present version of the theory. But it is probably true that short-term memory fills very quickly in this task and there is some rehearsal and organization and a lot of retroactive interference. The weaker players report that there is a tremendous amount of forgetting, and all players report that they tend to recall the most recently attended pieces first.

to derive from the EPAM net the information about the location of pieces in the chunk, and the result is the reproduction of each pattern that has been recognized.

To test their theory, Simon and Gilmartin first grew EPAM nets of various sizes--the largest containing about 4,000 nodes of which about 1,000 were terminal nodes. Their largest net was therefore able to recognize about 1,000 different patterns. The authors selected their patterns in an informal way--simply choosing chess positions from books and magazines and then breaking these positions down into patterns that seemed intuitively reasonable to the second author (KG). The selection of patterns was largely independent of the patterns that we obtained from our human players, since the selector (KG) had only a passing familiarity with those patterns. Standard EPAM learning techniques, of little interest here, were used for the actual mechanism of the net-growing process (see Feigenbaum, 1961).

The first question Simon and Gilmartin asked was how well the program recognizes patterns. Table 8 shows these data for the five middle game positions and the nine quiet positions that we used in our earlier research (Chase & Simon, 1973). The simulation, with a repertoire of about 1,000 patterns, does about as well as the Class A player, but significantly poorer than the Master. Notice also that the theory shows nearly the same proportionate improvement in performance as the humans on the nine quiet positions as compared with the five middle game positions.

A comparison of which pieces are remembered and which pieces are not remembered by human chess players

Table 8. Percentage of Pieces Placed Correctly by Master, Class A Player, and the Theory in two Sets of Positions

Positions	Master	Class A	Theory
Five Middle Game	62	34	43
Nine Quiet Puzzle	81	49	54
Row 2 / Row 1 Ratio	1.305	1.438	1.255

and by the theory, revealed a considerable overlap.
For example, the simulation recalled 51% of pieces
placed by the Master in the five middle game positions
and 60% in the nine quiet positions, but only about 30%
of the pieces that the Master missed in these positions.

Finally, Simon and Gilmartin demonstrated the
similarity between the humans' chunks and the chunks
derived by the simulation in a third way. The within-
chunk and between-chunk boundaries can be defined ob-
jectively from the output of the simulation since the
chunks in the internal net from which the output is
derived can be examined directly. The statistics on
the chess relations--attack, defense, proximity, same
color, same piece--between successively placed pieces
were partitioned into within-chunk and between-chunk
placements, and then compared with the corresponding
statistics obtained from human chess players (Chase &
Simon, 1973). Comparing the data from the five middle
game positions, the results are fairly clear: the
same kinds of correlations occurred for the within-
chunk placements as for the short-latency and within-
glance data of the human players, and the between-chunk
placements were pretty much random, as were the long
latency and between-glance data of the human players.

In sum, the simulation shows a good correspondence
with the human data in terms of the percentage of pieces
recalled correctly, in terms of which particular pieces
are remembered and which are forgotten, and even in
terms of the fine-grained detail of the order in which
pieces are placed on the board.

Simon and Gilmartin also estimated how many
patterns a Master would need in long-term memory in
order to perform well on the 5-second recall task. For
the quiet positions, the simulation recognizes about
50% of each position with about 1,000 patterns in
memory, whereas the Master averages over 80%. How many
more patterns would the simulation need in order to
perform as well as the Master?

Simon and Gilmartin assumed that the frequency
distribution of these patterns was similar to the distributions of frequency of words in natural language

prose, which is usually well approximated by the harmonic distribution--the most frequent pattern occurring with frequency f, the next most frequent pattern with frequency $1/2\ f$, the third most frequent with frequency $1/3\ f$, and so on. If we start with a net containing the 1,000 most frequent patterns, and if these account for 50% of all pattern occurrences, how many more patterns would have to be added in order to include about 80% of all occurrences? The answer is about 30,000.

Using this and other ways of estimating the size of the Master's repertoire of patterns, Simon and Gilmartin concluded that the size of his vocabulary lies between 10,000 and 100,000 patterns. Similar estimates have been obtained from quite different considerations (Simon & Barenfeld, 1969). The estimate also seems reasonable because it is about as large as a good reader's recognition vocabulary, which is consistent with the fact that chess Masters spend as much time viewing chess positions as good readers do reading.

Taken in perspective, then, what does the theory suggest about skilled chess performance? First, there is a very large repertoire of patterns in long-term memory--patterns that are held together by a small set of chess relations something like those we found in our earlier research. Second, there is a mechanism that scans the board, that recognizes pieces and the functional relations between pieces, and that finds the important pieces to build these little patterns around. And third, there are severe limits on the capacity of short-term memory, where the internal names of the patterns are stored.

There is one important mechanism, however, that is missing in the Simon-Gilmartin theory, as it is presently formulated. The simulation (unlike the earlier Simon-Barenfeld program) makes no provision for the perception of meaningful but unfamiliar patterns; only familiar patterns stored in long-term memory are recognized. As we mentioned earlier, there is a real possibility that if a player notices a relation between one or more pieces, this structural information may be

stored in short-term memory. Such a structure is not
a chunk, in the sense in which that term is now generally used, because in order to remember it, some details of the structure, and not just its internal name,
must be retained in short-term memory.

The issue we are raising is that there must be
some mechanism for perceiving meaningful structures--
meaningful in the sense that the pieces comprising the
structure are functionally related in some way--even
though the structure is unfamiliar. This mechanism
would be needed in order for such structures to become
familiar in the first place. And the basic functions
are undoubtedly the geometric and chess functions we
have been studying.

One way of thinking about this mechanism is in
terms of a set of production rules that create new
structures, given certain inputs. For example, *if A
attacks B and A attacks C, then A forks B and C.* The
production in this case would consist of a condition
side (*A attacks B, and A attacks C*) which needs to be
fulfilled before any action is taken. The action in
this case is to construct a new structure containing
the pieces A, B, and C. This structure is meaningful
because it is organized around the concept of a fork,
but this particular fork need not be familiar. The
structure would contain information about the relative
locations of the three pieces, as well as the more
abstract relation, *A forks B and C.* This relation
might enter into a still more complicated production
that takes a fork as a condition. And there must, of
course, be more elementary productions that take pieces
and the squares they control as input and construct
relations like *A attacks B.*[10] A collection of rules
of this form is called a production system (Newell &
Simon, 1972).

Regardless of the organization of these rules,
the perception of meaningful structures must be more
rule-bound (generative) than is necessary for the

---

[10]We point out, again, that the structure contains
the relative locations of the pieces as well as the
underlying functional relationship.

familiar structures. In the latter case, the recognition relies heavily on a simple mechanism with a few rules--the interpreter for the EPAM net--to sort through a large set of familiar patterns. Since familiar patterns are also meaningful, a familiar pattern might be recognized in two ways, although the recognition mechanism for familiar patterns is probably much faster.[11] The system for perceiving meaningful patterns is surely more elaborate for skilled players than for beginners.[12]

These processes are not necessarily organized as a production system or an EPAM net. That is a matter for further research. We merely wish to make the distinction between meaningful and familiar perceptual structures, and to point out that the Simon-Gilmartin simulation has only a mechanism for perceiving the familiar patterns.

---

[11]It is quite possible that this dual process is responsible for the results of the experiment on letter diagrams, as follows. Letter diagrams are initially unfamiliar, so the player has to notice pieces and relations individually as they are decoded, and he then uses this information to construct unfamiliar chunks. With a little learning, however, the player is able to modify his recognition mechanism to substitute letters for pieces, and the familiar patterns in long-term memory then become accessible.

[12]If it is true that some of the patterns are recalled because they are meaningful, and that the Master is better at perceiving meaningful but unfamiliar patterns, then Simon & Gilmartin have over-estimated the size of the Master's repertoire of familiar patterns. Also, in the present version of the program, patterns are associated with particular squares. However, it is probably the case that most patterns need not be tied to exact squares (cf. the data on placement errors in recall). If this restriction is relaxed, Simon & Gilmartin's estimate could be substantially lowered.

While this theory is simply a rough first approximation, it does offer a concrete application of cognitive principles to the task of playing skilled chess, and these principles are not derived or applied *ad hoc:* the basic elements of the theory--the EPAM organization of long-term memory, the elementary perceptual processes of PERCEIVER, and the limited capacity of short-term memory--are derived from an already existing body of theory about cognitive psychology that stands on a considerable data base of its own.

Further Experiments on Chess Skill

We have presented an empirical and theoretical treatment of the immediate perceptual processing of a chess position which specifies cognitive processes to account for the remarkable ability of chess Masters to remember so much from a brief exposure of a position. Other kinds of chess-like tasks show an equally dramatic effect of chess skill. In this section of the paper, we present our experiments on these other tasks along with our speculations about the underlying processes.

Long-Term Memory for Positions

In this experiment, we asked chess players to memorize a game until it was well learned, and then to reconstruct the position at a certain point in the game. The cue for recall was simply a move of the game, such as "White's twenty-third move: Bishop takes Knight." The player's task was then to reconstruct the position at that point.

We wanted to know if recall of these positions showed as large an effect of chess skill as the immediate recall of positions. We were further interested in the kind of chunks that would be revealed in this task. We conjectured that in order to recall these positions, the players would have to rely in part on their memory for the dynamic move sequences, and we were therefore expecting a different kind of chunk in the recall of these positions than we found in the immediate recall experiments. We were expecting, for example, less reliance on spatial properties, such as proximity, and more reliance on the chess functions, such as attack.

For this experiment, our three chess players--the Master, the Class A player, and the beginner--learned the moves of a 25-move game (50 plies) until they could reproduce the same perfectly twice in a row. The game was learned by the study-test method where each move (ply) was read out at the rate of 5 seconds per move, and the player then executed the move for himself on a chess board. During the test phase, the player tried to recall each move for himself by playing it on a chess board, and he was told the correct move if he made a wrong move or if 10 seconds had elapsed since the previous move. When the player had reproduced the whole sequence of moves perfectly, each move (ply) being made in less than 10 seconds, a second test trial was administered immediately. Upon successful completion of the second test trial, the player was then asked to reproduce the position after a specified move (e.g., after White's tenth move: Knight to Bishop Three). On five subsequent days following this learning session, the players returned for a single test trial on the same game, and then another reproduction of a different position from the game. We thus have six reproductions of positions taken from the same game, but widely spaced at different points throughout the game. All of this behavior was videotaped and analyzed by the same methods as were used in the earlier experiments.

Table 9 shows the simple statistics on recall of positions after a game had been learned. First of all, the Master just doesn't make many errors (99% correct) but the beginner does extremely well also (90% correct). The beginner, in fact, reproduces more of these positions than the Master did after the 5-second exposure (81%). With respect to chunk size, defined by the same 2-second pause as previously, it turns out that the Master recalls about 4 pieces per chunk, and the Class A player about 2 or 3 pieces per chunk. Thus, these

Table 9. Recall of Positions from Long-Term Memory

Player	Percent Correct	Pieces per Chunk	Chunks per Position
Master	99	4.0	7.7
Class A	95	2.5	10.5
Beginner	90	1.2	22.8

chunks are about the same size as the first chunk recalled after the 5-second exposures of the middle game positions. However, chunk size is relatively constant here; it does not fall off with successively recalled chunks as it did for the 5-second exposures. Also, the number of chunks per position varies inversely with the chunk size since all players were able to recall most of the positions from long-term memory. (Clearly, number of chunks recalled in this experiment should be independent of short-term memory limits.)

Looking at the beginner's data, we see something very interesting. His chunk size is smaller than before; in fact, his average chunk size is hardly more than one piece. Some 82% of his chunks contained only a single piece, whereas this percentage was much smaller for the Master and Class A player (26 and 37 percent, respectively). Apparently, the beginner doesn't have access to many patterns in long-term memory. He virtually has to reconstruct the position piece by piece from the moves of the game.

The next thing we looked at was the relationship between the interpiece latencies and the chess relations. Figure 10 shows that there is a strong (negative) correlation between the number of relations between two pieces and their interpiece latency. But unlike the case of the 5-second recall data, there is an interaction with chess skill. When two pieces, placed sequentially in the output, are highly related, then both the Master and the Class A player place them in rapid succession. However, with the pieces having few relations (0, 1, and possibly 2), the Master's

interpiece intervals are about half as long as the
Class A player's intervals. The average intervals for
the beginner are longer than the skilled players, even
for the highly related pieces. This reflects the fact
that the beginner had only a few intervals less than
2 seconds (18%), and these were for the highly related
pieces (2, 3, and 4 relations).

Thus, the recall of positions from a game is
accelerated by recalling them in chunks of related
pieces. Although there is also a difference in the
amount of material recalled as a function of chess
skill, this difference isn't nearly as impressive as
in the 5-second recall task; but there is a striking
difference in the speed of recall.

We interpret these data in the following way.
Once a chunk has been retrieved from long-term memory,
recall of the pieces is equally fast for all levels of
chess skill (probably a second or less per piece).
However, the differences in chess skill manifest themselves in the speed with which successive new chunks

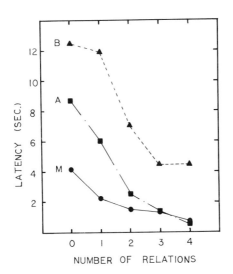

Fig. 10. Average interpiece latencies for the
Master (M), Class A player (A), and beginner (B) as a
function of the number of relations between the two
pieces.

are retrieved from long-term memory: 3 or 4 seconds
for the Master, 6 or 8 seconds for the Class A player,
and about 12 seconds for the beginner. This is a tremendous range of times when it is considered that most
simple mental operations take place in only a few tenths
of a second!

Finally, when we ask what kinds of chunks are being
recalled, we find that they look just like the chunks in
the 5-second recall task. For short pauses (less than
2 seconds) there is a lot of structure, and the structure is the same: a preponderance of Pawn chains and
local clusters of pieces of the same color that mutually
defend each other. The expected more frequent appearance of the attack relation failed to occur. These data
for the short pauses apply mostly to the Master and the
Class A player, since the beginner had few latencies
under 2 seconds.

For the longer interpiece latencies (greater than
2 seconds), the relations again looked almost as if the
two pieces were chosen randomly. Table 10 compares the
frequencies of the 16 possible interpiece relations by
examining the correlations between the various conditions involving long and short interpiece latencies for
short-term and long-term recall tasks. There are two
clusters of high correlations in this table: (1)
between interpiece relations for short pauses in both
long-term and short-term recall, and (2) between interpiece relations for long pauses in both long-term and

Table 10. Intercorrelation Matrix for Short-Term Memory,
Long-Term Memory, and Random Chess Relation Probabilities

Task	1	2	3	4	5
1 STM Less Than 2 Sec.		.86	.23	.26	-.03
2 LTM Less Than 2 Sec.			.26	.37	.03
3 STM Greater Than 2 Sec.				.92	.87
4 LTM Greater Than 2 Sec.					.81
5 Random					

short-term recall and the *a priori* random relations.
In short, these data show that for skilled chess
players (but perhaps not for the beginner), the same
kinds of perceptual structures are recalled in short-
term recall of briefly viewed positions and in recall
of positions from the long-term memory of a game.

Another interesting finding that we haven't documented very well yet is worth mentioning at this point.
From the verbal protocols it appears that the first
piece in a chunk is recalled dynamically--in terms of
the moves of the game--and then its neighbors are filled
in by reference to the local features with strong spatial components that are characteristic of the perceptual structures we have been studying. The most common
reasons given by players for remembering these initial
pieces are in terms of a move made earlier in the game,
together with the purpose of the move.

The fact that skilled chess players recall these
positions from long-term memory by means of perceptual
structures suggests that they are organizing the moves
of the game in terms of these structures and their
alternations as the game goes along. Of course, there
is more to remembering a game than this: the moves
themselves must be remembered, and these are undoubtedly
organized according to the semantics of the game (we
will say more about this later). But part of the
remembered organization of a game involves the perceptual structures.

The beginner, however, doesn't seem to make use
of these structures, which suggests that he doesn't have
a very large repertoire of chunks in long-term memory.
When it comes to recalling a position from the game,
the beginner is reduced to generating the positions of
the pieces from his rote memory of the moves. This
doesn't say that the beginner makes no use of perceptual
structures. It means that he has to build such structures from pieces and relations that he notices on the
board, since he doesn't have them familiarized for easy
recognition in long-term memory. In the 5-second recall
task, the beginner needs visual access to the board in
order to build these structures, and, we have hypothesized, he has a smaller memory span than the skilled

257

players for these structures because they are not simple chunks. He has to store considerable information about the relations of pieces in short-term memory. In the long-term recall of positions, however, the beginner doesn't have visual access to the position, so he can't build any structures, and he has long since lost from short-term memory any structures that he had originally assembled from the position.

Long-Term Memory for Games

In this experiment, we asked how chess players organize a game in memory. When a player recalls the moves of a game, we suspect that here, too, he organizes his sequences of moves in bursts which are held together closely by chess relations, and which are segmented by longer pauses. We further hypothesized that forgetting ought to be very selective. That is, with forgetting, the game ought to come apart at the seams, so to speak, with long pauses and errors at those points in the game where new chunks begin.

The data we consider here are the learning and recall of moves for the 25-move game mentioned in the previous section. We recorded the recall of moves, as well as positions, on video tape, including the trials to criterion on Day 1 and the recall trials on the 5 subsequent days.

The results show conclusively that rates of learning and forgetting the moves of a game strongly depend upon chess skill. In terms of trials to criterion, errors to criterion, and total learning time, the Master learned very rapidly (as rapidly as the moves were given to him), whereas the beginner spent considerable time and effort memorizing the game, and the Class A player was intermediate between these two. Table 11 shows the actual data. So here is another task, like memory for positions, that shows a very strong effect of chess skill.

Further, if we categorize each move in terms of its chess function, the latencies are very different for moves with different functions. We categorized

Table 11. Long-Term Memory for Games

Player	Trials to Criterion	Errors to Criterion	Learning Time (Minutes)
Master	2	4	10
Class A	5	13	29
Beginner	12	94	81

moves into six simple categories: (1) Opening: these moves are in the beginning of the game that develop the pieces. These moves usually follow fairly stereo- typed patterns that are well known to skilled chess players. (2) Exchange: the exchange of one piece for another. (3) Defense: a move which defends an attacked piece or square. (4) Attack: a move that threatens to win material or gain a favorable position. (5) Counter- attack: a move that counters an attacking move with a threat of its own. (6) Quiet: a move that is none of the above. In a game between skilled players, these latter moves generally represent the maneuvering for a favorable position according to some strategic plan (e.g., to gain control of the dark squares on the King's side). Against weaker opponents, the "quiet" and attacking moves are the ones that Masters make which usually lead to wins.

The latency data, shown in Table 12, indicate that latencies are generally longer for quiet moves and

Table 12. Move Latencies (Sec.) and their
Standard Errors (in Parentheses) for Long-Term Recall of Moves

Move	Learning			Recall		
	Master	Class A	Beginner	Master	Class A	Beginner
Opening	1.0 (.08)	1.7 (.18)	2.1 (.13)	1.3 (.11)	1.9 (.31)	1.5 (.08)
Exchange	1.8 (.51)	1.6 (.19)	2.5 (.19)	1.1 (.05)	1.2 (.08)	1.5 (.10)
Defense	2.0 (.56)	2.2 (.37)	3.4 (.34)	1.2 (.07)	1.6 (.15)	1.4 (.12)
Attack	3.0 (.92)	2.5 (.25)	3.9 (.26)	1.6 (.10)	2.1 (.21)	2.4 (.20)
Counterattack	1.6 (.11)	2.5 (.60)	3.3 (.50)	1.0 (.11)	1.1 (.10)	1.6 (.23)
Quiet	4.4 (.81)	3.0 (.33)	3.7 (.23)	1.6 (.10)	2.5 (.21)	2.5 (.25)

attacking moves than for the others. This seems to be true both for the test trials during learning and the recall trials over the 5 days following learning, although there are occasional deviations from this generalization. For example, the Class A player had repeated trouble recalling one move in the opening, and this single instance was enough to increase significantly his average opening-move latencies relative to the average latencies for exchange, defense, and counter-attack moves.

Too much significance should not be attached to these data since they are based on a single game. The standard errors, for example, vary widely because the number of observations vary for different conditions. (For example, in the learning trials there were only two trials for the Master and twelve trials for the beginner.) Also, there weren't many errors, particularly in the recall phase: .4, 1.7, and 2.1 percent for the Master, Class A player, and beginner, respectively. The memory for this game was highly tenacious over a period of a week. Thus, with this one game, we were unable to see if forgetting would occur at the chunk boundaries.

However, one result seems fairly robust in these data: the relatively long pauses associated with the quiet and attacking moves. We take this to mean that chunks (sometimes involving only a single move) are organized around the ideas (semantics) behind the quiet and attacking moves. Recall of these moves is slow because the underlying idea must be retrieved from long-term memory. Associated with this idea may be a series of more or less stereotyped moves-- exchanges, and defensive or counterattacking moves-- which are chunked together by virtue of their relation (hierarchical) to the underlying idea. These chunks are generally only a few plies deep (say 2-4), whereas the openings usually run at least 10 plies. Although there are underlying semantics associated with the opening moves, these moves are overlearned by experienced players and usually are played by rote.

This leads us to consider how memory for games is organized. Skilled chess players have hundreds and perhaps thousands of sequences of moves stored away in long-term memory. The top players have thousands of opening variations--some running over 40 plies deep-- committed to memory. There are also hundreds, perhaps thousands, of traps and winning combinations of moves that every Master knows. The question is whether most chunks comprising a game beyond the opening--simple exchanges, defensive moves, etc.--are also represented somewhere in this vast repertoire of move sequences, or whether these moves can be executed with a minimum of information because of the redundancy associated with the underlying idea behind the chunk. This is a question we can't resolve at the moment. It is clear, however, that the skilled player's recall of a game involves recognition memory for perceptual structures as well as sequences of moves, both of which must some- how be accessed in long-term memory.

Immediate Recall of Moves

In this experiment, we were interested in seeing if immediate recall of moves from a game yielded analo- gous results to those for immediate recall of a briefly exposed position. Specifically, we expected that immediate recall of a coherent sequence of moves from a real game would depend upon the level of chess skill, whereas memory for a random sequence of moves would be uniformly poor for all levels of chess skill. And we further expected that longer pauses and errors ought to occur on the same type of moves as in the previous section.

The Master, Class A player, and beginner were each given twenty 10-move sequences (20 plies) for immediate recall.[13] Half the move sequences were taken from

---

[13]We lost half the beginner's data due to a defec- tive tape recorder, but the data we did obtain are enough for comparisons with the Master and Class A player's data.

Master games and half were random sequences. The initial positions were all taken from a book of Dr. Lasker's games (Lasker, 1935), with the restrictions that the sequence begin around Move 20, that it begin with a move by White, that there be at least 10 more moves in the game, and that there be at least 18 pieces on the board. The real sequences of 10 moves were taken from the game from that point, and the random sequences were generated from that point by randomly selecting a piece of the correct color, and then randomly selecting a move from the set of legal moves for that piece.

To familiarize the players with each initial position, they were required to set up the position on a board in front of them by viewing a diagram of the position. The players were then allowed 30 seconds to study the position before the sequence of moves was presented.

Following this initial familiarization, the next 10 moves (20 plies) were read to the player at the rate of 5 seconds per ply, and the player executed each move (ply) on the board as he heard it. Five seconds after the last move was executed, the board was removed, the video tape was turned on, and a new board containing the initial position was placed in front of the player. There was about a 10-second delay between removal of the final position and presentation of the initial position. The player then immediately began to recall the sequence of moves by executing the moves on the board. The correct move was given to the player only if he made a wrong move, or if 10 seconds had elapsed since the previous move.

The first important result, shown in Table 13, is that the Master was virtually perfect at recalling the real game moves. The Class A player was also good at recalling the real move sequences, but the beginner made over 40% errors. This result confirms our expectation that immediate recall of moves is a function of chess skill. Contrary to our expectation, however, was the finding that even for the random sequences of moves, accuracy of recall depended upon the level of chess skill. Apparently, the skilled players were able to find some meaning in the randomly generated moves.

Table 13. Percent Errors for Short-Term Recall of Moves

Move	Real Moves			Random Moves		
	Master	Class A	Beginner	Master	Class A	Beginner
Exchange	0	0	29	10	23	73
Defense	4	0	25	25	13	50
Attack	3	11	39	25	28	67
Quiet	0	8	57	25	36	85
Average	1	6	43	22	31	85

Second, there was some indication that errors were more likely to occur on the attacking and quiet moves than on the exchange and defensive moves. This is true only for the real moves, and only for those players who made errors—the Master made only 2 errors on the real moves. (We have eliminated the counter-attacking moves from this analysis since they were so rare.)

The latency data, shown in Table 14, reveal that for all levels of chess skill, the attacking and quiet moves from real games were recalled relatively more slowly, on the average, than the exchange and defensive moves. Not surprisingly, there were few systematic latency differences among the different moves when they were randomly generated. Also, the latency differences were not systematically related to chess skill; the only consistent difference was that between the beginner and the two skilled players. Finally, for all levels of chess skill, average latencies were longer for the random moves than for the real moves.

The results of this experiment parallel those of the 5-second recall task in that recall of a coherent sequence of moves from a game is far superior to that of a random sequence of moves, and further, performance depends upon the level of chess skill, with the Master showing virtually perfect recall. However, unlike the 5-second recall task, performance on the random sequences also depends on chess skill.

263

Table 14. Move Latencies (Sec.) and their
Standard Errors (in Parentheses) for Short-Term Recall of Moves

Move	Real Moves			Random Moves		
	Master	Class A	Beginner	Master	Class A	Beginner
Exchange	2.2 (.22)	2.2 (.34)	4.2 (.86)	4.3 (.47)	3.6 (.58)	6.9 (1.21)
Defense	2.1 (.29)	2.0 (.32)	4.4 (.71)	2.8 (.52)	4.5 (.83)	4.8 (1.50)
Attack	2.5 (.28)	3.4 (.47)	6.4 (.80)	4.0 (.45)	4.2 (.58)	7.1 (1.06)
Quiet	3.5 (.23)	3.8 (.27)	6.5 (.58)	5.1 (.33)	4.4 (.35)	8.3 (.56)
Average	2.8	3.1	5.7	4.6	4.3	7.3

We should point out that there is less reliance on short-term memory for immediate recall of moves than for recall of positions because total presentation time of moves is almost 2 minutes before recall. In this amount of time, a great deal of organization and more permanent storage almost certainly occurs.

Finally, these results, taken in conjunction with those in the previous section on long-term memory for moves, suggest that pauses and errors in recalling the moves of a game give a clue as to how this memory is structured. Memory for moves is probably segmented into little episodes, each organized around some goal. These episodes begin with a high information move which may represent a direct threat (attack), or some more subtle plan. These latter moves are categorized as "quiet" since the purpose or plan that motivates them is not always readily apparent. Sometimes, episodes are only a single ply deep--such is the nature of chess that the game can change completely with a single move-- and sometimes these episodes continue with more predictable moves involving exchanges, defenses, counter-attacks, and probably more attacks. It is probably true that the moves are organized hierarchically, with higher level plans involving episodes within episodes; our research represents only a modest beginning in understanding how these memories are structured.

The Knight's Tour

There is another task, described in a recent chess magazine (Radojcic, 1971), which purports to measure chess talent, i.e., the *potential* to play skilled chess. Figure 11 shows the task, which is to move the Knight from its initial position at Queen's Rook One to each successive square until it finally ends up on the Queen's Rook Eight square. The Knight can make only legal moves, and it must progress by touching successive squares in a rank. That is, it must go next to the QN1 square, which it can do via the route QB2-QR3-QN1. Then the next target square is QB1, and so on, until it reaches the KR1 square at the end of the First Rank. Then the Knight must traverse the Second Rank, starting with the KR2 square, which it can reach via KB2 and KN4. The Knight proceeds thus, rank by rank, until it ends up on the QR8 square. An additional requirement makes the task interesting: the Knight cannot go to a square where it can be taken by one of the black Pawns, nor can it capture a black Pawn. The strategically placed Pawns

Black

White

Fig. 11. Starting position for the Knight's tour.

thus break up any stereotyped pattern of moves by the Knight, and they force the player to search for the right sequence of moves. The idea is to see how fast the player can do this.

This task was calibrated several years ago on a large sample of chess-playing school children in Czechoslovakia. Four children were far faster than all the others in their age group, and the boy who performed best on this test is currently one of the strongest players in the world, and was a candidate for the World's Championship this year. The other three children who solved the problem rapidly all turned out to be Grandmasters or International Masters. Radojcic also reports that the times on this task are correlated with the playing strengths of various Masters. Masters usually complete the task in 2 to 5 minutes.

We have confirmed the fact that this task measures chess skill. Our Master performed the task in 3 minutes, the Class A player in 7 minutes, and the beginner in 25 minutes. Perhaps the task also measures talent, the potential for chess skill, but we don't have the right data to answer that question. Our main concern here is with understanding the cognition of already existing chess skill, and we will leave open the question of chess talent.

One additional interesting phenomenon was the manner in which players executed the Knight moves. The skilled players (Master and Class A) invariably paused after reaching each successive target square. During the pause, they would search for the next series of Knight moves that would get the Knight to the next target square, and then execute these moves very rapidly (usually less than 1/2 second per move). It was at the pauses, when the players searched for the series of moves to the next target square, where chess skill had its effect. The Master averaged about 3 seconds per pause whereas the Class A player averaged over 7 seconds per pause. These times are similar to the chunk retrieval times in the long-term memory task, but perhaps this is a coincidence. Further, the length of the pause was strongly correlated with the number of moves necessary to reach the next target square, and this time interacted with chess skill (Table 15). For the short sequences, both players were about equally fast, but for the two longer sequences, the Master showed increasing superiority over the Class A player. Also, the Class A player executed three sequences that were longer than necessary.

For the beginner, there was no such neat division of the latencies, although his latencies did appear to consist of pauses followed by a series of more or less rapid moves. It seems fairly clear from the beginner's verbal report that he too was pausing to search for the correct path, but he often got lost. He sometimes executed partial solutions, and sometimes, after failing to discover a path, he would simply try to find a solution by trial and error.

We think the ability that underlies this task is very similar to that underlying the 5-second recall task: the ability to perceive a familiar pattern--in this case, the pattern of squares representing the Knight's path to the next target square. Here, too, the Master's perceptual processes appear to be all-important.

Cognitive Processes in Chess

All of our studies point to the perceptual processing--the ability to perceive familiar patterns quickly--as the basic ability underlying chess skill. We have surveyed several tasks that measure chess skill, and we believe that in each case we were measuring similar perceptual abilities. We think that is true for the Knight's Tour, and true even for the memory of the moves

Table 15. Pause Time (Sec.) Before a Move Sequence

| Player | Sequence Length | | | |
	2	3	5	Average
Master	1.5	2.6	10.5	2.9
Class A	2.1	5.6	28.6	7.4

of a game; we will outline our ideas on these tasks later in more detail. We first summarize our current thinking about the cognitive processes underlying chess skill.

The Contents of Thought

The slow, partly conscious, inferential processes that are available from verbal protocols just won't tell us very much about chess skill. Chess protocols are filled with statements like, "If I take him, then he takes that piece, then I go there . . ." and so on. de Groot showed that the structure of a player's thought processes while he is doing this are the same for all levels of chess skill. It is the *contents* of thought, not the structure of thought, that really makes the difference in quality of outcome. And we suggest that the contents of thought are mainly these perceptual structures that skilled chess players retrieve, for the most part, from long-term memory.[14]

Finding Good Moves

We believe we are in a position now to answer-- albeit speculatively--the following question: Why, as has often been observed, does the Master so frequently hit upon good moves before he has even analyzed the consequences of various alternatives? Because, we conjecture, when he stares at the chess board, the familiar perceptual structures that are evoked from long-term memory by the patterns on the board act as move generators. In the Master's long-term memory-- at the end of his EPAM net, or wherever that information is stored--there is associated with the internal name,

---

[14]Probably the moves derived from these structures, sequences of moves retrieved from long-term memory, and perhaps some strategic plans (e.g., center control) are also important.

268

structural information about the pattern that he can use to build an internal representation (a simulacrum in the mind's eye), and information about plausible good moves for some of the patterns. It is this organization of stored information that permits the Master to come up with good moves almost instantaneously, seemingly by instinct and intuition.

We can conceive this part of long-term memory to be organized as a production system (see Newell & Simon, 1972, pp. 728-735). Each familiar pattern serves as the *condition* part of a production. When this condition is satisfied by recognition of the pattern, the resulting *action* is to evoke a move associated with this pattern and to bring the move into short-term memory for consideration.

Forward Search in Chess

When the Master is staring at a chess board trying to choose his next move, he is engaged in a forward search through some kind of problem space. The problem space has generally been characterized as a branching tree where the initial node is the current board position, the branches represent moves, and the next nodes off these branches represent the new board positions reached by those moves (Newell & Simon, 1972, p. 665). But the Master's problem space is certainly more complicated than this, because he doesn't have the board position organized in short-term memory as a single unitary structure. As we have shown, the board is organized into smaller units representing more local clusters of pieces. Since some of these patterns have plausible moves associated with them in long-term memory, the Master will start his search by taking one of these moves and analyzing its consequences.

Since some of the recognizable patterns will be relevant, and some irrelevant, to his analysis, we hypothesize that he constructs a more concrete internal representation of the relevant patterns in the mind's eye, and then modifies these patterns to reflect the consequences of making the evoked move. The information processing operations needed to perform this perturbation, whatever they are, are akin to the mental rotation processes studied by Shepard (cf. Cooper & Shepard's chapter in this volume) and the mental processes for solving cube-painting and cube-cutting puzzles studied by Baylor (1971). When the move is made in the mind's eye--that is, when the internal representation of the position is updated--the result is then passed back through the pattern perception system and new patterns are perceived. These patterns in turn will suggest new moves, and the search continues.

External memory (Sperling, 1960), eye movements, and peripheral vision are also important for the search. When the player executes a move in the mind's eye, he generally looks at the location on the actual, external board where the piece would be, imagines the piece at that location, and somehow forms a composite image of the generated piece together with pieces on the board. Peripheral vision is important because the fovea can resolve only a very few squares (perhaps 4), so that verification of the location of the pieces within the image requires detection of cues in the periphery. Thus, forward search involves coordinating information available externally on the visible chess board with updating information held in the mind's eye. (For eye-movement studies of the coordination of external with internally stored information in a different problem-solving task, see Winikoff, 1967.)

If the Master wants to reconstruct his path of moves through the problem space, all he needs to store in short-term memory are the internal names of the relevant quiet patterns along the path, since the rest of the information can be retrieved, as we have seen, from long-term memory. This provides a tremendous saving of space in short-term memory for other operations, and time for the subsequent progressive deepening that is so often seen in the protocols.

We thus conceive of search through the problem space as involving an iteration of the pattern system's processes, and repeated updating of information in the mind's eye. Only the barest outline of this complex process is explicit in the verbal protocols. Given the known time constants for the mind's eye and for long-term memory retrieval (cf. Cavanagh, 1972; Cooper & Shepard's chapter; Sternberg, 1969), each iteration takes perhaps half a second.

The Properties of the Mind's Eye

What goes on in the mind's eye, then, would seem to be of central importance for the search process, and we should spell out in more detail the properties of this system, as they are revealed by human performance in tasks calling for visualization.

We conceive of the mind's eye as a system that stores perceptual structures and permits them to be subjected to certain mental operations. The perceptual system then has access to these new structures in order to perceive the consequences of these changes. Although the repertory of operations that can be performed in the mind's eye is yet to be determined, they are often analo- gous to external operations that cause visual-structural changes of objects in the real world. "Painting," "cutting," and rotating objects spatially are operations that have been shown experimentally to be performable.

Perhaps the most important (and "eye-like") property of the mind's eye is that spatial relations can be readily derived from the image. This property is illus- trated as follows. Suppose an image is a structure describable in the two propositions: *A is to the left of B* and *B is above C*. Then people know directly from their image that *A* is above and to the left of *C*. By directly, we mean that people can use the perceptual system to abstract quickly from the mind's eye a new spatial proposition, something like *A is northwest of C*. Although people could also "problem-solve" such a prop- osition inferentially, this information is more quickly derived by taking advantage of the spatial operators of the mind's eye.

This property of the mind's eye probably also underlies much simple problem-solving behavior. For example, DeSoto, London, and Hendel (1965) were the first to point out that people seem to solve problems of the form *If A is better than B, and C is worse than B, then who is best?* by placing *A*, *B*, and *C* in a mental image and replacing *better* by the spatial relation *above*. Then to find *best* or *worst*, people find the top or bottom item, respectively, in the image. People seem to solve these problems faster by this "spatial paralogic" than by the use of deductive reasoning.[15]

There appear to be severe constraints on how much detail can be held at any moment in the mind's eye. It is not clear whether the source of this limitation is in the mind's eye itself or in short-term memory, which presumably contains the perceptual structure (the input), the instructions needed to generate and transform the image (the control structures), and the new structures which are abstracted from the transformed image (the output). Because of this limited capacity, the mind's eye may image only part of a perceptual structure at a time.

Although an exact characterization of the mind's eye has yet to be worked out, we emphasize four properties of this system: (1) it is the meeting point where current visual information is coordinated and combined with remembered visual information stored in long-term and short-term memory; (2) it can be operated on by processes isomorphic to those that cause visual-structural changes of objects in the external world; (3) it can be operated on by the perceptual processes that abstract new information; and (4) it contains relational structures, hence the unstructured images and the feature-extractors of the visual system lie between it and the retina.

---

[15]We should point out that the relative difficulty of solving these syllogisms has been shown by Clark (1969) to be due primarily to the linguistic processes needed to comprehend the sentences in the first place.

Characteristics of Perceptual Structures

Although the precise manner in which perceptual structures are represented internally is not known, some of their abstract properties have been determined by experiment. The psycholinguist tends to conceive of them as somehow analogous to "kernel sentences." "Propositions" would be a better term, provided we interpret it abstractly and provided we do not attribute specifically verbal or linguistic characteristics to the structures.

In artificial intelligence studies (e.g., Baylor, 1971; Baylor & Simon, 1966; Coles, 1972; Quillian, 1966; T. Williams, 1972), perceptual structures are represented as assemblages of description lists, the elementary components of which are propositions asserting that certain relations hold among elements (e.g., *A is to the right of B*). We will here refer to perceptual structures as relational structures whose components are propositions. It should be understood that they are generally web-like or network-like, rather than tree-like in overall topology.

If this interpretation be accepted, then the "deep structures" postulated by psycholinguists, the "schemas" postulated by psychologists of perception, and the "internal representations" postulated by information processing psychologists are not to be regarded as separate entities, but simply as different ways of naming a single system of representations and processes for acting on those representations. Images in the mind's eye can be generated from such structures derived from visual inputs, from verbal inputs (as in the experiments of Baylor), or from structures stored in long-term memory, by the processes we have just described.

For the representation of abstract information, most investigators have concluded that a propositional or relational format is necessary (see Baylor, 1971; Clark & Chase, 1972; Kintsch, 1972; Newell & Simon, 1972, pp. 23-28, for examples). We hypothesize that perceptual structures are organizations of propositions about the three-dimensional world we live in (e.g., *X is blue*, *X is above*, *X attacks Y*, etc.) where the relations (*blue*, *above*, . . .) and their arguments (*X*, *Y*, . . .) should be thought of as abstract symbols representing the meaning of objects, actions, spatial relations, and the like.

Relations and arguments in turn can sometimes be represented in terms of more elementary relational structures (Kintsch, 1972). *Above*, for example, might in turn be represented (+ *Polar*, + *Vertical*), semantic features for markedness and verticality (Clark & Chase, 1972). Objects can also have multiple representations. The symbol +, for example, might be represented as the single symbol representing "plus" or as a proposition with vertical and horizontal lines as arguments and their proper juxtaposition in space as the relation. Chess pieces (e.g., Queen) and chess relations (e.g., attack) can be represented in terms of more primitive features. Thus, there is no *a priori* reason why a sensory feature, such as a contour of a certain orientation, can't also appear as an argument in a perceptual structure. This hierarchical organization has certain practical advantages, since one would want to hold only the relevant propositions in short-term memory; other information in the hierarchy can be retrieved from long-term memory or generated from redundancy rules upon demand.

The most important question about these perceptual structures is how each is organized. Although this is an an empirical question, we think of these structures, for chess at least, as description list structures or directed graphs comprised of object-relation-object triples. In chess, the directed graph of a chunk would usually involve pieces or squares at the nodes and chess relations as pointers to new pieces or squares. The size of such a structure, the number of redundant relations, and the detail of information at the nodes depend upon how much learning (or forgetting) has taken place.

These perceptual structures contain the "meaning" of a position in both senses of the word: to the extent that the representations contain structure, they have meaning in the Gestalt sense; and to the extent that there are internal labels that stand for familiar configurations in long-term memory, they have meaning in the sense of designation (cf. Garner, 1962; Newell & Simon, 1972, p. 24). These representations are abstract in the sense that they are built out of functional chess relations (e.g., defense), but they also have strong geometric components.

The Mind's Eye in Recalling a Game

We have already discussed the presumptive role of the mind's eye in the search process when a skilled player is trying to find a good move. We hypothesize that these perceptual structures and the mind's eye play a similar role in recall of moves from a game. In this view, a player's memory for a game involves both perceptual structures and their changes during the course of a game. Players store the game as a series of quiet positions along with information, mostly in chunks in long-term memory, that allows the player to get from one quiet position to the next. There is no need to remember the intermediate positions if they can be regenerated from more general information, from the redundancy of the position, or from plausible moves stored with these positions.

Thus, the perceptual structures relevant to the next move can be used to generate an image in the mind's eye, some transformation can be applied to the structure, and the next few moves can be abstracted from the mind's eye. A series of forced exchanges, for example, would be particularly suited to this process. The tendency of players to recall positions from a game in terms of chunks is evidence that these structures have been stored in memory as the game was memorized; and the inability of players to recall non-quiet positions is evidence that these positions are usually remembered only as transformations of quiet positions.

The Mind's Eye in the Knight's Tour

Performance in the Knight's Tour also depends upon basic processes involving perceptual structures and the mind's eye. The scope of the Knight--the eight squares of opposite color situated in a circle about the square containing the Knight--is stored as a perceptual structure in long-term memory. Perhaps the advantage of skilled players lies in the speed with which this structure can be retrieved from long-term memory, an image built in the mind's eye, and a new structure generated for the path of the Knight to its next location. As the search branches out, the skilled player holds an advantage in his ability to retrieve a sequence of moves as a chunk--in this case as a sequence of stereotyped moves to get the Knight to an adjoining square. The pattern of squares is generated in the mind's eye to see if the path works--that is, reaches the desired square without illegal intermediate moves.

Another principle illustrated by the Knight's Tour is the ability to superimpose a representation from memory onto the external representation. When the player is searching for the next series of Knight moves, he might imagine the Knight on successive squares and then construct the sequence of squares representing the potential next moves (phenomenally, these squares stand out as a pattern). From this pattern, he chooses the next move to be executed in the mind's eye, and the search continues.

This process is not unique to the Knight's Tour, but must also underlie the general ability to search ahead for a good move. In order to perceive chess relations, players must be able to visualize the path of a piece in order to see what lies in the path. This process is probably the same as that described by Hayes (this volume), when people generate, as a mnemonic device, images of partial solutions imposed on visually presented arithmetic problems. This capacity to construct an image combining perceptual structures from internal memory with sensory features from external memory is probably one of the very basic cognitive processes.

Organization of the Perceptual Processor

The processes and representational structures we have outlined here are frankly speculative and sketchy. We have speculated in some detail about the nature of the representations that hold perceptual information, but we have been deliberately vague about the system of memories that holds this information, and about the relation of the mind's eye to other memory structures. Our excuse for this vagueness is that the available empirical evidence does not choose among several alternative possibilities nor make one of them much more plausible than others.

The mind's eye is the meeting point where visual information from the external world is combined and coordinated with visual representations stored in short-term and long-term memory. Let us call the whole complex collection of visual processes and storage points for visual information that lie between the retina and this meeting point the "visual vestibule." The vestibular representation is by no means an unprocessed pictorial replica of the external world: contours are enhanced, the fovea is disproportionately represented, and there is a loss of resolution in the periphery. Within this vestibular passage there take place, for example, the processes of feature extraction --colors, contours, and shapes that serve to identify pieces and squares on the chess board--and probably also the short-term storage of visual information revealed by Sperling's (1960, 1963) experiments. Although we have not placed much emphasis on this vestibular memory in our research, evidence for such a memory in chess is provided, for example, by the difficulty an average player experiences in trying to play blindfold chess. The point we make here is that the mind's eye is located at the interface between this visual vestibule and the organized memories.

With this description of the visual system, imaging can be described as involving the interaction of three components, or memories: (1) An abstract representation in short-term or long-term memory where structural

277

information about clusters of pieces is stored. (2) The
"vestibule" memory, described above, where a fairly
concrete representation of the board is maintained.
(3) An image in the mind's eye that combines, in a
common format, information from both short-term memory
and vestibule. Unlike the vestibular memory, the image
has structure based on meaning and familiarity, and
unlike the representations in long-term and short-term
memory, the image contains features in specific spatial
locations.

The proposed theory has the attractive property
that it explains why we should expect eye movements to
accompany mental imaging. If the eyes normally extract
information about the same part of the visual scene
which short-term memory is structuring, and if these
two sources of information are to be combined in the
mind's eye, then it is essential that the imaging processes control eye movements to bring about this coordination.

Before we take our hypothesized memory systems too
seriously, we will need to examine them in relation to
many known perceptual phenomena. In particular, it is
not obvious that the system, which postulates that the
mind's eye contains relational structures similar to
those in short-term and long-term memory, can accommodate the mental rotation experiments of Shepard (and
perhaps the interference experiments of Brooks, 1968,
and Segal & Fusella, 1970) which have sometimes been
interpreted as implying an analog system (cf. Cooper &
Shepard's chapter), rather than relational symbol structures, as the heart of visual memory. But further
evaluation of these and other possibilities will have
to be left to later studies.

Conclusion

Our specific aim in the experiments described in
this paper has been to explain why it has been impossibl
to find non-chess tasks (such as general memory span)
that measure chess skill, and to give some account of
where that skill lies. Our answer is that chess skil

depends in large part upon a vast, organized long-term memory of specific information about chessboard patterns. Only chess-related tasks that tap this organization (such as the 5-second recall task) are sensitive to chess skill. Although there clearly must be a set of specific aptitudes (e.g., aptitudes for handling spatial relations) that together comprise a talent for chess, individual differences in such aptitudes are largely overshadowed by immense individual differences in chess experience. Hence, the overriding factor in chess skill is practice. The organization of the Master's elaborate repertoire of information takes thousands of hours to build up, and the same is true of any skilled task (e.g., football, music). That is why *practice* is the major independent variable in the acquisition of skill.

References

Alekhine, A. *My best games of chess 1908-1923.* New York: McKay, 1927.

Baylor, G. W., Jr. A treatise on the mind's eye: an empirical investigation of visual mental imagery. Unpublished doctoral dissertation, Carnegie-Mellon University, 1971.

Baylor, G. W., Jr. & Simon, H. A. A chess mating combinations program. *AFIPS Conference Proceedings, 1966 Spring Joint Computer Conference,* 1966, 28, 431-447.

Brooks, L. R. Spatial and verbal components of the act of recall. *Canadian Journal of Psychology,* 1968, 72, 349-368.

Cavanaugh, J. P. Relation between the immediate memory span and the memory search rate. *Psychological Review,* 1972, In press.

Chase, W. G., & Simon, H. A. Perception in chess. *Cognitive Psychology,* 1973, In press.

Clark, H. H. Linguistic processes in deductive reasoning. *Psychological Review,* 1969, 76, 387-404.

Clark, H. H., & Chase, W. G. On the process of comparing sentences against pictures. *Cognitive Psychology,* 1972, 3, 472-517.

Coles, L. S. Syntax directed interpretation of natural language. In H. A. Simon & L. Siklóssy (Eds.), *Representation and meaning*. Englewood Cliffs, N.J.: Prentice-Hall, 1972.

de Groot, A. *Thought and choice in chess*. The Hague: Mouton, 1965.

de Groot, A. Perception and memory versus thought: some old ideas and recent findings. In B. Kleinmuntz (Ed.), *Problem solving*. New York: Wiley, 1966.

DeSoto, C., London, M., & Handel, S. Social reasoning and spatial paralogic. *Journal of Personality and Social Psychology*, 1965, 2, 513-521.

Feigenbaum, E. A. The simulation of verbal learning behavior. *Proceedings of the 1961 Western Joint Computer Conference*, 1961, 121-132.

Garner, W. R. *Uncertainty and structure as psychological concepts*. New York: Wiley, 1962.

Kintsch, W. Notes on the structure of semantic memory. In E. Tulving & W. Donaldson (Eds.), *Organization of memory*. New York: Academic Press, 1972.

Lasker, E. *Lasker's greatest chess games*. New York: Dover, 1935.

Miller, G. A. The magical number seven, plus or minus two: some limits on our capacity for processing information. *Psychological Review*, 1956, 63, 81-97.

Newell, A., & Simon, H. A. *Human problem solving*. Englewood Cliffs, N.J.: Prentice-Hall, 1972.

Quillian, M. R. *Semantic memory*. Cambridge, Mass.: Bolt, Beranek and Newman Scientific Report No. 2, 1966.

Radojcic, M. What is your chess IQ? *Chess Life and Review*, December 1971, 709-710.

Reinfeld, F. *Win at chess*. New York: Dover, 1945.

Segal, S. J., & Fusella, V. Influence of imagined pictures and sounds on detection of auditory and visual signals. *Journal of Experimental Psychology*, 1970, 81, 458-464.

Simon, H. A., & Barenfeld, M. Information processing
    analysis of perceptual processes in problem solv-
    ing. *Psychological Review,* 1969, 76, 473-483.
Simon, H. A., & Gilmartin, K. A simulation of memory
    for chess positions. *Cognitive Psychology,* 1973,
    In press.
Sperling, G. The information available in brief visual
    presentations. *Psychological Monographs,* 1960,
    74, [11, Whole No. 498].
Sperling, G. A model for visual memory tasks. *Human
    Factors,* 1963, 5, 19-31.
Sternberg, S. Memory scanning: mental processes re-
    vealed by reaction-time experiments. *American
    Scientist,* 1969, 57, 421-457.
Williams, T. G. Some studies in game playing with a
    digital computer. In H. A. Simon & L. Siklóssy
    (Eds.), *Representation and meaning.* Englewood
    Cliffs, N.J.: Prentice-Hall, 1972.
Winikoff, A. Eye movements as an aid to protocol
    analysis of problem solving behavior. Unpublished
    doctoral dissertation, Carnegie-Mellon University,
    1967.

Acknowledgments

This research was supported by a grant from the
National Institutes of Mental Health (MH-07722), from
the Department of Health, Education and Welfare.
We wish to thank Larry Macupa for his help in
running subjects, analyzing data, and drawing graphs.
We are especially indebted to Hans Berliner for serv-
ing as our Master subject and for his many conversa-
tions about, and insights into, the mental life of a
chess Master. We thank Michelene Chi for her patience
as the beginner subject, and for her helpful comments
concerning the perspective of a novice chess player.
We owe a special debt of gratitude to Neil Charness,
who performed a major portion of the work in setting
up and conducting the experiments, analyzing data, and
who greatly contributed conceptually to all phases of
the research program.

YOU CAN'T PLAY 20 QUESTIONS WITH NATURE AND WIN: PROJECTIVE COMMENTS ON THE PAPERS OF THIS SYMPOSIUM

Allen Newell
Carnegie-Mellon University

I am a man who is half and half. Half of me is half distressed and half confused. Half of me is quite content and clear on where we are going.

My confused and distressed half has been roused by my assignment to comment on the papers of this symposium. It is curious that it should be so. We have just listened to a sample of the best work in current experimental psychology. For instance, the beautifully symmetric RT data of Cooper and Shepard (Chapter 3) make me positively envious. It is a pleasure to watch Dave Klahr (Chapter 1) clean up the subitizing data. The demonstrations of Bransford and Johnson (Chapter 8) produce a special sort of impact. And so it goes. Furthermore, independent of the particular papers presented here, the speakers constitute a large proportion of my all-time favorite experimenters--Chase, Clark, Posner, Shepard. Not only this, but almost all of the material shown here serves to further a view of man as a processor of information, agreeing with my current theoretical disposition. Half of me is ecstatic.

Still, I am distressed. I can illustrate it by the way I was going to start my comments, though I could not in fact bring myself to do so. I was going to draw a line on the blackboard and, picking one of the speakers of the day at random, note on the line the time at which he got his PhD and the current time (in mid-career). Then, taking his total production of papers like those in the present symposium, I was going to compute a rate of productivity of such excellent work. Moving, finally, to the date of my chosen target's retirement, I was going to compute the total

future additon of such papers to the (putative) end of
this man's scientific career. Then I was going to pose,
in my role as discussant, a question: Suppose you had
all those additional papers, just like those of today
(except being on new aspects of the problem), *where will
psychology then be?* Will we have achieved a science of
man adequate in power and commensurate with his complexity? And if so, how will this have happened via
these papers that I have just granted you? Or will we
be asking for yet another quota of papers in the next
dollop of time?

Such an approach seems fairly harsh, expecially to
visit upon visitors. It almost made me subtitle my
comments "The Time of the Walrus," as those of you who
know their Alice Through the Looking Glass can appreciate. The Walrus and the Carpenter invited a passel
of oysters to take a pleasant walk with them--and ended
up having them for lunch. Thus, I thought I'd try a
different way.

Detection

Psychology, in its current style of operation,
deals with phenomena. Looking just at the local scene,
we have Cooper and Shepard dealing with the phenomenon
of apparent rotation, Posner (Chapter 2) dealing with
the phenomenon of coding, Klahr dealing with the phenomenon of subitizing, and so on. There is, today, an
amazing number of such phenomena that we deal with.
The number is so large it scares me. Figure 1 gives a
list of some--hardly all--that I generated in a few
minutes. With each I've associated a name or two, not
so much as originators (for this is not a scholarly
review I am writing), but simply as an aid to identification.

How are these phenomena dealt with by Experimental
Psychology, once brought into existence by some clever
experimental discovery? Every time we find a new
phenomenon--every time we find PI release, or marking,
or linear search, or what-not--we produce a flurry of
experiments to investigate it. We explore what it is

PHENOMENA

1. Physical - name match difference (Posner)
2. Continuous rotation effect (Shepard)
3. Subitizing (Klahr)
4. Chess position perception (DeGroot)
5. Chunks in STM (Miller)
6. Recency effect in free recall (Murdock)
7. Instructions to forget (Bjork)
8. PI release (Wickens)
9. Linear search in sets in STM (Sternberg)
10. Non-improvement of STM search on success (Sternberg)
11. Linear search on displays (Neisser)
12. Non-difference of single and multiple targets in display search (Neisser)
13. Rapid STM loss with interpolated task (Peterson and Peterson)
14. Acoustic confusions in STM (Conrad)
15. High recognition rates for large set of pictures (Teghtsoonian and Shepard)
16. Visual icon (Sperling)
17. LTM hierarchy (Collins and Quillian)
18. LTM principle of economy (Collins and Quillian)
19. Successive versus paired recall in dichotic listening (Broadbent)
20. Click shift in linguistic expressions (Ladefoged and Broadbent)
21. Consistent extra delay for negation (Wason)
22. Saturation effect on constrained free recall (?)
23. Conservative probabilitistic behavior (Edwards)
24. Clustering in free recall (Bousefield)
25. Constant recall per category in free recall (Tulving)
26. Serial position effect in free recall (?)
27. Backward associations (Ebenholtz and Asch)
28. Einstellung (Luchins)
29. Functional fixity (Dunker)
30. Two-state concept models (all or none learning) (Bower and Trabasso)

Fig. 1. A partial list of psychological phenomena and investigators (parentheses).

a function of, and the combinational variations flow from our experimental laboratories. Each of the items in Figure 1 has been the source of such a flurry. I insisted on knowing at least one "second study" in order to include the item in the figure; in general there are many more. Those phenomena form a veritable horn of plenty for our experimental life—the spiral of

PHENOMENA (cont'd)

31. Concept difficulty ordering: conjunct, disjunct, cond, ... (Hovland)
32. Reversal learning (Kendlers)
33. von Restorff effect
34. Log dependency in disjunctive RT
35. Forward masking
36. Backward masking
37. Correlation between RT and EEG
38. Moon illusion (Boring)
39. Perceptual illusions (Mueller-Lyer, etc.)
40. Ambiguous figures (Necker cube)
41. Cyclopean perception (Julesz)
42. Imagery and recall (Pavio)
43. Constant time learning (Murdock, Bugelski)
44. Probability matching (Humphreys)
45. Transmission capacity in bits (Quastler)
46. Pupillary response to interest (Hess)
47. Stabilized images (Ditchburn)
48. Meaningful decay of the stabilized image (Hebb)
49. Categorical concepts (phonemes) (Lieberman)
50. Effect of marking (Clark)
51. Negative effect in part-whole free recall learning (Tulving)
52. Storage of semantic content over linguistic expression (Bransford)
53. Information addition (Anderson)
54. Induced chunking (Neal Johnson, Gregg and McLean)
55. Rehearsal
56. Repetitive eye scanning (Noton and Stark)
57. Positive effects of redundancy on learning (syntactic, semantic)
58. Effects of sentence transformations on recall (Miller)
59. Effect of irrelevant dimensions in concept learning (Restle)

Fig. 1 (continued).

the horn itself growing all the while it pours forth the requirements for secondary experiments.

Do not let my description put you off. Such fecundity is a sign of vitality. We do not stay, like the medieval scholastics, forever notating and annotating the same small set of questions. The phenomena are assuredly real, the investigations surely warrented to verify their reality and confirm their nature.

Psychology also attempts to conceptualize what it
is doing, as a guide to investigating these phenomena.
How do we do that? Mostly, so it seems to me, by the
construction of oppositions--usually binary ones. We
worry about nature versus nurture, about central versus
peripheral, about serial versus parallel, and so on.
To bring this point home, I give in Figure 2 a list of
oppositions that have currency in psychology. These
issues, I claim--about whether one or the other characterizes or explains some phenomenon--serve to drive a
large part of the experimental endeavor. There are,
to be sure, a few strands of theory of a different
stripe, where the theory strives for some kind of quantitative explanation over a class of phenomena, para-
metrically expressed. I do not wish to deny these
studies; neither do they dominate the current style of
research enough to quiet my concern.

I stand by my assertion that the two constructs
that drive our current experimental style are (1) at a
low level, the discovery and empirical exploration of
phenomena such as are shown in Figure 1; and (2) at the
middle level, the formulation of questions to be put to
nature that center on the resolution of binary oppositions. At the high level of grand theory, we may be
driven by quite general concerns: to explore development; to discover how language is used; to show that
man is a processor of information; to show he is solely
analysable in terms of contingencies of reinforcement
responded to. But it is through the mediation of these
lower two levels that we generate our actual experiments
and give our actual explanations. Indeed, psychology
with its penchant for being explicit about its methodology has created special terms, such as "orienting
attitudes" and "pretheoretical dispositions," to convey
the large distance that separates the highest levels
of theory from the immediate decisions of day to day
science.

Accept this view, then for the moment, despite the
fact that psychology like all human endeavors is too
diverse to be forced into such an iron maiden. Suppose
that in the next thirty years we continued as we are
now going. Another hundred phenomena, give or take a

287

BINARY OPPOSITIONS

1. Nature versus nurture
2. Peripheral versus central
3. Continuous versus all-or-none learning
4. Uniprocess versus duoprocess learning (Harlow)
5. Single memory versus dual memory (STM-LTM) (Melton)
6. Massed versus distributed practice
7. Serial versus parallel processing
8. Exhaustive versus self-terminating search
9. Spatial logic versus deep structure
10. Analog versus digital
11. Single code versus multiple codes
12. Contextual versus independent interpretation
13. Trace decay versus interference forgetting
14. Stages versus continuous development
15. Innate versus learned grammars (Chomsky)
16. Existence versus non-existence of latent learning
17. Existence versus non-existence of subliminal perception
18. Grammars versus associations for language (reality of grammar)
19. Conscious versus unconscious
20. Channels versus categorizing in auditory perception (Broadbent)
21. Features versus templates
22. Motor versus pure perception in perceptual learning
23. Learning on non-error trials versus learning only on error trials
24. Preattentive versus attentive

Fig. 2. A partial list of binary oppositions in psychology.

few dozen, will have been discovered and explored. Another forty oppositions will have been posited and their resolution initiated. Will psychology then have come of age? Will it provide the kind of encompassing of its subject matter--the behavior of man--that we all posit as a characteristic of a mature science? And if so, how will the transformation be accomplished by this succession of phenomena and oppositions? Same question as before, just a different lead in.

As I examine the fate of our oppositions, looking at those already in existence as a guide to how they fare and shape the course of science, it seems to me that clarity is never achieved. Matters simply become

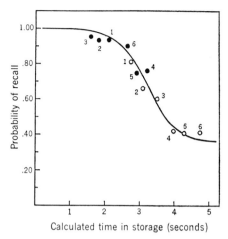

Fig. 3. Probability of recall of successive report (filled circles) and pair-by-pair report (open circles) as a function of storage time in STM (after Wingfield and Byrnes, 1972).

muddier and muddier as we go down through time. Thus, far from providing the rungs of a ladder by which psychology gradually climbs to clarity, this form of conceptual structure leads rather to an ever increasing pile of issues, which we weary of or become diverted from, but never really settle.

As I was preparing these comments an inadvertent illustration happened my way. The new *Science* came across my desk. Sure enough, there was an article by Wingfield and Byrnes (1972) entitled "Decay of Information in Short Term Memory." They are concerned with dichotic listening. The phenomenon is that if you hear a series of stimuli simultaneously in both ears at a rapid rate there are differences in the difficulty of reporting the stimuli, depending on how they are to be grouped. If the left ear gets stimuli L1, L2, L3 and the right ear R1, R2, R3, then *successive* reporting (L1, L2, L3, R1, R2, R3) is easier than so-called *simultaneous* reporting (L1, R1, L2, R2, L3, R3). The paper reports a new explanation for the phenomenon, which is most easily understood from Figure 3 (reproduced from their article). If one considers a uniform decay curve for memory, dependent only on the length of time an item is in short term memory, then both

results follow from a detailed calculation of the
lengths of time each item is in store. Thus, the
grouping itself is not the operative consideration,
but simply an indirect way of determining how long
items must remain in memory, hence be subject to
differential decay.

The original experiments showing the phenomenon
and the original explanations, in terms of time to
switch a channel go back 18 years to Broadbent (1958).
Furthermore, this phenomenon of simultaneous versus
sequential grouping has occasioned some hundreds of
papers over the intervening years, in an attempt to
clarify the issues (was it channel switching or not?).
Now Wingfield and Byrnes provide yet one more explanation. Regardless of the exact merits of their case--
and for my purposes here I need not judge them--it can
be stated with confidence that their article does not
settle the issue. Theirs is just one more entry in
what seems like a forever ending series of so-called
clarifying experiments. With due apologies to Wingfield
and Byrnes for using their work in this way (it was in
fact the random occurrence noted above), it provides
good evidence for the general proposition that psychological issues have difficulty even fading away.

There is, I submit, a view of the scientific endeavor that is implicit (and sometimes explicit) in the
picture I have presented above. Science advances by
playing twenty questions with nature. The *proper*
tactic is to frame a general question, hopefully binary, that can be attacked experimentally. Having
settled that bits-worth, one can proceed to the next.
The policy appears optimal--one never risks much, there
is feedback from nature at every step, and progress is
inevitable. Unfortunately, the questions never seem
to be really answered, the strategy does not seem to
work.

Of course I caricature. But I must get your
attention. And the caricature is not so great as to
be without merit.

Why do these considerations rise in me upon
attempting to comment on the papers in this symposium?

First, I took as my assignment from Bill Chase to comment on them all, to the extent that I was able. To do so was probably a fateful error. Second, since I was playing the theorist, I adopted the set of trying to put them all together. *Put them all together.* No doubt a compounding of the error. For not only could I not put them all together, I did not see how they themselves were putting them all together. It was exceedingly clear that each paper made a contribution. I was not exaggerating when I asserted that we have witnessed here an exceptionally fine set of experimental results and theoretical interpretations based thereon. But as I tried to put them all together, I was led back from the particular results described to a set of results that these papers referenced and used, in a qualitative sort of way. These led me back to yet other papers, many by the same group of authors and of equal merit and precision. It became less and less clear to me that all these papers were cumulating. Only the barest fraction of each prior paper found its way into the next (though fortunately there were some exceptions), and these experiments I was considering (those today) seemed destined to play a similar role *vis à vis* the future.

As I considered the issues raised (single code versus multiple code, continuous versus discrete representation, etc.) I found myself conjuring up this model of the current scientific process in psychology—of phenomena to be explored and their explanation by essentially oppositional concepts. And I coundn't convince myself that it would add up, even in thirty more years of trying, even if one had another 300 papers of similar, excellent ilk.

In opting for worrying about this larger issue, I am not trying thereby to shirk my duty as a reviewer of the particular papers under consideration. (How often have I been annoyed as someone who **was** to review *my* paper simply took it as the opportunity to go his own way with what *he* wanted to talk about!) As an earnest of my good faith, I record herewith a sample of the direct responses generated by the specifics of the papers.

291

To Mike Posner: Certainly, I agree that
there are multiple codes. That turns out to
be almost a logical necessity. You certainly
would seem to have knocked out one particular
simple view. However, it would seem impossible,
on the evidence that you present, to distinguish
codes in the sense of the content of a representation with codes in the sense of implying
separate boxes in an architectural memory
structure.

To Lynn Cooper and Roger Shepard: I am
extraordinarily impressed by your data. However, it seems to me quite unlikely that there
is a physical process of continuous rotation
involved. I do not take this belief from a
general bias for discrete symbolic processing
(though I have that bias). Much of what is
known about the visual system tells us that
it is like a sampled data system--that it
doesn't work continuously either in space or
time (Hubel & Wiesel, 1962; Stark, 1968).
It would be surprising if (1) the visual system
itself, considered as a tracking and eye-
movement-controlling device, were a sampled
data system, yet (2) inside that (that is,
centerward from the processing of the stimulus)
it became continuous again to deal with
rotation. For the intuition behind the
belief that rotation is to be accomplished
by a continuous system is that the outside
world is continuous and this should be
mirrored in the internal mechanism.

To Bill Chase and Herb Simon: You have
clearly established that there is a phenomenon
associated with chess skill, and that we have
a theory now to explain how this phenomenon
could arise--and arise in chess masters to a
degree that it would not in experts or beginners.
This correlational fact, however, does not
yet explain why chess masters are better chess

players than beginners or experts. A natural
theory is at hand given the type of theory
provided; namely, a chess player will have
specific actions associated with each pattern.
(This is, in fact, the scheme proposed in
Newell and Simon (1965) for guiding the
tactical search, where the actions were
functional move generators.) However, the
theory as you present it only lays the ground-
work for a theory of master level skill,
and does not in any sense provide evidence
for it. It requires that someone construct
a program with such an arrangement and see
if it plays as prescribed.

And so it might go. But it didn't seem to me to
add up to much. What I wanted was for these excellent
pieces of the experimental mosiac to add up to the
psychology that we all wished to foresee. They didn't,
not because of any lack of excellence locally, but
because most of them seemed part of a pattern of
psychological activity that didn't seem able to
cumulate.

Diagnosis

Let me turn, then, from detection to diagnosis--
from assertions that we have certain difficulties that
are manifest in the current pattern of our research,
to an attempt to say why that is the case.

On Methods

The most fundamental fact about behavior is that
it is programmable. That is to say, behavior is under
the control of the subject to shape in the service of
his own ends. There is a sort of symbolic formula that
we use in information processing psychology. To predict
a subject you must know: (1) his goals; (2) the structure of the task environment; and (3) the invariant
structure of his processing mechanisms. From this you

can pretty well predict what methods are available to
the subject; and from the method you can predict what
the subject will do. Without these things, most importantly without the method, you cannot predict what he
will do.

We may translate this assertion:[1]

> *First Injunction of Psychological
> Experimentation:* Know the method
> your subject is using to perform
> the experimental task.

Uncertainty over what method the subject is using drives
a substantial amount of discussion of experimental
results. It is quite in evidence in the present set
of papers. Klahr's discussion of why the last point
in his Figure 6 (Chapter 1) is a little lower hinges
on asserting the subject knows there cannot be more
than five elements so he can terminate the loop early.
That is, it is argued that the subject has a special
method that can capitalize timewise on a bit of knowledge that we know exists in the task environment.

In Cooper and Shepard's piece (Chapter 3) there
is a similar concern, for instance, at what choices the
subject is making at the bottom--whether to rotate to
the left or right. In Chase and Simon's paper (Chapter
5), the entire data analysis rests, in some sense, on
the method attributed to the subject for doing the
tasks; and much of the side calculations (e.g., those
on chunking) are done to confirm the method. Again,
so it goes. In short, we are totally engaged, in
psychological experimentation, in the discovery and
verification of the specific methods used by the subjec
in doing the experimental tasks.

---

[1]An earlier form was the injunction to know the
effective stimulus. The present formulation seems more
adequate to the complexities of human behavior.

The above considerations lead directly to the next assertion:

Second Injunction of Psychological Experimentation: Never average over methods.

To do so conceals, rather than reveals. You get garbage or, even worse, spurious regularity. The classic example of the failure to heed this injunction is the averaging of single-shot learning curves to yield continuous learning curves. However, we have two almost perfect examples in the present papers--perfect, not because an error was made, but because in each the authors provide data both before and after, so to speak, so one can appreciate the mis-interpretation, narrowly missed.

The first is the Cooper-Shepard data given in their Figure 5. It shows that RT is non-linear with angle of rotation. Their Figure 13 shows, however, that time is linear with angle. The explanation of the latter, as noted by Cooper and Shepard, is that it averages over all the different starting points. If they had settled for this latter data, having obtained it first, then the problem of interpretation of the non-linear curves would not have arisen--and we could have been led down a lovely garden path of over-simplified regularity.

The second example is from the Klahr paper. Gradually he purifies the subitizing data. At one stage (his Figure 5) we get the curve with a slope of 66 ms. However, he then separates out the instances with eye movement, leaving an additionally purified sample of response done with a single fixation and with a single subject: The slope drops to 25 ms per point in the subitizing set (his Figure 7). We are grateful for the unmixing of the methods. Can we assume to have touched bottom and that interpretation can now commence?

The point of all these remarks is that an immense amount of effort is devoted to such clarifications-- that, in fact, much of the ability of the field

continually and forever to dispute and question interpretations arises from the possibility of the subject's
having done the task by a not-til-then-thought-of
method or by the set of subjects having adopted a
mixture of methods so the regularities produced were
not what they seemed.

To put this in general terms again, our task in
psychology is first to discover that structure which
is fixed and invariant so that we can theoretically
infer the method. Given the goal of the subject and
the task environment which he faces, we can generate
the (small) collection of methods that are likely to
be used by him to perform the task (given his processing limits). Then, by means of careful design of the
experiments or by suitable *post-hoc* analysis of the
subject's performance we can settle what method he did
indeed use. Without such a framework within which to
work, the generation of new methods, hence new explanations, for old phenomena, will go on *ad nauseum*.
There will be no discipline for it, as there is none
now.

Let me push this branch of the diagnosis one step
further. The papers of our symposium proceed by ex-
tracting for consideration a couple of mechanisms out
of the totality of those required for the job. They
then proceed by means of experimental technique to
verify their existence, or to measure some of their
properties (e.g., duration). Thus, Posner (Chapter 2)
attempts (successfully, in my view) to deal with encoding of visual and auditory information, to determine
whether they are the same. Sometimes more detail of
a total process is presented: the flow diagrams in
Cooper-Shepard, in Klahr, and in other presentations
of Clark's work (Clark & Chase, 1972). These flow
diagrams serve to assert the existence of an entire
set of processing stages or components and some order-
ings between them.

All of the above, especially including the flow
diagrams, represent major progress, both in our experimental technique and in our frameworks of interpretation. I am not here to challenge that. However,

296

they have in common that they leave open the total
method being used. They do not operate within a frame
that constrains what other methods might also be evoked
to perform the same task. In short, they do not model
the *control* structure.

What is that, the control structure? It is best
illustrated by programming languages. A language such
as FORTRAN (or any other, for that matter) may be seen
as a device to evoke a sequence of primitive operations,
the exact sequence being conditional upon the data.
The primitive operations in FORTRAN are the arithmetic
operations, the given functions (sine, cosine, logarithm, etc.), the assignment of a value to a variable,
the input and output operations, etc. Each of these
has a name in the language (+, -, SIN, LOG, etc.).
However, just having names for the operations is not
enough. Specifying the conditional sequence is also
required and what does that is called the control
structure. In FORTRAN it includes the syntax of algebraic expressions, which governs how the arithmetic
operations are evoked, the order of statements, which
implies that the operations specified by these statements are to be done in order, the syntax of the iteration statement (the DO statement), the format of the
conditional and unconditional branch. Given the control structure, there exists a definite problem of
programming to get a task done. Given only the basic
operations, but not control structure, it is not possible to say what sequences of operations are or are
not possible, or are possible within constraints of
time and space.

Much of the new progress in the experimental
analysis of the information processing of humans has
eschewed attention to the control strurture. The
present papers of this symposium are no exception.
However, my best example (my canonical one, so to
speak) is the deservedly well-known paper by Atkinson
and Shiffrin (1968) entitled: "Human Memory: A proposed system and its control processes." The model of
memory is there all right, and is applied to a number
of tasks with quantitative precision. However, the

297

control structure is completely absent and is used as a *deus ex machina* to concoct separate models for each task. Criticism is not directed at that justly influential piece of work. But it does illustrate well the current state of the theoretical art. As long as the control structure—the glue—is missing, so long will it be possible to suggest an indefinite sequence of alternative possibilities for how a given task was performed, hence to keep theoretical issues from becoming settled.

Putting it Together

There is a second source of our difficulties, distinct from the one discussed above, though not unrelated to it. We never seem in the experimental literature to put the results of all the experiments together. The paper by Posner in the present symposium is an excellent example—excellent both in showing the skillful attempts we do currently make and in showing how far short this falls of really integrating the results. We do—Posner does—relate sets of experiments. But the linkage is extraordinarily loose. One picks and chooses among the qualitative summaries of a given experiment what to bring forward and juxtapose with the concerns of a present treatment.

This aspect of our current scientific style is abetted by our tendency noted at the beginning to case the results of experiments in terms of their support or refutation of various binary oppositions. Thus, what is brought forward from an experiment is supposed to be just such qualitative summaries. Innumerable aspect of the situations are permitted to be suppressed. Thus no way exists of knowing whether the earlier studies a in fact commensurate with whatever ones are under pres ent scrutiny, or are in fact contradictory. Only if the contradiction is blatant, so to speak—e.g., asser ing a single memory structure versus two, a long-term and a short-term memory—will the appropriate clash occur. Of course, it is not true that these other aspects are suppressed. They remain available to be dug up by any reviewer who cares to do so, thus to keep the cycle of uncertainty and re-interpretation going.

The article of Wingfield and Byrnes in *Science*, discussed above, provides a good example of what is permissible in our present experimental style. A single result is permitted, so to speak, to challenge a rather large edifice. So loose jointed are our edifices that a divide and conquer strategy can be used. A part of the totality can be pulled out and attacked in isolation with seeming impunity.

What should be the case? A challenge to one part of a pattern of experimental results should not be permitted unless it can successfully challenge (or be shown to be consistent with) a substantial part of the total existing pattern. It is a question of where scientific responsibility lays. The warp and woof of our experimental web hangs so loose that it comes as a novel suggestion that a paper such as the Wingfield-Byrnes one is being theoretically irresponsible.

A reaction of protest, or at least annoyance, should by now surely have set in. Am I not being harsh? How do I expect experimental work and inter-pretation to proceed? Isn't this the way all sciences proceed? As to the latter (since I get to give the answers, I get to select the questions), the other sciences may not have had such a slippery eel to con-tend with. That the same human subject can adopt many (radically different) methods for the same basic task, depending on goal, background knowledge, and minor details of payoff structure and task texture--all this-- implies that the "normal" means of science may not suffice. As to the first question, the harshness, I restate my initial point: this is my confused and distressed half speaking. My other half is tickled pink at how fast and how far we have come in the last decade, not to speak of the last two days.

Let me stress as well that nothing in my concern implies a lessened dependence on the extraction of experimental fact or the need to develop experimental techniques. The benefits yielded to this symposium

from the chronometric analysis of reaction times, a
tool that the last five years has honed to a fine edge,
are immense. In fact, I really approve of all those
phenomena in Figure 1. They are examples of the kinds
of experimental insights that we reap from our current
investigations. I do in fact hope they double in the
next ten years. My concern, to state it once more, is
with how they will add up.

Prognosis

What can be done about these concerns, assuming I
have convinced you to take them seriously, at least by
half? I will spend no time arguing that what is needed
is to view man as an information processing system.
This has been argued at length in several places (e.g.,
see Newell and Simon, 1972, for our contribution).
More important, all of the papers in the present symposium are executed enough within that conceptual view
to demonstrate that the lack of such a metaview is not
the culprit. From this vantage point the work of Cooper
and Shepard, raising as it does the possibility of
continuous processing mechanisms, is as much a scientific exemplar of an information processing view as is,
say, the discrete symbolic models of Chase and Simon.
I will not assert that I know exactly what should
be done. My distress is genuine. I am worried that
our efforts, even the excellent ones I see occurring
here, will not add up. Let me, however, discuss at
least three possible (non-exclusive) courses of action.
These might be viewed as possible paradigms within
which to operate experimentally.

Complete Processing Models

The first suggestion is to construct complete processing models rather than the partial ones we now do.
In the present company the work of Chase and Simon fits
this mold best, expecially when you add to it the sim-
ulations of Simon and Gilmartin (1973). This theory,
embodied in the simulation, actually carries out the
experimental task, thus is fairly tight.

As I noted earlier, the attempts in some of the other papers to move toward a process model by giving a flow diagram (Cooper-Shepard and Klahr[2]) seem to me not to be tight enough. Too much is left unspecified and unconstrained. To make the comparison with Chase and Simon somewhat sharp, these flow diagrams are not sufficient to perform their tasks. That flow diagrams may leave something to be desired as a scheme for cumulating knowledge might be inferred from a comparison of Donald Broadbent's two books (1958 and 1971), both of which contain flow diagrams representing what is known (at each respective date) about short-term memory and the immediate processor.

In one important respect, however, the Chase and Simon (and Gilmartin) work is deficient for present purposes. It does not employ a psychologically relevant model of the control processes. I argued above (and I believe) that until one has a model of the control processes (along with a model of the memories and the primitive operations) we will not be able to bring the problem of specifying subjects' methods under control.

At the moment I know of only one model of the human control processes, that of production systems (Newell & Simon, 1972; Newell, 1972). These are a form of programming system that have proved useful in discussing complex cognitive tasks (such as the cryptarithmetic, logic and chess tasks treated in Newell and Simon, 1972). At one level they are like any programming language, providing a way of specifying a conditional sequence of primitive operations to be applied. However, in most work on simulation programs the control structure has been treated about as casually as it is in the flow diagrams declared above to be deficient (see for instance Johnson, 1964). The production systems, by a route that need not be recounted, have become tied in with a model of the structure of memory. They

---

[2]Excluding the material in Klahr's second paper (Chapter 11).

thus find themselves providing a detailed model of the control processes.

It is not my main purpose in these comments to extol the advantages of production systems. However, as noted they are the sole exemplars to my knowledge of human control processes (though they will surely not be the last). Since the notion of modeling the control and the benefits that accrue thereby in putting experimental results together is not familiar, it seems incumbent on me to provide an illustration. The attempt to do this, though it fits in this comment as a single paragraph, so to speak, is extensive enough to require an independent statement. This I have done in a companion article (Chapter 10). One should simply imagine it inserted in this essay at this point.

Let me summarize the results of that excursion *vis à vis* the present argument. It is possible to construct models of the detailed control structure coupled with equally detailed assumptions about memories and elementary processes. Within such a system the question of what method the subject employs in an experimental task can be investigated in the same fashion as discovering a program in a given programming language to perform a specified task. Just as with programming, several organizations may lead to adequate performance of the task. However, each method makes definite predictions as to time and space used, providing the basis for experimental operations to determine which method was actually operating.

There is an immense space of possible control organization and each provides a scheme within which almost any method can be programmed. Thus, the problem of determining what control system is used by the human is analogous to determining what machine language is used by a computer, given that you can never see any written code, but only the outputs of running programs. However, each control organization has different detail of encoding, processing time, and memory load. They provide a basis for identifying the system experimentally if a sufficiently large and diverse set of tasks is analysed.

Analyze a Complex Task

The second experimental strategy, or paradigm, to help overcome the difficulties enumerated earlier is to accept a single complex task and do all of it. The current experimental style is to design specific small experiments to attempt to settle specific small questions--often as not, as I've said, dictated by the empirical exploration of a new phenomenon or by one of the polar issues. Whenever a coordinated series of experiments is created, it is usually phenomenon driven, e.g., one thinks of the sequences by Underwood and colleagues on verbal learning. The effect of this is to keep each experiment a thing-in-itself--disparate enough to guarantee the sort of loose jointed fabric I've bemoaned.

An alternative is to focus a series of experimental and theoretical studies around a single complex task, the aim being to demonstrate that one has a sufficient theory of a genuine slab of human behavior. All of the studies would be designed to fit together and add up to a total picture in detail. Such a paradigm is best described by illustration. Unfortunately, I know of no single example which successfully shows this scheme at work. I attribute this not to its difficulty but to its not really having been tried. However, let me give several partial examples.

The work of Dave Klahr provides, I believe, one example. The paper presented at this symposium is a component of a general attack on some problems of development. Initial work with a Piagetian set-inclusion task (Klahr & Wallace, 1970) led to a model that depended on quantification operators. There followed a paper (Klahr & Wallace, 1972) that attempted to construct a theory of quantification operators, to be used in pursuing the larger plan. The paper we heard here is a further subcomponent--the attempt to obtain some fresh data to solidify the models of quan-tification operators. Thus, the entire program of research is built to produce, ultimately, a complete model of the developmental set-inclusion task. I've

never explicitly asked Klahr about the strategy, but
it serves my purposes to interpret it so.

A second example is a thesis done awhile ago by
Donald Dansereau on mental multiplication (Dansereau,
1969). The goal was a theory of how people did tasks
such as 17 x 638 = ?, all in their heads. Dansereau
constructed an information processing model of the
process and simulated it to predict the results. That
model had half a dozen or more parameters: memory
transfer times, operation times, etc. The important
point, for our purposes, was that he estimated all
these parameters, not by fitting the simulation results
to the timing data, but by conducting a series of
independent micro-studies. Each of these studies was
built to supply one or more parameter values to be used
in the larger model. Thus, he forced a close coupling
between the entire set of experimental results.

A final example, clearly mostly prospect, would be
to take chess as the target super-task. We know already
from existing work that the task involves forms of
reasoning and search (de Groot, 1965; Newell & Simon,
1972; Wagner & Scurrah, 1972) and complex perceptual
and memorial processes (de Groot, 1966; Chase & Simon,
This volume, Chapter 5). From more general considerations we know that it also involves planning, evaluation, means-ends analysis, and redefinition of the
situation, as well as several varieties of learning--
short term, *post-hoc* analysis, preparatory analysis,
study from books, etc. Why should one not accept the
task of understanding thoroughly how chess is learned
and played and how this interacts with the general
capabilities brought to the game? To the query of why
pick chess, the response must be, Why not? Or pick
another. It doesn't matter much what task is picked as
long as we settle on a total complex task to force all
studies into intimate relation to each other. To the
point that there are lots of important mental activities
not well represented by chess, the answer must be that
no task is universal. What is important is to rise up
a couple of levels of integration over the disaggregated
scattering of tasks we now address. Concern with completeness can be saved for later iterations.

304

One Program for Many Tasks

The third alternative paradigm I have in mind is to stay with the diverse collection of small experimental tasks, as now, but to construct a single system to perform them all. This single system (this model of the human information processor) would have to take the instructions for each, as well as carry out the task. For it must truly be a single system in order to provide the integration that we seek.

The companion piece on productions systems (Newell, this volume, Chapter 10) in conjunction with Klahr's production system (Klahr, this volume, Chapter 11) indicates how such an endeavor might go. It is only a beginning, but it shows already a certain promise, it seems to me.

An alternative mold for such a task is to construct a single program that would take a standard intelligence test, say the WAIS or the Stanford-Binet. This is actually an enterprise that was called for much earlier (Green, 1964), but only recently has anything really stirred (Hunt, Frost, & Lunneborg, 1972).

Conclusion

My distressed and confused half has held the ascendency throughout this paper. I do not believe that it is just a commentator's ploy, though it emerged in the act of reviewing the papers of this symposium. It is certainly not a universal complaint I voice wherever occasion offers. Another half of my life is concerned with artificial intelligence, a part of computer science devoted to the construction of artifacts that do what mind can do--an enterprise not unrelated to the psychology of thought, though still distinct (Newell, 1970). There, despite the constant chorus of critics, whose universal complaint is that man and machine are of different categories, hence that progress is not possible in principle, and illusory at best, I feel that we have the ingredients of accumulation. Winograd's system (1972) is a genuine advance over the first natural language efforts. The robots do significantly better than they once did. Challengers keep showing up with programs that do all that their predecessors did and more besides.

Thus, I diagnose my concern as real. And I take seriously my call that we find some way to put it all together--even though this is voiced in an era when we have never been so successful experimentally and conceptually, and at a symposium where the papers exhibit so perfectly this success.

Maybe we are reaching the day of the theorist in psychology, much as it exists in other sciences such as physics. Then the task of putting things together falls to them, and experimentalists can proceed their own way. (That is not quite the way it works in physics, but no matter.) This does not seem to me our present case, but it could be.

Maybe we should cooperate in working on larger experimental wholes than we now do. My positive suggestions in the prior section were proposals of how to do that. They all have in common forcing enough detail and scope to tighten the inferential web that ties our experimental studies together. This is what I think would be good for the field.

Maybe we should all simply continue playing our collective game of 20 questions. Maybe all is well, as my other half assures me, and when we arrive in 1992 (the retirement date I pick might as well be my own) we will have homed in to the essential structure of the mind.

References

Atkinson, R. C., & Shiffrin, R. M. Human Memory: A proposed system and its control processes. In K. W. Spence & J. T. Spence (Eds.), *The psychology of learning and motivation: Advances in research and theory*. Vol. II. New York: Academic Press, 1968.

Broadbent, D. E. *Perception and communication*. New York: Pergamon, 1958.

Broadbent, D. E. *Decision and stress*. New York: Academic Press, 1971.

Clark, H. H., & Chase, W. G. On the process of comparing sentences against pictures. *Cognitive Psychology*, 1972, 3, 472-517.

Dansereau, D. An information processing model of mental multiplication. Unpublished doctoral dissertation, Carnegie-Mellon University, 1969.

de Groot, A. *Thought and choice in chess*. The Hague: Mouton, 1965.

de Groot, A. Perception and memory versus thought: some old ideas and recent findings. In B. Kleinmuntz (Ed.), *Problem solving*. New York: Wiley, 1966.

Green, B. F. Intelligence and computer simulation. *Transactions of the New York Academy of Sciences*, 1964, Ser. II, 27, 55-63.

Hubel, D. H., & Wiesel, T. N. Receptive fields, binocular interaction and functional architecture in the cat's visual cortex. *Journal of Physiology*, 1962, 160, 106-154.

Hunt, E., Frost, N., & Lunneborg, C. Individual differences in cognition. In G. Bower (Ed.), *Advances in learning and memory*, Vol. 7. New York: Academic Press, 1973.

Johnson, E. S. An information processing model of one kind of problem solving. *Psychological Monographs*, Whole No. 581, 1964.

Klahr, D., & Wallace, J. G. An information processing analysis of some Piagetian experimental tasks. *Cognitive Psychology*, 1970, 1, 358-387.

Klahr, D., & Wallace, J. G. Class inclusion processes. In S. Farnham-Diggory (Ed.), *Information processing in children*. New York: Academic Press, 1972.

Newell, A. Remarks on the relationship between artificial intelligence and cognitive psychology. In R. B. Banerji & M. D. Mesarovic (Eds.), *Theoretical approaches to non-numerical problem solving*. Berlin: Springer Verlag, 1970.

Newell, A. A theoretical exploration of mechanisms for coding the stimulus. In A. W. Melton & E. Martin (Eds.), *Coding processes in human memory*. Washington D. C.: Winston, 1972.

Newell, A., & Simon, H. A. An example of human chess playing in the light of chess playing programs. In N. Wiener & J. P. Schade (Eds.), *Progress in biocybernetics*, Vol. 2. Amsterdam: Elsevier, 1965.

Newell, A., & Simon, H. A. *Human problem solving*. Englewood Cliffs, N. J.: Prentice-Hall, 1972.

Simon, H. A., & Gilmartin, K. A simulation of memory for chess positions. *Cognitive Psychology*, 1973, in press.

Stark, L. *Neurological control systems*. New York: Plenum, 1968.

Wagner, D. A., & Scurrah, M. J. Some characteristics of human problem solving in chess. *Cognitive Psychology*, 1971, 2, 454–478.

Wingfield, A., & Byrnes, D. L. Decay of information in short-term memory. *Science*, 1972, 176, 690–691.

Winograd, T. Understanding natural language. *Cognitive Psychology*, 1972, 3, 1–191.

Acknowledgments

This work was supported by Public Health Service Research Grant MH-07722 from the National Institute of Mental Health.

PART II
VISUAL PROCESSES IN LINGUISTIC COMPREHENSION

ON THE MEETING OF SEMANTICS AND PERCEPTION

Herbert H. Clark, Patricia A. Carpenter,
and Marcel Adam Just**
Stanford University

Among the most important functions of language
is the communication of perceptual experience. Language affords each of us the ability to have a private
perceptual experience and then tell other people what
we have seen or heard. And because they know the same
language as we do, our audience can in some sense
"understand" this perceptual experience without actually going through it themselves. While this is
obviously an important linguistic capacity, we know
very little about the process by which people "transform" their perceptions into language, nor about the
processes by which people "transform" someone else's
description into an "understanding" of a perceptual
experience. Our goal in this paper is simply to suggest one plausible way of viewing this meeting of
language and perception. In doing so, we will attempt
a tentative formulation of the relation between certain linguistic and perceptual processes; review the
previous literature relevant to this formulation; and
offer new evidence in support of this point of view.
Obviously, our hope in this pursuit is not to present
the ultimate theory for the interface between meaning
and perception. Rather, we would like to define the
problem area itself, indicate some considerations
that must be faced up to in such a theory, and lay out
some phenomena that suggest that there are intriguing
psychological questions waiting to be answered.

In the present paper we take the view that perceptual events, like linguistic events, are interpreted when they are processed. That is, when we perceive objects and events, we do not merely store them

*Now at Carnegie-Mellon University

as visual or auditory entities, but rather we ultimately interpret them semantically and store these interpretations. The formation of such interpretations depends on a number of conditions. Someone else's description might induce us to interpret objects or events in one way rather than another, or some other previous context might bias our interpretation. But in the absence of such prior influences, we have some very general rules for interpreting our perceptions. These rules, we will argue, are a reflection of certain perceptual constancies and therefore constitute the most efficient and informative procedure for coding perceptual events.

As a working hypothesis, we further assume that such interpretations of perceptual events consist of amalgams of abstract, elementary propositions--i.e., functions with one or more arguments. This assumption is not new, but has evolved from previous work carried out by William Chase and the first author (Chase & Clark, 1971, 1972; Clark, 1970, 1971, 1972; Clark & Chase, 1972) and by the second and third authors (Carpenter & Just, 1972; Just & Carpenter, 1971). In the Chase and Clark work, there was evidence that people had to code a picture of an A above a B as something like (*A above B*) or (*B below A*) before they were able to use the picture as evidence for the truth or falsity of a sentence like *A is above B*.[1] The argument for this conclusion was straightforward. To compare a sentence against a picture, people must at some stage represent the sentence and picture in a compatible mental format. Since it is the interpretation, not the direct perceptual characteristics, of the picture that is the basis for verification, it is the interpretation that must be coded and compared against the sentence. The results of the Clark and Chase experiments were consistent with this model and also enabled Clark and Chase to rule out at least several plausible alternative candidates for this common format--for example,

---

[1]For convenience, we will denote the abstract interpretations given pictures by use of abbreviated propositions placed within parentheses, as in (*A above B*).

certain types of mental images. In the present paper,
we will continue to assume that perceptual events are
coded in an abstract, propositional format and will
add weight to this assumption with the new evidence we
will present.

Most, and perhaps even all, perceptual events can
be coded, or interpreted, in many different ways. There
are a number of obvious examples. The best known, perhaps, is the Necker cube, which is seen sometimes with
one vertex nearest the onlooker, sometimes with another.
This ambiguity occurs despite the fact that the same
pattern of contours, lines, and angles strikes the eye
under both interpretations. That is, although the
stimulus itself does not change, the interpretation
given that pattern does. Other examples include
Wittgenstein's "rabbit-duck" drawing, which is seen
either as a duck going in one direction or as a rabbit
going in the other direction, the drawing used by Leeper
and Boring (see Hilgard, Atkinson, and Atkinson, 1971),
which is interpreted as either an old woman or a young
woman, and Rubin's famous vase-face figure-ground
illusion, which is seen either as a white vase against
a black background or as two face silhouettes looking
at each other against a white background. In all these
instances, the picture is the same for two very different interpretations. These examples are striking but
hardly atypical. It would seem impossible to find a
perceptual experience that could not be interpreted in
alternative ways. Such differences in interpretation,
of course, affect how the onlooker would describe the
perceptual experience at hand. If the observer interpreted the duck-rabbit ambiguous figure as a duck, he
would call it a duck, not a rabbit. That is, our
descriptions of perceptual events spring from our
interpretations of those experiences. The most basic
question, therefore, is why people interpret a particular perceptual experience in one way rather than
another under various circumstances.

Because we assume that alternative linguistic
descriptions of a perceptual event arise from alternative interpretations of that event, the structure

of English itself ought to reveal how such an event
might be variously coded. Indeed, in the course of
this paper, we will examine four types of English
constructions commonly used in describing perceptual
events and examine what they imply about our perceptual codings. The first construction is the negative.
Shown a picture of a woman, we could say either "That
is a woman" in a positive form or "That's not a man"
in a negative form. Negation is a regular device all
languages have for expressing alternative interpretations of a perceptual event. The next construction is
the locative--an expression that contains a spatial
preposition. Such prepositions often come in pairs,
allowing us to describe the same event in two ways:
A is above B and *B is below A*; *A is over B* and *B is
under A*; *A is in front of B* and *B is in back of A*;
A is ahead of B and *B is behind A*; and so on. Although
each pair of descriptions can often refer to the same
event, we will argue that they derive from quite different interpretations of that event. The next construction is the comparative, which also comes in pairs:
for example, *A is higher than B* and *B is lower than A*;
A is deeper than B and *B is shallower than A*; and
A is longer than B and *B is shorter than A*. Like the
locatives, these alternative expressions for the same
perceptual event can be shown to be based on different
interpretations of that event. The final construction
we will look at is the dimensional term and its deriva-
tives, words like *length, depth, height, width,* and
their kin. These terms also enable us to express
different interpretations of the same physical dimension. The long dimension of a garage or box, for
example, can be called its length or its depth, depending on how one views the garage or box. Similarly, one
box below another can be said to be *lower* under certain
conditions, but *deeper* under others. Thus, we will
discuss some of the linguistic properties of these
alternative expressions, suggest how they might arise
from different interpretations of a perceptual event,
and then examine critical psychological evidence relevant to this view.

Our conception of the interface between language and perception could potentially apply to an enormous number of psychological phenomena. To keep from being overwhelmed, we will confine ourselves to a relatively tractable type of task in which people are given sentences and pictures and are required to judge whether the sentence is true or false of the picture or are required to answer questions about the picture. The subject in this task is typically timed as he makes his response, and it is this response latency that is of interest. Properly designed, these tasks make it possible to infer the *form* of the subject's perceptual codings. The basic idea is that some forms of the codes lead to the prediction that response latencies should be long and other forms to the opposite prediction. In this manner, we can explore a wide range of perceptual phenomena, discovering how they are coded in various contexts.

Three Hypotheses

We now turn to three general hypotheses we wish to explore with respect to negatives, locatives, comparatives, and dimensional terms. The utility of these hypotheses is not so much that they make specific predictions about perceptual coding, but rather that they serve as schemata for organizing a number of old and new facts about the relation between linguistic descriptions and perceptual events. For convenience, we will state these hypotheses using the terms "sentence" and "picture" in place of the more general locutions "linguistic description" and "perceptual event," respectively. These terms are used only as a shorthand, for we do not mean to imply that these hypotheses should necessarily apply only to single sentences or only to visual perception, even though this is where most of the empirical evidence will be found.

Hypothesis A: People prefer certain codings or interpretations of a picture to others;

315

these preferences arise from a tightly organized *a priori* conception of perceptual space
that appears to be common to humans regardless
of their language.

This hypothesis, perhaps the most basic of the
three, derives from the notion that humans view the
world in terms of a particular framework, and that this
framework comes about because people live in a world
with gravity and a horizontal ground-level, have eyes
in front of their heads, walk in a characteristic
direction, and so on. The particular properties of
this perceptual space have been spelled in more detail
previously (Clark, in press) and have been shown to be
consistent with certain fundamental linguistic characteristics of the spatial and temporal terms found in
English. For example, our perceptual space contains
the dimension of verticality, and this is the same
dimension that is expressed in such terms as *high*,
low, *tall*, *short*, *above*, and *below*. But, in addition,
the asymmetry in verticality found in our perceptual
space is also present in these spatial terms such that
one type of expression (e.g., *A is above B*) is preferred to its alternative (here, *B is below A*). These
and other similar consequences will be examined for the
four types of contructions.

> *Hypothesis B*: If a sentence describing a
> picture is presented prior to the picture,
> that sentence will normally determine the
> initial coding, or interpretation, of that
> picture.

This hypothesis merely makes explicit what we all
assume must happen in the normal case where there are
two plausible alternative codings of a picture. If we
tell someone, "I am going to show you a picture of a
rabbit," and then present him with the rabbit-duck
ambiguous figure, we would expect him to interpret the
picture as a rabbit, not a duck, on first inspection.
Obvious though this hypothesis is, it has certain
interesting consequences in sentence verification tasks.

Hypothesis C: Under certain conditions, the perceptual properties intrinsic to a picture will determine its coding, or interpretation, even when a sentence with a conflicting interpretation is presented prior to that picture.

This hypothesis posits that there will be exceptions to Hypothesis B that arise from extremely potent perceptual characteristics of the picture. We will give examples of pictures that can be coded in alternative ways, but appear to have such strong perceptual characteristics that one of the alternatives is extremely difficult to choose, even when the alternative is "primed" beforehand. Not surprisingly, these inflexible interpretations of a picture will enable us to draw some rather interesting conclusions about the process of perceptual coding.

These three hypotheses can be nicely illustrated with three constructions that have been widely studied in English: negatives, locatives, and comparatives. We will review the pertinent evidence (some of it new) for each of these constructions before turning to our own experiments on dimensional terms.

Negatives

Evidence for Hypothesis A

As a general rule, we code pictures in positive terms. When we look at a picture of an apple, for instance, we think of it in terms of what it is--an apple--not in terms of what it is not--an orange, a United States senator, a beach ball, an Indian pony, or a tuba. The reason seems clear. A positive code is a concise and informative designation, whereas normally there are many possible negative codes, each of which contains very little information. According to Hypothesis A, there should be a normal means for coding a picture on the positive-negative dimension. The rule we might propose is as follows:

Rule 1: People normally code pictures in positive terms.

This rule should apply at least whenever the picture being coded appears before a sentence that is meant to describe it. That this is the case has been nicely demonstrated in a verification task reported by Trabasso, Rollins, and Shaughnessy (1971). In their Experiment IX, they presented subjects with a picture (an orange or green color patch) followed by a sentence (a positive or negative description of the color patch) and then required the subjects to say whether the description was true or false of the picture as quickly as possible. The. measure of interest was the latency of the true-false judgments. To take a specific example, the orange patch in their experiment could be followed by one of the following four sentences.[2]

1. True Affirmative (TA): The patch is orange.
2. False Affirmative (FA): The patch is green.
3. True Negative (TN): The patch isn't green.
4. False Negative (FN): The patch isn't orange.

According to Rule 1, we assume, along with Trabasso *et al.*, that the orange patch is coded in a positive form, say as (*patch is orange*). Also, we assume that when the picture code matches the sentence code in the color name (*green* or *orange*), then response latencies ought to be shorter; and when the picture code matches the sentence code in polarity (positive or negative), then response latencies ought to be shorter by an independent amount. According to these two assumptions, TA should be faster than FA, and FN faster than TN, because only TA and FN match the picture code in the color term (here, *orange*); also Affirmatives should be faster than Negatives, since the former match the picture code in polarity. These predictions are

---

[2]Trabasso *et al.* actually used abbreviated forms of these sentences (e.g., *kov green*, which means "The patch isn't green").

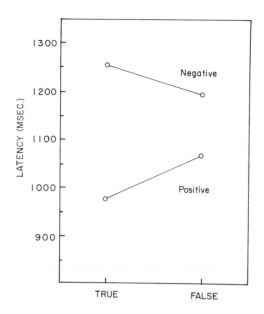

Fig. 1. Latencies to verify affirmative and negative sentences as true or false. Data from Trabasso, Rollins, and Shaughnessy (1971).

borne out in Trabasso *et al*.'s response latencies, shown in Figure 1. Thus, their evidence is consistent with Rule 1, that pictures are normally coded in a positive form.[3]

Rule 1, however, contains the word "normally," indicating that it is not necessarily the case that a picture will be coded in a positive form. To find a case of negative coding, however, one has to look hard for relatively contrived pictures. Consider, for example, the two pictures in (5):

---

[3]This result is also consistent with the findings of other studies, including Clark and Chase (1972) and Just and Carpenter (1971).

319

(5)　　a. 　b.

When told that (5a) illustrates the presence of a hole, and (5b) its absence, one finds it very difficult to code in anything but a negative form. Under these circumstances, (5a) would be coded as, say (*hole present*) and (5b), as (*false* (*hole present*)). This latter code consists of a positive proposition (*hole present*) that is negated by an embedding second proposition, represented here as (*false* ()); that is, (*false* (*hole present*)) represents the more complex negative coding (see Clark, 1970, 1971, 1972; Clark & Chase, 1972; Just & Carpenter, 1971, for discussion of this type of coding). Normally, of course, (5a) would be coded as something akin to the linguistic description "square with a circle inside" and (5b) as something akin to "square." It is only when the viewer knows that (5b) is meant to depict the absence of a hole that he will code it in an implicitly negative form reflecting that it is a "square without a hole," which we have represented as (*false* (*hole present*)).

To demonstrate just such a negative code for pictures, Clark (unpublished) gave subjects a picture followed by a sentence and required them to make true-false judgments of the sentence as quickly as possible, while they were timed. The sentence-picture combinations were of two kinds. In the first, the sentences included *The plus/star is present/absent*, and these were paired with pictures of either a plus (+) or a star (*). Since *present* is positive and *absent* a type of negative, the sentences were one of the four types-- TA, FA, TN, and FN. It was assumed in this case that the pictures would both be coded in positive form, and so the four sentence types were expected to form a pattern just like Trabasso *et al.*'s sentences. The second type of sentence-picture combination consisted of *The hole is present/absent* paired with either one of the two pictures in (5). When paired with these particular pictures, these sentences also form TA, FA,

TN, and FN sentences, as shown in Table 1. Now, if (5a) and (5b) are coded in positive and negative forms, respectively, then the pattern for these sentences should be quite different. The four sentences, their presumed underlying codes, and the picture codes are all shown in Table 1, and they lead to rather simple predictions. Note that the only discrepancy possible between the sentence and picture codes is polarity-- the embedding negative (*false* ())--and this occurs only for FA and FN. Thus, TA should be faster than FA, and TN faster than FN, independently of any difference between Affirmative and Negative sentences. Indeed, the results, shown in Fig. 2, bear out the predictions for both groups of sentences. The *star/plus* sentences, shown on the left, pattern like the color-patch in Fig. 1, just as expected. But in the pattern on the right for the *hole* sentences, TN is faster than FN, quite unlike the *star/plus* pattern, but exactly as predicted under the assumption of a negative representation for picture (5b).

One might suppose, however, that picture (5b) was coded as a negative because it did not contain the circle in its physical representation, and not because it was "interpreted" as the absence of the hole. To check out this possibility, Clark ran a second group of subjects using the same two pictures in (5) followed by the sentences *The lid is present/absent*. In this instance, the subjects were to interpret picture (5b)

Table 1. Sentences, Pictures, Sentence Codes, and Picture Codes for Verification task by Clark (Unpublished)

	Sentence	Picture	Sentence Code	Picture Code
TA:	The hole is present.	▢o	(hole present)	(hole present)
FA:	The hole is present.	▢	(hole present)	(false (hole present))
TN:	The hole is absent.	▢	(false (hole present))	(false (hole present))
FN:	The hole is absent.	▢o	(false (hole present))	(hole present)

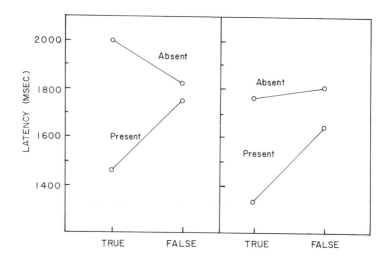

Fig. 2. Latencies to verify *The star is present/absent* as true or false (on the left) and to verify *The hole is present/absent* as true or false (on the right). Data from Clark (unpublished).

as the presence of a lid, and picture (5a) as its absence. Thus, the *presence* of the circle was to be "interpreted" as the absence of the lid. Significantly, these sentences yielded the same pattern as the *hole* sentences, with the TN taking less time than the FN in accordance with the assumption that it is (5a) now that is coded as a negative. Thus, these results are consistent with the hypothesis that pictures can, under special circumstances, be interpreted in a negative form, even though they would normally be coded in a positive form.

Evidence for Hypothesis B

According to Hypothesis B, we should be able to show that a sentence presented before the picture it describes can in some instances influence how that picture is coded. Such an influence has been demonstrated with negatives in a series of experiments on sentence verification by Just and Carpenter (1971, 1972). Their demonstration relied on the fact that in English there are a number of alternative ways of describing a picture that contains, say, 14 black dots and only two red dots. Four of these alternatives are shown in (6) and (7):

(6)   a. A majority of the dots are black.
       b. A minority of the dots are red.

(7)   a. Many of the dots are black.
       b. Few of the dots are red.

Linguistically, there are several fundamental differences among these sentences. Sentence (6a), with *majority*, asserts that the larger group of dots are colored black, while sentence (6b), with *minority*, asserts that the smaller group of dots are colored red. Sentence (7a), with *many*, asserts that the larger subset of dots is colored black, and in this sense, it is similar to sentence (6a). Sentence (7b) with *few*, is the odd one. Instead of asserting something positive about the smaller subset as (6b) does, (7b) denies that the larger subset is red. Its function as a denial comes from the fact that *few* is an explicit negative, with syntactic properties like *not*, *never*, and the other elements normally considered to be negative (see Klima, 1964); none of the other quantifiers--*many*, *majority*, or *minority*--has this property. The important linguistic fact, then, is that even though (6b) and (7b) both make reference to the color of the smaller subset in the picture, their meaning is quite different: *few* refers to the larger subset and says what it is not, while *minority* refers to the smaller subset and says what it is.

    Just and Carpenter (1971) argued that if *few* and *minority* differ in this way linguistically, they ought to induce a person to code a picture that follows in different ways. In particular, the *minority* sentence (6b) should induce a person to code a picture in terms of the smaller subset, whereas the *few* sentence (7b), since it refers to the larger subset, should induce a person to code the picture in terms of the larger subset. To demonstrate this, subjects were given sentences like those in (6) and (7) followed by a picture and were asked to say whether the sentence was true or false of the picture as quickly as possible. Again, latency was the measure of interest.

The predictions in this experiment come about roughly as follows. Consider the *many* and *few* sentences in (8), which are followed by the picture code they are assumed to induce for a picture containing 14 black dots and 2 red ones:

> (8) a. TA: Many are black.
>   (larger subset is black)
>   b. FA: Many are red.
>   (larger subset is black)
>   c. TN: Few are red.
>   (larger subset is black)
>   d. FN: Few are black.
>   (larger subset is black)

According to Just and Carpenter's proposal, all four sentences induce the subject to code the picture in terms of the larger subset of dots. In accordance with the logic used with the Trabasso *et al.* and Clark examples discussed previously, sentences are easier to verify when the color in the predicate (*red* or *black*) is the same in the sentence and picture codes. Thus, for the affirmative sentences, TA should be faster than FA, but for negatives, FN should be faster than TN. This is just what Just and Carpenter found for *many* and *few*, as shown in Fig. 3. But consider the *majority* and *minority* sentences in (9), again followed by the picture code they are assumed to induce for a picture of 14 black dots and 2 red ones:

> (9) a. TA: Majority are black.
>   (larger subset is black)
>   b. FA: Majority are red.
>   (larger subset is black)

    c. TN: Minority are red.
           (smaller subset is red)
    d. FN: Minority are black.
           (smaller subset is red)

The difference here is that when the sentence contains
minority, the subject is assumed to code the *smaller*
subset of dots, as we argued above. It is just this
difference in picture coding that leads to a change in
predicted latencies. According to the same logic as
before, TA should be faster than FA, as with the *many*
sentences, but here, TN should be faster, not slower,
than FN, exactly contrary to the prediction for the
few sentences. These predictions were borne out in the
results, which are also shown in Fig. 3.
    In several additional experiments, Just and
Carpenter were able to demonstrate this difference in
picture coding in several different ways, thereby secur-
ing their explanation for this particular pattern of

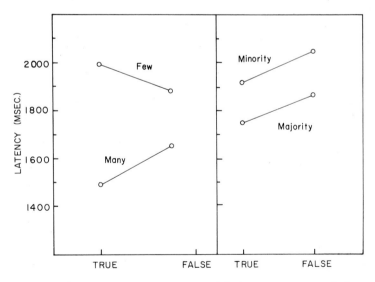

Fig. 3. Latencies to verify sentences with
unmarked affirmative (*many*, *majority*), marked affirmative (*minority*), or implicitly negative (*few*) quanti-
fiers as true or false. Data from Just and Carpenter
(1971).

latencies. In short, these results demonstrate that subtle differences in the type of negation in a sentence--here, *few* vs. *minority*--can lead to quite distinct codes for the same picture.

More recently, Carpenter and Just (1972) have shown that not only do *minority* and *few* induce different picture codes, but they induce measurable differences in the way subjects scan the pictures. The technique in this case was to monitor the subject's eye-movements as he looked at a picture in order to verify a sentence he had just read. Carpenter and Just used the same sentences as before, examples of which are shown (in abbreviated form) in (8) and (9). In the previous experiment, subjects were assumed to code the picture in terms of its larger subset whenever the sentence contained *many*, *few*, or *majority*, but in terms of the smaller subset whenever the sentence contained *minority*. If this is so, argued Carpenter and Just, the subject ought to look at the larger subset first with *many*, *few*, and *majority*, but at the smaller subset first with *minority*. Their results upheld this prediction. The interesting contrast again is between sentences containing *few* and *minority*: although both make reference to the color of the smaller subset, the first induces the subject to look first at the larger subset--since it is a negative sentence about the larger subset--while the second induces the subject to look first at the smaller subset.

Evidence for Hypothesis C

According to this hypothesis, there should be cases where the perceptual properties of the picture determine its code even when a conflicting sentence describing it appears before the picture. The work on negatives, in fact, is for the most part completely consistent with this hypothesis. Rule 1--that pictures are coded positively--is apparently a very potent rule, applying when a negative sentence precedes the picture, too. Consider the *present/absent* experiment, presented above and in Fig. 2, in which the objects in the picture were either

326

a plus (+) or a star (*). In the experiment reported, the pictures were presented before the sentence. In a second experiment, this sequence was reversed, yet the results were approximately the same as in the picture-first experiment. To account for this similarity, one need only assume that subjects coded the plus and star positively even when the preceding sentence was a negative. When presented *The star is absent* followed by a plus (+), the subject would be assumed to code the picture as (*plus present*), not as (*false (star present)*). In fact, this explanation--that pictures are coded positively even when preceded by negative sentences--is consistent with the results of Clark & Chase (1972), Just & Carpenter (1971), and Trabasso *et al.* (1971) as well.

But just as the positive code seems mandatory for most pictures, so is a negative code mandatory for certain other pictures. The hole/lid sentences described previously, for example, were also used in a verification task in which the sentences were presented before the pictures. The results in this experiment, too, were approximately the same as in the picture-first experiment. This is consistent with the supposition that the absence of the hole was coded negatively, even when preceded by a positive sentence.

The role of negation in picture coding might, therefore, be summarized as follows. First, pictures are normally coded in positive terms, even when preceded by negative sentences. The single exception we have found to this rule is interesting. It appears to show that a person can be induced to code a picture negatively if he knows that the picture represents a negative situation--e.g., the absence of a hole. It is not too difficult to think of pictures that depict such situations, but they probably do not appear very often in real situations. Second, positive and negative sentences that refer to subsets of objects in a picture have been shown to induce different codings of that picture. For example, genuine negative sentences containing *few* tend to induce people to code the larger subset, while referentially equivalent sentences

containing *minority* tend to induce people to code the
smaller subset instead. It should be noted, however,
that in either case, the coded subset is represented
in a positive form, in agreement with Rule 1.

Locatives

Turning now to locatives (expressions with spatial
prepositions), we must begin to make use of an important
assumption underlying the present view of perceptual
coding, namely, that the general rules for coding perceptual events arise fundamentally from characteristics
of man's perceptual apparatus. This view, which has
been detailed and justified more thoroughly in Clark
(1971), takes the following form. Man's perceptual
space is constrained in certain quite specific ways.
The space has a vertical dimension determined by gravity
and a reference plane at ground level, both of which are
independent of the perceiver. The perceiver himself is
another invariant point of reference in his own perceptual space. Thus, objects can almost always be coded
with respect to vertical, ground level, and the perceiver. In addition, upwardness from ground level is
positive on the vertical dimension, and forwardness
from the perceiver is positive in the front-back dimension. These two claims derive from the fact that the
only visible, fully perceptible part of the perceptual
field is that quadrant of space in front of the perceiver and above ground level: man's perceptual apparatus is not geared to perceive objects behind him or
below ground level. Man's perceptual space is, therefore, a type of coordinate system: ground level is
the zero point on the vertical dimension, with up as
the positive direction; and man is the zero point on
the front-back dimension, with front as the positive
direction. These considerations suggest the following
extension of Rule 1:

Rule 2: People prefer to code the locations of
objects positively, where upwardness and forwardness are positive directions.

328

But what does Rule 2 have to do with locative expressions? To answer this, we must look at one important property of locatives--the notion of reference point. In *A is above B*, the two nominals A and B do not serve equivalent functions (see Clark, 1971, 1972, in press). Linguistically, it can be shown that this sentence locates A with respect to B, where B is said to be a reference point. In this regard, *A is above B* differs from *B is below A*, where A is the reference point. Because of this asymmetry, one can speak of the directionality of a locative. *A is above B* locates A in an upward direction from B: it does *not* locate B in a downward direction from A. Combined with Rule 2, this suggests that people should prefer to represent one object above another in terms of the coding (*A above B*), not (*B below A*); and they should prefer to represent one object in front of another in terms of the coding (*A in front of B*), not (*B behind A*).

Evidence for Hypothesis A

Hypothesis A would therefore claim that, all other things being equal, people will code spatial locations according to Rule 2. This claim has been demonstrated very nicely in a series of experiments by Chase and Clark. In their most direct test, Clark and Chase (in preparation) simply asked subjects to describe a symmetrical picture of one object above another in a "single, simple sentence." Of the subjects who made reference at all to the vertical dimension (using expressions like *above, below, over, under,* and the like), 80% used *above* or its synonyms to describe the picture, but only 20% used *below* or its synonyms. Thus, Rule 2 accounts for the preferred descriptions in this experiment.

This relatively crude measure of preference, however, was corroborated in a verification task in which subjects were first shown a picture of one object above another and were then presented a sentence to judge as true or false (Chase & Clark, 1972; Clark & Chase, 1972). By Rule 2, a picture of an A above a B (where A and B are geometric figures) should normally be coded in a positive form, represented here as (*A above B*). Consider four of the sentences that could follow this picture, whose code is repeated at the right for each case:

(10)   a.   True Above: A is above B. (A above B)
         b.   False Above: B is above A. (A above B)
         c.   True Below: B is below A. (A above B)
         d.   False Below: A is below B. (A above B)

The picture code (*A above B*) is directly congruent with the True Above sentence (10a), but not with the True Below sentence (10c). Thus, True Above should be easier to verify than True Below. The picture code (*A above B*) however, is not congruent with either of the false sentences: while it has only the same preposition as the False Above (10b) sentence, it has only the same subject as the False Below sentence (10d). Crudely speaking, then, we should expect the difference in verification times between True Above and True Below to be considerable, but the difference between False Above and False Below to be much smaller. Indeed, this is the case, as shown in the left-hand side of Fig. 4. To demonstrate further that the picture is coded as (*A above B*), Chase and Clark carried out converging experiments. In one verification experiment, subjects were asked to "attend" to the top or bottom figure in coding the picture (before reading the sentence to be verified). When subjects attended to the top and presumably coded the picture as (*A above B*), the result was like that in the left-hand side of Fig. 4; however, when they attended to the bottom and presumably coded the picture as (*B below A*), the result was very different and consistent with a coding using *below*.

Underlying Rule 2 is the idea that upwardness and forwardness are positive directions in man's naturally occurring perceptual space because the ground level and the perceiver himself constitute two prominent and invariant reference points in this space and because up and forward are the perceptible directions from these reference points. In any particular scene, however, there could be a particularly prominent object or surface which would define a new reference point overriding these prior conditions. Positive would then be taken as the direction away from that reference point. Thus, with no real change in conceptualization, Rule 2 could be extended to Rule 3 for pictures that contain such overriding reference points:

> Rule 3: If one of two objects in a picture is perceptually prominent, then it will normally serve as a reference point, and the other object will be coded with respect to it.

This rule expresses the fact that it seems normal to describe a socket as above or below a blackboard, but odd to describe the blackboard as above or below the socket. The blackboard is somehow more "perceptually prominent"--an expression left undefined here--and would

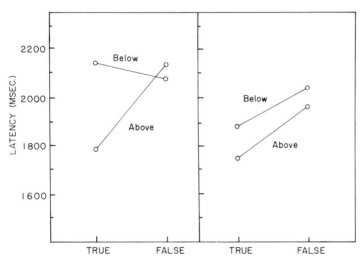

Fig. 4. Latencies to verify A *is above* B and B *is below* A as true or false when the subject attended to the picture first (on the left) or to the sentence first (on the right). Data from Clark and Chase (1972).

normally be taken to be the reference point. The less
prominent socket is therefore described with respect to
it in sentences like *The socket is above the blackboard.*

Clark and Chase (in preparation) examined this rule
with respect to the two pictures shown in (11):

(11) a. _____*_____   b. _____
                                          *

Since the line in (11) is perceptually prominent, Clark
and Chase assumed that the picture code should be
(*star above line*) for (11a) and (*star below line*) for
(11b). To test this directly, they again asked subjects
to describe the pictures with simple sentences. Of
those subjects using vertical terms, 89% used *above* for
(11a), while 69% used *below* for (11b). So it appears
that there is the expected preference based on Rule 3,
even though there is another superimposed preference
(61% to 39%) to use *above* for both pictures, consistent
with Rule 2. In further verification experiments,
Clark and Chase found that (11a) and (11b) were indeed
coded according to Rule 3 by many subjects, but were
coded according to Rule 2 (invariably using codes containing *above*) by other subjects; no subject invariably
used a picture code containing *below*. These experiments
then, demonstrate the validity of Rules 2 and 3, at
least in these restricted contexts.

Evidence for Hypothesis B

According to Hypothesis B, a prior sentence can
guide the perceiver into coding the picture one way
rather than another. This is nicely demonstrated in
an experiment by Chase and Clark on locative sentences
containing *above* and *below*. In that experiment, the
subjects read the sentence to be verified before looking
at a picture of an A above a B (where A and B were
alternative geometric forms). Since the sentences came
first in the sequence, they could clearly influence how
subjects coded the picture--say, as (*A above B*) or as
(*B below A*). One form this inducement could take is to

lead the subject to code the picture as (A *above* B) whenever the sentence contained *above*, but as (B *below* A) whenever the sentence contained *below*. Under this arrangement, the four positive sentences and their presumed picture codes would be as follows:

(12)   a. True Above: A is above B.   (A above B)
       b. False Above: B is above A.   (A above B)
       c. True Below: B is below A.   (B below A)
       d. False Below: A is below B.   (B below A)

Note that if these were the codes used, then True Above (12a) should be faster than False Above (12b), since in the latter case the sentence and picture codes are incongruent; furthermore, True Below (12c) should be faster than False Below (12d) by about the same amount, since the same form of incongruence holds for False Below as for False Above. These predictions were confirmed by the results of Chase and Clark, which are shown in the right-hand side of Fig. 4. In addition, this figure shows how the sentence-first task just considered yields quite a different pattern of latencies from the picture-first task considered earlier, in accordance with Hypothesis B.

Interestingly enough, this contingent coding scheme --where the code of the picture is contingent on which sentence preceded it--can be quite powerful. In another verification task using the asymmetrical pictures in (11), Clark and Chase (in preparation) asked subjects to read the sentences before viewing the pictures. In this case, too, the subjects were apparently strongly induced to code the picture as (A *above* B) when the sentence contained *above*, and as (B *below* A) when the sentence contained *below*. This happened even though in half of these cases, this coding would *not* be the preferred one according to Rule 3. That is, the inducement to code the pictures contingent on the sentences was apparently so powerful that it overrode the *a priori* coding preferences.

Evidence for Hypothesis C

Hypothesis C claims that certain perceptual situations are able to induce a particular coding regardless of what sentence preceded it. Evidence for this claim is found in an important series of experiments by Huttenlocher and by Bem on the difficulties children have in following instructions to place blocks into physical arrays (Bem, 1970; Huttenlocher, Eisenberg, & Strauss, 1968; Huttenlocher & Strauss, 1968; Huttenlocher & Weiner, 1971). In these experiments, the child is typically shown a ladder-like construction with a block on one of its middle rungs. The block, let us say, is colored red. Then the child is handed a blue block and is instructed, "Make it so that the blue block is on top of the red block." The child's task is to insert the blue block into the array in accordance with the description. The perceptual situation, however, could have been just the reverse for the child: the blue block could have been fixed and the red block mobile. Schematically, then, the task consists of a sentence (e.g., *A is above B*) and a perceptual situation in which (1) A is mobile and B is fixed, or (2) B is mobile and A is fixed. The results of these studies have been very consistent, showing that the instruction is easier to follow under situation (1) than situation (2).

These results constitute evidence for Hypothesis C if we make certain obvious assumptions about how the child has coded these two perceptual situations. Consider situation (1), in which A is mobile and B is fixed. It seems natural to consider the fixed object (B) to be a reference point and the mobile object (A) something that is to be placed with respect to B. The child is therefore induced to code this event in a semantic form corresponding to "A is somewhere with respect to B." Note that this is congruent in its underlying form with the instruction *A is above B*; however, perceptual situation (2), coded as "B is somewhere with respect to A," is not. From our previous discussions of congruent codes, we should expect that situation (1) should be easier to handle than situation (2), and this is borne

334

out in all of the results. The suggestion is, then, that even when the instruction *A is above B* precedes situation (2), in which B is mobile and A is fixed, the child cannot readily code the situation with B as the reference point and A as the item to be located with respect to it: the perceptual properties are so "extreme" that they invariably induce the other coding. The same argument can be made for comparatives like *A is higher than B* based on a parallel set of experiments carried out on adults by Clark (1972).

Our discussion of locatives, then, revolves around the notion of reference point. First, man's perceptual apparatus defines two naturally occurring reference points--ground level and the perceiver himself--and these normally determine one's coding of a perceptual event. That is, the perceiver usually codes the location of objects positively with respect to these reference points, in accordance with Hypothesis A. But some pictures contain prominent or immobile objects which can be viewed as reference points themselves, and they can supersede the naturally occurring reference points in determining the codes for the locations of objects, in accordance with Hypothesis C. Finally, a previous sentence can influence which object in a picture will be chosen as the reference point, and this is in accordance with Hypothesis B. In every case, the perceptual code is an asymmetrical characterication of two objects: the code describes the location of one object, and in doing so, gives its relation with respect to the reference point.

Comparatives

Comparatives are in many respects like locatives. The comparative *A is taller than B* is like the locative *A is above B* in that it locates A with respect to B, and not vice versa, and in that it does this on a specific underlying dimension. But comparatives are of additional interest because of the tremendous variety of dimensions that can underlie such expressions. Indeed, two objects can be compared on any dimension for which there is an adjectival name in English, e.g., *larger, smaller, more gigantic, tinier, grosser, broader, steeper, more rectangular,* and so on. This makes it possible for people to conceptualize and express comparisons of the same two objects in a variety of ways. We will be concerned with three of the parameters that determine how a comparison will be conceptualized: (1) reference points (e.g., B in *A is taller than B*); (2) underlying dimensions (e.g., *height* in *A is taller than B*); and (3) the polarity of certain dimensions (e.g., *taller* versus *shorter*). More specifically, we will be interested in the properties of some spatial dimensions underlying comparatives and in what they tell us about the conceptual basis for our linguistic and perceptual codes.

Evidence for Hypothesis A

According to Hypothesis A, people prefer certain interpretations of pictures over others, and these preferences arise from a tightly organized *a priori* conception of man's perceptual space. Some particularly important properties of this conception are revealed in the most common spatial adjectives in English. Most of these adjectives come in pairs, like *high* and *low*, such that the second member of the pair is marked, or more complex, with respect to the first (see Bierwisch, 1967; Clark, 1969, 1971; Greenberg, 1966). As most commonly used, *high* and *low* are merely contrastive: *high* refers to distance above some standard height (as in *The fence is high*), and *low*, to distance below that standard (as in *The fence is low*). Nevertheless, *high* and *low* are asymmetrical in that *high* can also be used "normally" to denote the entire dimension of height with ground level as its zero point, whereas *low* cannot. In such expressions as *height, How high is the window?*, and *six feet high*, the adjective *high* simply denotes extension from the zero point upwards; the comparable expressions with *low*--i.e., *lowness, How low is the window?*, and the unacceptable *six feet low*--do not. Interestingly enough, the use of *high* as the name for the overall dimension is consistent with certain perceptual considerations. Note that the "contrastive" sense of *high* denotes distance in the positive direction (upwards) from standard height, or what we will call the "secondary" reference point, and *low* denotes distance in the negative direction. It is natural, then, for *high* to also denote distance in the same positive direction from zero, the "primary" reference point. The use of *low* instead would lead to inconsistent directions of measurement on the overall dimension and the *low* sub-dimension. This and other evidence demonstrates that *high* has two senses: the nominal sense denotes the overall scale, the dimension called *height*; and the contrastive sense denotes the upper portion of this scale, the sub-dimension we will call *highness*. In contrast, *low* has only a contrastive sense: it denotes the lower portion of the scale--the sub-dimension called *lowness*. The same asymmetry is also found in *tall-short*, *far-near*, *long-short*, *deep-shallow*, *wide-narrow*, *broad-narrow*, *thick-thin*, *large-small*, *big-little*, and *much-little*. In each case, the first member of the pair can also take on a nominal sense, denoting the entire underlying dimension.

These properties of spatial adjectives may arise because perceptual and linguistic codes both reflect constraints on man's perceptual apparatus. The main property of this apparatus is that it can perceive physical extent, and indeed, all of these pairs of adjectives indicate extent: in each case the overall dimension measures extend from a zero point outwards. But as we noted above, there are two main organizing dimensions in man's perceptual space: verticality, with ground level as its zero point; and horizontal distance, with the perceiver as its zero point. These two dimensions are realized in English as *height* (*high-low* and *tall-short*) and as *distance* (*far-near*) or *length* (*long-short*). That is, the two fundamental reference objects in man's perceptual space (ground level and the perceiver himself) commonly serve as the primary reference points, or zeroes, for several of the spatial adjectival dimensions in English (see Clark, in press).

To indicate underlying dimensions, comparative sentences make use of specific adjectives. The important point is that these adjectives indicate quite precisely what dimension is meant. For example, when one says *A is richer than B*, one is comparing A and B quite specifically as to how rich they are, not simply as to how much money they have or whatever. Thus, this comparative is not equivalent to *B is poorer than A*, in which one is comparing A and B instead as to how poor they are. One consequence of this is that the sentence *Rockefeller was richer than Carnegie* can be legitimately used to compare these two men as to how rich they were; but it sounds odd to compare multimillionaires such as Rockefeller and Carnegie as to how poor they were, as in *Carnegie was poorer than Rockefeller*, except in some ironic sense. For this reason, *A is richer than B* is said to presuppose that A and B lie on a scale of richness. The same point can be illustrated for any adjective one can choose: *more competent, braver, tinier, more gigantic, redder*, and so on. It therefore becomes critically important to spell out the properties of the adjectives in their non-comparative forms—*competent, brave, tiny, gigantic, red*, and so on—for these will tell us precisely what the underlying dimensions are.

Bearing this in mind, we can now specify the underlying dimensions for comparative constructions that contain the spatial adjectives we have just discussed. For example, *A is higher than B* can be used to compare A and B as to how high they are. Recall, however, that *high* has two uses—a nominal use (as in six feet *high*) and a contrastive use (as in *The balloon is high*). Since this is the case, *A is higher than B* could presuppose either (1) that A and B lie on the full dimension of height, or (2) that they lie on the sub-dimension of highness. It is an open question at present whether *higher* presupposes the first possibility, the second possibility, or both at various times. In any case, *high* indicates extent in a positive, upward direction from a reference point, and so *A is higher than B* locates A in a positive direction from B on the underlying dimension. On the other hand, *low* can only be used contrastively to denote extent in a downwards, negative direction from some arbitrary reference point (as in *The balloon is low*). So *B is lower than A* will always locate B in a negative direction from A on the *lowness* sub-dimension. Since this analysis quite clearly defines which directions are positive and which are negative, we can easily say how a preference for coding pictures positively (see Rule 1) would manifest itself in the domain of comparatives:

> Rule 4: People prefer to code perceptual comparisons in a positive form on the underlying dimension or sub-dimension.

This rule implies that the perceiver prefers to code comparisons of *height, length, width,* and so on in terms of the perceptual codes (*A higher B*), (*A longer B*), (*A wider B*), etc., rather than their "negative" converses (*B lower A*), (*B shorter A*), (*B narrower A*), etc.

Rule 4 was motivated by the consideration that overall dimensions like height, distance, length, and so on are directed. That is, they each indicate extension in a positive direction from a zero point. And it is this, we proposed, that leads to the linguistic marking in pairs like *high* and *low, long* and *short,* etc. Although this explanation is satisfactory at one level. it relates linguistic marking only to the physical properties of the overall dimensions. It does not relate linguistic marking to an actual perceptual process. It would be significant, then, if we could find more direct evidence that people *perceive* physical dimensions in an asymmetrical manner. This would give us a more fundamental reason for the fact that people conceive of physical dimensions like height and length as directed. Indeed, it would be best to demonstrate that people make use of perceptual strategies that take in the properties of physical dimensions asymmetrically.

A recent study by Parkman (1971) suggests just such a mechanism which might account for the asymmetry of physical dimensions. In that study, he asked subjects

to say as quickly as possible which of two digits was
larger, or smaller, while he timed them. As others had
found, reaction times decreased the greater the difference between the two digits. But Parkman noted an
important additional effect. Reaction time also
appeared to increase in a linear fashion with the size
of the lesser of the two digits. Thus, it took longer
to judge which was larger of the pair 3 and 7 than of
the pair 2 and 6. Surprisingly, however, there was no
corresponding correlation between reaction time and the
size of the *larger* of the two digits. From these data,
Parkman suggested the following very interesting model
for choosing the larger or smaller of two digits. The
subject is assumed to increment a comparison digit from
zero upwards first looking for 1's, then 2's, then 3's,
and so on. As soon as he finds one of the given two
digits to match the comparison digit, the subject marks
that digit--let us call it B--as the reference point
(in our terminology) and locates the second digit--
let us call it A--with respect to B in a code containing
the term *larger*, specifically, (*A larger B*). If the
question asked is *Which is larger?* he can immediately
answer it with A. But if the question is *Which is
smaller?*, then he must translate this code (*A larger B*)
into its converse (*B smaller A*) before he can derive
the answer B. This last operation implies that it should
take the subjects longer to answer *Which is smaller?*
than *Which is larger?*, a prediction confirmed in
Parkman's data.

Our interest in Parkman's model stems from his
important observations about the greater and lesser of
the two digits: reaction times vary with the lesser of
the two, but not with the greater. It was this criterion
that led him to posit that digits are "scanned" in a
positive direction from zero--not in some other way--
and that the lesser digit serves as a reference point
(in our terminology). If the same phenomenon could be
demonstrated in a purely perceptual domain, then we
could be even more certain of the role of scanning processes. Therefore, Gajdos and Clark (in preparation)
decided to repeat Parkman's study with different lengths

of lines in place of the digits. They found essentially
the same results as Parkman. Reaction times varied
somewhat with the difference between the two line
lengths; they also varied directly with the length of
the shorter line, but not with the length of the longer
line. One could therefore apply a similar model to
these data, supposing that line lengths are "scanned"
from zero length outward in a positive direction (with
longer scans taking longer time) and that the perceptual
code is invariably constructed in a positive form, i.e.,
(A longer B). If this model is correct—and obviously
further tests need to be made—then it provides a perceptual basis for a number of the linguistic phenomena
we have just discussed. First, this model postulates
that people scan a dimension outwards from the primary
reference point of that dimension to locate the proximal
object. The proximal object (say, B) then becomes a
secondary reference point, and the position of the other
object (say, A) is established with respect to this
secondary reference point. As research by Clark (1972)
has shown, it is easier to say where A is than where B
is whenever A is located relative to the reference
point B. For this reason, it should be easier to indicate the position of the object distal from the zero
point, since it is represented with the proximal object
as its reference point, as in (A longer B). Thus, it
should be easier to judge which is longer or larger than
which is shorter or smaller. This explanation could
perhaps be extended to account for the advantage of
unmarked over marked adjectives in a variety of other
situations too, as in deductive reasoning (Clark, 1969)
and sentence verification (Just & Carpenter, 1971).

Finally, there is other fairly direct evidence for
Rule 4, that people prefer to compare objects positively
on underlying dimensions. In part of a study by Flores
d'Arcais (1970), ten subjects were asked to describe
some simple pictures depicting the comparative lengths
of lines. Flores d'Arcais reports that the comparisons
they used always contained the unmarked adjective
longer. Less direct evidence is found in frequency
counts of words like longer, shorter, higher, lower,
etc. If positive codes are generally preferred, then

this should be reflected in the frequency counts, with *longer* more frequent than *shorter*, etc. The count by Kučera and Francis (1967) confirms this for all the adjectives considered above except those in which the same term (e.g., *smaller*) is the common opposite of two terms (*bigger* and *larger*), thereby raising its count relative to its positive counterparts.

Evidence for Hypothesis C

Hypothesis C states that perceptual properties intrinsic to a picture will sometimes determine the coding or interpretation given to the picture, even when a conflicting sentence has preceded this coding. The most complete set of experiments relevant to this issue has been carried out by Audley and Wallis (1964) and Wallis and Audley (1964) on comparative judgments of brightness and pitch. In the brightness experiments, the subject was shown a pair of lights on each trial and was asked to choose the brighter one (on one block of trials) or the darker one (on another block of trials). The subject was timed while he made this judgment. Audley and Wallis's interest was in the absolute intensity of the pair of lights. On half the trials, the two lights were very bright (while differing slightly in intensity), and on the other half, they were very dim. Audley and Wallis found what we will call the "congruity" effect. In general, it was relatively easier to choose the brighter of the two absolutely bright lights and the darker of the two absolutely dark lights. Audley and Wallis repeated this experiment under a number of conditions, and yet this basic result appeared again and again, although with slightly different concomitant findings.

These results can be accounted for quite directly by the present view of comparatives, their underlying dimensions, and picture coding. Consider the two pairs of lights (the bright pair and the dark pair) when viewed against a black background, as in one of Audley and Wallis's experiments. There appear to be two methods for coding these two pairs. First, both pairs could be

seen as falling on the brightness dimension, since the
black background serves as a primary reference point
(the zero point) for the judgment of intensity. If
this is so, Rule 4 implies that the two pairs should
be coded as follows:

(13)   a. Two bright lights: (A brighter B)
       b. Two dark lights: (C brighter D)

Second, the two pairs could nevertheless be seen as
lying on the two sub-dimensions brightness and darkness,
with the secondary reference point (separating the
absolutely bright lights from the absolutely dark lights)
falling half-way between the two pairs. Thus, the two
bright lights would be on the brightness sub-dimension,
and the two dark lights on the darkness sub-dimension.
If this were the case, then the following codes should
be used:

(14)   a. Two bright lights: (A brighter B)
       b. Two dark lights: (D darker C)

   Now consider the two questions *Which is brighter?*
and *Which is darker?* as presented in (15):

(15)   a. Which is brighter? (X brighter Y)
       b. Which is darker?   (X darker Y)

The subject's job is to compare the question asked,
say (15a), with his representation of the picture,
say (13a), make sure the adjectives match, and replace
X by the corresponding term in the picture representation (here, A), and respond with A. The question
Which is brighter? matches (13a) and (13b) directly,
so it should be relatively fast; *Which is darker?* does
not match either (13a) or (13b), so it should be relatively slow. Thus, if the subject is coding all stimuli
on the brightness dimension, *Which is brighter?* should
be faster than *Which is darker?* for both pairs. But if
the subject is using the coding scheme in (14), then by
the same logic *Which is brighter?* should be faster for

343

the pair of bright lights and *Which is darker?* for the
pair of dark lights. Audley and Wallis's results for
this experiment, shown on the left in Fig. 5, suggest
that subjects were using both schemes. *Which is
brighter?* was the easier question overall, and yet
there was a congruity effect as predicted by the second
coding scheme.

This analysis would be strengthened if subjects
could be induced to use the second coding scheme more
readily than the first, thereby reducing the overall
advantage of *Which is brighter?* over *Which is darker?*
while retaining the congruity effect. Fortunately,
Audley and Wallis repeated their experiment with a
background that was about half-way between the two
pairs in intensity. This arrangement would be expected
to emphasize the sub-dimensions (hence the second coding
scheme) and to deemphasize the overall brightness dimension (hence the first coding scheme). The results of

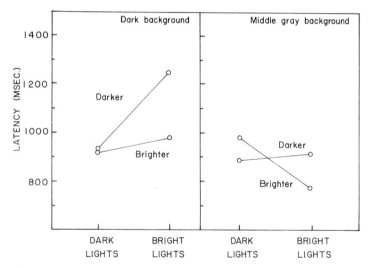

Fig. 5. Latencies to judge which of two very
bright or very dark lights was brighter, or which was
darker. For the latencies on the left the background
illumination was black; for those on the right it was
a middle gray. Data from Audley and Wallis (1964).

this experiment, shown in Fig. 5 on the right, are consistent with such an expectation. In this pattern of latencies, there is very little advantage of *Which is brighter?* over *Which is darker?* overall, but the congruity effect is still there. These two experiments, therefore, show (a) that subjects do code comparative judgments on what they perceive to be the underlying dimensions of the stimuli and (b) that the background illumination of the presented stimuli influences what subjects perceive as the underlying dimension.

Other experiments have confirmed Audley and Wallis's original findings in some detail. Wallis and Audley (1964) gave subjects pairs of tones, one tone right after the other. They showed that when the two tones were high in frequency, it was easier to answer *Which is higher?* than *Which is lower?* Conversely, when the two tones were low in frequency, the comparative difficulty of the two questions reversed, thereby yielding the congruity effect. More recently, Ellis (1972) gave subjects pictures of pairs of people and asked them to judge *Which is older?* or *Which is younger?* The pairs consisted either of two adults or of two children. Consistent with the congruity effect, Ellis found that it was easier to choose the older of the two adults but the younger of the two children. And Marks (1972) has demonstrated much the same effect on latencies when people are asked to judge the more or less likely of two likely or unlikely events. While the Wallis–Audley and Ellis experiments showed little overall advantage for the overall dimensions *higher* over *lower* for the tones and *older* over *younger* for the people, Marks showed a considerable overall advantage for *more likely* over *less likely*. At present, it is not clear under what conditions the subject makes use of the overall dimension and under what conditions he does not.

Evidence for Hypothesis B

Hypothesis B implies that there should be cases in which the previously seen sentence induces one particular coding of the picture over another. Just such

345

instances have been found in several experiments
carried out by Clark and by Flores d'Arcais. In the
experiment by Clark (unpublished), subjects were
required to verify sentences like *Blue is longer/shorter
than pink* against pictures of blue and pink lines. They
were asked to read the sentence, then look at the
picture (of one blue and one pink line, one longer than
the other, and one above the other), and indicate
whether the sentence was true or false of the picture,
all while timed. Assume that the presence of the sentence determines how the subject codes the picture.
One such contingent coding scheme for the four sentence
types is shown in (16), where the hypothesized code of a
picture of an A longer than a B is given to the right of
each sentence:

(16)   a. True Longer:
              A is longer than B.   (A longer B)
       b. False Longer:
              B is longer than A.   (B shorter A)
       c. True Shorter:
              B is shorter than A.   (B shorter A)
       d. False Shorter:
              A is shorter than B.   (A longer B)

Under this scheme, the picture is coded with the same
topic and reference point as the sentence; that is, if
the two terms in the sentence are A and B, respectively,
the subject looks for the A in the picture and codes it
with respect to the B as (*A longer B*). This causes the
True Longer and True Shorter sentences to be fully congruent with their picture codes, and the False Longer
and False Shorter sentences to be incongruent with their
picture codes; furthermore, the False Longer and False
Shorter sentences are incongruent with their picture
codes in exactly the same way. All this leads to the
prediction that True Longer should be faster than False
Longer, and that True Shorter should be faster than
False Shorter by approximately the same amount. This
prediction is borne out in the results in Fig. 6. The
two lines deviate from parallel by less than 1 msec.

One further piece of evidence favored this particular contingent coding scheme over alternative ones: the latencies were approximately 200 msec. faster (independent of the other latency differences) when the topic of the comparison (as opposed to the reference line) referred to the upper line in the picture. This fact suggests that subjects did scan the picture for the topic of comparison and that they did so from top down, taking less time when it was the upper line.

It *is* certain, however, that the pattern in Fig. 6 cannot be accounted for under a non-contingent coding scheme. Consider the one shown in (17):

(17) a. True Longer:
           A is longer than B.   (A longer B)
      b. False Longer:
           B is longer than A.   (A longer B)
      c. True Shorter:
           B is shorter than A.   (A longer B)
      d. False Shorter:
           A is shorter than B.   (A longer B)

Here it is assumed that Rule 4 holds and that the picture is invariably coded as (*A longer B*) regardless

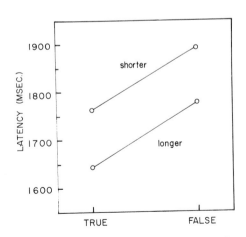

Fig. 6. Latencies to verify *A is longer/shorter than B* as true or false. Data from Clark (unpublished).

of the previous sentence. In this scheme, True Longer is fully congruent with the picture code, False Longer and False Shorter are partially congruent, and True Shorter is fully incongruent. This pattern of congruence would lead to a True-False by Longer-Shorter interaction, with True Longer the fastest sentence and True Shorter the slowest. Such an interaction, of course, did not occur. Other non-contingent coding schemes would lead to the same incorrect prediction. Thus, we are left with the contingent coding scheme in (16) as the best account for the results.

Flores d'Arcais (1966) has carried out a comparable set of experiments in Italian with much the same results. In one experiment, he read subjects sentences like *The policeman is less fat than the thief* and then, while timing them, showed them appropriate confirming or disconfirming pictures to which they were to respond true or false. In Italian, unlike English, comparatives always contain either *more* or *less* plus an adjective. Thus, Flores d'Arcais could examine *more* versus *less* on a number of common underlying dimensions. The pattern of latencies he found was precisely like those in the Clark experiment just described. True More was faster than False More, and in parallel, True Less was the same amount faster than False Less. This pattern therefore argues for a contingent scheme for coding the pictures (comparable to (16)). In another experiment, Flores d'Arcais (1970) repeated his first experiment but with physical dimensions such as size and length and came up with almost exactly the same results.

Both Clark's and Flores d'Arcais's results, however, raise an important question about the coding of perceptual comparisons. Recall that in the Parkman experiment, it was assumed that people invariably represented digits in terms of the code (*A larger B*). This was a non-contingent coding scheme in which people preferred to code the comparisons positively, as stated in Rule 4. But in Clark's and Flores d'Arcais's experiments, the conclusion was that people coded line lengths contingent on the sentence—sometimes as (*A longer B*) and sometimes as (*B shorter A*). Yet in both types of

348

experiments, the sentence preceded the picture. How could this apparent contradiction come about? One critical difference between the two experiments is that the former used questions such as *Which is larger?* or *Which is smaller?*, while the latter used full sentences such as *Pink is longer than blue*. Apparently, when the sentence contains an explicit topic or comparison term (the word *pink*) and an explicit reference point (the word *blue*), as in the latter sentence, the topic can then govern the strategy for searching the picture and constructing a perceptual code. But since the questions *Which is larger?* and *Which is smaller?* do not designate a topic or reference point, the perceiver has to rely on other strategies—e.g., Parkman's counting model—for coding the two objects comparatively. The same logic applies to the Audley and Wallis experiments, where the presence of questions—not sentences—led to the coding of the lights on what were perceived to be their underlying dimensions.

In summary, comparatives are like locatives in that both contain topics, reference points, and underlying dimensions. From the evidence we have examined, there appear to be four general strategies people use in coding the perceptual comparison of two objects. (1) Given a topic from previous context, the perceiver will search the picture for the topic and code the topic with respect to the reference point. The topic could be specified by the previous sentence (as in Clark's and Flores d'Arcais's experiments) or it could arise in other ways —for example, as the topic of conversation or as the focus of a question like *Where is the blue line?* (2) If the picture itself contains a prominent object, the perceiver will treat it as a reference point and code the other object with respect to it. We have examined instances in which an object was prominent on perceptual grounds—because it was large or immobile—but such prominence could also be based on conceptual grounds. For example, it seems preferable to code lesser known objects with respect to better known ones rather than vice versa; compare *Pacifica is smaller than San Francisco* to *San Francisco is larger than Pacifica*.

349

(3) If the picture contains an underlying dimension with a well defined secondary reference point (or standard) on it, then the perceiver may use the standard to specify two subdimensions and then code the two objects on their subdimension. This strategy is illustrated in the Audley and Wallis results. (4) In the absence of previous topics, prominent objects, and secondary reference points, the perceiver will fall back on his *a priori* conception of space, coding the two objects being compared on the underlying dimension of extent, preferring upwardness from the ground level and forwardness from himself as dimensions for coding. These four strategies seem to form an approximate hierarchy in that if (1) applies, it seems to take precedence over (2) and so on. At present, however, we cannot be sure of such an ordering, and indeed it seems plausible that the four factors considered separately (topic, perceptual prominence, secondary reference points, and *a priori* dimensions) could determine perceptual codes jointly rather than in an all-or-none fashion.

Spatial Adjectives

Adjectives that describe spatial relations are especially well suited for the study of the interface between linguistic and perceptual processes, for they illustrate how the same spatial relation can be conceptualized or interpreted in different ways. For example, two different adjectives may engender different interpretations of the same picture. This idea is the same as we surmised would happen with the rabbit-duck ambiguous figure: it would be interpreted as a duck when called a duck and as a rabbit when called a rabbit. The difficulty with the rabbit-duck figure, however, is that one cannot specify the conceptual difference between rabbits and ducks in any simple way. With spatial adjectives, on the other hand, one can often specify the differences in interpretation. For example, the spatial adjectives *tall*, *short*, *deep*, and *shallow* all may denote how extended an object is on a single vertical dimension from a particular reference point. They differ, however, in what is presupposed to be the direction in which this extent is to be measured: *tall-short* presupposes that the dimension is vertical and that measurement is upward from some reference point; *deep-shallow* presupposes that the dimension is the direction into some interior from its surface. These characterizations delimit what can be termed the "conditions of application" of the dimensional terms: certain conditions must be assumed to hold before the term can be applied to a particular picture. To put it in terms of the present hypothesis, the perceptual code must satisfy certain criteria before the linguistic term can be applied.

The experiments that follow were devised to determine how the conditions of application of a particular adjective enter into the process of making comparative judgments. The basic technique was to ask people to make comparative judgments about a variety of objects on several dimensions (e.g., *Which can is deeper?* *Which can is taller?*, etc.) and time them while they did so. In these experiments, we entertained two general hypotheses. The first was that the more explicitly a picture satisfied the conditions of application of a spatial adjective, the easier it would be to make a comparative judgment with respect to that adjective. To put it another way, given a particular perceptual event, it is easier to apply certain interpretations than others. The differences in such interpretations are those found in the conditions of application of various adjectives. By varying the pictures, then, we can manipulate the "fit" of the picture to the conditions of application of an adjective. The second hypothesis was concerned with "marking" of a pair of terms with otherwise identical conditions of application--*long-short*, *high-low*, and *deep-shallow*, for instance. The hypothesis states that it is easier to make judgments about greater extent (*longer*, *higher*, *deeper*) than about lesser extent (*shorter*, *lower*, *shallower*) in accord with the previous discussion of marking.

351

Height vs. Depth

Hypothesis B suggests that sentences influence picture coding. To see how spatial adjectives might do so, we followed the same procedure as before and required people to read a sentence before they look at a picture. In this case the sentence contained adjectives with differing conditions of application. The first experiments to be reported were concerned with the two pairs *tall-short* and *deep-shallow*, as they are applied to objects like, say, garbage cans.

Even though both *tall-short* and *deep-shallow* can be used to describe the vertical extent of a garbage can, they actually describe quite different dimensions, as is obvious once we spell out their different conditions of application. Note that *tall* and *short* require the objects they describe to be at least two-dimensional and the dimensions they denote to be either vertical or canonically vertical (that is, vertical when the object is in its normal position, e.g., a *tall* boy lying down). Furthermore, they require that vertical extent be measured upwards from some reference line or plane. To see this, picture a garbage can--and then make it taller. The height added to the garbage can was probably added to the top of the can, increasing it vertically upwards. All these considerations suggest the following rough characterization for the conditions of application of *tall-short:*

(18) tall-short:

     a. The object described must have at least two dimensions.
     b. The dimension measured must be vertical or canonically vertical.
     c. The reference line or plane is bottom-most.
     d. The extent measured is one-dimensional.

On the other hand, *deep* and *shallow* refer to the one-dimensional extent of an enclosed space, where that extent is measured from the surface or opening of that space. The direction to which *deep* and *shallow* refer is usually vertically downward (as in depth into a mine or well), but they may also refer to other directions, such as a horizontal direction into a forest or a drawer. Most often, the reference plane for *deep* and *shallow* is ground level, and the terms refer to extent in a downward direction from ground level. Thus, the conditions of application for *deep* and *shallow* might look something like this:

(19) deep-shallow:

    a. The object described must have three dimensions.
    b. The object described must have an interior space.
    c. The reference plane is the surface or an opening in that surface.
    d. The extent measured is one-dimensional.

A priori, it is difficult to say whether the conditions in (18) are more or less complex than those in (19), although on intuitive grounds, those in (19) for *deep-shallow* seem more complex. But we can find concrete evidence to back up our intuitions in certain linguistic properties of these terms. Note that there are two sets of terms--*tall-short* and *high-low*--for referring to upward vertical measurement. *Tall-short* refers to the vertical extent of an object, while *high-low* refers to the vertical position of an object. In contrast, there is only one set of terms for measurements into an interior space. *Deep-shallow* refers to the vertical extent, as we have just described, and *deep* (but not *shallow*) refers to vertical position-- as in *The submarine is deep (*shallow) in the ocean.* That is, measurement into an interior is a defective case in English because it is partially syncretized and is missing a term. According to Greenberg's (1966) criteria of complexity, that is an indication that *deep-shallow* is the linguistically more complex set of

terms in English. If our present thesis is true, and
linguistic properties do arise from perceptual codes
and reflect their properties, then it follows that
measurement into something is coded in a more complex
form than measurement up from a reference point.
Experiment I was designed in part to test this
hypothesis.

Experiment I. In this experiment, we asked subjects to answer the questions in (20) about the pair
of rectangles in (21):

(20) a. Which is taller?
      b. Which is shorter?
      c. Which is deeper?
      d. Which is shallower?

(21)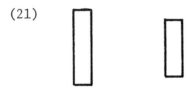

The two rectangles were actually 1 x 3 cm and 1 x 4 cm,
were about 4 cm apart, and were centered with respect
to each other about their horizontal midlines. The
subjects were told to think of the rectangles as side
views of garbage cans. We measured how long subjects
took in answering each question for this pair of
rectangles.
   The general procedure in this and the later experiments was as follows. The subject viewed the sentences
and pictures at 16 in. in a tachistoscope and responded
by pressing a left or right button on a response panel.
He started each trial by pressing a middle button.
Half a second later, the question (typed in elite type)
appeared in the top half of the field and remained on
for 1.5 sec. At that point the sentence disappeared,
the picture appeared in the bottom half of the field,
and a timer began. In the present experiment, for
example, the picture consisted of the two rectangles

in (21). The subject was required to answer the question by pressing the left button if the left rectangle was the correct answer, and the right button if the right rectangle was correct. The moment the response button was pressed, the picture disappeared and the timer stopped, thereby ending the trial. Typically, the subject was run for 16 practice trials and 160 experimental trials, where the experimental trials were broken down into ten blocks of 16 trials or five blocks of 32 trials. In the present experiment, for example, there were eight distinct displays (four questions and two responses), which were duplicated, making a set of 16 displays. The displays were presented in a shuffled order within each block, and there were ten experimental blocks. Care was always taken to balance everything-- the left-right position of the correct response, the order of various conditions, and so on. Finally, there were 12 subjects in this and most of the following experiments. For any one experiment they were either all volunteer or all paid Stanford University students, and they were recruited separately for each experiment.

In this first experiment we were interested in examining both whether there were differences in the initial comprehension of the four questions and whether there were differences in the coding of the rectangles contingent on the four questions. For this reason we ran two conditions. In the first, the rectangles were presented simultaneously with the question, and in the second they were presented 1.5 sec. after the question. In both conditions the subject was to read the sentence before looking at the rectangles, but in the first he could do this *ad libitum*. Timing was always from the onset of the picture. Thus, if the adjectives differ only in their linguistic encoding time, this difference should be present in the simultaneous condition but not the sequential condition; and if the rectangles are more difficult to code for depth than height, this should appear in both the simultaneous and sequential conditions. Indeed, we chose the 1.5 sec. since the subjects in the simultaneous condition were able to understand the adjectives, make a judgment, and respond in much less than 1.5 sec. Thus, 1.5 sec. is ample time to understand the adjectives completely. The two display intervals were given in an order that was counter-balanced both within and between subjects.

The results of this experiment were analyzed as follows, and this was typical of the following experiments, too. For each subject we calculated the mean latency of his 10 or fewer correct responses for each of 16 distinct conditions in the experiment (eight displays by two intervals). We then used these means (a) for calculating overall means by collapsing across subjects and the side of the response and (b) for doing an analysis of variance. The error rate was typically low--below 5%--so we did not analyze errors other than to note whether they were discrepant with the latencies, which they were not.

The overall mean latencies, shown in Fig. 7, indicate that it is faster to compare the rectangles in terms of height[4] (*taller* and *shorter*) than to compare the very same rectangles in terms of depth (*deeper* and *shallower*). *Taller-shorter* took 30 msec. less than

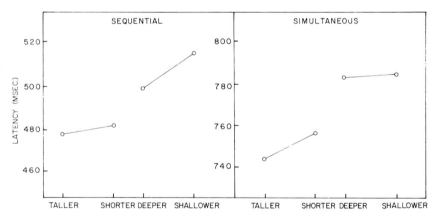

Fig. 7. Latencies to judge *Which is taller/shorter/deeper/shallower?* where there were 1.5 ("sequential") or 0 ("simultaneous") seconds between the appearance of the sentence and the displays.

---

[4]For convenience, we will use the word *height* in this section to refer to the entire *tall-short* dimension, not the *high-low* dimension.

356

deeper-shallower overall, $F(1, 11) = 17.17$, $p < .01$.
This difference was found in both the simultaneous and
sequential conditions, showing that the effect is not
due to linguistic encoding, but to picture coding or
the comparison process. In addition, the latencies at
both display intervals were consistent with the marking
hypothesis, which states that it would to be easier to
code a picture in terms of unmarked adjectives (*taller*,
deeper) than marked adjectives (*shorter*, *shallower*).
This difference was 9 msec. overall and just failed to
reach significance: $F(1, 11) = 4.69$. The difference
between unmarked and marked adjectives, however, was
considerably smaller here than in previous experiments,
where it was typically around 100 msec. In the previous experiments, the subjects were required to verify
statements as true or false or to answer questions from
information in the sentences (see, for example, Just
and Carpenter, 1971; Clark, 1972). Just how these
previous tasks differ from the present in their use of
unmarked and marked adjectives is not clear at this
time.

Somewhat surprisingly, the simultaneous and sequential conditions did not interact at all with any
variable. That is, this experiment showed no reading
or linguistic encoding difference among the four adjectives *taller*, *shorter*, *deeper*, and *shallower*.

What this experiment demonstrates is that how a
particular perceptual dimension is to be interpreted
affects how long it takes people to compare objects
along that dimension. Comparative judgments about the
vertical dimension of two rectangles took about 30 msec.
longer if the dimension was coded as depth than if it
was coded as height. Moreover, this difference is
attributable to the perceptual coding and comparison
processes rather than to the linguistic encoding of the
question. But the question is, where exactly does this
difference come from? What are the subjects doing
during those 30 msec? Our hypothesis is that they are
constructing an interpretation of the picture which
satisfies the conditions of application of the adjective. *Deep-shallow* may require construction of a

component of an interpretation that *tall-short* do not require. The problem is that the conditions of applications for height and depth (in (18) and (19)) differ in a number of ways, and the advantage of height over depth could be due to any one of them. One contrast between height and depth, for example, is that measurement is upwards from a reference line or plane for height, but downwards for depth. A second contrast is that the dimension measured is an exterior extension for for height, but an interior space for depth. These two contrasts were examined in Experiments II and III, respectively.

Experiment II. If height is measurement upward and depth measurement downward from a reference plane, then we should be able to construct pictures that emphasize these criteria in favor of height or in favor of depth. Consider the two pictures in (22):

(22) a.   b.

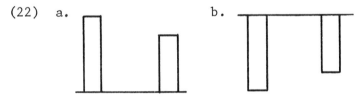

In (22a), the bottom edges of the two rectangles are colinear; this fact is further emphasized by the explicit line on which the two rectangles are resting. In contrast, (22b) has the tops of the two rectangles colinear so that they are both hanging, so to speak, from the same line. Since height denotes measurement upward, height should be easier to judge from the common reference line in (22a) than (22b); the reverse should hold for depth since it denotes measurement downward. In our present framework, it should be easier to code (22a) in terms of height and (22b) in terms of depth.

Experiment II was similar to the sequential condition in Experiment I. The subject was shown one of the four questions in (20) followed 1.5 sec. later by either (22a) or (22b)--or the same pictures with left and right reversed. The rectangles were of the same dimensions as those in Experiment I; the only differenc

was in their placement and the extra reference line.
Again, reaction times were measured from the onset of
the picture to the response.

The mean latencies, shown in Fig. 8, largely bear
out our expectations. To begin with, *taller-shorter*
was still faster than *deeper-shallower* overall, this
time by 25 msec., $F(1,11) = 5.98$, $p < .05$. But this
factor interacted with the position of the reference
line, just as expected, $F(1,11) = 5.21$, $p < .05$. The
interaction took a particular form. While there was
no difference between the two types of pictures for
depth judgments, there was a consistent one for height
judgments: height was easier to judge when the explicit
reference line was at the bottom than when it was at the
top, as expected. And again, the unmarked adjectives
took less time than the marked adjectives, by 16 msec.,
although this was not significant $F(1,11) = 2.31$.

These results rule out a type of "conversion"
explanation for the added difficulty of *deeper-shallower*
over *taller-shorter*. This explanation would have the
subject converting *deeper* and *shallower* into *taller* and

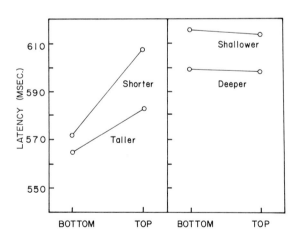

Fig. 8. Latencies to judge *Which is taller/
shorter/deeper/shallower?* when the two rectangles were
aligned either at the bottom or at the top.

shorter, respectively, before the linguistic and perceptual representations are compared. This strategy would have made the judgments of height differ from those of depth by a constant for the two positions of the reference line. Since this did not happen, such a conversion explanation can be dismissed.

What did happen was that judgments of height were a significant 27 msec. faster when the reference line was at the bottom than when it was at the top. This is consistent with the postulated condition of application that height extends in an upward direction. It is apparently easier to decide about comparative extent upward when the two extents begin at the same point. Moreover, the presence of a reference line at the bottom fosters an interpretation of upward extent. When the reference line is at the top, however, perhaps the rectangles have to be mentally "normalized," so that their upward extent can be compared to a common starting point. Furthermore the interpretation of upward extent may be more difficult to construct when there are explicit reference lines at the top. Construction of these two features of the interpretation may account for the 27 msec. difference between the two types of alignments of the rectangles for *taller-shorter* judgments.

The question remains as to why depth was no easier to judge when the rectangles were aligned at the top than at the bottom, whereas height was easier when they were aligned at the bottom than at the top. One possibility is that height is judged with reference to some extrinsic plane--usually ground level in normal situations--and this plane is not perceived as being part of the object being measured. In contrast, depth is judged with reference to its own surface, or opening in its surface, where the reference line or plane is perceived as being an intrinsic part of the object being measured. If this were the case, efficient judgments of height would be facilitated when the extrinsic reference planes at the bottom of the two rectangles being compared were coplanar. In contrast, it might be less important for judgments of depth as to whether the two intrinsic reference lines at the top of the rectangle are aligned, since they would not necessarily have to be related to each other, but only to their own rectangles. At present, however, we have no hard evidence for this or any other explanation.

Experiment III. In Experiment III we examined another possible explanation for the difference between height and depth. In discussing the conditions of application for height and depth above, we pointed out that depth was a measurement of an interior space, whereas height (i.e., tallness) was not. In fact, *tall-short* is normally used to measure the vertical extent of an exterior dimension--of something other than an interior space. We would not normally say that a well (an interior space) is tall or short, although we could say that it is deep or shallow. This contrast might be a partial source for the difference between height and depth. We reasoned that if the drawings of the objects to be compared emphasized the interior aspect of the objects, then depth judgments should become relatively easier than height judgments. We therefore chose pairs of rectangular boxes with openings at their tops and showed them from one of five views: from the side, where the interior aspect of the boxes is not obvious; from the top, where the view is directly into the interior of the boxes; and from three intermediate viewing angles. The five pairs of boxes used are shown in Fig. 9. They were presented 1.5 sec. after each one of the questions in (20), and latencies were measured from the onset of the picture.

The latencies were quite consistent with the expected interaction between the viewing angle and the relative ease of height and depth judgments. While height judgments were 108 msec. faster than depth judgments for the boxes viewed from the side, depth judgments were 78 msec. faster for boxes viewed from the top. The overall interaction between viewing angle and the height-depth difference, shown in Fig. 10, was significant, $F(4,44) = 6.82$, $p < .01$. Indeed, the linear component of this interaction (where viewing angle is treated as if it were a linear scale) is highly

H. H. CLARK, P. A. CARPENTER, AND M. A. JUST

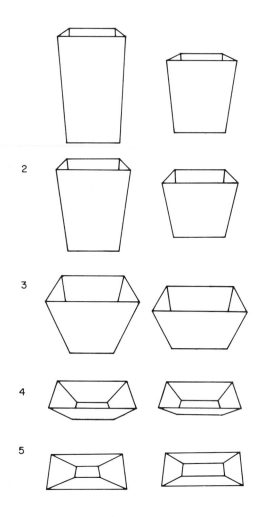

Fig. 9. The figures used in judgments of
Which is taller/shorter/deeper/shallower? in
Experiment III.

362

significant, $F(1,44) = 19.74$, $p < .01$, and the residual is non-significant, $F(3,44) = 2.53$. Thus the data are consistent with the view that encoding an entirely upright box as tall is easier than encoding one that is slightly tilted, and that the more the inside dimension of the box is visible, the easier depth judgments become. Such a view predicts a strict monotonic trend in the difference between height and depth as a function of the tilt, and this was consistent with the results. A close examination of Fig. 10, however, suggests that there might be a discontinuity between the displays in which the bottom does not show (1, 2, and 3) and the displays in which the bottom does show (4 and 5). It is, therefore, possible that rather than a true linear trend, these data reflect an underlying all-or-none process in which the exposure of any part of the bottom of the box makes the box much easier to encode in terms of depth. At this point it seems premature to attempt to choose between these two interpretations of Fig. 10.

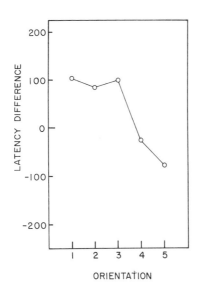

Fig. 10. Differences in latencies between judgments of *Which is taller/shorter?* and *Which is deeper/shallower?* for the various rotated figures in Experiment III shown in Fig. 9.

363

In addition to this main result are several others. First, height judgments were 38 msec. faster overall than depth judgments, $F(1,11) = 7.10$, $p < .05$, suggesting that if the viewing angles are truly representative, there is still greater difficulty in coding the depth of an object. Second, the unmarked adjectives (*taller*, *deeper*) were again found to be faster than the marked adjectives (*shorter*, *shallower*), and by 46 msec., $F(1,11) = 10.55$, $p < .01$; however, the *taller-shorter* difference (72 msec.) was significantly larger than the *deeper-shallower* difference (21 msec.) for some reason, $F(1,11) = 5.53$, $p < .05$. Finally, there were wide variations in the difficulty of the five viewing angles, $F(4,44) = 70.62$, $p < .01$. Since these differences clearly arose from the uneven discriminability within the five pairs of boxes used for the five viewing angles, this effect is of little interest here.

What can we conclude from these three experiments? Clearly, *deeper* and *taller* presuppose different qualities of the objects and situations to which they can apply. From these data we can argue that the subject attempts to code different aspects of the picture depending on whether he is judging height or depth. Furthermore, some pictures match the conditions of application better for height, whereas other pictures match better for depth. In particular, emphasizing the reference plane at the bottom of two objects makes it easier to code height, although it does not affect depth; and emphasizing the interior aspect of a three-dimensional box facilitates the coding of depth relative to height. In general we can conclude that comparative judgments of a spatial dimension are made relative to a particular interpretation of that dimension: the more closely the features of the picture match the conditions of application of the adjective underlying the comparison, the faster the two figures can be interpreted and compared.

Size vs. Height and Width

The next dimensional terms of interest are *larger-smaller*, *taller-shorter*, and *wider-narrower*. The main

contrast among them is that *larger-smaller* denotes
two- (or three-) dimensional extent, while *taller-
shorter* and *wider-narrower* denote only one-dimensional
extent. Secondarily, height and width differ as to
whether they denote vertical or horizontal extent, at
least for rectangles. Consider the pair of rectangles
in (23), which differ only in height:

(23)
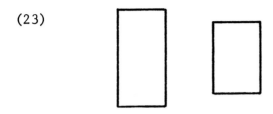

We could ask subjects to judge *Which is larger?* or
Which is taller? and in either case, the subject should
point to the left rectangle. In the most literal sense,
the subject must do the same thing for both judgments:
he must ascertain that the vertical extent of the left
rectangle is greater than that of the right, and decide
therefore that the left one is taller or larger. But
if we assume that the subject is attempting to code the
rectangle in terms of size and height, respectively, he
should code the figures quite differently under the two
questions, for he must represent them in terms of the
conditions of application for size and height, respectively.
    What are the conditions of application for size,
height, and width? Roughly speaking, *large-small*
presupposes that the object or space being measured is
at least two-dimensional. What is measured can be
either a solid object or an interior space; it must
simply have a definable boundary. In this sense, size
is more general than height. But it is most difficult
to specify the extent which size measures, for it is
obviously an amalgam of all the linear dimensions that
the thing measured can vary on. In fact, when Shepard
(personal communication) asked subjects to make size
judgments of various types of rectangles, he found that
some subjects used the length of the perimeter of the

365

rectangles for their physical correlate of size, while other subjects used area (i.e., length times width). Size is apparently not very well defined, then, in terms of any unique physical measurement. It should be obvious that these considerations make it difficult to set up a neat set of conditions of application for *large-small*, although they might be roughly as follows:

(24) large-small

    a. The object or space measured must have at least two dimensions.
    b. The extent measured is two- or three-dimensional.

We have already examined the conditions of application for height, which are repeated in (25) for reference:

(25) tall-short

    a. The object described must have at least two dimensions.
    b. The dimension measured must be vertical or canonically vertical.
    c. The extent measure is one-dimensional.
    d. The reference line or plane is bottom-most.

Width is even more difficult to specify than height (see Clark, 1971). When used with length, it is the major dimension that is left over once length has been specified (as in *the width of a board*); the tertiary dimension is then normally called thickness. When used with height, width is again the major dimension that is left over once height has been specified (as in *the width of a door*), although there are other constraints that could apply. For example, if the viewer sees himself as part of the perceptual event, width becomes the lateral left-to-right dimension of the object with respect to the viewer (as in *the width of a desk or a sofa*). Furthermore, there is no single reference point or direction of measurement for width. In the last instance mentioned, measurement could be from left to right, from right to left, or from the middle outward; there appears to be no *a priori* means for deciding on a direction of measurement, as there is with height. We will give only a very rough set of conditions of application, and this is only for width as it contrasts with height (not length):

(26)   wide-narrow

    a. The object described must have at least two dimensions.
    b. The dimension measured must be secondary to the vertical or canonically vertical.
    c. The extent measured is one-dimensional.
    d. The reference line or plane can be at either end of the dimension.

In the present experiments, however, we will make little use of the difference in conditions of application for height and width.

Experiment IV. Our purpose in Experiment IV was simply to demonstrate that the different conditions of application for size, height, and width lead to different codings of the same picture and therefore to different patterns of judgment latencies. We made use of pairs of figures consisting of one square and one rectangle (differing from the square on only one dimension). The two pairs that differed only in height are the following:

(27)   a.   b.

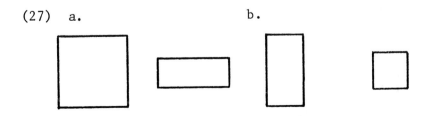

For these two pairs, subjects were asked to judge either
the relative size or the relative height of the two
rectangles:

    (28)   a. Which is taller?
             b. Which is shorter?
             c. Which is bigger?
             d. Which is smaller?

The second two pairs differed only in width:

    (29) a.   b.

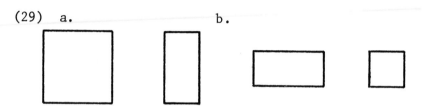

For these pairs subjects judged only relative size and
relative width:

    (30)   a. Which is wider?
             b. Which is narrower?
             c. Which is bigger?
             d. Which is smaller?

The larger sides of these rectangles were always 1.5
in. and the smaller side .75 in.; the two rectangles
were centered about their horizontal midline, and their
centers were separated by about 3 in. As in Experiments
II and III, the picture appeared 1.5 sec. after the
question, and the subject was timed from the onset of
the picture to his response.
    The results are best understood as resulting from
a contrast between one-dimensional terms (*tall-short*
and *wide-narrow*) and two-dimensional terms (*big-small*).
Subjects apparently found it easier to make size judgments about the square in each pair of figures, but
height and width judgments about the rectangle. In
(27a), for example, subjects were able to judge that
the left figure (a square) was larger more quickly than

that the right figure (a rectangle) was smaller; in contrast, they were able to judge that the right figure (a rectangle) was shorter more quickly than that the left figure (a square) was taller. This striking effect appeared for each pair of figures no matter whether the contrast was between size and height or between size and width. This higher order interaction averaged a sizable 55 msec. and was highly significant, $F(1,11) = 18.74$, $p < .001$. The effect is pictured in Fig. 11, which shows the reaction times as a function of the shape of the correct figure and the number of dimensions of the adjective.

Although marking was confounded with the shape of the referenced figure (i.e., whether it was a square or a rectangle), there was still an overall difference between unmarked and marked terms. Unmarked terms were 25 msec. easier to respond to than marked, $F(1,11) = 5.53$, $p < .05$. There was, however, an interaction between marking and the dimensionality (one vs. two) of the judgments, $F(1,11) = 6.85$, $p < .05$; this interaction occurred because there was essentially no overall *bigger-smaller* difference, while the marked terms *shorter* and *narrower* took 46 msec. longer than their unmarked counterparts, *taller* and *wider*. In addition, there were two other effects that could be

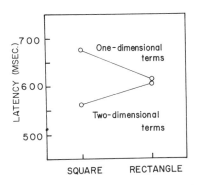

Fig. 11. Latencies to make one-dimensional judgments (*Which is taller/shorter/wider/narrower?*) or two-dimensional judgments (*Which is bigger/smaller?*) as a function of whether the answer designated a square or a rectangle.

specific to this experiment. First, judgments of size
(*bigger-smaller*) were faster overall than judgments of
individual dimensions (*taller-shorter* and *wider-narrower*)
by 60 msec. $F(1,11) = 10.62$, $p < .01$. Although this
difference could have arisen from simpler conditions of
application for size than for height or width, this
explanation is questioned by the results of the next
experiment. Second, subjects were able to make judgments about the two pairs of figures in (27) more
quickly than about the two pairs of figures in (29).
This result should be evaluated with some caution too,
since the sides to be compared are adjacent for vertical judgments (27), but not for the horizontal judgments (29).

This experiment clearly demonstrates how the perceptual characteristics of a picture can make it easier
or harder to code the picture in terms of different
dimensions. When the two figures being compared
differed only in height, it was easier to judge the
square as larger or smaller, but easier to judge the
rectangle as taller or shorter. The analogous result
held for two figures that differed only in width. But
what might account for this close affinity between
squares and size and between rectangles and height and
width? We will examine one explanation that relies on
the notion that height and width are easier to judge
of asymmetrical figures (rectangles), and size of
symmetrical figures. The former advantage might arise
because asymmetrical (elongated) figures make it easier
to separate out the two distinct dimensions, and the
second advantage might arise because size judgments
require measurement taking both dimensions into account,
a process that is aided by symmetry and hindered by
asymmetry.

To account for these results, we will assume that
when a perceiver makes size judgments, he codes the
size of the symmetrical figure (the square) with respect
to the asymmetrical one (the rectangle), but when making
height or width judgments, he does the reverse. Consider, for example, the pair of figures in (27a), in
which the square is taller than the rectangle. When the

perceiver is asked *Which is larger/smaller?* he knows
he must code the relative size of the two figures, and
so, by our assumption, he codes the pair as (31):

(31) (square larger rectangle)

It follows (in parallel with our discussion of the
Audley-Wallis experiments) that the perceiver should be
able to answer *Which is larger?*--i.e., (X *larger* y)--
more quickly than *Which is smaller?*--i.e., (X *smaller* y)
--since the first question is congruent with the coding
in (31) whereas the second question is not. On the
other hand, when the perceiver is asked *Which is taller
/shorter?* he knows he must code the relative height of
the pair. By our assumption, this code is:

(32) (rectangle shorter square)

By the same logic, the perceiver should be able to
answer *Which is shorter?* faster than *Which is taller?*
Such an assumption about coding, therefore, accounts for
the pattern of latencies found in this experiment.
   The critical step in this explanation, obviously,
is the assumption that squares are coded with respect
to rectangles for size, but vice versa for height.
Given this assumption everything else follows. But is
this assumption plausible? We have argued that squares
can be coded more readily in terms of size, and rectangles more readily in terms of height or width. More
importantly, we want to argue that when two objects are
compared on a scale to which one is more applicable than
the other, the most applicable object will be chosen as
the topic of the comparative. Thus, the square would
be selected as the topic of a comparison for size (as
in (31)), and the rectangle, as the topic of comparison
for height (as in (32)). To pursue this argument, consider a comparison of midgets and cars on the dimension
of height. One of the most distinctive features of the
midgets is that they are very short, while cars are not
normally coded as tall or short. If our argument is
correct, then midgets should serve better as the topic

than as the reference point in a comparison of heights of midgets and cars, and this appears to be the case: *Midgets are shorter than cars* seems more apt as a description than *Cars are taller than midgets*. To put it another way, objects that are easy to code on a dimension will normally be compared to other objects that are not so easy to code on that dimension.

The results of Experiment IV, therefore, suggest the following hypothesis about size, height, and width. It is easier to code a figure for its comparative size the more symmetrical it is, while it is easier to code a figure for its comparative height or width the more asymmetrical it is. The pairs of figures used in Experiment IV, however, were not optimal for testing this hypothesis to its fullest extent, for there were basically only two figures: a square, and a rectangle with wides in a 2:1 ratio. The evidence for this hypothesis (and our explanation of Experiment IV) would be much stronger if we could show that this generalization held for wide variations in symmetry--for example, for figures ranging much farther over the squareness-rectangularity dimension. This was the purpose of Experiment V.

Experiment V. In this experiment, we made use of four rectangles which were taller than they were wide, but varied in their squareness or rectangularity. The height-to-width ratios (in cm) were 5:3, 4:3, 5:2, and 4:2; these figures are actually not all that different from each other in appearance. As in the previous experiment, subjects made judgments of size and height (with the questions in (28)) for the two pairs of figures that differed only in height:

(33) a.   b.

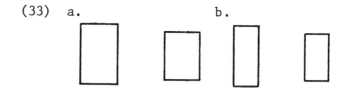

The following two pairs of figures were used for judgments of size and width (with the questions in (30)):

(34) a.   b.

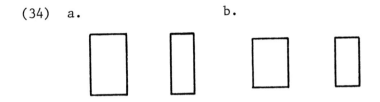

In all other respects, Experiment V was identical to
Experiment IV.

The main results of Experiment V conformed to our
expectations. The first result duplicated the main
effect found in Experiment IV. For each pair of rectangles, the squarer or more symmetrical the rectangle
was, the faster subjects were able to say it was bigger
or smaller and the slower they were able to say it was
taller, shorter, wider, or narrower. The interaction
between the symmetry of the figures and the dimensionality of the judgment (one- vs. two-dimensions) was
highly significant, $F(1,11) = 9.85$, $p < .01$. This
interaction, shown in Fig. 12, was again a sizable 37
msec. effect, even though the differences in symmetry
among the rectangles used were relatively subtle.

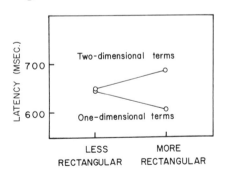

Fig. 12. Latencies to make one-dimensional judgments (*Which is taller/shorter/wider/narrower?*) or two-
dimensional judgments (*Which is bigger/smaller?*) as a
function of whether the answer designated a figure that
was less or more rectangular.

But this experiment added an important new piece of evidence for the affinity between size and symmetry and between height and width and asymmetry. Note that the four pairs of rectangles in (33) and (34) vary in how symmetrical or asymmetrical they are *as a pair*. For example, (33b) contains two relatively asymmetrical rectangles. If our hypothesis about these affinities is correct, then we should expect size judgments to be more difficult relative to height or width judgments the more elongated the pair of rectangles is. As a measure of elongation (or asymmetry) for each pair we simply summed the height-to-width ratios for the two rectangles in the pair. For example, the two relatively elongated rectangles in (33b) have height-to-width ratios of 5:2 and 4:2, so the elongation measure for this pair is 2.5 + 2.0, or 4.5. Then we computed the mean latency difference between size and height, or size and width, for each pair of rectangles. Figure 13 shows these four latency differences plotted as a function of the elongation measure. As this figure clearly shows, the difficulty of size judgments relative to height or width judgments increased monotonically as elongation (or asymmetry) increased, thereby bearing out our hypothesis. In addition, size judgments took an average of 41 msec. longer than height or width judgments in this experiment, $F(1,11) = 10.92$, $p < .01$; this is to be contrasted with the 60 msec. difference in the opposite direction in the previous experiment. This reversal is also consistent with the affinity hypothesis, for the figures were more asymmetrical on the average in Experiment V than in Experiment IV (with average elongation measures of 3.75 and 3.0, respectively), hence size judgments should be more difficult in Experiment IV, as they were found to be.

Because of Experiment V, we can be more certain of the following general thesis. Size is easier to judge of rectangles the more symmetrical they are, and height and width easier to judge of rectangles the more asymmetrical they are. This was shown most strikingly in the latencies plotted in Fig. 13, where height and width were progressively easier to judge relative to

374

size the more asymmetrical (or elongated) the rectangles
were as a pair. To account for the remaining results
we must make the following assumption: in making perceptual comparisons the perceiver prefers to code the
object that more naturally lies on the underlying dimension with respect to the other object. With this
assumption it follows directly that comparative size
will be coded with the more symmetrical figure as topic,
whereas comparative height and width will be coded with
the more asymmetrical figure as topic. This is consistent with the latencies plotted in Figs. 11 and 12.
Finally, it should be noted that it is the asymmetry of
elongated rectangles, rather than the prominence of the
interrogated dimensions, that makes height and width

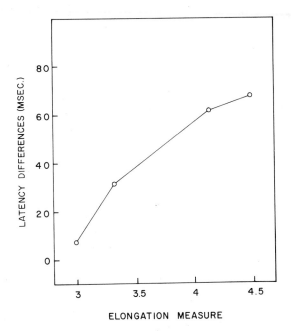

Fig. 13. Latency differences between two-
dimensional judgments (*Which is bigger/smaller?*) and
one-dimensional judgments (*Which is taller/shorter/
wider/narrower?*) as a function of the elongation of the
two rectangles in a display.

easier to judge for such rectangles. In Experiment IV, for example, height judgments were easier than size judgments not only when the rectangles were taller than they were wide, but also when they were wider than they were tall. That is, height can be made easier to judge without making that dimension prominent by its size. Rather, height becomes easier to judge simply by greater asymmetry, which apparently makes it easier to separate out height from width. These generalizations, of course, also hold for width.

Like Experiments I, II, and III, Experiments IV and V demonstrate how the perceiver coding a picture is influenced by a sentence preceding the picture just as Hypothesis B asserts should happen. In these experiments, the preceding sentence (e.g., *Which is larger?*) selects the dimension along which the comparison is to be made (here, size). But once this choice has been made, it is the shapes of the objects that determine the exact codes and their relative difficulty. Thus, the perceiver finds it easier to code the same two rectangles (say, A and B) on one dimension than on another, depending on their shape. Furthermore, he might prefer to code A with respect to B if he is representing them on one dimension, but just the reverse if he is representing them on another dimension. The coding process, then, is a relatively complex one, for although the preceding sentence selects the coding dimension, it is the objects themselves that determine the exact form of coding.

Concluding Remarks

Most of what we know has been acquired through sensory perception and linguistic communication. The ability to relate perception and language is one of the most important functions of our cognitive system. From a psycholinguistic viewpoint, it is important to discover how perceptual and linguistic input are represented so that they can be compared to each other. It is also important to discover how input in one medium can affect the coding of input from the other medium. In this paper we have simply tried to explore one facet of this meeting of semantics and perception. We have pointed out that there are similarities between linguistic and perceptual representations that may have arisen from a basic conceptual organization of space. This conception, which we have assumed is molded in the main by constraints on our perceptual apparatus, appears to be directly reflected in the linguistic properties of spatial terms in English and how we process them (for a related developmental view, see E. Clark, in press).

Consider, for example, the differences between unmarked and marked adjectives in English. Previous work on deductive reasoning (see Clark, 1969) has consistently shown that unmarked comparatives (*longer*, *higher*) are easier to reason with than marked terms (*shorter*, *lower*). We have examined other evidence in this paper which argues that people also prefer to code perceptual events in terms of the semantic representations underlying unmarked adjectives. And the experiments just reported demonstrate that perceptual displays are generally coded more quickly in terms of the unmarked than the marked term. To add to the evidence, Klatzky, E. Clark, and Macken (in preparation) have recently shown that young children show the same asymmetry in applying nonsense syllables to perceptually extended and non-extended objects (corresponding to unmarked and marked adjectives, respectively). They have further argued that this asymmetry cannot be attributed to a purely linguistic asymmetry the children have already learned. In short, we could presume that all of these marking asymmetries arise in some complex way from the fact that people code extent, not lack of extent, along perceptual dimensions, a process that is fundamental to man's perceptual apparatus.

In this paper we have considered various sources of evidence in support of this point of view. In doing so, we have mainly relied on four concepts: polarity, reference point, underlying dimension, and conditions of application. The first section argued that the *polarity* of perceptual codes is normally positive. This rule was extended in later sections to include codes for

377

location (where certain propositions reflect a positive code) and for comparison (where unmarked adjectives reflect a positive code). The *reference point* was central to our discussions of representations of location and comparison, for people code the location of one object with respect to another and compare the value of one object on an underlying dimension with respect to another. Reference points were fundamental also to the specification of *underlying dimensions*. Such dimensions are defined as extension from a primary reference point (a zero): they can also contain a secondary reference point, or standard, which separates the positive half of the scale from the negative half. Finally, we found it necessary to bring in the notion of *conditions of application* to differentiate one underlying dimension from another--i.e., to distinguish one spatial adjective from another. We argued that the same physical dimension could be interpreted perceptually in terms of various underlying dimensions, and this depended on what conditions of application the perceptual dimension could be viewed as satisfying. In all, it is apparent from the available evidence that there is a very abstract, but well-organized, relation between language and perception: both linguistic and perceptual coding must rely on the common notions of polarity, reference point, underlying dimension, and conditions of application.

References

Audley, R. J., & Wallis, C. P. Response instructions and the speed of relative judgments. I. Some experiments on brightness discrimination. *British Journal of Psychology*, 1964, 55, 59-73.

Bem, S. L. The role of comprehension in children's problem solving. *Developmental Psychology*, 1970, 2, 351-358.

Bierwisch, M. Some semantic universals of German adjectives. *Foundations of Language*, 1967, 3, 1-36.

Carpenter, P. A., & Just, M. A. Semantic control of eye movements during picture scanning in a sentence-picture verification task. 1972, 12, 61-64.

Chase, W. G., & Clark, H. H. Mental operations in the comparison of sentences and pictures. In L. Gregg (Ed.), *Cognition in learning and memory.* New York: Wiley, 1972.

Chase, W. G., & Clark, H. H. Semantics in the perception of verticality. *British Journal of Psychology,* 1971, 62, 311-326.

Clark, E. V. What's in a word? On the child's acquisition of semantics in his first language. In T. E. Moore (Ed.), *Cognitive development and acquisition of language.* New York: Academic Press, in press.

Clark, H. H. Linguistic processes in deductive reasoning. *Psychological Review,* 1969, 76, 387-404.

Clark, H. H. How we understand negation. Paper presented at COBRE Workshop on Cognitive Organization and Psychological Processes. Huntington Beach, California, August, 1970(a).

Clark, H. H. Comprehending comparatives. In G. Flores d'Arcais & W. J. M. Levelt (Eds.), *Advances in Psycholinguistics.* Amsterdam: North Holland Press, 1970(b).

Clark, H. H. More about "Adjectives, comparatives, and syllogisms:" A reply to Huttenlocher and Higgins. *Psychological Review,* 1971, 78, 505-514.

Clark, H. H. Difficulties people have in answering the question, "Where is it?" *Journal of Verbal Learning and Verbal Behavior,* 1972, 11, 265-277.

Clark, H. H. Space, time, semantics, and the child. In T. E. Moore (Ed.), *Cognitive Development and the acquisition of language.* New York: Academic Press, in press.

Clark, H. H. Semantics and comprehension. In T. A. Sebeok (Ed.), *Current trends in linguistics, Vol. 12: Linguistics and adjacent arts and sciences.* The Hague: Mouton, in press.

Clark, H. H., & Chase, W. G. On the process of comparing sentences against pictures. *Cognitive Psychology,* 1972, 3, 472-517.

Ellis, S. H. Interaction of encoding and retrieval in relative age judgments: An extension of the "crossover" effect. *Journal of Experimental Psychology,* 1972, 94, 291-294.

Flores d'Arcais, G. B. On handling comparative sentences. Unpublished Research Report, Center for Cognitive Studies, Harvard University, 1966.

Flores d'Arcais, G. B. Semantic factors and perceptual reference in the comprehension of comparatives. Paper presented at the Second Meeting of the Psychologists of the Danubian Countries, Smolenice, September, 1970.

Greenberg, J. H. *Language universals*. The Hague: Mouton, 1966.

Hilgard, E. R., Atkinson, R. C., & Atkinson, R. L. *Introduction to psychology*. New York: Harcourt, Brace, and Jovanovich, 1971.

Huttenlocher, J., Eisenberg, K., & Strauss, S. Comprehension: Relation between perceived actor and logical subject. *Journal of Verbal Learning and Verbal Behavior*, 1968, 7, 300-304.

Huttenlocher, J., & Strauss, S. Comprehension and a statement's relation to the situation it describes. *Journal of Verbal Learning and Verbal Behavior*, 1968, 7, 527-530.

Huttenlocher, J., & Weiner, S. L. Comprehension of instructions in varying contexts. *Cognitive Psychology*, 1971, 2, 369-385.

Just, M., & Carpenter, P. Comprehension of negation with quantification. *Journal of Verbal Learning and Verbal Behavior*, 1971, 10, 244-253.

Klatsky, R. L., Clark, E. V., & Macken, M. Asymmetries in the acquisition of polar adjectives: Conceptual or linguistic? In preparation.

Klima, E. S. Negation in English. In J. A. Fodor & J. J. Katz (Eds.), *The structure of language*. Englewood Cliffs, N. J.: Prentice-Hall, 1964, 232-246.

Kučera, H., & Francis, W. *Computational analysis of present-day American English*. Providence: Brown University Press, 1967.

Marks, D. F. Relative judgment: A phenomenon and a theory. *Perception and Psychophysics*, 1972, 11, 156-160.

Parkman, J. M. Temporal aspects of digit and letter inequality judgments. *Journal of Experimental Psychology*, 1971, 91, 191-205.

Trabasso, T., Rollins, H., & Shaughnessy, E. Storage and verification stages in processing concepts. *Cognitive Psychology*, 1971, 2, 239-289.

Wallis, C. P., & Audley, R. J. Response instructions and the speed of relative judgments. II. Pitch discrimination. *British Journal of Psychology*, 1964, 55, 133-142.

Acknowledgements

The research reported in this paper was supported in part by Public Health Research Grant MH-20021 from the National Institute of Mental Health. We are deeply indebted to Susan L. Weiner for running all of the experiments and to Eve V. Clark for her suggestions on the manuscript.

CONSIDERATIONS OF SOME PROBLEMS
OF COMPREHENSION

John D. Bransford and Marcia K. Johnson
State University of New York at Stony Brook

Since 1957 (Chomsky, 1957), the area of language
has received increasing attention from psychologists.
Linguistic characterizations of sentence structure
have played important roles in formulating theories
of sentence perception, comprehension and memory.
The emphasis on characterization of the linguistic
system has tended to overshadow another problem, however, namely that a language is a symbol system that
is used by individuals. A consideration of the individual's contributions to the processes of creating,
comprehending and remembering linguistic utterances
may thus involve principles beyond those necessary
for characterizing the linguistic system *per se*.

The purpose of the present paper is to investigate some of the contributions made by listeners
while comprehending and remembering, and to demonstrate that the ability to understand linguistic
symbols is based not only on the comprehender's knowledge of his language, but also on his general knowledge of the world. Much of the extra-linguistic
knowledge affecting comprehension and memory may come
from visually presented information (e.g., perceptual
context), hence the present conference's concern with
visual processing can have important implications for
theories dealing with the comprehension and memory of
linguistic events.

The paper is divided into four major sections.
The first three present a number of studies which
illustrate some of the interplay between linguistic
inputs and extra-linguistic knowledge. In the fourth

section we attempt to highlight various implications
of these studies with respect to the problem of
characterizing the thought processes involved in comprehending language, and of characterizing the role
of comprehension factors in learning and memory.

Comprehension as a Process of
Creating Semantic Products

The studies in this section were designed to
allow some initial inferences about the comprehension
process based on the nature of the information available to a subject following comprehension. If understanding involves relating input information to
general knowledge, the semantic product resulting
from this process should often include more information than that directly expressed in the input. In
the following experiments, the basic research strategy
was to ask whether subjects would falsely recognize
information that could only be available to them by
inference.

Inferring Spatial Relations Among Objects

Consider the following set of sentences:

1. Three turtles rested *beside* a floating
   log and a fish swam beneath them.

2. Three turtles rested *on* a floating log
   and a fish swam beneath them.

These two sentences differ only in the lexical
items *on* or *beside*. Both sentences include information about a fish swimming beneath the turtles. The
critical difference is that in sentence (2), since
the turtles are on the log and the fish swam beneath
them, it follows that the fish swam beneath the log
as well. This information (that the fish swam beneath
the log) is not supplied by the linguistic input, but

is based on knowledge of spatial relations. Likewise, a knowledge of spatial relations allows the
conclusion that the fish did not necessarily swim
beneath the log in sentence (1).

Bransford, Barclay and Franks (in press) used
sets of sentences like those above in the acquisition
phase of a memory task. For example, an individual
subject's acquisition list included either sentence
(1) or sentence (2). Later, subjects were given a
recognition test. Recognition items were presented
successively and the subject's task was to indicate
which sentences they had heard during acquisition and
which they had not. In addition, they were asked to
rate their confidence in each response. Of interest
was the confidence with which subjects thought they
had heard recognition items in which the final pronoun of the acquisition sentence was changed. For
example, sentences (1') and (2') below are the recognition items corresponding to sentences (1) and (2),
respectively:

1'. Three turtles rested beside a floating
log and a fish swam beneath *it*.

2'. Three turtles rested on a floating log
and a fish swam beneath *it*.

If subjects store only the linguistic information underlying the input sentence, subjects hearing
either sentence (1) or (2) should be equally likely
to detect the pronoun change in the recognition item.
On the other hand, if subjects acquire information
about a situation based on the information conveyed
by the sentence in combination with their understanding of spatial relationships, a different pattern of
results would be expected. Subjects hearing sentence
(1) should reject the recognition item (1') since it
is neither consonant with the actual input sentence
nor with their understanding of the situation,
whereas subjects hearing sentence (2) should be more

385

likely to think they heard the recognition item (2')
since it is consonant with their understanding of the
situation. As expected, subjects' confidence ratings
indicated that they were not simply basing their
judgments on the information expressed solely by the
sentence. Rather, subjects were responding on the
basis of whether or not a change in pronoun produced
a sentence which was consistent with the overall spatial relationships among the objects that the input
sentence implied.

Bransford, Barclay and Franks reported a similar
finding in cases where sets of sentences were used to
communicate an overall understanding of the spatial
relationships among objects. For example, subjects
heard several descriptions of the following type:

> There is a tree with a box beside it, and a
> chair is on top of the box. The box is to the
> right of the tree. The tree is green and
> extremely tall.

The reasoning was that subjects hearing such descriptions should know more than simply that information
underlying the individual sentences in the description. For example, they should also know that *The
chair is to the right of the tree* or *The tree is to
the left of the chair*, even though this information
was never presented. In a recognition task in which
subjects were asked to choose which sentence they had
actually heard from among a set of alternatives,
subjects were much more likely to choose a sentence
like *The tree is to the left of the chair* than they
were to choose a sentence that violated the overall
set of relationships, e.g., *The chair is to the left
of the tree.*

Inferring Instruments Used to Carry Out Acts

Johnson, Bransford and Solomon (in press) investigated a class of items such as *The man was shot.*

386

Kintsch (in press) had earlier presented subjects with such sentences and asked them to indicate additional information that seemed to be true about the situations described. His subjects suggested that the man must be shot by something (i.e., there must be some *instrument* for carrying out the action, to use Fillmore's [1968] term), and most assumed that the instrument would be a gun. We asked whether subjects were likely to think they heard information based on such inferences.

The general design involved reading subjects a series of descriptive stories at acquisition and later giving them a recognition test in which they were to say Yes to sentences which were exactly like sentences in the stories and to say No to sentences which had been changed in any way. Subjects heard 20 stories in all, 6 of which are relevant to the present discussion. For the Experimental group, these stories were designed to suggest a particular inference regarding an instrument involved in the action described. For example,

1. John was trying to fix the bird house.
    He was *pounding* the nail when his father
    came out to watch him and to help him
    do the work.

For the Control group, the same story frames were used but in each case a verb was changed so that no object was implied or the implied object was different:

2. John was trying to fix the bird house.
    He was *looking for* the nail when his
    father came out to watch him and to
    help him do the work.

At recognition, both groups of subjects were presented with the same sentences. The critical Instrument-Inference item for the above story was:

387

> John was using the *hammer* to fix the bird
> house when his father came out to watch him
> and to help him do the work.

The mean number of Yes responses are shown in Table
1. As can be seen in Table 1, Experimental and Control subjects did not differ in the mean number of
Yes responses to Unrelated sentences (which conveyed
information inconsistent with the stories of both
groups) or to Old sentences (which were identical to
sentences in the stories of both groups). However,
the Experimental subjects were much more likely to
say Yes to the critical Instrument-Inference items
than were Control subjects.

Inferring Consequences of Input Events

In the study just described, we also investigated an additional class of items. In these items,
the experimental version of each story suggested some
probable consequence of the action described. In the
corresponding control stories, verb or prepositional
phrases were changed so that the probable consequence
of the action was changed. Two examples of acquisition stories are given below, with the changes made
for the control group given in parentheses and the
corresponding Consequence-Inference recognition item
given in italics.

Table 1. Mean Number of Yes Responses During Recognition

	Unrelated	Old	Inference	
			Instruments	Consequences
Number of Sentences	12	10	6	6
Experimental Group	.70	6.65	3.40	4.05
Control Group	.45	6.95	1.20	1.40

It was late at night when the phone rang and a
a voice gave a frantic cry. The spy threw
(pulled) the secret document into (from) the
fireplace just in time since 30 seconds longer
would have been too late. *The spy burned the
secret document just in time since 30 seconds
longer would have been too late.*

The river was narrow. A beaver hit the log
that a turtle was sitting on (beside) and the
log flipped over from the shock. The turtle
was very surprised by the event. *A beaver
hit the log and knocked the turtle into the
water.*

As can be seen in Table 1, subjects hearing the experimental version of the story were more likely to
think they had heard the critical recognition items
than subjects hearing the control version.

*Creating Situations that Justify the Relations
Between Two Events*

In collaboration with Nancy McCarrell, we have
recently used a similar false recognition paradigm
to investigate a class of items where the relations
between two events have to be justified. For example,
consider the sentence:

The floor was dirty *because* Sally used the mop.

Most people have little trouble understanding this
sentence, but they usually assume additional information in order to do so. For example, many people
assume that the mop was dirty. That is, people assume
an antecedent condition that explains or justifies the
relation between the two phrases. If the connective
is changed--

The floor was dirty *so* Sally used the mop.

389

--the sentence seems relatively "self-contained;" at least understanding it does not seem to require any special assumptions about the state of the mop.

As another example, compare the following two sentences:

John missed the bus *because* he knew he would have to walk to school.

John missed the bus *so* he knew he would have to walk to school.

The relationship between the two phrases can be justified in the *because* version if, for example, one assumes that John wanted to walk to school. On the other hand, this assumption does not seem to play any part in understanding the *so* version of the sentence. In the experiment, these types of sentences were embedded in short acquisition story frames. The experimental version of each sentence contained a *because* and the control version contained a *so*. The critical recognition items included the kind of information subjects were likely to infer given the experimental version of the story (e.g., that the mop was dirty or that John wanted to walk to school). The mean number of Yes responses to these critical recognition items was greater under the experimental than under the control condition. The data are given in Table 2.

Table 2. Mean Number of Yes Responses During Recognition

	Version During Acquisition	
	Because	So
Number of Sentences	3	3
Critical Justifications Recognition Items	1.54	.32

390

We think that the results of the studies in the present section are consistent with the notion that a subject's understanding depends not only on what he hears, but on the implications of this information in light of his prior knowledge.[1] Therefore, the subject's performance (e.g., in a recognition memory task) will be not only a function of what he heard, but of what he knows. These processes of making inferences and creating justifications probably occur quite frequently in the normal course of comprehending. Generally, we may not be aware of them. Sometimes, however, processes like justification can be quite elaborate. Our favorite example of this is to ask people to comprehend the sentence, *Bill is able to come to the party tonight because his car broke down*. As we have noted elsewhere (Bransford and Johnson, 1971), people generally indicate that they can comprehend this sentence *via* a process of fabricating a situation in which it makes sense. Most people come up with something like the following:

> Bill was originally going to leave town, but now he could not leave because his car broke down. Since he could not leave he could come to the party since the party was in town.

This act of creating an elaborate situation in order to understand the sentence is a far cry from merely interpreting the meanings of the phrases, "Bill is able to come to the party tonight" and "his car broke down." In some sense the *because* structure of the sentence acts as a cue to create a situation that

---

[1]Reaction time studies--in conjunction with false recognition data--might help distinguish between cases where inferences occur during acquisition and those where inferences are made during recognition. For some initial studies in this question, see Potts, 1971.

391

brings the two phrases into a meaningful relation. A listener is confronted with a problem-solving task of creating some situation in which the *because* structure makes sense. The studies in the next section indicate what happens if a listener fails in such problem-solving tasks.

Semantic Prerequisites for Comprehension

A description of the output of the comprehension process as a joint product of input information and prior knowledge allows for the possibility that a person *first* comprehends an input and *then* elaborates on its implications. However, the studies in the present section indicate that, under certain circumstances, this is not an accurate characterization of the comprehension process. Rather, there are cases in which certain knowledge may constitute a semantic prerequisite for comprehension; that is, where sentences presuppose knowledge of relevant information.[2] In the experiments presented below, the availability of prior knowledge is manipulated in order to assess its role in comprehending and remembering information.

Novel Contexts

One way to manipulate the information available to a listener is in terms of the contexts surrounding a message. As an example of how context can determine whether or not one can comprehend, consider the following passage:

> If the balloons popped the sound wouldn't be able to carry since everything would be too far away from the correct floor. A closed window would also present the sound from carrying, since most buildings tend

---

[2]For linguistic discussions of presuppositions see, for example, Fillmore and Langendoen, 1971.

to be well insulated. Since the whole
operation depends on a steady flow of elec-
tricity, a break in the middle of the wire
would also cause problems. Of course, the
fellow could shout, but the human voice is
not loud enough to carry that far. An additional problem is that a string could break on
the instrument. Then there could be no
accompaniment to the message. It is clear
that the best situation would involve less
distance. Then there would be fewer potential problems. With face to face contact,
the least number of things could go wrong.

In one experiment (Bransford and Johnson, in
press), subjects in the No Context (1) condition were
instructed to listen carefully to this passage and to
try to comprehend and remember it. They were informed
that they would later be asked to recall the passage
as accurately as possible. They then heard the passage once and were asked to rate it on 7-point comprehension scale (where 1 indicated "very hard" to
comprehend and 7 indicated "very easy"). The rating
task was followed by a recall task in which subjects
were encouraged to write down as many ideas from the
passage as they could.[3] The No Context (1) subjects

---

[3]We have adopted the following standard procedure
for scoring recall protocols of sentence materials or
prose passages: idea units are designated *a priori*
and correspond either to individual sentences, basic
semantic propositions, or phrases. Maximum possible
scores for the materials used in the experiments presented here are given in the appropriate tables. The
protocols, which cannot be identified as to condition,
are scored independently by two judges against the
list of idea units. Paraphrases are allowed. Inter-
judge reliability measures have been $\geq$ .91. Any differences in the assignment of scores to subjects are
resolved by a third judge. These adjusted scores are
then used in the final analysis of the data.

gave the passages very low comprehension ratings and recalled very few ideas. In contrast, subjects who were given 30 seconds to look at the picture in Figure 1 before hearing the passage (Context Before subjects) rated it as much more comprehensible and recalled twice as many ideas.

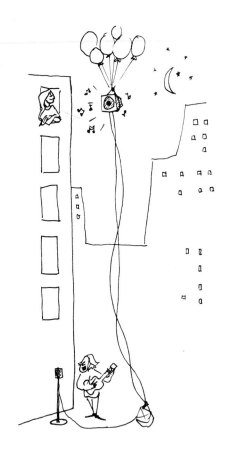

Fig. 1. Appropriate Context for the *balloon* passage.

There were three additional conditions in the study. Comprehension ratings and recall scores for all conditions are given in Table 3. No Context (2) subjects heard the passage twice in succession before the rating and recall tasks. A comparison between the No Context (2) group and the Context Before group indicates that subjects were actually better off in the present situation spending time looking at the picture (and then transferring to the to-be-learned items) than they were spending even more time on an additional study trial of the to-be-remembered material. This presents even stronger evidence that the picture constituted a prerequisite setting for comprehending the passage.

The other two conditions (Context After and Partial Context) were included to control for possible alternative explanations of the expected difference in recall between the Context Before and No Context conditions. Context After subjects saw the picture in Figure 1 after they heard the passage and before the comprehension rating and recall tasks. This did not seem to help them since they also rated the passage as quite incomprehensible and their recall scores were no better than those of subjects in the No Context group. The absence of a Context After effect suggests that subjects in the Context Before condition were not obtaining higher recall scores by simply generating ideas consonant with the picture. In fact, it is important to note that the passage did not simply describe the picture, but instead discussed events that could happen given the context as a conceptual base.

Table 3. Mean Comprehension Ratings and Mean Number of Ideas Recalled (Balloon Passage)

	No Context 1	No Context 2	Context After	Partial Context	Context Before	Maximum Score
Comprehension	2.30	3.60	3.30	3.70	6.10	7.00
Recall	3.60	3.80	3.60	4.00	8.00	14.00

As an alternative to the generation hypothesis, one might argue that the Context Before group benefited from a more available set of retrieval cues (i.e., the elements of the picture--balloons, wire, window, etc.) relative to the No Context groups. There are data to suggest that retrieval cues are important for recall and that it is important that these cues be present at input (e.g., Tulving & Osler, 1968). Therefore, Partial Context subjects saw the picture in Fig. 2 before hearing the passage. The partial context picture contained all of the objects represented in the appropriate picture, but

Fig. 2.   Partial Context for the *balloon* passage.

the objects were rearranged. Partial Context subjects were clearly inferior to Context Before subjects in both comprehension ratings and recall.

The question of differential retrievability of information was investigated in a different way in a study conducted by Stanley Nyberg and John Cleary in our laboratory at Stony Brook. Subjects in No Context (1), Context Before, and Context After conditions were asked to recall the *balloon* passage either with or without key words as retrieval cues. The retrieval cues were the following words selected from the passage: balloons, window, wire, human voice, instrument, contact. Providing retrieval cues did not diminish the differences between the Context Before subjects and those in the other two groups, despite the fact that the Context Before subjects had less room to improve (see Table 4).

The results of the preceding studies indicate that context has a marked effect on memory. We are not, however, suggesting that there is a one-to-one correspondence between comprehension and recall. A subject may remember (or learn with repeated exposures) material that he has not understood. Conversely, a subject will not invariably remember all the material that he has comprehended. Although considerable research is needed to assess the relative contributions of comprehension and retrieval processes to remembering, our results do indicate that the absence of an appropriate semantic context can under some conditions seriously affect the acquisition process.

Table 4. Mean Number of Ideas Recalled (Balloon Passage)

	No Context	Context After	Context Before	Maximum Score
No Cues	3.92	4.33	7.33	14.00
Key Word Cues	4.00	3.75	8.50	14.00

Several colleagues have suggested that one way in which the absence of an appropriate context may retard the acquisition process is that subjects in No Context conditions are not using their study time efficiently. Rather than trying to memorize the input, subjects are trying to figure out a context for it in order to understand the meaning of the information. Indeed, many subjects in the experiments above who were not provided with the appropriate picture prior to hearing the passage did report that they actively searched for a situation that the passage might be about. It is possible that subjects who are relieved of the problem of finding a context (Context Before subjects) can devote more time to applying strategies for learning the input materials. On the other hand, subjects in No Context conditions have to share their time between looking for contexts and trying to memorize.

A study by Elizabeth Cole and the present writers attempted to evaluate the above time-sharing notion. The *balloon* passage was used and Context Before and No Context (1) conditions were included. In addition, subjects received either comprehension instructions or memorization instructions. Comprehension instructions were essentially equivalent to those used in the prior studies. The memorization instructions emphasized that the subjects should not spend any time or effort trying to understand the passage they were about to hear. Instead, they should attempt to memorize as much of it as possible. The time-sharing hypothesis predicts that No Context subjects under instructions to memorize should do better than No Context subjects who received comprehension instructions. In addition, if the time-sharing variable completely accounts for the memory deficit, No Context memorization subjects should perform as well as subjects in Context Before groups. The instructional manipulation should have little effect in the Context Before conditions since both comprehension and memorization groups are free of the problem of finding or creating a context and the comprehension subjects are presumably devoting their time to memorizing the input.

The results of the experiment are given in Fig. 3. They did not provide any support for the time-sharing notion. In fact, the No Context subjects recalled slightly (though not significantly) more under instructions to comprehend than under instructions to memorize, and No Context Memorization subjects were far below subjects in the Context Before groups. Insofar as the instructional manipulation influenced the subjects' activities, these data indicate that those activities related to comprehending may also be those most conducive to learning prose materials. Of course, it should be possible to train subjects in better memorizing strategies than they presumably used in the present experiment. However, it is doubtful whether a good learning strategy will completely overcome the disadvantages arising from the problem of poor comprehension. We shall return to the question of how the context aids comprehension

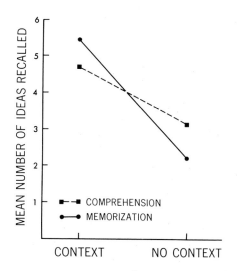

Fig. 3. Mean number of ideas recalled as a function of comprehension vs memorization instructions (*balloon* passage).

later in the paper. First we shall consider some additional studies that investigate the relation between prior knowledge, comprehension and recall.

Familiar Contexts

The *balloon* passage was constructed so that it would be very unlikely that the prerequisite semantic information would be part of the preexperimental knowledge of the subjects. The basic points made above, however, are applicable to situations where the semantic prerequisites are available from the subject's prior knowledge. Consider, for example, the following passage:

> The procedure is actually quite simple.
> First you arrange things into different
> groups. Of course, one pile may be suffi-
> cient depending on how much there is to do.
> If you have to go somewhere else due to lack
> of facilities that is the next step, other-
> wise you are pretty well set. It is impor-
> tant not to overdo things. That is, it is
> better to do too few things at once than too
> many. In the short run this may not seem
> important but complications can easily arise.
> A mistake can be expensive as well. At
> first the whole procedure will seem compli-
> cated. Soon, however, it will become just
> another facet of life. It is difficult to
> foresee any end to the necessity for this
> task in the immediate future, but then one
> never can tell. After the procedure is
> completed one arranges the materials into
> different groups again. Then they can be
> put into their appropriate places. Even-
> tually they will be used once more and the
> whole cycle will then have to be repeated.
> However, that is part of life.

Now consider the same passage again, but this time with the knowledge that the topic of the passage is *washing clothes*.

Comprehension ratings and recall scores from two different experiments (one using the above passage and one using a slightly different version of the above passage) are presented in Table 5. The procedure in these experiments was similar to that used in the initial *balloon* passage experiment outlined above. Subjects in the No Topic group produced low comprehension and recall scores, as did subjects who received information that the passage was about washing clothes after hearing the passage. Subjects in the Topic Before conditions showed higher comprehension and recall scores.

Dooling and Lachman (1971) recently reported a similar recall advantage for Topic Before subjects vs No Topic subjects. Their materials were metaphorical passages about *Christopher Columbus Discovering America* and *The First Space Trip to the Moon*. With Nancy Fenrick, we replicated the Dooling and Lachman

Table 5. Mean Comprehension Ratings and Mean Number of Ideas Recalled (Washing Clothes)

| | Experiment A | | | |
	No Topic	Topic After	Topic Before	Maximum Score
Comprehension	2.29	2.12	4.50	7.00
Recall	2.82	2.65	5.83	18.00

| | Experiment B | | |
	Topic After	Topic Before	Maximum Score
Comprehension	3.40	5.27	7.00
Recall	3.30	7.00	20.00

experiment with the addition of a Topic After condition. The words of the passage were presented successively *via* a carousel projector and protocols were scored for the number of correct words from the passage recalled. The mean number of words recalled in Topic Before, No Topic and Topic After conditions (collapsed across the two passages) were 22.6, 16.4 and 16.0, respectively. Again, Topic After did not augment recall.

These Topic After conditions seem particularly important in situations where the materials to-be-recalled convey information about familiar topics. The notion that subjects in Topic Before conditions achieve higher recall scores relative to No Topic subjects because they can generate (or reconstruct) ideas that are consistent with the topic and, coincidentally, with the passage, is much more persuasive in cases where the topics are familiar (as compared, for example, to the *balloon* passage). However, the results of the studies in the present section strongly indicate that, although generation of preexperimentally acquired ideas may sometimes operate in the recall of prose about familiar topics, this process alone cannot account for the large advantage of Topic Before subjects.[4]

In general, the results indicate that simply having relevant preexperimental knowledge is not sufficient to insure comprehension. This knowledge must be activated during the ongoing process of comprehension in order for it to be maximally useful.

---

[4]On the acquisition side, it has been suggested to us that providing a context makes it easier for the subject to image the input information (e.g., see Paivio, 1971; Bower, 1969, on the role of imagery in recall) or for the subject to organize the input information into a limited set of chunks or subjective units that may mediate efficient "storage" and subsequent recall (e.g., see Miller, 1956; Tulving, 1968;

Contexts and Sentence Acquisition

It seems reasonable to assume that had the No Context subjects in the above experiments thought of a relevant context during acquisition, their comprehension and recall scores would have improved. Therefore the present study, conducted in conjunction with Nancy McCarrell, explored the hypothesis that the difficulty of to-be-learned material is related to the likelihood that subjects will generate relevant contextual information. In order to have more than a single recall test as an index of the subjects' level of learning, the acquisition procedure involved three study-test trials. The materials consisted of a list of unrelated sentences and to minimize retrieval factors, cues for each sentence were provided on test trials.

The sentences were similar in form to the *because* sentences used earlier in the false recognition study (e.g., *John missed the bus because he knew he would have to walk to school*). On the basis of our intuitions we generated two classes of items: easy and hard. Easy sentences were those for which subjects should be able to find justifications for the relations between the two phrases with little difficulty. Hard sentences were designed to be ultimately comprehensible, but difficult to understand without help from the experimenter. For example:

Mandler, 1967). For example, materials like the *balloon* and *washing clothes* passages become intuitively more imagable when they become more comprehensible (i.e., in the context or topic before conditions). Likewise, when these passages are comprehensible, the number of cohesive ideas, and consequently organizational units, seems to be more circumscribed. However, from our point of view, images and subjective units are potential outputs of active comprehension processes but do not by themselves constitute a full analysis of such processes.

Easy: The account was low because Sally went
to the bank.
The car was moved because he had no
change.

Hard: The notes were sour because the seam
was split.
The haystack was important because the
cloth ripped.

Two groups of subjects were run in the study. One
group (No Context) received a list consisting of eight
easy and eight hard sentences, randomly intermixed.
On study trials, each sentence was preceded by the
subject noun (e.g., the account, the car, the notes,
the haystack). On the free-recall test trials, the
subject nouns were available as retrieval cues. For
this condition we expected easy sentences to be better
remembered than hard sentences, since the latter should
seem anomalous (see Marks & Miller, 1964, for memory
for anomalous vs. non-anomalous sentences). Figure 4
shows that there was a marked difference in the level
of recall of the easy and hard items, with the advantage of the easy items persisting over three study-
test trials.

The second group (Context) received conditions
identical to those of the first group except that each
sentence was preceded by a context cue rather than a
subject noun on study trials. The contexts for the
four sentences above were *withdrawal*, *parking meter*,
bagpipes, and *parachute*, respectively. The retrieval
cues on the recall tests were the subject nouns. As
can be seen in Fig. 4, the presentation of context cues
significantly reduced the difference between easy and
hard sentences. The differential difficulty of easy
and hard items was therefore not simply a function of
the sentences *per se*, but rather was a function of the
ease with which subjects could find solutions to the
comprehension problems they presented. For the Context
subjects, all sentences were presumably easy to comprehend; consequently subjects were learning instances

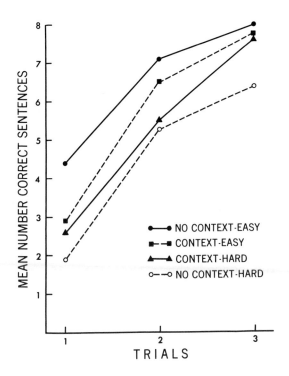

Fig. 4. Mean number of sentences recalled on successive learning trials (easy vs. hard *because* sentences.

of both classes of sentences rather than concentrating on only "easy" items (as seemed to be the case with subjects in the No Context group).

The results of the present study are consistent with the notion that context cues affected the degree to which hard sentences could be comprehended and that comprehension, in turn, affected the degree to which the individual sentences were learned and recalled. The results also support the notion that semantic anomaly is largely a function of the degree to which one can relate a sentence to some relevant aspect of his knowledge of the world (Olson, 1970).

*Situations in which Prior Activation of Relevant
Information Fails to Augment Comprehension or Recall*

A specification of the information that must be
available in order for a subject to arrive at a particular semantic product would involve a clarification
of the conditions under which the prior presentation
of relevant information does and does not augment
comprehension and recall. The two studies in the
present section suggest some of the factors that may
be important in determining whether or not providing
subjects with relevant information before a comprehension task will improve their performance. One study
indicates that the prior presentation of a relevant
topic for a passage may not be sufficient to activate
the critical features of the prerequisite semantic
context. The second shows that the effects of presenting a topic will depend on the availability of
contextual cues within the passage itself.

In the first study, the *balloon* passage mentioned
earlier was used. One group of subjects received the
topic *Possible breakdowns in communication during a
serenade* before hearing the passage. A second group
did not receive any information before the passage was
presented. Table 6 shows that providing a topic did
not augment comprehension ratings and recall scores
relative to the No Topic condition. Presumably,
information about the specific structure of the
serenade (which is supplied in the context picture in
Fig. 1) is necessary for understanding the balloon
passage. Knowledge of a relevant topic alone was not

Table 6. Mean Comprehension Ratings and Mean
Number of Ideas Recalled (Balloon Passage)

	No Topic	Topic After	Topic Before	Maximum Score
Comprehension	2.78	2.33	3.10	7.00
Recall	3.78	3.56	3.90	14.00

sufficient to increase comprehension and recall scores. From prior studies it is clear that subjects do not need any advance information about the topic in order for the context picture to greatly facilitate comprehension and recall. In addition, the picture does not "contain" the topic in that various passages (with different topics) could be built around the picture. Given that this is the case, it is possible that subjects might derive additional benefit from a condition in which the topic is provided along with the context picture. However, since the topic may be inferred from the content of the passage (in combination, of course, with the picture), providing it ahead of time may contribute little additional information. Although we have not run this topic-plus-context condition, the next study is relevant to this issue.

In conjunction with Carol Raye, we conducted a study designed to assess the role of prior activation of topics in two situations, one in which the passage in isolation was relatively incomprehensible, the other in which the passage in isolation was comprehensible. Two versions of the same passage were prepared for this experiment, one abstract and one concrete. The abstract version was similar to the *washing clothes* passage presented earlier. For the concrete version, concrete words were substituted for more abstract words in the passage. Two of the 11 substitutions were *clothes* for *items* and *laundromat* for *somewhere else*. Four groups of subjects were run in the experiment: Topic Before-Concrete, Topic Before-Abstract, No Topic-Concrete, No Topic-Abstract. The topic was *washing clothes*.

From previous studies we expected the topic-before manipulation to have a large effect on comprehension and recall scores for subjects receiving the abstract passage. One primary question was whether the prior information about the topic would augment performance in the concrete case, where the passage itself included many cues to the appropriate context. An additional point of interest was the degree to which the Topic Before-Abstract subjects' performance would approximate that of subjects in the concrete group.

Table 7 shows the comprehension ratings and mean number of ideas recalled for the four conditions. The maximum score was 17; therefore, the groups were all well below ceiling. Recall scores for the concrete version of the passage were not affected by the topic variable. As in previous results, the topic increased comprehension and recall scores for subjects receiving the abstract version of the passage. In addition, the Topic Before-Abstract group remained significantly below the corresponding concrete condition.

We think that this residual advantage of the concrete passage can be attributed to the fact that substituting concrete words did help make some of the individual sentences in the passage more comprehensible. Therefore, although both Concrete subjects and Abstract-plus-Topic subjects had relevant semantic information activated, concrete words probably had greater cue value for specific details of the meaning of the passage than did abstract words. The fact that subjects in the Topic Before-Abstract group produced significantly lower comprehension ratings than subjects in the concrete groups supports this point of view.[5]

Table 7. Mean Comprehension Ratings and Mean Number of Ideas Recalled

	Comprehension[a]		Recall[b]	
	Abstract	Concrete	Abstract	Concrete
Topic	6.00	6.89	9.00	11.67
No Topic	3.67	6.67	4.87	10.56

[a]Scale from 0-7

[b]Maximum Score = 17

---

[5]Concreteness and comprehensibility are, in fact, confounded in many experiments. See, for example, Johnson, Bransford, Nyberg and Cleary's (in press) analysis of Begg and Paivio's (1969) study of memory for abstract versus concrete sentences.

*Situations in which Prior Activation of Certain
Information Retards Comprehension and Recall*

The experiments above indicate that relating information to relevant aspects of prior knowledge is a critical part of the comprehension process. Presenting subjects with a context or, more generally, a cue to a context) made relatively incomprehensible materials much more comprehensible. Postexperimental interviews indicated that, when left to their own devices (no context, no topic or no cue conditions), many subjects attempted to find or generate information that would make sense of the materials. Occasionally they appeared to be somewhat successful in making parts of the input idiosyncratically meaningful. In this section, we will consider what happens when subjects are specifically misdirected in their attempts to find a useful context for difficult material. Although we do not have a great deal of evidence on this point, the data below suggest that subjects may be better off creating their own context than attempting to find relationships between an input and the wrong context.

One indication that wrong contexts might retard performance was obtained in our replication (mentioned above) of the Dooling and Lachman experiment. In addition to the conditions previously discussed, this study included a condition in which subjects were presented with irrelevant topics just prior to acquisition. The irrelevant topics were *Writing a letter to a Friend* and *Reading a Magazine at Lunch* for the *Christopher Columbus Discovering America* and *The First Space Trip to the Moon* passages, respectively. As can be seen in Table 8, there was a slight

Table 8. Mean Number of Words Recalled
(Columbus and Moon Passages Combined)

No Topic	Topic After	Irrelevant Topic	Topic Before	Maximum Score
16.40	16.05	15.25	22.65	77.00

detrimental effect on recall as a consequence of presenting the irrelevant topics, but the difference between irrelevant and no topic conditions was not significant.

With different materials and procedure, a subsequent experiment (Doll, Lapinsky, Bransford, & Johnson, in preparation) resulted in a much more marked effect of irrelevant information on recall. The subjects were presented with 16 sentences for three study-test trials. The sentences were relatively short, and seemingly anomalous in isolation (e.g., *The streak blocked the light; The man saw his face in the body*). The design consisted of three cue conditions combined factorially with two acquisition rates and for the present purposes the data are collapsed across this latter factor. For No Cue subjects, each sentence was preceded by the word ready during acquisition. For Cue subjects, each sentence was preceded by a context cue; for example, the cues corresponding to the sentences above were *a window* and *new car*, respectively. For the Irrelevant Cue condition, these cues were randomly paired with the sentences. Subjects in the Cue and Irrelevant Cue conditions were told that the cues might help them remember the sentences, but that the cues themselves would never have to be recalled. A free recall test procedure was used and no cues were provided on test trials.

The mean number of sentences recalled on each of the three trials is shown in Fig. 5. As expected, the Cue subjects were at a considerable advantage. More important for the present discussion, the performance of the Irrelevant Cue subjects was significantly worse than that of the No Cue subjects. It seems likely that many of the No Cue subjects were able to find contexts for some of the sentences. On the other hand, providing irrelevant cues hurt the subjects' performance presumably because they were attempting to understand the sentences in light of the presented contexts and therefore were not as likely to discover better contexts of their own.

The sentences used above were difficult to understand in isolation, but even basically comprehensible information can be rendered incomprehensible by an inappropriate context. A sentence that can be understood in isolation is presumably one that provides sufficient cues so that the comprehender can make whichever semantic contributions are necessary. However, from the present point of view, comprehension problems should arise with such sentences when the context active at the time of input is inappropriate or when the subject cannot create a relationship between the sentence and the context. To test this notion, we used the following passage.[6] The passage was read once at a

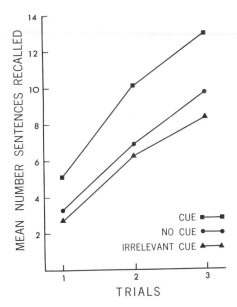

Fig. 5. Mean number of sentences recalled on successive learning trials under three input cueing conditions (Cue, Irrelevant Cue, and No Cue).

---

[6]This study grew out of an undergraduate project conducted by Paula M. Mintzies. We are indebted to her for her interest and her work.

normal rate, so the subjects did not have time to linger over any particular sentence. The subjects were instructed that they would later be asked to recall as much as they could.

Watching a Peace March from the 40th Floor

The view was breathtaking. From the window one could see the crowd below. Everything looked extremely small from such a distance, but the colorful costumes could still be seen. Everyone seemed to be moving in one direction in an orderly fashion and there seemed to be little children as well as adults. The landing was gentle, and luckily the atmosphere was such that no special suits had to be worn. At first there was a great deal of activity. Later, when the speeches started, the crowd quieted down. The man with the television camera took many shots of the setting and the crowd. Everyone was very friendly and seemed glad when the music started.

The conditions of the experiment and the recall data will be presented below. For the moment, consider some informally gathered introspective reports. People are generally able to understand this passage quite easily until they hear the sentence, "The landing was gentle and luckily the atmosphere was such that no special suits had to be worn." At this point they usually become confused or surprised. A few people come up with a "rationale" for the sentence. For example, that a helicopter landed in the middle of the parade to control the crowds, that the peace march moved to the airport to meet someone, or that the "landing" referred to a platform outside the hotel-room window and that the "atmosphere" part of the sentence referred to the fact that the weather was warm. These reports represent the most creative attempts to incorporate the sentence into the ongoing context suggested by the title and the rest of the passage. Most people report that they could not figure out what the sentence meant.

Now consider the same passage again and assume that the title has been changed to *A Space Trip to an Inhabited Planet*. Under this title condition, people generally do not have any special trouble with the *landing* sentence.

There were four conditions in the actual experiment using this passage. Two conditions (one with each title above) were included to make sure that the *Space Trip* title did not simply activate a better overall context for the passage. Therefore, in these conditions, the *landing* sentence was deleted; otherwise the passage was the same as above. With the *landing* sentence deleted, recall was not influenced by the title manipulation. For the other two conditions, the passage contained the *landing* sentence. In this case, overall recall under the *Space Trip* title was slightly (but not significantly) greater than under the *Peace March* title. Therefore, the presence of the critical sentence did not appreciably disrupt the overall performance of the subjects in the *Peace March* condition.

Of primary interest were the recall scores on the *landing* sentence as a function of the title condition. As can be seen in Table 9, a significantly greater number of subjects in the *Space Trip* than in the *Peace March* condition recalled at least one of the two critical idea units (landing gentle; atmosphere did not require suits) from the *landing* sentence. To assess whether this expected difference in recall was due simply to subjects' tendency to recall only ideas consistent with their respective topics, the subjects received a second type of retention test immediately following the free recall test. They were provided with a printed "cue outline" of the passage in which many words were deleted (similar to a "cloze" technique). The subject's task was to fill in the missing parts of the passage. The scores for the frame, "Luckily the landing _____ and the atmosphere _____ " are also included in Table 9. As is apparent, the cued recall procedure did not reduce the advantage of the subjects in the *Space Trip* title condition.

Table 9. Recall Scores with
The *Landing* Sentence Deleted or Present

Mean Number of Ideas Recalled		
	Landing Sentence Deleted	with *Landing* Sentence
Space Trip	5.57	7.41
Peace March	5.86	5.82
Number of Subjects per Condition	14	17
Maximum Score	16	18

Number of Subjects Recalling at least One Idea from *Landing* Sentence		
	Uncued	Cued
Space Trip	9	14
Peace March	3	5
Number of Subjects per Condition	17	17
Maximum Score	17	17

Taken together, the studies presented in this section indicate that potentially meaningful material can remain relatively incomprehensible when subjects do not have prerequisite semantic information activated at the time of input. In addition, it is possible to impede the subjects' ability to find useful relations between an input and what he already knows by presenting him with an irrelevant context. A logical inference from these results is that the meaning of an input cannot be determined independently of the context into which an individual is trying to assimilate it. For example, the *Peace March/Space Trip* passage is a message whose meaning varies depending on the cognitive orientation from which it is viewed.

Alternative Contexts

Meaning as a Function of Context

In the present section, we would like to mention briefly some further implications of the notion that what is understood from a message depends on the activated semantic context. The studies above indicate that comprehension ratings and recall measures are quite sensitive to the presence or absence of an appropriate context. However, the general orientation suggested by the above studies should be applicable to situations where material is readily comprehensible without additional cues but where alternative contexts yield different semantic products. In these cases, differences in semantic products will not always be reflected in the number or objective characteristics of the ideas recalled. Nevertheless, the characteristics of the semantic product should vary with different contexts and these differences should have consequences for subsequent tasks.

As an example of the influence of alternative contexts, and of how their activation may depend on minimal changes in the input, consider the following passage:

The man stood before the mirror and combed his hair. He checked his face carefully for any places he might have missed shaving and then put on the conservative tie he had decided to wear. At breakfast, he studied the newspaper carefully and, over coffee, discussed the possibility of buying a new washing machine with his wife. Then he made several phone calls. As he was leaving the house he thought about the fact that his children would probably want to go to that private camp again this summer. When the car didn't start, he got out, slammed the door, and walked down to the bus stop in a very angry mood. Now he would be late.

415

Now consider the passage again, but assume that it includes an adjective that lets you know that the man is out of work: "The *unemployed* man stood before the mirror...."

Intuitively it seems that adding this single adjective changes the characteristics of what is understood about the passage. For example, the events described in the passage (e.g., reading a paper, making phone calls, putting on a conservative tie, etc.) might be structured into a semantic product that not only includes information *that* certain things took place, but also inferences about *why* they took place. An individual may be likely to infer that the unemployed man is getting ready for a job interview, that he studied the want ads over breakfast, and that he probably cannot afford to buy the washing machine or send his children to camp. Different contexts allow different types of inferences. For example, if *stockbroker* is substituted for *unemployed man*, the individual should be more likely to conclude that the man was getting ready for work, that he studied the financial page over breakfast, and that he probably could afford to buy the washing machine and send his children to camp. These differences in understanding should have empirical consequences for subsequent performance. For example, question answering should reflect the meanings understood in light of the context (e.g., what section of the paper do you think the man was reading?), and the kinds of cues that will remind one of aspects of a story or seem consonant with that story should be determined by the way that it was initially understood (e.g., see Light & Carter-Sobell, 1970; Tulving & Osler, 1968; Tulving & Thomson, 1971).

Restructuring Information in Retrospect

As we can ask whether the activation of various contexts results in different meanings for the same or similar passages, we can ask whether a change in context *after* an initial understanding has been obtained will allow an individual to retrospectively comprehend (recomprehend). A pilot study, conducted with Nancy Fenrick, provides some information about this question. It involved reading subjects a passage and providing them with "inference cues" that might remind them of aspects of the story. These cues were designed to be effective for subjects hearing the story from an "appropriate topic" perspective, but not for subjects hearing it from its "natural" (i.e., no topic) perspective. The passage is provided below:

It was 5:30 in the morning and the sun was not yet up. The man got up quietly so as not to awaken anyone and silently got dressed. It was Saturday--a day he had long been looking forward to--and he was glad it had arrived. Once outside he walked along the fence for a while until he came to the break that formed an opening. There he headed for the forest that he so loved.

Since it was spring there was lots of foliage, so the forest was quite dense. He walked for quite a while and enjoyed the view. After some time he thought he heard voices. He looked around but could not see anyone else.

The man came to a clearing in the forest. It was muddy because of the previous day's rain, and his boots sank in deeply. When he came to a little stream he walked up it for quite a while before crossing to the other side.

In front of him darted a rabbit. At first he had an urge to shoot it, but then decided to let it be.

When he finally came to the lake he found his little boat that was moored among the rushes. He had spent many childhood days fishing from this craft, and it was still quite seaworthy. He rowed out to the little island where he and his brother had built their shack for hunting. Everything was as

they had left it the last time. Once inside
he took off his shirt and put on his long-
loved lumber jacket. It felt much more
comfortable than his other clothes, and he
liked the looks much better too.

The man turned on his radio to catch a
glimpse of what was happening in civiliza-
tion, and then relaxed with his pipe.

His brother should arrive shortly, and
together they would follow the lakes even
more deeply into the wilderness, and follow
trails where few men had gone before.

Examples of "inference cues" are as follows:

Evidence of pursuers
A concern with the trail and a way to
    eliminate it
Worry about the sound
A desire to eliminate old identifying factors

From prior experience we knew that most subjects
in the No Topic conditions would assume that the above
passage was either about a hunter or a man walking
through the forest, and we did not expect the above
cues to suggest ideas from the information yielded by
these points of view. Topic Before subjects, however,
were told that the story was about an *escaped convict*.
For these subjects, we anticipated a higher probability
of the cues mapping into the meanings they had acquired
(e.g., that evidence of pursuers referred to the man
hearing voices, that a way to eliminate the trail
referred to his walking up the river for awhile, that
a desire to eliminate old identifying factors referred
to his changing out of his prison shirt, etc.).

After all subjects recalled the passage, they were
provided with "inference cues" like those mentioned
above and told to use them to aid their recall of
things they had forgotten. Then they were to answer
some questions about the information value of the
cues. The cues did not augment recall of the Topic

Before subjects. However, subjects' answers to questions about the information value of the cues suggest some interesting leads. Most subjects in the Topic Before condition (who knew that the passage was about an escaped convict) seemed to feel that the cues related to the story. Some felt that many of the cues made sense immediately, some felt that they had to think awhile before seeing their relevance, and some felt that the cues actually helped them understand the story better. Only one subject said that he failed to see a meaningful relation between the initial story and any of the cues. The responses of the No Topic subjects were quite different. Over half (56%) of the subjects wrote spontaneous comments indicating that the cues actually made them change their initial interpretation of the story or doubt that they had correctly understood the story when it had initially been read. For example, "After thinking about the cues for about 5 minutes I realized that this story was in fact about a man who had a hunting shack but was now using it as a hide-out from the police. I put the story sections I remembered together with the cues and it occurred to me to have a completely different story than the one I described (recalled) first."

Although they are difficult to classify, the subjective reports indicate that the above "information after" condition caused some of the subjects to recomprehend the story--to understand it from a different point of view. The No Topic subjects presumably tried to find some relationship between the cues and the story, and when they were unsuccessful they changed their interpretation of the story in order to accommodate the cues.

Note that this possibility for retrospective comprehension is in contrast to the results of previous studies. For example, there was little effect on comprehension ratings and recall for topic after conditions in the *balloon* or *washing clothes* passages. The lack of context or topic-after effects with these latter passages is probably due to the fact that, unlike the *hunter* passage, these stories were not comprehensible

419

in isolation; thus, subjects had a difficult time
retaining much of what they heard. In order for information to be retrospectively comprehended it must somehow be available, which is unlikely with relatively
long, incomprehensible passages after only one acquisition trial. With shorter materials retrospective comprehension is possible and seems to produce the subjective feeling of the "aha-experience" (Buhler, cf.
Blumenthal, 1970, p. 51). For example, we have informally presented subjects with sentences like *The notes
were sour because the seam was split* and after a few
seconds' delay have presented them with relevant contextual information (e.g., bagpipes). The "insight"
or "aha-experience" seemed to occur in a very sudden
way. The "aha-experience" in the context of a single
sentence seems to be a limiting case where non-compre-
hended information is temporarily available since the
material in question is not long enough to tax the
limits of short-term memory. Using longer passages,
it would be interesting to assess the speed with which
inputs may be retrospectively comprehended. In some
cases, subjects probably have to recall mentally an
initially comprehended story and, in effect, present
themselves with a new comprehension trial with a new
context in mind. In other cases, the retrospective
process might be more abrupt with new information
restructuring old information more or less all at once.
Studies of the processes by which subjects retrospectively comprehend information should provide interesting
hypotheses about some of the ways in which individuals
can manipulate and modify what they already know.

Towards a Schematic Characterization of the Problem of Comprehension

The preceding studies, we think, implicate an
approach to comprehension that focuses on the relation
between input information and the general knowledge
available to the subject. Their dominant theme is the
reminder that a language is a symbol system that is
generally used by individuals for the purpose of

communication, and that the effective use of this symbol system depends on other knowledge available to its users. One implication of this orientation is that an account of comprehension must concern itself not only with an analysis of the linguistic symbol system for communication, but also with a consideration of the knowledge structures to which the symbols are assumed to refer.

The basis for an approach to comprehension that focuses on the relation between input information and general knowledge was provided some time ago by Karl Buhler (cf. Blumenthal, 1971) who emphasized the interdependence between inputs and "fields." According to Blumenthal:

> Buhler's field concept was most important. Given two speakers of the same language, no matter how well one of them structures a sentence his utterance will fail if both parties do not share the same field to some degree. . . There are inner aspects of the field, such as an area of knowledge, or outer aspects, such as objects in the environment. Indeed, the field can be analyzed into many aspects. The total field (Umfeld) consists not only of the practical situation (Ziegfeld) in which an utterance occurs, but also the symbol field (Symbolfeld) which is the context of language segments preceding the segment under consideration. . . . The structure of any particular language is largely field-independent, being determined by its own particular conventional rules, but the field determines how the rules are applied . . . with a 'rich' external field less needs to be specified in the sentence (p. 56).[7]

---

[7]If the "field" is rich enough, a series of ideas can probably be communicated with minimal input cues and little processing time. For example, at Stony

The studies presented here seem quite compatible with
Buhler's general framework. In the present section we
shall further consider some theoretical implications
of these studies. Although the following discussion
is divided into sub-sections, the points discussed are
all interrelated, differing more in emphasis than in
kind.

*Linguistic Inputs Presuppose Appropriate Knowledge
of the World*

The studies using the *balloon* and *washing clothes*
passages were explicitly designed to investigate the
consequences of a subject's failure to identify appropriate knowledge domains that were presupposed by input
information. Such failures markedly reduced his recall
of the material. Although No Context and No Topic
subjects reported attempting to discover or generate
circumstances that would render the materials meaningful, their lack of success was clearly reflected in
the low comprehension ratings they gave the materials.
These results suggest that comprehensibility (and
presumably linguistic acceptability) is affected by
extra-linguistic information. That is, a linguistic
input may seem acceptable to one listener and unacceptable to another, depending on the contributions they
are able to make from their past experience.[8]

Brook, Carol Ray has presented subjects with three
successive lists like the following: Mailman, box,
plastic, room, hose, sheet, cigarette, flood. Overall
recall scores of subjects receiving an appropriate
theme for each list (e.g., *new waterbed*) were higher
than those of subjects in several other instructional
conditions (e.g., method of loci). Additional pilot
data suggest that increasing the presentation rate to
1.5 sec. (from 5.0 sec.) per item has much less of a
detrimental effect on the performance of Theme subjects
than on that of Method of Loci subjects.

[8]Many recent papers in linguistics discuss the
notion that the acceptability of a sentence can be

The dependence between linguistic comprehensibility and general knowledge was also illustrated in the sentence acquisition studies (Figs. 4 and 5). Sentences such as *The house turned to water because the fire got too hot* become readily comprehensible (and were much better recalled) in light of additional information that helps specify referential situations (e.g., *igloo*). This sentence is difficult to comprehend and remember, not because it violates some syntactic constraint governing the use of the word *house*, but because it conflicts with the knowledge that houses do not usually turn to water. Identifying a kind of house that could turn to water, however, renders the sentence intelligible. A similar example is apparent from the sentence *The haystack was important because the cloth ripped*, which is more readily understood in combination with the cue *parachute*. Here the word *parachute* does not simply specify a reading for cloth. It also sets up conditions for realizing the relations between the cloth and the haystack, namely that the parachute was above the haystack when it ripped. These examples illustrate that the contributions that an individual must often make in order to comprehend include more than a specification of appropriate individual referents. He must also generate appropriate relations among entities as well.[9]

---

affected by knowledge from other sources (e.g., see Fillmore and Langedoen, 1971), and the false recognition data shown in Table 2 suggest that subjects often make extra-sentential assumptions in order to justify sentences. The notion that acceptability can be affected by extra-linguistic information implies that a sentence may be acceptable to one individual and unacceptable to another. Perhaps this helps explain why some examples of linguistic "clear-cases" and "non-cases" are not always convincing to everyone, and, more importantly, why one's intuitions about acceptability may change.

[9]The notion that subjects must often be able to specify rather precise conditions in order to comprehend an input suggests that it may be fruitful to view

The fact that information about presupposed knowledge structures may be prerequisite for comprehending inputs indicates that sentences are not always first understood as independent entities and then amalgamated with other information. Instead, there may be important dependencies between activated knowledge structures and comprehension of the inputs themselves.[10]

The Same Inputs Can Have Different Meanings Depending on the Knowledge Structures to which they are Referred

A related aspect of the dependency between activated knowledge structures and comprehension is that not only may such structures be prerequisite for comprehension, but the same inputs may have different meanings depending on the knowledge structures to which they are assumed to refer. The passages about the *Peach March/Space Trip* and *Man/Unemployed/Man* illustrate this point.

---

words or phrases as providing cues to semantic structure. A sentence like *The man put the airplane in the envelope*, for example, may be more quickly comprehended if it contains the adjective *toy* (i.e., *The man put the toy plane in the envelope*). Similarly, the sentence *The man escaped from the ice cream cone* may be more readily understood when it includes an adjective that suggests relational aspects of the referential situation (i.e., *The man escaped from the falling ice cream cone*). In ordinary prose or conversation, of course, the referential situation is often given by preceding inputs. For example, a paragraph from a well-known study by Sachs (1967) contains the sentence *On the next night all were to the west*. The preceding sentences indicate that the sentence referred to Galileo looking at Jupiter's moons.

[10]Other studies showing that the situation to which an input refers can affect how easily it is understood include Slobin (1966); Huttenlocker, Eisenberg and Strauss (1968); Huttenlocker and Strauss (1968); Huttenlocker and Weiner (1971).

At first glance it may appear that examples such as these show only that sentences can be ambiguous, and that different knowledge structures may disambiguate sentences in different ways. We think that the relation between linguistic inputs and referential knowledge structures can be much more dynamic than is implied by the general notion of linguistic disambiguation, however. To illustrate with an example that is somewhat simpler than a whole passage, consider the sentence *The woman was worried that the rope might break* in light of the four situations (contexts) shown in Fig. 6. Each context suggests different reasons for worrying about the rope breaking: e.g., (a) because the mirror would fall (and might break); (b) because the lamp would fall (and maybe break the mirror); (c) because the clothes would fall; (d) because the man would fall. The availability of these reasons is based on perceived implications of the input (i.e., of the rope breaking) in light of each context.[11] In addition, the perceived implications of inputs may yield referential situations that are presupposed by subsequent inputs. For example, the sentences *The rope broke/The woman was angry about the mirror* are interrelated sentences from the perspective of the first two contexts (e.g., they could be connected by *so*) but not from the perspective of contexts (c) and (d). Thus, inputs modify structures and these modified structures are, in turn, referents for subsequent inputs. In general, the meaning derived from inputs should depend on their implications for the structures to which they are referred.

---

[11]The following sentence is a similar example: *The man escaped from the situation.* If the situation in question is an airplane, *escape* may involve parachuting, whereas if the situation is a boat, *escape* may involve swimming. It might be profitable to consider word meanings as abstract constraints governing more precise specifications that occur in particular contexts. This would seem to allow for the possibility of variance as well as abstract invariance in meaning.

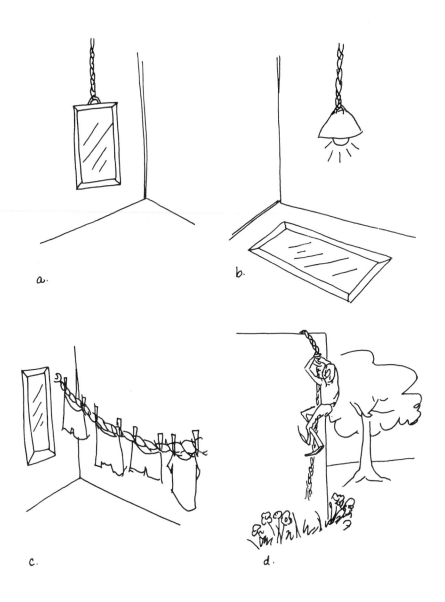

Fig. 6. Four contexts for *The woman was worried that the rope might break.*

A consideration of the dynamic interplay between inputs and knowledge structures suggests some speculations about why the appropriate context (Fig. 1) for the *balloon* passage aided comprehension but the partial context (Fig. 2) did not. Given either context, the subjects' initial assumption was probably that the sentences in the passage referred to the context provided. For the appropriate context, the first phrase of the passage (i.e., *If the balloons popped . . .*) had definite implications, namely that the speaker would fall. Since the distance between the ground and the girl was considerable, a possible consequence of the speaker falling was that the girl could no longer hear the boy's voice. The availability of the latter information thus allowed the subject to understand what was being referred to by the phrase *the sound could not carry* (which was the second phrase of the passage).

For the subjects receiving the partial context picture, the phrase *If the balloons popped* also had certain potential implications (e.g., that the balloons would no longer tug at the strings held by the boy) but none which could easily serve as a basis for relating *the sound could not carry* to the situation suggested by the initial phrase. Of course, given different information the partial context could serve as an adequate referential structure. In short, the notion of an "appropriate" context is relative to the input information that is to be processed.[12]

---

[12]It should be possible to develop experimental situations which are sensitive to the processes by which inputs are related to other knowledge structures. For example, if different structures require different amounts of modification in order to accommodate an input (or if different inputs require different amounts of modification of the same context), measures of comprehension time might reflect the number of implicational steps involved. Such a paradigm might provide more systematic information about the processes by which subjects amalgamate input information with other available knowledge.

Memory may Include Extra-Linguistic Information

Many theories of language processing tacitly assume that sentences are treated as self-contained objects. They thus assume that the semantic reading directly assigned to a sentence exhaustively characterizes what is understood and stored (e.g., Katz & Postal, 1964). Although it is possible, of course, for subjects to treat linguistic inputs as objects to be remembered, recent evidence from memory studies indicates that subjects often are not simply storing either the surface (Sachs, 1967) or the deep structures (Bransford, Barclay, & Franks, in press; Bransford & Franks, 1971) of individual sentences. For example, when related sentences are included in an acquisition list, the subjects' performance in a recognition task may be based on an integration of the ideas expressed by several sentences (Bransford & Franks, 1971). And input sentences may be amalgamated with previous knowledge to yield semantic products specifying more information than was expressed in the input. False recognition studies indicate that subjects are likely to make assumptions about spatial relations (Bransford, Barclay & Franks, in press), and about instruments (*John was using the hammer* . . .), consequences (*The spy burned the secret document* . . .) and antecedent conditions (*John wanted to walk to school* . . .).

The general pattern of these results indicates that subjects spontaneously make assumptions about extra-linguistic circumstances and draw on a wide range of prior knowledge in doing so. The subject's memory for a sentence or sets of sentences will therefore be a function of how he uses what he knows to interpret what he hears, and of how he uses this interpretation to modify what he already knows.[13]

---

[13]The view that subjects may treat sentences as cues to activate and modify general knowledge structures --rather than simply as information to be stored--may help in understanding the bases for some idiosyncratic distortions in recall. For example, subjects sometimes recall sentences which are related to input information

What is Understood and Remembered can Depend on the
Uses to which Information is Put

In the preceding sections we have argued that what
is understood and remembered about an input depends on
the knowledge structures to which it is related. In the
present section we shall consider implications of the
fact that an input can be related to a particular knowledge structure in different ways. For example, an input
may be judged true or false with respect to another
source of information. Presumably this process of verification may proceed without significantly altering the
referential knowledge structure. On the other hand, an
input can be viewed as further information about some
knowledge structure. The input may then cause a restructuring of (or an elaboration of) the old structure such
that new information is acquired. The manner in which
an input is related to a knowledge structure may thus
influence the processes of knowledge acquisition. We
think that this is demonstrated in the pilot study
below.

In conjunction with Nancy McCarrell, we conducted
an experiment designed to manipulate the manner in which
inputs were related to a specific structure. All subjects were tested simultaneously and each subject
received one of three sets of written instructions.
All instructional conditions informed the subjects
that they were in a two-part experiment and that during
Part 1 they would hear a story. One group of subjects
(Verification) was told that in Part 2 they would hear
a series of statements and that their task was to decide
(and to write down on an answer sheet) whether each
statement was true or false with respect to the story.

---

but which cannot be said to be direct paraphrases of
input information. Thus, a sentence like *The University*
President demanded that the barricades be removed imme-
diately might be recalled as *The University President*
demanded that the students immediately leave the occu-
pied building.

They were instructed that true referred to any reasonable paraphrase of events described in the story and
that false meant that the statement contradicted information conveyed by the story. The other two instructional conditions will be described after the stimulus
materials are presented. Parts 1 and 2 are given below
(consider them in light of the above instructional
condition):

Part 1

The man got into his pick-up truck and
drove to the store in the nearby city. He
knew that this was the last day of the special
sale. He wanted to buy a hat and coat while
the special prices were still in effect. The
streets near the store were very crowded and
there was no place to park. He drove round
and round. After 10 minutes he returned to
a dead-end alley he had noticed earlier. The
alley was a couple of blocks away from the
store. The man parked in the alley, got out
of his truck and started walking. It began
to drizzle and he worried whether the store
was as close as he thought it was.

Part 2

The man returned to the alley/ The man
got into his pickup truck and drove towards the
the store/ After searching, the man finally
saw a place to park/ The parking space was
only a few feet from an entrance to the store/
The man was not worried about the rain/ The
man bought a specially priced coat but not a
hat/ The man was happy about the sale/

Subjects in the other two conditions, Acquisition
(U/P) and Acquisition (Y/N), were informed that each
statement in Part 2 represented a continuation of
Part 1 in order to induce them to view the statements

as a potential source of further information about the man's activities. These two conditions differed with respect to the written rating task the subjects performed during Part 2. Acquisition (U/P) subjects were to decide whether each statement seemed pleasant or unpleasant given the initial story. Acquisition (Y/N) subjects were instructed to write "yes" if a statement in Part 2 represented a comprehensible extension of Part 1 and to write "no" if it did not.

One minute after the completion of the Part 2 task, all subjects were given a surprise recall test. They were informed that information in Part 2 really represented an extension of Part 1, and were asked to attempt to recall the information in order of presentation if they could, but were encouraged to recall in any order if they could not remember the exact order in which events occurred.

Following the recall test, all subjects were informed about the experiment and were told to listen to both Parts 1 and 2 as a single story. Subjects were then asked to indicate whether, during the actual experiment, they had been aware of the fact that information in Part 2 could have represented a continuation of Part 1. If subjects indicated that they had noticed this relationship, they were also asked to indicate whether they had noted a little, a moderate, or a lot. Of course, we expected subjects in the two Acquisition conditions to indicate that they had noticed the continuation since they had been led to expect it by instruction. Of primary interest was whether or not Verification subjects would detect the potential continuation relationship between Parts 1 and 2. As can be seen in Table 10, most subjects in the Verification

Table 10. Awareness Ratings

	Verification	Acquisition (U/P)	Acquisition (Y/N)
No	16	1	1
Yes			
A Little	8	1	4
Moderate	1	6	6
A Lot	0	18	14

condition were not aware that Part 2 could be an
extension of Part 1. Further, most of the subjects
who did respond "yes" were only slightly aware of the
continuation.

The mean number of ideas recalled (scored for
paraphrases and without regard for correct serial order)
are given in Table 11. The three conditions exhibited
equivalent Part 1 recall. In recalling Part 2, however,
subjects in the verification condition were markedly
inferior to subjects in the other two conditions.

The awareness data in combination with the recall
data suggest that under conditions where all subjects
are processing information semantically, the consequences of this processing may depend on the assumed
relationship between an input and the presupposed referential structure. That is, with the same inputs, different things may be understood.[14]

Table 11. Mean Number of Ideas Recalled

	Verification	Acquisition (U/P)	Acquisition (Y/N)	Maximum Score
Part 1	9.36	9.08	8.80	11.00
Part 2	2.84	5.84	5.00	7.00

[14]Recent evidence (e.g., Bobrow & Bower, 1969;
Hyde & Jenkins, 1969; Johnston & Jenkins, 1971) indicates that memory for words is better if subjects are
asked to perform tasks during acquisition that presuppose semantic processing than if they are directed
to perform tasks that require them to focus on more
formal properties of the inputs. The results of the
present pilot study suggest that even when subjects are
presumably successfully processing the information
semantically, the uses to which the information is put
may influence its availability on a subsequent recall
task.

Recently, many investigators have concentrated on processes involved in verifying the relation between sentences and knowledge structures (e.g., Chase & Clark, 1972; Clark, in press; Collins & Quillian, 1969, 1970; Trabasso, in press). Our experiments have generally involved situations where the subject is attempting to modify or acquire new information about knowledge structures. It would appear fruitful to compare more carefully the effects on comprehension of different task sets.[15]

Although additional research is needed, the above study also suggests the possibility of a very complex relation between comprehension and knowledge acquisition. Semantic processing may involve options such as whether or not to modify various knowledge structures, whether or not to create new ones, whether or not to judge the truth value of a statement or presuppose its truth value and see what its implications might be.[16] What is acquired from an input may thus depend on the ways in which it is related to existing knowledge domains.

---

[15]See Dooling (in press) for an example where comprehension times are affected by differences in task set.

[16]Different syntactic forms probably influence the way subjects react to various inputs. For example, we have asked subjects to write down their first response (from the set of responses *True, False, Comprehensible*) to each of a list of unrelated sentences. Sentences like *Girls wear dresses* and *Canaries eat cigarettes* generally are given True and False responses, respectively. In contrast, subjects tend to respond Comprehensible to sentences like *The girls wore dresses* and *The canaries ate the cigarettes*. In further investigating how subjects draw upon knowledge available from long-term memory in processing information (e.g., Collins & Quillian, 1969, 1972), it might be interesting to compare the time to verify sentences like *Sharks have large fins* and *Sharks have tough skin* with comprehension times for sentences like *The sharks had large fins* and *The sharks had tough skin*.

Concluding Comments

The present paper has been concerned with the question of linguistic comprehension. We have tried to show that one may not be able to process linguistic inputs effectively without access to a substrate of additional information. Such prerequisite information may be derived from non-linguistic experiences (e.g., visual inputs) as well as from prior sentences. Therefore, questions about linguistic processing cannot be completely separated from questions about the processing of other information.

The results of the studies reported here do not dictate a detailed model of comprehension, but they suggest to us a general orientation towards the problem of linguistic comprehension that places it squarely within the domain of cognitive psychology, and that generates questions for future research. We have emphasized that aspects of the comprehension process may involve mental operations on knowledge structures and the realization of the implications of these operations. In addition, we have argued that information about the consequences of such operations—rather than information only about the input itself—may be necessary for comprehending subsequent inputs and may be an important part of what is available in memory tasks. Hopefully, the development of paradigms to investigate comprehension as a function of the degree of modification of knowledge structures which is required, and of paradigms to determine the locus and time course of inferences, will clarify the thinking processes involved in comprehension and will clarify the relationship of understanding to the acquisition and retention of information.

References

Begg, I., & Paivio, A. Concreteness and imagery in sentence memory. *Journal of Verbal Learning and Verbal Behavior*, 1969, 8, 821-827.

Blumenthal, A. L. *Language and psychology*. New York: John Wiley and Sons, Inc., 1970.

Bobrow, S. A., & Bower, G. H. Comprehension and recall of sentences. *Journal of Experimental Psychology*, 1969, 80, 455–461.

Bower, G. H. Mental imagery and associative learning. In L. Gregg (Ed.), *Cognition in learning and memory*. New York: John Wiley and Sons, Inc., 1969.

Bransford, J. D., Barclay, J. R., & Franks, J. J. Sentence memory: A constructive versus interpretive approach. *Cognitive Psychology*, In press.

Bransford, J. D., & Franks, J. J. The abstraction of linguistic ideas. *Cognitive Psychology*, 1971, 2, 331–350.

Bransford, J. D., & Franks, J. J. The abstraction of linguistic ideas: A review. *International Journal of Cognitive Psychology*, In press.

Bransford, J. D., & Johnson, M. K. Semantic prerequisites for comprehending prose. Paper presented at Eastern Verbal Investigators League meetings, October, 1971.

Bransford, J. D., & Johnson, M. K. Contextual prerequisites for understanding: Some investigations of comprehension and recall. *Journal of Verbal Learning and Verbal Behavior*, In press.

Chase, W. G., & Clark, H. H. Mental operations in the comparison of sentences and pictures. In L. Gregg (Ed.), *Cognition in learning and memory*, New York: John Wiley and Sons, Inc., 1972.

Chomsky, N. *Syntactic structures*. London: Mouton and Company, 1957.

Clark, H. H. Semantics and comprehension. In T. A. Sebeok (Ed.), *Current trends in linguistics, Vol. 12: Linguistics and adjacent arts and sciences*. The Hague: Mouton, In press.

Collins, A. M., & Quillian, M. R. Retrieval time from semantic memory. *Journal of Verbal Learning and Verbal Behavior*, 1969, 8, 240–247.

Collins, A. M., & Quillian, M. R. Experiments on
  semantic memory and language comprehension. In
  L. Gregg (Ed.), *Cognition in learning and memory*.
  New York: John Wiley and Sons, Inc., 1972.
Dooling, D. J. Some context effects in the speeded
  comprehension of sentences, *Journal of Experimen-
  tal Psychology,* In press.
Dooling, D. J., & Lachman, R. Effects of comprehen-
  sion on retention of prose. *Journal of Experi-
  mental Psychology,* 1971, 88, 216-222.
Fillmore, C. J. The case for case. In E. Bach &
  R. T. Harms (Eds.), *Universals in linguistic
  theory*. New York: Holt, Rinehart and Winston,
  Inc., 1968.
Fillmore, C. J., & Langendoen, D. T. (Eds.). *Studies
  in linguistic semantics*. New York: Holt,
  Rinehart and Winston, Inc., 1971.
Huttenlocher, J., Eisenberg, K., & Strauss, S. Com-
  prehension: relation between perceived actor and
  logical subject. *Journal of Verbal Learning and
  Verbal Behavior,* 1968, 7, 527-530.
Huttenlocher, J., & Strauss, S. Comprehension and a
  statement's relation to the situation it describes. *Journal of Verbal Learning and Verbal
  Behavior,* 1968, 7, 300-304.
Huttenlocher, J., & Weiner, S. Comprehension of in-
  structions in varying contexts. *Cognitive Psy-
  chology,* 1971, 2, 369-385.
Hyde, T. S., & Jenkins, J. J. Differential effects of
  incidental tasks on the organization of recall
  of a list of highly associated words. *Journal
  of Experimental Psychology,* 1969, 82, 472-481.
Johnson, M. K., Bransford, J. D., Nyberg, S., &
  Cleary, J. Comprehension factors in interpret-
  ing memory for abstract and concrete sentences.
  Journal of Verbal Learning and Verbal Behavior,
  In press.
Johnson, M. K., Bransford, J. D., & Solomon, S.
  Memory for tacit implications of sentences.
  Journal of Experimental Psychology, In press.

Johnston, C. D., & Jenkins, J. J. Two more inciden-
    tal tasks that differentially affect associative
    clustering in recall. *Journal of Experimental
    Psychology,* 1971, 89, 92-95.
Katz, J. J., & Postal, P. M. *An integrated theory
    of linguistic descriptions.* Cambridge: M.I.T.
    Press, 1964.
Kintsch, W. Notes on the semantic structure of
    memory. In E. Tulving & W. Donaldson, (Eds.),
    Organization and memory. New York: Academic
    Press, In press.
Light, L. L., & Carter-Sobell, L. Effects of changed
    semantic context on recognition memory. *Journal
    of Verbal Learning and Verbal Behavior,* 1970,
    9, 1-11.
Mandler, G. Organization and memory. In K. W.
    Spence & J. T. Spence (Eds.), *The psychology
    of learning and motivation, Vol. 1.* New York:
    Academic Press, 1967.
Marks, L. E., & Miller, G. A. The role of semantic
    and syntactic constraints in the memorization
    of English sentences. *Journal of Verbal Learning
    and Verbal Behavior,* 1964, 3, 1-5.
Miller, G. A. The magical number seven plus-or-minus
    two: Some limits on our capacity for processing
    information. *Psychological Review,* 1956, 63,
    81-97.
Olson, D. R. Language and thought: Aspects of a cog-
    nitive theory of semantics. *Psychological Re-
    view,* 1970, 77, 237-273.
Paivio, A. *Imagery and verbal processes.* New York:
    Holt, Rinehart and Winston, 1971.
Potts, G. A cognitive approach to the encoding of
    meaningful verbal material. Unpublished doc-
    toral dissertation, University of Indiana, 1971.
Sachs, J. Recognition memory for syntactic and
    semantic aspects of connected discourse. *Per-
    ception and Psychophysics,* 1967, 2, 437-442.
Slobin, D. I. Grammatical transformations and sen-
    tence comprehension in childhood and adulthood.
    Journal of Verbal Learning and Verbal Behavior,
    1966, 5, 219-227.

Trabasso, T. Mental operations in language comprehension. In J. B. Carroll & R. O. Freedle (Eds.), *Language comprehension and the acquisition of knowledge*. Washington: V. H. Winston and Sons, In press.

Tulving, E. Theoretical issues in free recall. In T. R. Dixon & D. L. Horton (Eds.), *Verbal Behavior and general behavior theory*. Englewood Cliffs, New Jersey: Prentice-Hall, 1968.

Tulving, E., & Osler, S. Effectiveness of retrieval cues in memory for words. *Journal of Experimental Psychology*, 1968, 77, 593-601.

Tulving, E., & Thomson, D. M. Retrieval processes in recognition memory: Effects of associative context. *Journal of Experimental Psychology*, 1971, 87, 116-124.

Acknowledgments

We would like to give special thanks to the following students for their entheusiastic assistance and collaborative contributions: John Cleary, Elizabeth Cole, Nancy Fenrick, Cynthia Kaplan, Stanley Nyberg and Carol Ray (State University of New York at Stony Brook) and Nancy McCarrell (visiting from the University of Minnesota).

Discussion of the Papers by
Bransford and Johnson and
Clark, Carpenter, and Just:
Language and Cognition

Tom Trabasso
Princeton University

Each of the papers succeeds in achieving its
specific aim. In what I can only describe as a bril-
liant *tour de force*, Bransford and Johnson have convinced us that the interpretation of an utterance is
possible only when we can find a relevant context in
our conceptual knowledge about the world. In like
manner, Clark, Carpenter, and Just have examined how
several lexical items in English might linguistically
encode our perceptual knowledge about the world,
derived from relationships of the physical location of
one's self in Euclidian space.

The above phrase, "knowledge about the world," was
deliberate. I believe that we are to be indebted to
these authors for at least two general contributions.
Their efforts place language in the realm of cognitive
psychology (a bias I share) and bear upon the familiar
linguistic relativity (Whorfian) *hypothesis*. While
much of my discussion will focus on the relation of
language and cognitive processes, a revision of the
Whorfian hypothesis appears to be in order.

According to one interpretation of the Whorfian
hypothesis, our perception of the world and our dealings
with it are determined by the structure and lexicon of
the language we speak (see Fishman, 1960, for a fuller
treatment). It is language which is organized, not the
input from the world. To illustrate this assumption,
we need only to quote Whorf:

We dissect nature along lines laid down by our native languages. The categories and types that we isolate from the world of phenomena we do not find there because they stare every observer in the face; on the contrary, *The world is presented in a kaleidoscopic flux of impressions* which has to be organized by our minds--and this means largely the linguistic systems in our minds. We cut nature up, organize it into concepts, and ascribe significances as we do, largely because we are parties to an agreement to organize it this way--an agreement that holds throughout our speech community and is codified in the patterns of our language. (Whorf, 1956, p. 213. Italics added.)

I am aware that Whorf's view now has the status of being a straw man and I do not wish to use it as such. I raise the hypothesis as a contrast to Clark, Carpenter, and Just's position: the physical environment and our location in it imposes severe constraints on how we interpret and represent that world and our language codes rather than molds these constraints. Second, the focus on linguistics by psychologists during the past decade was motivated, at least in part, by an implicit view not unlike Whorf's, namely, the study of the structure of language was the study of the structure (competence) of the mind. It is the recent focus on isolated sentences that contrasts sharply with work of Bransford and Johnson. One has to doubt the value of studying sentences in isolation; clearly, reference and context can no longer be denied as important contributors to how people go about processing sentential information (cf. Olson, 1970).

If one were to rewrite the Whorfian hypothesis in the light of the present papers, one would conclude that language is determined by cognitive processes which derive structures from complex but organized environments. A study of the lexical content or comprehension of language enables one to see how perceptual experiences are encoded or which presuppositions are implicit in an utterance. It is knowledge, both linguistic and perceptual, which determines our interpretation of the world.

Having noted a common thread which ties these two papers together, I would now like to comment critically on each in turn.

Clark, Carptenter, and Just

Clark, Carpenter, and Just (hereafter, CC&J) assume that an important function of language is to communicate perceptual experience. The key working assumption is that in the structure of English one can find how alternative interpretations of perceptual experience are encoded. While the locus of the structure of English (is it in our knowledge structure?) is not specified, this assumption entails an *intuitive* examination of the presuppositions of English with reference to perceptual events. The constraints imposed by the latter and how they are realized in the coding system follow a linguistic analysis, rather than vice versa. If it is the constraints of one perceiving objects and relations in Euclidian space which determine the semantic interpretation or coding, then examining the linguistic coding rather than the perceptual one would seem to put the cart before the horse. The reason for the emphasis on lexical items in propositions by CC&J appears historical--the present paper represents a decided shift from a strongly linguistic orientation, using principles such as semantic features, the scope of negation or lexical marking as explanations for psychological difficulty in processing information (cf. Clark & Chase, 1972). The shift to perceptual events and their relation to the language structure is a welcome and promising development.

It is curious that CC&J omit a discussion of work related to theirs by Huttenlocher (Huttenlocher, 1968; Huttenlocher & Higgins, 1971) which entails an analysis of linguistic-perceptual relations. (Huttenlocher, 1968, used the term *imagery*, thereby stressing perceptual encoding rather than the physical stimulus, a distinction not clearly drawn by CC&J.) The Huttenlocher and Higgins paper deals with similar issues--adjectives and comparatives--and relates them to reference points and extents, using these physical properties to distinguish between marked and unmarked forms. After Bierwisch (1967), they too indicate that unmarked adjectives or comparatives have positive polarity, and a property which can extend indefinitely in an upward direction (as "above"). Marked forms indicate the absence of the property (hence have negative polarity), the extreme lower point being zero. Unmarked adjectives refer to the entire dimension. If the scale is a ratio scale, unmarked adjectives designate the property; marked ones designate its absence (e.g., length). If the scale is ordinal, the scale seems to extend in both directions (e.g., good-bad) so that unmarked scales can extend indefinitely but on a negative polarity. Since with ordinal scales, there exists a zero point, one can have "subdimensions" such as *goodness* or *badness*; the choice of the unmarked forms seems to depend upon positive affect of polarity.

I recognize that the paper by CC&J is a beginning onto the problem of relating language and perception. Clearly, these structures are related. However, the assumption that all perceptual experience is interpreted semantically appears too strong. Perceptual encodings can have existence independent of linguistic ones and there is some dispute about the isomorphic or one-to-one correspondence between the perceptual encodings and the physical world. CC&J seem to share with Gibson (1966) an isomorphic view and they further assume some direct relation based upon features between the encoded percept and language structure. Since their experimental tasks require some common *semantic* format for internal representations, it is not surprising that they are led into a view that assumes all perceptual experience is so encoded. We should not, however, let the demand characteristics of our particular experimental paradigms determine our general assumptions. Franks (personal communication) in an unpublished paper on the relation of language to perception suggests five *perceptual classes* which can be related to language:

1) nouns to *objects*
2) intransitive verbs to *transformations*
3) adjectives to *properties of objects*
4) adverbs to *properties of transformations*
5) prepositions and transitive verbs to *spatial-temporal relations among objects*

The work of CC&J appears to treat only the third and fifth relations. If the relation between perceptual classes and language structure is causal, then this analysis may give a firm basis for linguistic universals which are not strictly biological in nature. The information and regularities in the physical stimuli would determine the perceptual and linguistic structures; our cognitive abilities are those processes which allow us to abstract this information.

The organizing hypotheses of CC&J cover all possibilities and given the evidence in favor of each, hardly anyone is likely to disagree. A paraphrase of Jenkins' (1969) characterization of the relation of thought and language as a series of answers to a multiple-choice question may be made here:

What is the relation between language and perception?

1) Perception is dependent upon language (Hypothesis B)
2) Language is dependent upon perception (Hypothesis C)
3) Perception is (coded as) language (in preferred ways) (Hypothesis A)

An information processing analysis may help here. The complexity of the perceptual event determines the cost in real-time application of the linguistic code. Complexity refers to the number of perceptual-semantic features and the relations among them in the concept.

443

For example, to apply *deep-shallow* encodings, one must proceed through several stages:

1) perceive three dimensions (length, width and depth) of two objects
2) perceive an interior space for each object
3) locate a reference plane which is a surface (or an opening into that surface) on each object
4) measure downward (rather than the preferred upward direction) on each object simultaneously
5) as soon as the measurement of one object is concluded, the object upon which measurement is continued is encoded "deep;" the other object is "shallow"

In this analysis we note that it is not the language code (i.e., name) which determines how the perceptual event is encoded, but what set of *criterial features* must be present and *perceived* for the application of the code. This analysis is precisely that of Hunt, Marin, & Stone (1966) for the application of the *name* of a concept. The process model simply enumerates the operations of detecting and operating on the features (see Trabasso, Rollins, & Shaughnessy, 1971, for tests of Hunt *et al*.'s concept learning system). The main purpose of applying the linguistic codes would appear to be for making match-mismatch decisions required by CC&J's experimental tasks. The generalization to linguistic coding for communication of perceptual events *to others* (rather than the self in verification tasks) is by analogy. The information necessary for application of a linguistic code is stored in a rule system and feature list so that one can either generate the code from a knowledge of the perceptual features or test its appropriateness given the lexical item in a proposition. That is, either linguistic or perceptual codes access the system. If a lexical item occurs first, the rule system sets into motion a series of operations which encode perceptually the physical object and test the feature list for applicability of the linguistic code (concept name). When all the perceptual features pass, the code is applied; if they fail, either another appropriate code is applied or further searching and tests occur.

This analysis accounts for Answer 3 (Hypothesis A) since "preferred" positive codes are determined by prominent features of the objects in the absence of prior linguistic codes. Answer 1 (Hypothesis B) is supported where the linguistic code precedes the physical event and determines how to code it by providing the feature test list; and Answer 2 (Hypothesis C) is likely to be supported when the perceptual feature lists for the linguistic and perceptual event are incompatible (i.e., the tests fail but further search is made for the lexical item corresponding to the features of the perceptual event).

Of particular importance for CC&J is that the ease or difficulty of applying a linguistic code to a perceptual event depends not only on the semantic feature list of the linguistic code but on all the other operations as well. Time is consumed by perceptually encoding the features, and as in the experiments on *tall-short* versus *deep-shallow*, the use of two-dimensional drawings favor perceptual encoding of *tall-short* but not *deep-shallow*. Here the subject must either imagine a third dimension or an interior surface or reencode tall onto deep and short onto shallow. Thus the faster times for *tall-short* may be due not to semantic complexity but to the paucity of the physical array.

We see here where a failure to make explicit the process model underlying the linguistic-perceptual relationship as well as the necessary conditions for prior perceptual coding leads to possible misleading conclusions. It would seem that CC&J should be more explicit about *all* the stages of processing within the encoding stage, including that of encoding the physical stimuli. Otherwise their use of the reaction-time experiments and chronometric stage analysis remains at the level of testing vaguely formulated hypotheses.

445

Correlations of time data with linguistic taxonomies are not sufficient. One needs to specify the processes underlying each encoding system and their relationship.

Polarity, reference points, underlying dimensions and conditions of application are abstract notions which implicitly assume several processes. Polarity involves both frequency of occurrence and evaluative components (Boucher & Osgood, 1969), both of which affect coding and matching decisions, especially in the limited and ambiguous contexts studied by CC&J. Reference points are necessary for the starting point of several perceptual processes, especially scanning dimensions on their vertical or horizontal extents. While the organizing hypotheses and abstract principles are useful for summarizing the set of findings by CC&J, we now need more mechanism and less taxonomy.

CC&J use explicit process models to predict reaction times *after encoding is assumed to occur*. The apparent success of these models in fitting data is misleading since, as emphasized, the reaction times depend directly upon the number of stages in which operations occur. The stages involve the number of matching operations or truth-index changes when a mismatch occurs. By assuming a different set of codings and stages, one can obtain the same set of predictions. Consider the Just and Carpenter (1971) experiment on *many-few* versus *majority-minority*. Assume that the sentences have *no* effect on how the perceptual events are encoded. Rather, salient features such as the relative number of dots of a given color determine the code (e.g., "Many of the dots are black" in Scheme (8) of CC&J.) I have indicated elsewhere (Trabasso, 1970; in press) that subjects use optional strategies in dealing with linguistic codes depending upon a number of factors. Prominent among them are so-called "conversion" strategies. Suppose we assume that subjects convert "Few are red" into "Many are black." Since TN (true negative) sentences would lead to two operations (conversion plus match) and FN (false negative) sentences, three operations (conversion, plus mismatch, plus change in truth-index), one would predict

446

TN's to be processed more quickly. Since FN sentences were processed faster, a conversion model does not apply here, and we end up with the same model as CC&J for *few-many*. But, consider CC&J's Scheme (9) where majority and minority are used. Again, assuming that the codes are the same as Scheme (8) and are independent of the propositions, the conversion model fits the data. TN sentences are predicted and observed to be faster than FN. What are we to conclude here? Either Hypothesis B is supported or not, depending upon whether or not one assumes a conversion operation. We have to consider what alternative or optional strategies subjects use to process information in addition to the codes and relations among them.

Consider CC&J's Scheme (12) where *above-below* propositions precede the pictures. It is not specified by CC&J whether people code the perceptual array by *subject* or *preposition* of the sentence. Suppose the subject of the sentence determines the code. Then False Below codes are: (B above A) *vs.* (B below A) and take longer than True Above codes since there is a mismatch on the preposition. False Below codes take longer than True Below ones for the same reason. If people use the prepositions to determine the code, then mismatches occur on *subjects* of the codes and we get the same predictions. This problem again arises (and is recognized by CC&J) in Scheme (16) where the *subject of the proposition* (A or B) rather than the *comparative* (longer or shorter) is now assumed to determine the code versus in Scheme (17) where the comparative is assumed to be the determiner. Although CC&J resolve the conflict in favor of subject coding (Scheme (16)), the resolution is *post hoc* and does not resolve the dilemma for Scheme (12).

Thus, the models are not explicit in specifying *a priori* which lexical items of the proposition are to be used to code perceptual events. The problem of conversion strategies further complicates interpretation. As long as options exist, people will use them and then we are studying strategies for specific task demands as much as linguistic-perceptual relations.

Both are equally important and we should not be blind to their presence.

One final comment on CC&J's work. The experiment on *deep-shallow* using three-dimensional representations (containers) by CC&J is not without alternative explanations. They recognize this in passing but I believe more elaboration is necessary. While they try to vary the degree of depth by rotating the top of the containers toward the viewer, the data indicate (see Fig. 10) that pairs 1-3 take identical times while pairs 4 and 5 are considerably faster and about equal. Examination of the objects suggests strongly that pairs 1-3 involve *longer-shorter* judgments since the interior dimension is not shown (i.e., only length can be used as in the prior two-dimensional drawings); in pairs 4 and 5, width of the bottom determines depth (i.e., using size-distance relations, one can judge that the container with the smaller rectangle is deeper). Since pairs 4 and 5, which clearly involve depth cues (interior dimension), are processed more quickly than pairs 1-3 which do not, the difference in processing times for *deep-shallow* versus *long-short* would seem to depend upon *which* dimensions or ends are shown visually, rather than their semantic interpretation. My earlier remark on the content of the physical stimuli influencing ease of coding applies with force here. If physical cues—their salience, presence or absence—vary, then we can expect variation in ease of perceptual coding independent of ease of linguistic coding. Once one specifies the conditions of application for a code to a physical array, then ease of applying the code depends directly on the presence (or absence) of the features required as well as the number of operations (feature tests). Once again, explicitness of the process model is of direct value to the construction and interpretation of experiments.

Bransford and Johnson

Bransford and Johnson (hereafter B&J) have amply demonstrated that the input from the environment may contain information of minimal meaning unless one can find in it (or elsewhere) cues to retrieve knowledge that allows for interpretation and elaboration of that input. Their work shows the importance of matching highly organized, internal knowledge in long-term memory with sensory inputs, a key assumption in Norman's (1969) model for memory and attention.

My previous comments stressed the organized character of information emanating from external environments; B&J have demonstrated the importance of the internal environment. The stored knowledge used to interpret utterances, often called "presuppositions" by linguists, was also assumed to underly semantic interpretation of perceptual inputs by CC&J. My previous stress on environmental input and complexity was made since I was concerned about how the physical environment and task demands gave rise to the conditions of application for the lexical codings used by knowledgeable adults. One can speculate on the developmental importance of external versus internal sources of knowledge. Since children do not begin with an internal store, their information processing may be more concerned with extraction of information from regularities of occurrence in external environmental inputs. Adult information processing rests on the other extreme: minimal external inputs are used to access and operate upon highly organized, internal linguistic and perceptual structures.

Although B&J are concerned about comprehension of linguistic inputs, they do not define comprehension or the nature of long-term memory nor do they resort to formal, linguistic analyses of their material. Since their aim is primarily to demonstrate the role of context in the "comprehension" and recall of linguistic information, this is not a necessary requirement but one may, for purposes of discussion, raise some questions about both of these issues.

In examing their tasks, all of which are memorial in character, B&J intuitively selected passages which involve extensively the use of conjunctions such as "because," "if . . . then" and "so," or utterances which contain sequential time and spatial relations among the clauses as well as verbs which, of course, provide case relation information. For example:

John missed the bus *because* he knew he would have to walk to school.

Or:

A beaver hit the log that a turtle was sitting on (beside) and the log flipped over from the shock.

Or:

The man was shot.

These causal, time and space or case relations allow one to make *inferences:* missing the bus presupposes walking or finding other transportation; if one is on a log which rolls, then one is likely to fall into the water; the verb shot implies an instrument.

This analysis applies with equal force to the balloon and washing clothes passages. In the balloon passage, one finds "If . . . then . . . since . . . since . . . but . . . then . . . then" connecting clauses. In the washing clothes example, one finds time markers and conditionals:

First . . . if . . . otherwise . . . but . . . at first . . . soon . . . but . . . after . . . then . . . Eventually . . . .

The same analysis applies to the Peace March-Space Trip passage (where the *landing* sentence is temporally and spatially *out of place* in the first context), the Stockbroker-Unemployed man passage, and the Hunter-Convict passage.

Recall measures are the main indication of comprehension (rating scales are used only in the early experiments on the balloon passage). This is critical in deciding what is meant by comprehension. We know that information that is organized or stored in pre-existing or organizational structures leads to better recall (e.g., Tulving & Donaldson, 1972). An outcome of the act of comprehension in the B&J tasks would appear to be storage of the input in an organized structure and then access to this structure at the point of recall. This is analogous, as B&J note, to the known importance of retrieval cues first found by Tulving (1968) and his associates.

How is this organization achieved? The first problem seems to be to find cues in the input or from some other source (e.g., the "Topic") which the person can use to retrieve an organized set of knowledge against which the content and *consequences* can be tested. If the consequences are tested and pass (by being congruent with known information), then the input is already "organized" (e.g., turtle on log--log rolls --turtle falls in water). If the consequences "mismatch," then another set of searches are made to make them congruent with other known information (e.g., "John came to the party because his car broke down" leads to incongruent presuppositions: "John came" implies he was transported but his car was not the means). Hence, new organizations which justify the initially incongruent presuppositions or inferences result.

An interesting question is whether or not these justified organizations lead to better recall than the ones which the presuppositions or inferences match. That is, is recall or recognition better for "The floor was dirty *because* Sally used the mop" than for "The floor was dirty *so* Sally used the mop?" If the incongruent sentence is recalled better, this would be a demonstration of a case where recall was superior for sentences which are not easy to comprehend. One would conclude that the additional information processing of finding justification for the conflicting inferences and the resulting organization was responsible for superior recall and not "comprehension" as measured by how easy it is to find a context or congruent inferences.

In contrast to CC&J, who derived their initial set of lexical items from linguistic considerations (and belatedly examined the perceptual referents), B&J avoid entirely any linguistic analysis. One reason may be that linguists have generally avoided context (although not entirely; for example, Chafe, in press, has discussed the role of knowledge in comprehension and uses the notion of foregrounding in relating prior context to pronominalization), and the study of isolated sentences has little to offer analysis of connected discourse. But some analysis would seem to be in order. For example, contrasts of *so* and *because* indicate reversal of temporal-causal relations. With *because* the order is consequent-antecedent; with *so*, it is antecedent-consequent. There may be interactions between states or processes (cf. Chafe, 1970) in the first clause and whether one anticipates an antecedent or consequential action in the second. In the example of Sally and the mop, "the floor was dirty" is a state which leads to expectation of a consequent action (e.g., cleaning). *Because* denotes an antecedent action and a semantic anomaly between the cleaning function of the mop and the dirty state of the floor results. I don't know how far one can push this kind of linguistic analysis, but it might elucidate in each instance the kind of mechanism underlying further justification. The bother here is that we remain at the level of demonstration and avoid explanation. A linguistic (semantic) analysis of temporal-spatial relations and inferences would seem to be of value.

Since B&J use recall or recognition paradigms throughout, comprehension, storage and retrieval processes are all involved in their tasks. One could describe the behavior in their tasks in information-processing terms, i.e., one could create a memory model for their results which includes inference making, testing and organizing operations. While this may be of value, we don't know much at all about the structure of long-term memory (semantic memory or knowledge for that matter) and we also don't know much about how presuppositions or inferences are made.

One question that plagues me is whether inferences are made concurrently with initial comprehension or must they be forced? Frase's (in press) work seems of value here. If one is looking for a causal link across a series of sentences (by having a question prior to a passage), recall of the intermediary links is increased. Of necessity, the inferences were made; otherwise the question could not be answered. Inferences and organization of sentences outside of the question are not made, and subsequent recall is poor. Since one experiences an initial lack of comprehension followed by subsequent attempts at justification in B&J's examples, these inferences apparently are made unconsciously. This seems to also occur in the work by Bransford, Barclay, and Franks (1972).

Inference-making and congruence-testing across clauses is dramatically illustrated in the balloon passage. Consider the first sentence:

> If the balloons popped the sound wouldn't be able to carry since everything would be too far away from the correct floor.

In the absence of the picture context, the sound must refer to popping, but the third phrase provides no way to verify what is meant by the assertion that the sound would not carry. "Correct floor" and distance are without reference here. Hence, subjects would judge this sentence not comprehensible, i.e., they cannot relate the causal clause. The picture context is highly organized and allows immediate identification of referents, testing and *relating* of clauses plus a visual storage location. Together, these operations allow for comprehension (i.e., relating constitutent clauses of the sentence or sentences semantically) and storage of the relations in an organized image. The balloon picture, in some sense, illustrates an internal knowledge context.

Cognitive Strategies

In discussing the work of both sets of authors, I have sketched some process models which suggest cognitive operations used by subjects in verification and recall tasks. These were intended to help specify the role that mental operations may play in language processing. In our work on comprehension and verification (Trabasso *et al.*, 1971; Trabasso, 1970; 1972; Wald, 1972), we have been struck by the range of operations or strategies that college students use to perform the tasks efficiently and optimally. Instead of focusing on structures (linguistic or perceptual), our interest has turned to the kind of optional strategies subjects use and their relationship to the various stages of processing identified in the chronometric data. While structures undoubtedly are involved, the way in which subjects operate upon them and relate them seems to us to be of equal importance. If we are unable to decide upon what operations are used, we cannot be sure that our assumed structure is the one present. This argumen may be illustrated with a brief description of a senior thesis by Jerry Wald at Princeton which Sam Glucksberg and I directed.

Wald had college students verify sentences against pictures (or vice versa) where the voice (active-passive) and subject-object reversibility were varied. Examples of the sentences are:

1) The pole is pulled by the car.
2) The train passed the bus.
3) The bus passed the fence.
4) The truck is hit by the train.

Sentence 1 is a passive, nonreversible sentence (the pole cannot pull the car). Sentence 2 is an active, reversible sentence (the bus can pass the train). Sentence 3 is an active, nonreversible sentence. Combinations of (car, truck, bus, train), (hit, passed, pulled) and (fence, pole, tree) were used to generate these sentences and their corresponding pictorial referents. Of particular importance is the way in which *False* events were constructed: sentences were falsified by a mismatch on only one constituent, either the subject, the action, or the object. The sentences were presented before or after the pictures and the amount of time the college students spent encoding the first and verifying the second stimuli was recorded.

The encoding times were affected by only one variable and that occurred only for encoding *pictures*: reversible pictures took longer to encode. This result may have to do with the ease of discriminating objects; a car is more difficult to discriminate from another vehicle than it is from a tree. The reversibility effect suggests that Slobin's (1966) widely cited finding was a *perceptual* and *not a linguistic* effect.

I shall not go into all of the verification results. In order to make my point, let me summarize them by listing the steps in information processing which captured most of the findings. I shall restrict my description to that for the condition where the sentence occurred first, keeping in mind that the model for the picture-first condition is very similar.

The subject first encodes the sentence, marking case function, potency and voice, and then in verification, he carries out the following steps:

1) Do *actions* match? If "Yes," continue; if "No," change response index and respond "False."

2) Is the grammatical subject in picture? If "Yes," continue; if "No," respond "False."

3) Is the grammatical object in picture? If "Yes," continue; if "No," respond "False."

4) Encode picture as a proposition: (noun verb noun), marking potency and agent-recipient functions of each noun.

5) Are the potency markers of the first and second nouns in the proposition the same? If "No," respond "True;" if "Yes," continue.

6) Is the agentive noun of the sentence the same as the first noun of the picture and is the latter an agent? If "Yes," respond "True;" otherwise continue.

7) Is the agentive noun of the sentence the same as the second noun of the picture and is the latter an agent? If "Yes," respond "True."

Steps 1, 2, and 3 reflect the fact that the reaction times were *fastest* for false sentences where the verbs mismatched followed by mismatch times for the grammatical subject and grammatical object, in that order. Since there was *no* reversibility effect on the false verb times, the picture was *not* encoded until after feature (constituent) coding and testing was done on the nouns. This is Step 4.

After Step 4, grammatical complexities having to do with case grammar enter into the process. However, these variables affect only the times for *true* sentences. That is, the subjects optimally selected feature tests on verbs, grammatical subjects and objects first since these yielded the most information. It is only when these tests were passed that they moved to tests involving more abstract linguistic (semantic) classifications.

Step 5 is based on the assumption that the propositions were encoded in a case grammar format, with potency and agentive-recipient markers. Since true nonreversible sentences were processed faster than true reversible sentences, this could be accomplished in Step 5 by noting that the nouns differed in potency (e.g., car and tree). Active-passive differences do not play a role here, although they contribute to Steps 2 and 3.

Step 6 is required if both nouns are potent, since one could have a voice difference (e.g., the car hit

456

the truck versus the car was hit by the truck). The subject tests to see whether the first noun of the second code is the same as that of the first code and is an agent. If so, he can stop and respond "True," and active reversible sentences are completed here.

Step 7 requires the subject to test whether the agent of the sentence is the same as the second noun of the picture (e.g., the truck was hit by the car versus the car hit the truck). If so, he can respond "True," and passive reversible sentences are completed here.

One striking observation on this model is that as one goes from Step 1 to Step 7, the amount and level of abstraction of the information required to reach a decision increases. The verb is checked first in Step 1, since it is most informative in the sense of efficient information processing. Since the college students made a total of 192 verifications, and the data were so orderly, they apparently discovered these strategies quickly.

A second observation is that the number of stages identified correspond directly to the complexity of the environment presented. That is, in simple verification tasks with negation, we and others (Trabasso, in press; Clark & Chase, 1972) find only two stages: negation and congruence (matching grammatical subjects). Here with increases in grammatical complexity (voice and reversibility), more stages are required by the task and our subjects reflect this requirement in their processing. That is, they are able to use their cognitive abilities to extract from the environment information for all the critical tests that are necessary to decide upon a match between internal representations. Since the complexity of the environment (i.e., its information processing demands) is what varies, I think we have here a good example of what Herb Simon (1969) meant when he said in *The Sciences of the Artificial*: "Environments are complex; people are simple." However, given both contributions reviewed here, a paraphrase of Simon's remark might be:

People are simple; knowledge is complex.

References

Bierwisch, M. Some semantic universals of German adjectivals. *Foundations of Language*, 1967, 3, 1-36.

Boucher, J., & Osgood, C. E. The Pollyanna hypothesis. *Journal of Verbal Learning and Verbal Behavior*, 1969, 8, 1-8.

Bransford, J. D., Barclay, J. R., & Franks, J. H. Sentence memory: A constructive versus interpretive approach. *Cognitive Psychology*, 1972, 3, 193-209.

Chafe, W. L. Discourse structure and human knowledge. In J. B. Carrol & R. O. Freedle (Eds.), *Language comprehension and the acquisition of knowledge*. Washington: V. H. Winston, in press.

Chafe, W. L. *Meaning and the structure of language*. Chicago: University of Chicago Press, 1970.

Clark, H. H., & Chase, W. G. On the process of comparing sentences against pictures. *Cognitive Psychology*, 1972, 3, 472-517.

Fishman, J. A. A systematization of the Whorfian hypothesis. *Behavioral Science*, 1960, 5, 323-339.

Franks, J. J. Toward a psychological theory of knowledge. Unpublished manuscript.

Frase, L. T. Maintenance and control in the acquisition of knowledge from written materials. In J. B. Carroll & R. O. Freedle (Eds.), *Language comprehension and the acquisition of knowledge*. Washington: V. H. Winston, in press.

Gibson, J. J. *The senses considered as perceptual systems*. Boston: Houghton Mifflin Company, 1966.

Hunt, E., Marin, J., & Stone, P. *Experiments in induction*. New York: Academic Press, 1966.

Huttenlocher, J. Constructing spatial images. *Psychological Review*, 1968, 75, 550-560.

Huttenlocher, J., & Higgins, E. T. Adjectives, comparatives and syllogisms. *Psychological Review*, 1971, 78, 487-504.

Jenkins, J. J. Language and thought. In J. F. Voss (Ed.), *Approaches to thought*. Columbus: C. E. Merrill, 1969, 211-237.

Just, M. A., & Carpenter, P. A.   Comprehension of
    negation with quantification.   *Journal of Verbal
    Learning and Verbal Behavior*, 1971, 10, 219-225.
Norman, D. A.   *Memory and attention: An introduction
    to human information processing.*   New York:
    Wiley, 1969.
Olson, D. R.   Language and thought: Aspects of a
    cognitive theory of semantics.   *Psychological
    Review*, 1970, 77, 257-273.
Simon, H. A.   *The sciences of the artificial.*
    Cambridge: MIT Press, 1969.
Slobin, D. I.   Grammatical transformations and sentence
    comprehension in children and adults.   *Journal of
    Verbal Learning and Verbal Behavior*, 1966, 5,
    219-227.
Trabasso, T.   Reasoning and the processing of negative
    information.   Invited Address, Division 3, 78th
    Annual Convention, APA, 1970.
Trabasso, T.   Mental operations in language comprehen-
    sion.   In J. B. Carroll & R. O. Freedle (Eds.),
    *Language comprehension and the acquisition of
    knowledge.*   Washington: V. H. Winston, in press.
Trabasso, T., Rollings, H., & Shaughnessy, E.   Storage
    and verification stages in processing concepts.
    Cognitive Psychology, 1971, 2, 239-289.
Tulving, E.   Theoretical issues in free recall.   In
    T. R. Dixon & D. L. Horton (Eds.), *Verbal behavior
    and general behavior theory.*   Englewood Cliffs,
    New Jersey: Prentice-Hall, 1968, 2-36.
Tulving, E., & Donaldson, W.   *Organization of memory.*
    New York: Academic Press, 1972.
Wald, J.   Encoding and comparison processes in the
    verification of pictures and sentences.   Unpub-
    lished Senior Thesis, Princeton University, 1972.
Whorf, B. L.   *Language, thought and reality.*   New
    York: Wiley, 1956.

Acknowledgment

Preparation of this paper was supported by United
States Public Health Service, National Institutes of
Mental Health Grant MH-19223.

PART III

INFORMATION PROCESSING MODELS

PRODUCTION SYSTEMS: MODELS OF CONTROL STRUCTURES

Allen Newell
Carnegie-Mellon University

A production system is a scheme for specifying an
information processing system. It consists of a set
of productions, each production consisting of a condition and an action. It has also a collection of
data structures: expressions that encode the information upon which the production system works--on which
the actions operate and on which the conditions can be
determined to be true or false.

A production system, starting with an initially
given set of data structures, operates as follows.
That production whose condition is true of the current
data (assume there is only one) is executed, that is,
the action is taken. The result is to modify the current data structures. This leads in the next instant
to another (possibly the same) production being executed,
leading to still further modification. So it goes,
action after action being taken to carry out an entire
program of processing, each evoked by its condition
becoming true of the momentarily current collection of
data structures. The entire process halts either when
no condition is true (hence nothing is evoked) or when
an action containing a stop operation occurs.

Much remains to be specified in the above scheme
to yield a definite information processing system. What
happens (a likely occurrence) if more than one production is satisfied at once? What is the actual scheme
for encoding information? What sort of collection of
data structures constitutes the current state of knowledge on which the system works? What sort of tests
are expressible in the conditions of productions? What
sort of primitive operations are performable on the data
and what collections of these are expressible in the

actions of productions? What sorts of additional
memories are available and how are they accessed and
written into? How is the production system itself
modified from within, or is this possible? How much
time (or effort) is taken by the various components of
the system and how do they combine to yield a total
time for an entire processing?

There are many questions which can be answered in
many different ways. Each assemblage of answers yields
a different production system with different properties
from its siblings. Taken in all, they constitute a
family of schemes for specifying information processing
systems. Within this family can be found almost any
process specification scheme one could like--though not
in fact all possible schemes. There are other ways of
specifying the information processing to be done. There
are languages, such as Algol and Fortran, that take as
their basis a specified sequence of operating-processes
to be performed, punctuated by test-processes that
explicitly direct processing to switch to another
sequence. There are languages, such as SNOBOL, that
use productions (conditions associating to actions),
but each production explicitly switches the processing
this way or that to other sequences of production.

Look at the situation a different way. Suppose
you know about an information processing system: its
memories, its encodings and its primitive operations
(both tests and manipulations). What more would you
require to obtain a complete picture? You need to know
how the system organizes these primitives into an effective processing of its knowledge. This additional
organization is called the *control structure*. Production systems are a type of control structure.

The purpose of this paper is to illustrate the
possibility of having a theory of the control structure
of human information processing. Gains seem possible
in many forms: completeness of the microtheories of how
various miniscule experimental tasks are performed; the
ability to pose meaningfully the problem of what method
a subject is using; the ability to suggest new mechanisms for accomplishing a task; the facilitation of

comparing behavior on diverse tasks.

We illustrate by actually proposing a theory of the control structure. We are in earnest about the theory; in this respect we are being more than illustrative. However, to be taken seriously, a theory of control should encompass a substantially greater scope of experiments than we are able to deal with here. This also appears to be the first explicit model of the control structure at this level of detail. It would hardly seem that details of the structure are right-- even if (as I currently believe) a production system of some sort appears to be a suitable model of the human control.

Our plan is to present a particular production system, noting its psychological properties, but with no attempt to defend it against variant schemes. Using this system we will conduct an analysis of the basic Sternberg paradigm, which underlies several of the experiments discussed in the present symposium. With this basic analysis in hand, we will then discuss in varying levels of detail the potentialites of production systems as models for human control and the issues raised thereby.

PSG: A Particular Production System

The particular production system presented here, PSG (for production system version G), was developed as a continuation of work with problem solving in crypt-arithmetic (Newell & Simon, 1972, Chapters 5-7). The original data that PSG was designed to deal with were about an order of magnitude grosser than the reaction time data that currently seem most appropriate to defining the behavior of the immediate processor-- i.e., it worked with freely produced phrases of a few seconds duration. A recent paper (Newell, 1972) describes PSG and begins the task of applying it to the more detailed situation, focussing on the problem of stimulus encoding.

The overall architecture of the system is shown in Figure 1. All of the action in the system takes

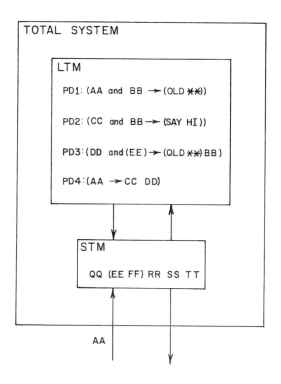

Fig. 1.   Overall architecture of PSG.

place in the Short Term Memory (STM), which contains
a set of symbolic expressions. STM is to be identified
with the memory of Miller (1956) and Waugh and Norman
(1965),[1] its size is some small number of chunks
(proverbially 7 ± 2).

---

[1]We prefer not to use the terms primary and secondary memory introduced by Waugh and Norman, since the
terms conflict directly with their use in computer
science. There, primary memory is the memory that a
processor can access for its program, secondary memory
being more remote (e.g., a disk or magnetic tape, see
Bell & Newell, 1971). What Waugh and Norman call primary memory would be called a scratchpad memory or a
working memory. STM seems suitable as a name.

There is no direct representation in PSG of the various buffer memories that appear to be part of the immediate processor of the human: the visual icon of Sperling (1960), (possibly) the precategorical auditory store of Crowder and Morton (1969), and others. The interface to the senses is not represented as well, nor is the decoding on the motor side. Such deficiencies in the architectural model undoubtedly limit the scope and adequacy of the system, but will not be of first importance in this paper.

The STM holds an ordered set of symbolic expressions (i.e., chunks). The ordering shows up, as will be seen later, in that new expressions always enter STM at the front and that the conditions examine the expressions in order starting at the front (hence the frontal expressions may preempt later ones). As can be seen in Figure 1, a symbolic expression may be simply a symbol (e.g., CC) or it may consist of an ordered collection of symbolic expressions (e.g., (EE (AA DD))). Thus, symbolic expressions may be built up in a nested fashion, and we can represent them in the manner of algebraic expressions. STM may be taken as holding symbol tokens (i.e., pointers) to the expressions, or it may be taken as holding the expressions themselves. Operationally, there is no way of telling the difference. The degree to which an element in STM is opaque (Johnson, 1970) is determined by the conditions of the productions, which in essence are a description of what aspects of an expression can be responded to.

The Long Term Memory (LTM) consists entirely of an ordered set of productions. Each production is written with the condition on the left separated from the action on the right by an arrow. In Figure 1 only four productions are shown, PD1, PD2, PD3 and PD4. Some of the conditions (e.g., that of PD4) consist of only a single symbolic expression (e.g., PD4 has AA); others have a conjunction of two (e.g., PD1 has AA and BB). Some actions consist of a single symbolic expression (e.g., PD3 with BB), some have a sequence of expressions (e.g., PD4 with CC followed by DD), some have expressions that indicate operations to be performed (e.g., the SAY in PD2).

467

We will not, for the purposes of this paper, be considering either the question of other types of LTM or of storing new information (new productions) in LTM. This imposes a substantial restriction on the classes of experiments we can consider, but this class still includes many of those in the present symposium. Our assumption about LTM implies a form of homogeniety, but not one that precludes having essentially distinct memories for (say) distinct modalities--the distinctiveness arises from the content of the conditions, not from the structure of the memory itself. The creation of new expressions in STM is not to be taken as creating them in LTM as well. Thus chunking is separated from storing the chunks in LTM so they can be retrieved later.

As the system stands initially, none of the productions is satisfied by the contents of STM and nothing happens. However, we have shown an AA about to enter into STM from the external world. When it does so we get the situation of Figure 2. Here we have shifted to the representation of the system we will use from now on. All the essential elements in Figure 1 are represented, only the various enclosing boxes and input/output arrows are missing. STM now holds the AA and has lost the TT from the far right. (The STMI in the figure is the initial contents of STM.)

In Figure 3 we show the trace of the run, as it is produced by the system.[2] At each cycle the production that is true (i.e., the first whose condition is true) is noted, followed by each action when it is taken. Then the new state of STM is printed and the cycle repeats. The numbers to the left are a count of the number of actions that have occurred so far in the run.

```
00100   PS.ONE: (PD1 PD2 PD3 PD4)
00200   ;
00300   PD1: (AA AND BB --> (OLD **))
00400   PD2: (CC AND BB --> (SAY HI))
00500   PD3: (DD AND (EE) --> BB)
00600   PD4: (AA --> CC DD)
00700   ;
00800   STMI: (AA QQ (EE FF) RR SS)
```

Fig. 2.   Example production system PS.ONE

```
00100   0. STM: (AA QQ (EE FF) RR SS)
00200   PD4 TRUE
00300   0. ACTION- CC
00400   1. ACTION- DD
00500   2. STM: (DD CC AA QQ (EE FF))
00600   PD3 TRUE
00700   2. ACTION- BB
00800   3. STM: (BB DD (EE FF) CC AA)
00900   PD1 TRUE
01000   3. ACTION- (OLD **)
01100   4. STM: ((OLD AA) BB DD (EE FF) CC)
01200   PD2 TRUE
01300   4. ACTION- (SAY HI)
01400
01500   ********** HI
01600
01700   5. STM: (CC BB (OLD AA) DD (EE FF))
01800   PD2 TRUE
01900   5. ACTION- (SAY HI)
02000
02100   ********** HI
02200
02300   6. STM: (CC BB (OLD AA) DD (EE FF))
02400   PD2 TRUE
```

Fig. 3.   Run of PS.ONE

Let us work through the trace, explaining how the conditions and actions operate. The only condition of the four productions satisfied is that of PD4, the AA on the left side of PD4 matching the AA in STM. This leads to the action of PD4 being evoked, first the CC then the DD. Notice that AA is still in STM but RR and SS have disappeared off the end. This can be seen in Figure 3 at Line 500 where the contents of STM are printed after all actions for production PD4 have been taken.

A production (PD4) having been successfully evoked, the system starts the cycle over. PD4 is of course still satisfied since AA is still in STM. But PD3 is also satisfied since the DD matches the DD in STM and the (EE) also matches the (EE (EE FF)) in STM. This

---

[2]PSG is a programming system coded in a system building language called L*(G) (see Newell, McCracken, Robertson and Freeman (1971) for an overview of L*(F), the immediate predecessor of L*(G)). PSG operates on a PDP10 and the runs in this paper were made on the PDP10 system of the CMU Computer Science Department.

latter follows from one of several matching rules in
PSG. This one says that a match occurs if the condition matches completely, starting with the first symbol
in the STM expression but optionally skipping some.
Thus (EE) would also match (EE (FF GG)), but would not
match an expression without EE at the front, e.g.,
(FF EE).

When two productions are simultaneously satisfied,
the rule for resolving such conflicts is to take the
first one in order--here PD3. The result of PD3's
action is to put BB into STM as shown at Step 2.

Notice that when PD3 was evoked the two items in
its condition moved up to the front of STM in the same
order as in the condition. Thus, attended items stay
current in STM, while the others drift down toward the
end, ultimately to be lost. This mechanism provides a
form of automatic rehearsal, though it does not pre-
clude deliberate rehearsal. It also implies that the
order of the items in STM does not remain fixed, but
flops around with the details of processing.

At the next cycle PD1 is evoked, being the first
of the productions satisfied, which includes PD2, PD3
and PD4. The action of PD1 introduces a basic encoding
(i.e., construction) operation. (OLD**) is a new
expression, which will go into STM like any other. But
** is a variable whose value is the front element in
STM.[3] In the case in point the front element is AA,
which was moved up by the automatic rehearsal when the
condition of PD1 was satisfied. Hence the new element
is (OLD AA). This element *replaces* the front element,
rather than simply pushing onto the front. The net
effect is to take the front element and embed it in a
larger expression. Any expression may be written with
**. For example, if the action of PD1 had been (XX **
(YY **)), then the new element replacing AA in STM

---

[3]The constructive operation using ** is an addition
to PSG beyond Newell (1972). There we used a replacement operation to modify STM elements; here no modification is possible.

would have been (XX AA(YY AA)), creating a rather
complex encoding. It is important that the AA no
longer exist in STM (i.e., as the second element, after
pushing in the code), since it is necessary to modify
STM so AA cannot re-evoke a production.

The import of PD1's action is that it deactivates
the STM item able to evoke PD4 (and itself, as well).
On the next cycle only PD2 is satisfied. Its action
involves SAY, which is a primitive operation of the
system that prints out the expression following it in
the element, i.e., it prints HI (as shown in the
figure).

We see from Figure 3 that the system continues to
evoke PD2 and say HI. Nothing happens to modify STM so
the condition of PD2 remains satisfied. If we had
written:

    PD2:   (CC AND BB --> (SAY HI) (OLD **))

then the production system would have turned off by
marking CC as old.

We have indicated by illustration a number of
details of PSG, enough to permit us to turn to the
analysis of a substantive example. The details given
so far are not sufficient. There is a somewhat wider
array of primitive operations and many more details of
the matching operation for conditions (Newell, 1972).
We will introduce the additional aspects of this
specification as required throughout the paper.

We can see, even at this stage, that many assumptions are required to specify a complete control structure. Some of them, such as the STM itself, its
encoding, and the automatic rehearsal, constitute
rather clear psychological postulates. Others, such
as the details of matching have psychological implications (presumably every aspect of the system does),
but it is hard to know how to state them directly as
independent postulates.

The Sternberg Paradigm

Let us consider the simplest of all binary classification tasks studied by Sternberg (1970). The
subject memorizes a small set of symbols, say digits.
This is called the *positive set*. In a trial of the
experiment proper the subject is given a ready signal,
followed by a digit after a short fixed delay. The
subject responds "yes" if this so-called probe digit
is a member of the positive set, "no" if it is not.
The "yes" and "no" responses are usually encoded into
button pressings. Many trials are given, so that the
task becomes well practiced, the goal being to respond
as quickly as possible while keeping a very low error
rate. The positive set is varied in blocks, both as to
size and composition. The measure taken is the response time (RT) from presentation of the signal to
response, measured in milliseconds (ms).

The results of this experiment are well known and
form a basis for a number of the experiments which are
discussed by Posner (Chapter 2) and Hayes (Chapter 4)
in the present symposium. Let us just summarize the
basic findings:

(1)   Response time is linear with the size
      of the positive set, the slope being in
      the range of 35-40 ms. The natural
      interpretation is that a search is made
      through the positive set.

(2)   The intercept is of the order of 350
      ms, but its absolute magnitude is never
      analysed in detail since it contains
      several unknown components (e.g.,
      motor response time).

(3)   The size of the positive set can be
      be up to the size normally associated
      with STM, i.e., around seven elements.

(4)   The slope for negative responses (when
the probe digit is not in the set) is
the same as for positive responses
(when the probe is in the set). This
violates the results expected if the
search is terminated whenever it found
the probe in the set (which would make
the positive set appear to be on the
average only half as large in the case
of positive responses). This gives
rise tó an interpretation of so-called
exhaustive search (as opposed to so-
called self-terminating search).

(5)   There is essentially no serial position
effect (the time it takes to respond
to a positive probe as a function of
where in the positive set the probe
digit occurs). This agrees with the
exhaustive search notion.

(6)   The negative response can differ from
the positive response by a constant
amount (independent of set size, so the
two linear curves lie parallel). The
amount is usually about 50 ms, depending
on experimental conditions.

Much more is known about this simple task, a full
list including all the qualifications to the above
would probably run to a hundred statements, rather than
the six above. The basic results are highly reproducible and robust. The total set of results, however,
is by no means easily seen to be consistent with any
simple model.
We can use this paradigm to illustrate concretely
what a model of the control system involves and how it
makes contact with experimental data. Since we want to
reveal the strengths and issues with respect to production systems we will not simply present a final system,
but will proceed by a process of step-wise refinement.

We will work our way through a series of production
systems until we arrive at one that seems appropriate
to the task and the data.

PS.ST1: *Immediate Recognition*

The obvious scheme, shown in Figure 4, is for STM
to contain the positive set, whence the probe is introduced, leading to the attempt at identification. We
cannot just have digits as the elements in STM, since
we need to distinguish the probe digit from the positive set digits. Thus, we encode the digits of the set
as (ELM <DIGIT>), where <DIGIT> means that any digit
can go in that place, e.g., (ELM 5); likewise we encode
the probe as (PROBE <DIGIT>). The class <DIGIT> is
defined explicitly at the top of the figure. STM is
initialized with a set of three elements and a ready
signal (Line 1500). This latter simply controls the
response to attend to the stimulus.

The labeling of items is responsive to a general
issue. STM may contain various odd expressions from
a diversity of sources. The subject must (normally)
be able to distinguish the relevant items from the
irrelevant. For instance, the positive set might consist of 2, 3, 4 and the subject (say) become aware of
the digit 5 upon a final rehearsal, so that 5 is in STM
upon presentation of the probe. We would not expect
the subject simply to take 5 as a member of the positive

```
00100   <DIGIT>: (CLASS 0 1 2 3 4 5 6 7 8 9)
00200   ANY: (VAR)
00300   ;
00400   RESPOND: (ACTION (NTC (RESPONSE ANY)) (SAY ANY) (OLD **))
00500   ATTEND: (OPR CALL.TO.USER)
00600   ;
00700   PS.ST1: (PD1 PD2 PD3 PD4)
00800   ;
00900   PD1: ((PROBE) AND (OLD (RESPONSE)) --> (OLD **))
01000   PD2: ((PROBE <DIGIT>) AND (ELM <DIGIT>) --> (RESPONSE YES)
01100        RESPOND)
01200   PD3: ((PROBE) AND (ELM) --> (RESPONSE NO) RESPOND)
01300   PD4: (READY --> ATTEND)
01400   ;
01500   STMI: (READY (ELM 1) (ELM 4) (ELM 9) NIL NIL)
```

Fig. 4.   PS.ST1:   Immediate recognition.

set, though whether some additional processing would be called for is not clear. In any event, the general use of codes that declare the nature of the item seems to be appropriate and we will do it throughout, without making special arguments each time.

The production system, PS.ST1, consists of four productions. The performance of the task is accomplished by PD2 and PD3. PD2 is satisfied if there is an ELM and a PROBE both of which have the same digit. Thus the occurrence of the class name <DIGIT> in an expression operates as a variable to match against the actual items in STM. The action of PD2 is to put into STM a response expression (in this case to respond YES) and then to fire an operator, RESPOND. This operator, shown at the top of the figure at Line 400, consists of a sequence of actions, i.e., essentially the right side of a production.[4] There are three actions in RESPOND. The first action is to notice anywhere in STM an element of the form (RESPONSE ANY), where ANY is a variable that can take any symbolic expression as value (it is declared at the top of the figure at Line 200). NTC is a primitive operation, that performs a recognition of the same sort as is performed in the matching on the condition side. The second action is to say the value of ANY, which is accomplished by the SAY operation used in PS.ONE. Finally, RESPOND marks the RESPONSE element old, so that the system now knows (in some sense) that it has said the response.

Production PD3 is sensitive to the occurrence of any ELM and any PROBE, and will respond with NO.

---

[4]It thus behaves like a subroutine from a control point of view. However, it works with the same STM as do all other actions. That is, there is no isolation of its data, as there is for instance with a subroutine for computing the sine, SIN(X), which operates in an isolated environment where it knows only about the value of the passed operand, X. Whether or not subroutine control occurs and whether or not subroutine data isolation occurs are psychological questions about the human control system.

However, it sits behind PD2 and thus will only be evoked if PD2 is not, i.e., only if the probe is not a member of the positive set. Thus, PS.ST1 composes its response to the task out of a recognition of membership and a recognition that it is appropriate to respond.

The other two productions in PS.ST1 provide some of the additional control to make the system behave. PD4 responds to READY as does the operator ATTEND. Since we have no model of the external environment, we finesse the matter by having ATTEND call to the console of the user to obtain the input[5] (which will be described in Figure 5, coming up). PD1 is an analog to PD1 in PS.ONE, which serves to recognize that the task is done and to encode this by marking the PROBE element. The effect of this is to keep the system from saying YES YES YES ..., as PS.ONE keeps saying HI HI HI ...

Figure 5 shows a run of PS.ST1, from which it can be seen that the system performs correctly in both the positive and negative cases. The system was reinitialized for the second trial (Line 2600).[6] When ATTEND fires it prints a message to the user. The user puts in the expression after the prompt and then executes a ↑Z to return control to PSG.[7]

Variables occur in two places in PS.ST1: ANY in RESPOND and <DIGIT> in the condition of PD2. In both cases they are assigned a value during the course of a match, in order to satisfy the match. But they perform distinct functions.

---

[5]Thus PSG operates in an essentially interactive mode. The main gain, besides the usual one of flexibility, is that there is no need to program an outer environment.

[6]We might have simply put in another probe at the end of the first session, without reinitializing. However, it would not have behaved properly (why?).

[7]This ↑Z is necessary, since the system allows the user to do whatever he pleases after ATTEND sends its message, hence cannot know until told when the user is finished and wishes to return control to it.

```
00100    PS.ST1 START!
00200    0.  STM: (READY (ELM 1) (ELM 4) (ELM 9) NIL NIL)
00300    PD4 TRUE
00400    0.  ACTION- ATTEND
00500        ATTENDING - INPUT NEXT STIMULUS = (PROBE 4)
00600    ~
00700    1.  ACTION- (PROBE 4)
00800    2.  STM: ((PROBE 4) READY (ELM 1) (ELM 4) (ELM 9) NIL)
00900    PD2 TRUE
01000    2.  ACTION- (RESPONSE YES)
01100    3.  ACTION- RESPOND
01200    4.  ACTION- (NTC (RESPONSE ANY))
01300    5.  ACTION- (SAY ANY)
01400
01500    ********** YES
01600
01700    6.  ACTION- (OLD **)
01800    7.  STM: ((OLD (RESPONSE YES)) (PROBE 4) (ELM 4) READY (ELM 1) (ELM 9))
01900    PD1 TRUE
02000    7.  ACTION- (OLD **)
02100    8.  STM: ((OLD (PROBE 4)) (OLD (RESPONSE YES)) (ELM 4) READY (ELM 1) (ELM 9))
02200    PD4 TRUE
02300    8.  ACTION- ATTEND
02400        ATTENDING - INPUT NEXT STIMULUS =
02500
02600    PS.ST1 START!
02700    0.  STM: (READY (ELM 1) (ELM 4) (ELM 9) NIL NIL)
02800    PD4 TRUE
02900    0.  ACTION- ATTEND
03000        ATTENDING - INPUT NEXT STIMULUS = (PROBE 8)
03100    ~
03200    1.  ACTION- (PROBE 8)
03300    2.  STM: ((PROBE 8) READY (ELM 1) (ELM 4) (ELM 9) NIL)
03400    PD3 TRUE
03500    2.  ACTION- (RESPONSE NO)
03600    3.  ACTION- RESPOND
03700    4.  ACTION- (NTC (RESPONSE ANY))
03800    5.  ACTION- (SAY ANY)
03900
04000    ********** NO
```

Fig. 5. Run of PS.ST1 on positive and negative cases.

The ANY in RESPOND is used to communicate between one action, which sets the value of ANY, and another, which needs to use it. This communication of values from one action to another occurring later, or from a condition to its action, implies the existence of memory. By the nature of things, this memory cannot be STM (which would lead to an infinite regress). On the other hand, this memory occurs only over the scope of a single production. This is a short time, providing we restrict the time taken by an action. For instance, we should not permit an entire production system to be evoked by one action before going on to the next action.[8] Thus, our control system must posit a very short term

477

buffer memory in addition to the STM working memory.

The <DIGIT> in PD2 serves to restrict the match to work on digits (so that e.g., (ELM BOAT) would not be recognized). No such restriction occurs with ANY. More important, it serves to enforce the equality between two occurrences of digits, since the value assigned at the first place will be used at the second and give a match only if the same digit recurs. Thus, the multiple occurrence is performing a major function of the task--the equality test of probe digit and member digit. Whether there can be multiple occurrences of variables in a condition is an independent psychological question. To replace it with the provision that a variable can occur but once on the condition side is tantamount to making only identification possible (including class membership). This would imply that a primitive operation of equality testing would be required, to be used in the action part. The processing implications of one assumption or the other is unclear, since what additional memory and control is required within the match to accomplish multiple occurrences depends on the mechanism used to implement the match (in particular the amount and kind of parallelism).[9]

How do we know this production system is the right sort of mechanism, given the results of experiments? We need to adopt an explicit timing model, so that we can compute the total time taken in performing the task. The central assumption we will make has three parts:

---

[8]Such facility represents good programming language design, in which one wants indefinite capabilities for recursion. However, we are trying to model the human control system, not construct a neat system.

[9]We state all these issues to show that the conventions of the production system, which may appear to be linguistic in nature, contain substantive psychological assumptions.

The time to evoke the next production is independent of:

(1)   the number of productions in the system;

(2)   the contents of STM;

(3)   the condition of the evoked productions.

The assumptions are meant only as a first approximation. However, they do rule out time being proportional to the number of productions (the assumption that comes naturally from the definition of a production system and its implementation on a digital computer).

In favor of Part (1) is the circumstance that in writing a production system (PS.ST1 or any other) we only put down a few of the conditions to which the subject is presumably sensitive and could respond to if the situation (i.e., the contents of STM) warranted: a wasp lighting on the apparatus, the smell of smoke, an irrelevant remark in the background, turning off the lights and so on, any of which would surely evoke a noticing operation and subsequent alteration of the contents of STM. While reaction to such conditions might be somewhat longer, in no way could the subject be imagined to iterate through all such possible conditions taking an increment of time per possibility. Thus, the set of productions we work with bears no relation to the set of productions that we envision constituting the LTM. More generally, the basic control structure is to be viewed as one of a recognition followed by an action followed by a recognition again-- the act of evoking the next action (or mini-sequence of actions) being the basic pulse of the system.[10]

Parts (2) and (3) of the assumption are not quite so compelling and alternatives can be imagined.[11] That

---

[10]This recognition-act cycle is to be contrasted with the basic fetch-decode-execute cycle which is the primitive control structure of the digital computer.

all the conditions are tested simultaneously implies that the time to determine the next production depends on all the unsatisfied conditions as well as the one that is chosen. Thus, no strong dependence could exist on the particular items, and in any event all the items in STM must be involved in the processing, not just those that enter into the selected production.

These three assumptions imply that it takes a constant amount of time, call it $T.evoke$, to determine the next production to be executed. Each production, of course, evokes a sequence of actions. The total time to accomplish the sequence may be variable, depending on the exact actions that occur. The simplest assumption is one of *seriality*: that each action takes a fixed amount of time and that the time for the sequence is the sum of the times for each action. Even simpler is the assumption that each action takes the same time, call it $T.action$. Under this assumption the time for a production with N actions can be written:

$$T.production = T.evoke + N * T.action$$

The special case of T.evoke = 0 is worth a moment's attention. The obvious interpretation is that it takes no time to evoke the production (i.e., to recognize what action sequence to perform) and all the time is taken by the performance of actions. An alternative interpretation is that only a single action can be evoked at a time. That is, writing of a sequence of N actions is simply a shorthand for writing N productions, each of which has a condition and a single action. We assert thereby that the conditions are so unique that only the production associated with the next action would fire. Under this assumption the total time of a production-as-written with N actions is:

---

[11]For instance, considering elements in order from the front of STM and evoking the first satisfied production would make the time dependent on the contents of STM.

T.production = N * (time-to-evoke + time-for-action)

The two times coalesce to form the T.action in the top formula.

    The simplicity of these assumptions should not be disturbing. Their complication can be left to the impact of specific data. Even in this simple form they offer guidance in the analysis of a production system. Notice, by the way, that the production system has a built in seriality in the sequence of production evocations, independent of whether we make the serial assumption for performing a sequence of actions for a given production. Roughly speaking, the time to do a task is proportional to the number of productions evoked to do the task.

    Given this much of a timing model, it can be seen from Figure 5 that PS.ST1 produces an answer in a time that is independent of the size of the positive set (essentially, T.evoke + 5*T.action). Thus PS.ST1 disagrees fundamentally with the empirical results. Consequently, let us explore other methods for the task (putting to one side for the moment what is implied by not using a scheme of action that seems possible a priori).

PS.ST2: Terminating Search

    Figure 6 shows a production system, PS.ST2, that performs the task by explicitly searching through each of the members of the positive set. PD2 in Figure 6 looks very similar to PD2 in Figure 4. However, there is a critical difference. In Figure 4 the digit selected by <DIGIT> is defined by the probe; thus this seeks out an element in STM that has the same digit. In

```
00100   PS.ST2: (PD1 PD2 PD3 PD4 PD5)
00200   ;
00300   PD1: ((PROBE) AND (OLD (RESPONSE)) --> (OLD **))
00400   PD2: ((ELM <DIGIT>) AND (PROBE <DIGIT>) --> (RESPONSE YES)
00500        RESPOND)
00600   PD3: ((ELM) AND (PROBE) --> (OLD **))
00700   PD4: ((PROBE) AND (ELM) ABS --> (RESPONSE NO) RESPOND)
00800   PD5: (READY --> ATTEND)
```

Fig. 6. PS.ST2: Linear terminating search.

Figure 6, the digit is selected by the first (ELM...)
in STM; only if this has the same digit as the probe,
will there be a match. If this doesn't occur, the next
production (PD3) then modifies the first element so that
it will not be sensed again by PD2. Thus, these two
productions work through the positive set and will find
a match if it exists. Only if no more elements exist
will PD4 be evoked and say NO. (PD1 and PD5 are identical to PD1 and PD4 respectively of PS.ST1.)

The condition of PD4 involves detecting the absence
of an element in STM, indicated by the ABS following
the element. Thus PD4 will not be evoked if there is
an item in STM of form (ELM...). This happens not to
be strictly necessary for PS.ST2 to work, but somehow
providing a production that could be triggered to say
NO on the occurrence of the probe alone seems risky.
Suppose, for instance, the probe arrived simultaneously
with the ready signal. PS.ST2 would behave right; a
system with only (PROBE) in the condition of PD4 would
not, producing NO immediately.

We have now introduced all but one of the ingredients of matching: (1) the matching of items in STM;
(2) the conjunction of condition elements, either for
presence or absence; (3) the use of variables and classes (which operate as variables with restricted domains);
and (4) the rules for matching an element (or subelement)
of the condition with an element (or subelement) of the
STM, namely subelement by subelement, working from the
front, but allowing the tail of the STM element to not
be matched (e.g., (EE) matches (EE FF)). The one addition (to occur in the next example) is (5) permitting
a variable to have an associated domain locally. An
example of this is:

$$(A \ X1 \ == \ (B \ C) \ D) \qquad \text{where X1:} \quad (VAR)$$

This says that X1 must match (B C). Thus the entire
condition element matches (A (B C) D), but not (A B C D),
((B C) D) or (A (C B) D).

Examination of the logic of PS.ST2 shows that the
time is indeed proportional to the size of the set

```
00100    0. STM: (READY (ELM 1) (ELM 4) (ELM 9) NIL NIL)
00200    PD5 TRUE
00300    0. ACTION- ATTEND
00400         ATTENDING - INPUT NEXT STIMULUS = (PROBE 4)
00500    ~
00600    1. ACTION- (PROBE 4)
00700    2. STM: ((PROBE 4) READY (ELM 1) (ELM 4) (ELM 9) NIL)
00800    PD3 TRUE
00900    2. ACTION- (OLD **)
01000    3. STM: ((OLD (ELM 1)) (PROBE 4) READY (ELM 4) (ELM 9) NIL)
01100    PD2 TRUE
01200    3. ACTION- (RESPONSE YES)
01300    4. ACTION- RESPOND
01400    5. ACTION- (NTC (RESPONSE ANY))
01500    6. ACTION- (SAY ANY)
01600
01700    ********** YES
```

Fig. 7. Run of PS.ST2 on positive case.

```
00100    0. STM: (READY (ELM 1) (ELM 4) (ELM 9) NIL NIL)
00200    PD5 TRUE
00300    0. ACTION- ATTEND
00400         ATTENDING - INPUT NEXT STIMULUS = (PROBE 8)
00500    ~
00600    1. ACTION- (PROBE 8)
00700    2. STM: ((PROBE 8) READY (ELM 1) (ELM 4) (ELM 9) NIL)
00800    PD3 TRUE
00900    2. ACTION- (OLD **)
01000    3. STM: ((OLD (ELM 1)) (PROBE 8) READY (ELM 4) (ELM 9) NIL)
01100    PD3 TRUE
01200    3. ACTION- (OLD **)
01300    4. STM: ((OLD (ELM 4)) (PROBE 8) (OLD (ELM 1)) READY (ELM 9) NIL)
01400    PD3 TRUE
01500    4. ACTION- (OLD **)
01600    5. STM: ((OLD (ELM 9)) (PROBE 8) (OLD (ELM 4)) (OLD (ELM 1)) READY NIL)
01700    PD4 TRUE
01800    5. ACTION- (RESPONSE NO)
01900    6. ACTION- RESPOND
02000    7. ACTION- (NTC (RESPONSE ANY))
02100    8. ACTION- (SAY ANY)
02200
02300    ********** NO
```

Fig. 8. Run of PS.ST2 on negative case.

searched requiring one evocation and one action for each
element examined that is not the probe and then one more
(PD2 if positive, PD4 if negative) to generate the response. However, as demonstrated in Figures 7 and 8,
PS.ST2 does a self-terminating search. It looks at all
the elements in the set in the negative case (Figure 8),
but only half the elements (on the average) in the positive case (Figure 7), thus making the slope of the positive case appear only half of what it is in the negative case. But, as noted earlier, the evidence is

483

unequivocal that the slopes are the same for the positive and negative cases. Furthermore, there is no
serial position effect (as there would be in PS.ST2).
Thus, we have not yet found a method for doing the
task that has the right characteristics.

PS.ST3 and PS.ST4: Encoded Representations

The system of Figure 9, PS.ST3, introduces the
notion that the set is actually held in an encoded
representation (i.e., as a chunk). Thus, we have
changed the STM to hold some irrelevant items prior to
the start of the trial. At the READY signal the encoded
positive set is brought into STM (PD5).
The positive set is encoded as a nested set, as can
be seen in the action side of PD5 for a set of three
elements. A set of five would have the form:
(X (X (X (X X)))). This means that a single production,
PD2, can perform the decoding by repeated application.
The point of introducing the decoding is that the entire
set must be decoded before any further processing is
done on it. Thus, the time to decode will be independent of whether the result is to be positive or negative. Thus, PS.ST3 satisfies the experimental results
that lead to the inference of the exhaustive search.
It does so, however, by attributing the time, not to
search (which is done in constant time by PD3 and PD4),
but to a linear time to decode the expression. Figures
10 and 11 show runs on PS.ST3 in the positive and negative case that illustrate this. It can be seen that
the time to do the task is:

$$T.total = 2*T.action + N*(T.evoke + 3*T.action)$$

Examination of PS.ST3 shows that what enforces the
compulsive decoding before testing is that PD2, the
decoding production, occurs before PD3 and PD4, the
comparison and response productions. Why don't we
simply reverse the order? Then we should catch the
elements as they are being decoded, and reinstitute a
termination search. Figure 12 shows the result, using
PS.ST3X which is simply a reordered version of PS.ST3.

```
00100   X1: (VAR)
00200   X2: (VAR)
00300   ;
00400   PS.ST3: (PD1 PD2 PD3 PD4 PD5 PD6)
00500   ;
00600   PD1: ((PROBE) AND (OLD (RESPONSE)) --> (OLD **))
00700   PD2: ((SET X1 X2) AND (PROBE) --> (OLD **) X2 X1)
00800   PD3: ((PROBE <DIGIT>) AND (ELM <DIGIT>) --> (RESPONSE YES)
00900        RESPOND)
01000   PD4: ((PROBE) AND (ELM) --> (RESPONSE NO) RESPOND)
01100   PD5: (READY AND (SET) ABS -->
01200        (SET (ELM 1) (SET (ELM 4) (ELM 9))) )
01300   PD6: (ANY --> ATTEND)
01400   ;
01500   STMI: (JUNK NIL NIL NIL NIL NIL NIL)
```

Fig. 9.   PS.ST3:   Nested representation.

```
00100   0.  STM: (JUNK NIL NIL NIL NIL NIL NIL)
00200   PD6 TRUE
00300   0.  ACTION- ATTEND
00400       ATTENDING - INPUT NEXT STIMULUS = READY
00500   ~
00600   1.  ACTION- READY
00700   2.  STM: (READY JUNK NIL NIL NIL NIL NIL)
00800   PD5 TRUE
00900   2.  ACTION- (SET (ELM 1) (SET (ELM 4) (ELM 9)))
01000   3.  STM: ((SET (ELM 1) (SET (ELM 4) (ELM 9))) READY JUNK NIL NIL NIL NIL)
01100   PD6 TRUE
01200   3.  ACTION- ATTEND
01300       ATTENDING - INPUT NEXT STIMULUS = (PROBE 4)
01400   ~
01500   4.  ACTION- (PROBE 4)
01600   5.  STM: ((PROBE 4) (SET (ELM 1) (SET (ELM 4) (ELM 9))) READY JUNK NIL NIL NIL)
01700   PD2 TRUE
01800   5.  ACTION- (OLD **)
01900   6.  ACTION- X2
02000   7.  ACTION- X1
02100   8.  STM: ((ELM 1) (SET (ELM 4) (ELM 9)) (OLD (SET (ELM 1) (SET (ELM 4) (ELM 9))))
02150       (PROBE 4) READY JUNK NIL)
02200   PD2 TRUE
02300   8.  ACTION- (OLD **)
02400   9.  ACTION- X2
02500   10. ACTION- X1
02600   11. STM: ((ELM 4) (ELM 9) (OLD (SET (ELM 4) (ELM 9))) (PROBE 4) (ELM 1)
02650       (OLD (SET (ELM 1) (SET (ELM 4) (ELM 9)))) READY)
02700   PD3 TRUE
02800   11. ACTION- (RESPONSE YES)
02900   12. ACTION- RESPOND
03000   13. ACTION- (NTC (RESPONSE ANY))
03100   14. ACTION- (SAY ANY)
03200
03300   ********** YES
```

Fig. 10.   Run of PS.ST3 on positive case.

485

```
00100    0. STM: (JUNK NIL NIL NIL NIL NIL NIL)
00200    PD6 TRUE
00300    0. ACTION- ATTEND
00400        ATTENDING - INPUT NEXT STIMULUS = READY
00500    ~
00600    1. ACTION- READY
00700    2. STM: (READY JUNK NIL NIL NIL NIL NIL)
00800    PD5 TRUE
00900    2. ACTION- (SET (ELM 1) (SET (ELM 4) (ELM 9)))
01000    3. STM: ((SET (ELM 1) (SET (ELM 4) (ELM 9))) READY JUNK NIL NIL NIL NIL)
01100    PD6 TRUE
01200    3. ACTION- ATTEND
01300        ATTENDING - INPUT NEXT STIMULUS = (PROBE 8)
01400    ~
01500    4. ACTION- (PROBE 8)
01600    5. STM: ((PROBE 8) (SET (ELM 1) (SET (ELM 4) (ELM 9))) READY JUNK NIL NIL NIL)
01700    PD2 TRUE
01800    5. ACTION- (OLD **)
01900    6. ACTION- X2
02000    7. ACTION- X1
02100    8. STM: ((ELM 1) (SET (ELM 4) (ELM 9)) (OLD (SET (ELM 1) (SET (ELM 4) (ELM 9))))
02150        (PROBE 8) READY JUNK NIL)
02200    PD2 TRUE
02300    8. ACTION- (OLD **)
02400    9. ACTION- X2
02500    10. ACTION- X1
02600    11. STM: ((ELM 4) (ELM 9) (OLD (SET (ELM 4) (ELM 9))) (PROBE 8) (ELM 1)
02675        (OLD (SET (ELM 1) (SET (ELM 4) (ELM 9)))) READY)
02700    PD4 TRUE
02800    11. ACTION- (RESPONSE NO)
02900    12. ACTION- RESPOND
03000    13. ACTION- (NTC (RESPONSE ANY))
03100    14. ACTION- (SAY ANY)
03200
03300    ********** NO
```

Fig. 11.   Run of PS.ST3 on negative case.

Trouble results, as we see, since PD4 responds to the
non-satisfaction of PD3 by declaring NO immediately,
thus causing an error.

What ways exist of patching up the system so it
avoids the difficulty of Figure 12, while preserving
the self-terminating features? PD4 must be inhibited
while decoding goes on, whereas PD3 must not be. The
simplest solution is to split the two productions,
putting PD3 ahead of PD2 and PD4 afterward. This works
just fine. Other alternatives involve making PD4
conditional upon the set being completely decoded. This
can be done, for instance, by changing PD4 to:

PD4:   ((PROBE) AND (SET) ABS --> (RESPONSE NO) RESPOND)

Thus, although introducing the idea of decoding permitted us to produce a version with the correct timing

```
00100   PS.ST3X: (PD1 PD2 PD3 PD4 PD5 PD6)
00200   PD1: ((PROBE) AND (OLD (RESPONSE)) --> (OLD **))
00300   PD3: ((PROBE <DIGIT>) AND (ELM <DIGIT>) --> (RESPONSE YES) RESPOND)
00400   PD4: ((PROBE) AND (ELM) --> (RESPONSE NO) RESPOND)
00500   PD2: ((SET X1 X2) AND (PROBE) --> (OLD **) X2 X1)
00600   PD5: (READY AND (SET) ABS --> (SET (ELM 1) (SET (ELM 4) (ELM 9))))
00700   PD6: (ANY --> ATTEND)
00800
00900   PS.ST3X START!
01000   0.  STM: (JUNK NIL NIL NIL NIL NIL NIL)
01100   PD6 TRUE
01200   0.  ACTION- ATTEND
01300        ATTENDING - INPUT NEXT STIMULUS = READY
01400   ~
01500   1.  ACTION- READY
01600   2.  STM: (READY JUNK NIL NIL NIL NIL NIL)
01700   PD5 TRUE
01800   2.  ACTION- (SET (ELM 1) (SET (ELM 4) (ELM 9)))
01900   3.  STM: ((SET (ELM 1) (SET (ELM 4) (ELM 9))) READY JUNK NIL NIL NIL NIL)
02000   PD6 TRUE
02100   3.  ACTION- ATTEND
02200        ATTENDING - INPUT NEXT STIMULUS = (PROBE 4)
02300   ~
02400   4.  ACTION- (PROBE 4)
02500   5.  STM: ((PROBE 4) (SET (ELM 1) (SET (ELM 4) (ELM 9))) READY JUNK NIL NIL NIL)
02600   PD2 TRUE
02700   5.  ACTION- (OLD **)
02800   6.  ACTION- X2
02900   7.  ACTION- X1
03000   8.  STM: ((ELM 1) (SET (ELM 4) (ELM 9)) (OLD (SET (ELM 1) (SET (ELM 4) (ELM 9))))
03050        (PROBE 4) READY JUNK NIL)
03100   PD4 TRUE
03200   8.  ACTION- (RESPONSE NO)
03300   9.  ACTION- RESPOND
03400   10.  ACTION- (NTC (RESPONSE ANY))
03500   11.  ACTION- (SAY ANY)
03600
03700   ********** NO
```

Fig. 12.   Run of PS.ST3X showing error.

```
00100   X1: (VAR)
00200   X2: (VAR)
00300   X3: (VAR)
00400   X4: (VAR)
00500   ;
00600   PS.ST4: (PD1 PD2 PD3 PD4 PD5 PD6 PD7 PD8 PD9)
00700   ;
00800   PD1: ((PROBE) AND (OLD (RESPONSE)) --> (OLD **))
00900   PD2: ((SET X1 X2 X3 X4) AND (PROBE) --> (OLD **) X4 X3 X2 X1)
01000   PD3: ((SET X1 X2 X3) AND (PROBE) --> (OLD **) X3 X2 X1)
01100   PD4: ((SET X1 X2) AND (PROBE) --> (OLD **) X2 X1)
01200   PD5: ((SET X1) AND (PROBE) --> (OLD **) X1)
01300   PD6: ((PROBE <DIGIT>) AND (ELM <DIGIT>) --> (RESPONSE YES)
01400        RESPOND)
01500   PD7: ((PROBE) AND (ELM) --> (RESPONSE NO) RESPOND)
01600   PD8: (READY AND (SET) ABS -->
01700        (SET (ELM 1) (ELM 4) (ELM 9)) )
01800   PD9: (ANY --> ATTEND)
```

Fig. 13.   PS.ST4:   Linear representation.

properties, we have found minor variations of the same
scheme that re-instate the terminating condition, and
appear to be somewhat more efficient than the exhaustive scheme.

Figure 13 shows an alternative form of encoded
representation that appears to overcome these difficulties. A set is now represented by a linear expression,
e.g., (SET A B C D). Such sets cannot be decoded re-
cursively, but require a set of productions, one member
for each set size. Thus, PD2 to PD5 in PS.ST4 accomplish jointly the decoding of a set in STM into its
elements. The recognition of the larger sets occur
before smaller ones, since by the matching rules of PSG
the productions for smaller sets would also be satisfied by larger sets. The maximum size set admitted in
PS.ST4 is four elements; it could be extended to any
specific upper limit.[12]

The decoding now occurs within the action sequence
of a single production. Thus, it takes minimal time
(N*T.action) and there is no opportunity to slip in the
evocation of a production (i.e., PD6) that would terminate the search. The rest of PS.ST4 is the same as in
PS.ST3. Figure 14 shows a run on a positive case that
illustrates how the decoding goes.

Throughout the discussion we have ignored where
the positive set came from. In the first examples
(PS.ST1 and PS.ST2) we simply posited the elements in
STM initially. In the later examples (PS.ST3 and
PS.ST4) we posited a set in LTM already assimilated into
a production and in the encoded form we wished to work
with. We have set to one side the way new productions
are created in LTM (i.e., the question of LTM acquisition as it shows up in our system), but the mechanics
of encoding are within our purview.

Figure 15 shows PS.ST5, which is an augmentation
of PS.ST4 to encode a sequence of incoming elements

---

[12]The capacity of STM would appear to limit the size
of the sets that could be successfully decoded; so also
could the capacity of the variable buffer store.

```
00100   0.  STM: (JUNK NIL NIL NIL NIL NIL NIL)
00200   PD9 TRUE
00300   0.  ACTION- ATTEND
00400       ATTENDING - INPUT NEXT STIMULUS = READY
00500   ~
00600   1.  ACTION- READY
00700   2.  STM: (READY JUNK NIL NIL NIL NIL NIL)
00800   PD8 TRUE
00900   2.  ACTION+ (SET (ELM 1) (ELM 4) (ELM 9))
01000   3.  STM: ((SET (ELM 1) (ELM 4) (ELM 9)) READY JUNK NIL NIL NIL NIL)
01100   PD9 TRUE
01200   3.  ACTION- ATTEND
01300       ATTENDING - INPUT NEXT STIMULUS = (PROBE 4)
01400   ~
01500   4.  ACTION- (PROBE 4)
01600   5.  STM: ((PROBE 4) (SET (ELM 1) (ELM 4) (ELM 9)) READY JUNK NIL NIL NIL)
01700   PD3 TRUE
01800   5.  ACTION- (OLD **)
01900   6.  ACTION- X3
02000   7.  ACTION- X2
02100   8.  ACTION- X1
02200   9.  STM: ((ELM 1) (ELM 4) (ELM 9) (OLD (SET (ELM 1) (ELM 4) (ELM 9)))
02250       (PROBE 4) READY JUNK)
02300   PD6 TRUE
02400   9.  ACTION- (RESPONSE YES)
02500   10. ACTION- RESPOND
02600   11. ACTION- (NTC (RESPONSE ANY))
02700   12. ACTION- (SAY ANY)
02800
02900   ********** YES
```

Fig. 14. Run of PS.ST4 on positive case.

into a set with the linear encoding. Figure 16 shows
a run where this encoding occurs, stopping at the point
where one would go into the rest of the Sternberg task
with a READY and a (PROBE). Again, there has to be a
separate production for each set size, since each item
of the set has to be acquired (with a variable) and
then the new set created. A similar program can be
written to construct sets in the nested representation.
In this case, only a pair of productions is needed (as
shown in Figure 17, which gives only the encoding part
of the complete system). This pair has the property
that it can construct indefinitely large sets, though
of course the sets must still be decoded step by step.
    We have attended primarily to the equality between
the slope of the response time for positive responses
and negative responses, when response time is plotted
against the size of the positive set. However the
negative response can differ from the positive response
(Point 6 in our list of empirical properties). This

```
00100   PS.ST5: (PD1 PD2 PD3 PD4 PD5 PD6 PD7 PD8 PD9 PD10 PD11 PD12)
00200   ;
00300   PD1: ((PROBE) AND (OLD (RESPONSE)) --> (OLD **))
00400   PD2: ((SET X1 X2 X3 X4) AND (PROBE) --> (OLD **) X4 X3 X2 X1)
00500   PD3: ((SET X1 X2 X3) AND (PROBE) --> (OLD **) X3 X2 X1)
00600   PD4: ((SET X1 X2) AND (PROBE) --> (OLD **) X2 X1)
00700   PD5: ((SET X1) AND (PROBE) --> (OLD **) X1)
00800   PD6: ((PROBE <DIGIT>) AND (ELM <DIGIT>) --> (RESPONSE YES)
00900       RESPOND)
01000   PD7: ((PROBE) AND (ELM) --> (RESPONSE NO) RESPOND)
01100   PD8: (X1 == (ELM) AND X2 == (ELM) AND READY -->
01200       (OLD **) (NTC (ELM)) (OLD **) (SET X2 X1))
01300   PD9: (X1 == (ELM) AND (SET X2 X3 X4) AND READY -->
01400       (OLD **) (NTC (SET)) (OLD **) (SET X2 X3 X4 X1))
01500   PD10: (X1 == (ELM) AND (SET X2 X3) AND READY -->
01600       (OLD **) (NTC (SET)) (OLD **) (SET X2 X3 X1))
01700   PD11: (X1 == (ELM) AND (SET X2) AND READY -->
01800       (OLD **) (NTC (SET)) (OLD **) (SET X2 X1))
01900   PD12: (ANY --> ATTEND)
```

Fig. 15.   PS.ST5:   Linear representation, encoding and decoding.

effect can be attributed to a response bias--that is, the subject sets himself to respond one way, e.g., YES so that the expected response occurs more rapidly than the unexpected one. Such a bias could presumably be adopted in either direction, which is in accord with the empirical findings. (For instance, if there is an appreciable frequency difference between the occurrences of positive and negative instances, then the response is quicker to the more frequent.)

Given a system such as we have been considering, we can ask how, or whether, a response bias can be programmed to permit a more rapid response in one or the other case. Figure 18 shows a solution, PS.ST7, that puts the (RESPONSE YES) element in STM in advance, so it does not have to be done by the positive response production (PD6). We do not show what determines which way the bias goes; from the structure of the production system it could be either way. The actual size of the bias depends on the difference between PD6, which now simply executes RESPOND, and PD7, which has the burden of changing the response to NO. We have shown three different productions, PD7A, PD7B and PD7C. The first does not bother to neutralize (RESPOND YES), but simply puts a (RESPOND NO) ahead of it in STM. Presumably this raises some problems about a freely wandering (RESPONSE YES), but perhaps this could be neutralized

```
00100   0.  STM: (JUNK NIL NIL NIL NIL NIL NIL)
00200   PD12 TRUE
00300   0.  ACTION- ATTEND
00400        ATTENDING - INPUT NEXT STiMULUS = READY
00500   ~
00600   1.  ACTION- READY
00700   2.  STM: (READY JUNK NIL NIL NIL NIL NIL)
00800   PD12 TRUE
00900   2.  ACTION- ATTEND
01000        ATTENDING - INPUT NEXT STIMULUS = (ELM 1)
01100   ~
01200   3.  ACTION- (ELM 1)
01300   4.  STM: ((ELM 1) READY JUNK NIL NIL NIL NIL)
01400   PD12 TRUE
01500   4.  ACTION- ATTEND
01600        ATTENDING - INPUT NEXT STIMULUS = (ELM 2)
01700   ~
01800   5.  ACTION- (ELM 2)
01900   6.  STM: ((ELM 2) (ELM 1) READY JUNK NIL NIL NIL)
02000   PD8 TRUE
02100   6.  ACTION- (OLD **)
02200   7.  ACTION- (NTC (ELM))
02300   8.  ACTION- (OLD **)
02400   9.  ACTION- (SET X2 X1)
02500   10. STM: ((SET (ELM 1) (ELM 2)) (OLD (ELM 1)) (OLD (ELM 2)) READY JUNK NIL NIL)
02600   PD12 TRUE
02700   10. ACTION- ATTEND
02800        ATTENDING - INPUT NEXT STIMULUS = (ELM 3)
02900   ~
03000   11. ACTION- (ELM 3)
03100   12. STM: ((ELM 3) (SET (ELM 1) (ELM 2)) (OLD (ELM 1)) (OLD (ELM 2)) READY JUNK NIL)
03200   PD10 TRUE
03300   12. ACTION- (OLD **)
03400   13. ACTION- (NTC (SET))
03500   14. ACTION- (OLD **)
03600   15. ACTION- (SET X2 X3 X1)
03700   16. STM: ((SET (ELM 1) (ELM 2) (ELM 3)) (OLD (SET (ELM 1) (ELM 2))) (OLD (ELM 3))
03750        READY (OLD (ELM 1)) (OLD (ELM 2)) JUNK)
03800   PD12 TRUE
03900   16. ACTION- ATTEND
04000        ATTENDING - INPUT NEXT STIMULUS = (PROBE 1)
```

Fig. 16.   Run of PS.ST5 on encoding part only.

```
00100   PD5: (X1 == (ELM) AND X2 == (ELM) AND READY -->
00200        (OLD **) (NTC (ELM)) (OLD **) (SET X2 X1))
00300   PD6: (X1 == (ELM) AND X2 == (SET) AND READY -->
00400        (OLD **) (NTC (SET)) (OLD **) (SET X2 X1))
```

Fig. 17.   Encoding productions for nested representation.

after the response was actually made. PD7B and PD7C
both mark the YES respond OLD. PD7B does so by locating
the response element in its condition part; PD7C takes
an extra NTC action to locate it. Thus, we have a range
of time differences depending on which mechanism we
opt for.

491

```
00100   PS.ST7: (PD1 PD2 PD3 PD4 PD5 PD6 PD7X PD8 PD9 PD10 PD11 PD12
00200          PD13)
00300   ;
00400   PD1: ((PROBE) AND (OLD (RESPONSE)) --> (OLD **))
00500   PD2: ((SET X1 X2 X3 X4) AND (PROBE) --> (OLD **) X4 X3 X2 X1)
00600   PD3: ((SET X1 X2 X3) AND (PROBE) --> (OLD **) X3 X2 X1)
00700   PD4: ((SET X1 X2) AND (PROBE) --> (OLD **) X2 X1)
00800   PD5: ((SET X1) AND (PROBE) --> (OLD **) X1)
00900   PD6: ((PROBE <DIGIT>) AND (ELM <DIGIT>) --> RESPOND)
01000   PD7A: ((PROBE) AND (ELM) --> (RESPONSE NO) RESPOND)
01100   PD7B: ((RESPONSE) AND (PROBE) AND (ELM) --> (OLD **)
01200          (RESPONSE NO) RESPOND)
01300   PD7C: ((PROBE) AND (ELM) --> (NTC (RESPOND)) (OLD **)
01400          (RESPONSE NO) RESPOND)
01500   PD8: (X1 == (ELM) AND X2 == (ELM) AND READY -->
01600          (OLD **) (NTC (ELM)) (OLD **) (SET X2 X1))
01700   PD9: (X1 == (ELM) AND (SET X2 X3 X4) AND READY -->
01800          (OLD **) (NTC (SET)) (OLD **) (SET X2 X3 X4 X1))
01900   PD10: (X1 == (ELM) AND (SET X2 X3) AND READY -->
02000          (OLD **) (NTC (SET)) (OLD **) (SET X2 X3 X1))
02100   PD11: (X1 == (ELM) AND (SET X2) AND READY -->
02200          (OLD **) (NTC (SET)) (OLD **) (SET X2 X1))
02300   PD12: (READY AND (RESPONSE) ABS --> (RESPONSE YES))
02400   PD13: (ANY --> ATTEND)
```

Fig. 18. PS.ST7: PS.ST5 with response bias.

Summary

   The final production system, PS.ST7, comes close
to satisfying the several empirical propositions listed
earlier: the linear dependence on set size, the
equality of slope for positive and negative cases, the
constant difference between positive and negative cases,
and the lack of a serial position effect.

   However, the situation is not perfect. We can
write the total response time as:

$$T = T.external + 3*T.evoke$$
$$+ (6 + X)*T.action + N*T.action$$

   where X = 0 for the positive case
          X = 1, 2, 3 for the negative case
             for PD7A, B, C respectively.

Actually, this equation contains a small addition to
the constant part. If the system is actually run
through both the encoding and decoding stages then
(RESPONSE) gets lost from STM before it is called by
(PROBE) after decoding. This can be avoided by the

492

addition of another production that brings (RESPONSE) to the front when (PROBE) is first detected:

PDX: (READY AND (PROBE) AND (RESPONSE) --> (OLD **))

This production goes right after PD1. It marks READY as old to avoid repetition of PDX itself; READY has in fact done its job of controlling the encoding and initiating the response when (PROBE) occurs. PDX adds one T.evoke and one T.action to the constant part of T above, since it is evoked on every occasion.

The experimental value of the slope of time against set size is around 35 ms. Hence from the equation above, T.action must be around 35 ms. The difference between positive and negative cases is either 1, 2, or 3 times T.action, which is to say, either about 35, 70, or 105 ms. Empirically this difference is often found to be around 50 ms, which lies halfway between the two values for A and B. Notice that both the slope and the positive-negative difference are determined solely by T.action. T.evoke enters the equation only as part of the total ordinate. since this also contains various peripheral perception and motor response times (here symbolized by T.external), there is no way to derive any independent information about T.evoke. The best we can do is make a check of reasonableness. Since the total ordinate is around 350 ms, there is about 140 ms available for T.external + 3*T.evoke, which does not seem out of bounds if T.evoke is not too large.

There is little point in attempting to assay the seriousness of the discrepancy between the theoretical and empirical values for the positive-negative difference or to explore various potential explanations. The model is still enough within the ball park to remain worth considering. Other more pressing issues need exposing

Let us note what the control structure has accomplished for us so far. First, we have been able to approach the task of binary classification in the Sternberg paradigm as a programming task. We could tell when an arrangement accomplished the task and when it did not.[13] Once a viable production system was discovered, all of its properties were fixed, to the extent that we had settled on an explicit timing model. Thus, explicit predictions follow for the entire range of inputs.

In this view PSG represents the basic structure of the human information processing system. It follows that *any* program written in PSG should be a viable program for the subject. Only such an assumption permits us simply to program the task in PSG. However, nothing has been provided to determine which of all the feasible production systems will come to govern the subject's behavior. Our example makes clear that the multiple production systems are possible. Without a theory of which system is selected the total view remains essentially incomplete.

General considerations of the adaptiveness of human behavior lead one to adopt the following:

> *Principle of adaptation*: Other things equal, the subject will adopt that production system that more closely obtains his goals.

It is, after all, a principle of this sort that leads us to believe that the subject will come to perform the task at all, once instructed. For we do not believe that the subject comes equipped with a preformed organization for doing the Sternberg task (before encountering it for the first time). This organization is composed in response to the demands of the task, i.e., the subject himself selects this organization, presumably from among others that he could adopt that would not solve the task. That he should also be able, say, to use one organization that takes less time than another is simply another application of the same principle.

Why then does not a subject use the more efficient

---

[13]We do face verifying that the program does in fact work, i.e., debugging the program. While simple for the task at hand, it can become a serious problem.

schemes, such as PS.ST1 which recognizes the action in a time independent of set size and (importantly) less than for the other systems? Resolution can be sought in several directions. Possibly the timing model is wrong, or the particular structure of PSG, or the general structure of production systems. A different sort of possibility is that additional constraints exist that limit the production systems that are possible or selected. For example, if the subject can't learn a given type of production system or assemble it on demand, then it can be excluded from the feasible set. Something of this sort, perhaps, makes us hesitate at splitting the response productions on both sides of the decoding productions in PS.ST3 (Figure 13). We have reason to be leery of the linear ordering of productions, since we do not interpret a production system as considering productions serially, but rather in parallel. If productions are not completely independent, but are developed in subsystems, arbitrary ordering may not be possible.

Notice that the set of all production systems plays a somewhat different role here than does, say, the set of all Markov processes in mathematical learning theory. In both cases the set in question is indeed the set of all theories under consideration. But with the Markov process the problem of selection is one of descriptive adequacy (i.e., of the fit to the data). In the present case, since the selection is ascribed to the subject (by a not yet formulated process, unfortunately) we must confront the issue of why psychologically one rather than another production system occurs—in addition to the question of whether it fits the data.

Leaving to one side for the moment the major issue just raised, working with the production systems has in fact led us down a somewhat new path in theorizing about the basic phenomena in the Sternberg paradigm. The basic linear effect is ascribed not to a search process but to a decoding process. This solution was discovered in the attempt to find a production system that fit the basic phenomena. One can find in the

literature some suggestions that encoding may be
involved (e.g., Sternberg, 1970), but no genuine
presentation of such a theory is known to me. This
at least illustrates that the additional level of
detail of a control system theory serves to generate
new hypotheses about the mechanisms involved.

This assumption about decoding is sufficiently
novel and sufficiently central to the model, that it
rates additional investigation. This will let us explore additional aspects of what a detailed theory of
control can provide.

The Decoding Hypothesis

We wish to explore the decoding hypothesis and
attempt to discover whether it is reasonable, or
whether (as introduced) it is to be viewed as a *deus
ex machina* to permit the construction of a production
system that happens to fit the empirical data. There
are two directions (at least) in which to look. First,
we can search for basic theoretical reasons why the
decoding should exist. Second, we can look at other
tasks to see whether they too seem to require the
decoding hypothesis.

Why Decode?

The argument starts from the generally accepted
view (within an information processing theory of human
behavior) that subjects encode stimuli ubiquitously.
Hence, the argument goes, the system is simply unable
to pick a production system that does not do the encoding, hence the decoding.

The argument has perhaps some force, though it is
better when kept rather general. In detail, it would
not seem to rule out the decoding of the set upon re-
ceipt of the ready signal, rather than the probe, so
that by the time the probe came along only the instan-
taneous matching productions would need to be evoked.
This would not be possible in the dynamic versions of
the task where the set is given sequentially right up
to the problem. But we know that the behavior in the

static task (the positive set in LTM) and the dynamic task (the positive set given each time) are essentially the same. Thus we must still face the issue: Why not decode the positive set into STM at the ready signal?

Let us return to the question of adaptive behavior raised in the prior section in a more pointed way: Why should the subject encode and decode a set rather than leave it in STM where the task can be performed in a single recognition (as in PS.ST1)? Consider the following assumption:

> *Assumption of Unreliable STM*: The contents of STM are sufficiently variable, noisy and unreliable that the subject will adopt production systems with lower risk from STM unreliability.

Unreliability of STM could be the case because it fades rapidly or because it is the confluence of uncontrolled input from many sources, both from LTM and from perception. The production system itself is consonant with such a view. Imagine, as argued earlier, that the small production system that we use to describe the program of the subject is really embedded in a very large system. From time to time other productions may be evoked instead of the ones in our set. The only effect of these, mostly, may be to add junk to the memory and to add some time to performance (a few T.evokes and T.actions). From a control point of view the process looks like cycle-stealing (as it goes on in most computers today for input/output). From a data point of view it makes the STM unreliable.

Given such a situation the rational way to obtain reliable behavior is to work with programs that are as safe as possible--in which the parts of the program are positively coupled. In the case at hand, if the total organization (our PS.ST7) both dumps the elements into STM and then tests for a match, then the test production can operate with the knowledge that the elements of the set are all there. It is a reliable method for solving the problem. If the system (PS.ST1) simply scans

whatever is in STM at the probe signal when the set
was dumped earlier at the ready signal, then it is not
safe. The chance of a spurious NO is appreciable and
even the chance of a spurious YES increases. What if
the subject thinks about some possible element during
the interval between READY and PROBE--he has no way of
guaranteeing that he will be able to distinguish it
from a true element. Note that he cannot process such
a stray thought, since processing conflicts with being
prepared to react to the PROBE when it comes.

This argument essentially introduces a second
criterion, reliability, in addition to speed as a
governor of the production system that the subject will
construct. We have thereby preserved the principle of
adaptation. Against this we have only a qualitative
notion so far of how to assess the reliability (as seen
by the subject) of a proposed production system. In
the case at hand, an *ad hoc* argument goes some ways
toward establishing that the speedier production system
is less reliable than the slower one (which is also the
empirically correct one). We should at least package
this assumption in a principle:

> *Principle of Coupled Systems*: When
> attempting to behave reliably the
> subject uses production systems
> where early evoked productions
> produce guarantees on the contents
> of STM that can be utilized by
> later productions (thereby coupling
> the productions together).

The argument above leads directly to two qualitative hypotheses, one rather easy to verify, another
much harder. First, if the selection of PS.ST7 over
PS.ST1 is due to a requirement for reliability, then
releasing that requirement should move subjects to
adopt PS.ST1. As mentioned at the beginning of the
paper, the conditions for the Sternberg paradigm are a
low error rate (of the order of a few percent). If one
permitted much higher error rates and paid off for speed
only, one should see the slope disappear. It is unknown

of course, how much the error rate would go up, since selection of the reliable system is based on a choice of the subject in the face of a task demand, not on demonstrated failure of the faster algorithm. This experiment should be rather easy to carry out and indeed the essential facts may already be known (though I don't know them).

The second hypothesis comes from noting that we have an instance of the speed-accuracy trade-off, which is a general phenomenon much studied in the literature. One of the features of that literature (which we cannot review here) is that no mechanisms are proposed as to how a speed-accuracy trade-off is possible. One often proposes to represent such a trade-off by a criterion parameter which can be changed. But (to my knowledge) this never is embedded within a model for how such a parameter effects a shift to greater speed at the expense of accuracy or vice versa. The hypothesis then is that the space of feasible programs is indeed relatively large and that selection (construction) of different production systems with slightly different speeds and reliabilities provides the underlying ability of the subject to trade off speed for accuracy. Within this hypothesis, the freedom of programmability of production systems, far from being a disturbing theoretical feature (reflecting a preference that a unique production system exist for a task), is an essential aspect of the human information processing system.

We state these two hypotheses to point out how having a specific theory of the control system is able to generate hypotheses of the rather global nature long favored by experimental psychology.

Memory Span

A major advantage of a theory of the control system is the applicability of the theory to a wide range of tasks. One should be able to test an hypothesis, such as the decoding hypothesis, against its indicated use in other tasks. A particularly transparent task from this viewpoint is the standard auditory memory span test.

We can take the task as receiving a sequence of
elements, each of which can be perceived as a chunk.
When the signal to repeat occurs, the subject is to
repeat the sequence exactly.

Figure 19 gives a production system PS.MS1, for
performing the memory span test in the most obvious
way. The subject lets the elements accumulate in STM
and then, upon REPEAT, proceeds to respond with each
one. It keeps from repeating an element by marking
each element used. Thus, we get a production system
of only three productions: PD1 to emit the response
and mark old; PD2 to terminate the trial by deactivat-
ing REPEAT when no more elements are left; and PD3 to
attend to the environment. We do not include an initial ready signal in this simple version.

Figure 20 gives a run of PS.MS1 on a sequence of
three elements. We have modified the executive structure so that the ATTEND operator goes to a list,
STIMULUS (given at the top of the figure), and attends
to each symbol successively. Although all members of
the sequence are emitted, the system does not obtain
them in the correct order. A moment's consideration
shows that this is not a fluke. The STM is indeed a
stack-like memory which performs generally in a last-
in first-out manner.

How can this order be reversed? There are two
directions to explore: reversing at response time; and
reversing at input time so that the response process
works off something in the right order. Let's consider
each in turn.

Simply tring to pick up the last element of a
given type in STM appears difficult. The subject
(i.e., the production system) knows about the elements
only that they belong to the same type (e.g., are marked
ELM). The nature of the match is such that the more

```
00100  PS.MS1: (PD1 PD2 PD3)
00200  ;
00300  PD1: ((ELM X1) AND REPEAT --> (OLD **) (RESPONSE X1) RESPOND)
00400  PD2: (REPEAT AND (ELM) ABS --> (OLD **))
00500  PD3: (ANY --> ATTEND)
```

Fig. 19. PS.MS1: Simple PS for memory span.

```
00100   STIMULUS: ((ELM A) (ELM B) (ELM C) REPEAT)
00200
00300   PS.MS1 START!
00400   0.  STM: (JUNK NIL NIL NIL NIL NIL NIL)
00500   PD3 TRUE
00600   0.  ACTION- ATTEND
00700   ATTEND TO: (ELM A)
00800   1.  ACTION- (ELM A)
00900   2.  STM: ((ELM A) JUNK NIL NIL NIL NIL NIL)
01000   PD3 TRUE
01100   2.  ACTION- ATTEND
01200   ATTEND TO: (ELM B)
01300   3.  ACTION- (ELM B)
01400   4.  STM: ((ELM B) (ELM A) JUNK NIL NIL NIL NIL)
01500   PD3 TRUE
01600   4.  ACTION- ATTEND
01700   ATTEND TO: (ELM C)
01800   5.  ACTION- (ELM C)
01900   6.  STM: ((ELM C) (ELM B) (ELM A) JUNK NIL NIL NIL)
02000   PD3 TRUE
02100   6.  ACTION- ATTEND
02200   ATTEND TO: REPEAT
02300   7.  ACTION- REPEAT
02400   8.  STM: (REPEAT (ELM C) (ELM B) (ELM A) JUNK NIL NIL)
02500   PD1 TRUE
02600   8.  ACTION- (OLD **)
02700   9.  ACTION- (RESPONSE X1)
02800   10.  ACTION- RESPOND
02900   11.  ACTION- (NTC (RESPONSE ANY))
03000   12.  ACTION- (SAY ANY)
03100
03200   ********** C
03300
03400   13.  ACTION- (OLD **)
03500   14.  STM: ((OLD (RESPONSE C)) (OLD (ELM C)) REPEAT (ELM B) (ELM A) JUNK NIL)
03600   PD1 TRUE
03700   14.  ACTION- (OLD **)
03800   15.  ACTION- (RESPONSE X1)
03900   16.  ACTION- RESPOND
04000   17.  ACTION- (NTC (RESPONSE ANY))
04100   18.  ACTION- (SAY ANY)
04200
04300   ********** B
04400
04500   19.  ACTION- (OLD **)
04600   20.  STM: ((OLD (RESPONSE B)) (OLD (ELM B)) REPEAT (OLD (RESPONSE C))
04650          (OLD (ELM C)) (ELM A) JUNK)
04700   PD1 TRUE
04800   20.  ACTION- (OLD **)
04900   21.  ACTION- (RESPONSE X1)
05000   22.  ACTION- RESPOND
05100   23.  ACTION- (NTC (RESPONSE ANY))
05200   24.  ACTION- (SAY ANY)
05300
05400   ********** A
```

Fig. 20. Run of PS.MS1.

recent elements will be selected first. Thus, the only
way to get the last element is by brute force--by productions that latch onto all preceding elements. One
needs a set of productions of the form:

$$X1 \text{ AND } X2 \text{ AND } X3 \text{ AND } X4 \longrightarrow \dots$$
$$X1 \text{ AND } X2 \text{ AND } X3 \longrightarrow \dots$$
$$X1 \text{ AND } X2 \longrightarrow \dots$$
$$X1 \longrightarrow \dots$$

While this bears some resemblance to the encoding productions, it still seems like an uncomfortable way to
do business.

   An alternative strategy is to mark each element
as it enters in a unique way so that that production
system can know about the first one. This essentially
produces an STM paired-associate structure, e.g.,

STM: (... (ELM3 C) ... (ELM2 B) ...(ELM1 A) ...)

With this arrangement the response productions have to
be an explicit set, knowing first to respond with
(ELM1), then with (ELM2), etc. Again, it seems a
possible, but awkward strategy. However, an attempt
on the part of a subject to use the 1-BUN, 2-SHOE, ...
mnemonic on the memory span test would be an application
of this. (General experience is that presentation rates
of 1 symbol/sec are too fast for this.)

   As a final example of the reverse-while-responding
strategy, the system could respond internally as in
Figure 20, which reverses the order, and then respond
again externally, thus emitting them in the right order.
This is also a conceivable strategy and in slightly
different circumstances can be detected (e.g., in recit-
ing an alphabet backwards, McLean & Gregg, 1967). It
seems an unlikely strategy in the simple memory span.
It should produce a substantial delay before the first
response; further, the task of repeating the set backwards should be easier than repeating it forwards and
should not have the delay. Empirically these seem not
to be the case.

Turning to strategies of reversing on input, the
attempt to do this for each element at each moment of
input creates a fair amount of thrashing, in which the
set of already ordered elements must be brought in
front of each new element and still left in the same
order.

A second scheme is to encode the elements on
input, just as we have done for the Sternberg task.
This leaves a single chunk in STM which is decoded in
the right order at response time. Figure 21 gives a
production system, PS.MS2, for this encoding. To show
the relationship to the Sternberg task we have labeled
the productions with the ones they correspond to in
PS.ST7 (Figure 18), the final production system for
the Sternberg task. Productions PD1 and PD1.1 are the
response productions and are unique to the task. Production PD1.1 is the response production for the memory span task, and takes the place of PD6 and PD7 in
the Sternberg task. PD12 in the Sternberg task sets
the response bias. This is not a feature of the memory
span task, so it is missing as well. Corresponding
productions are not all identical. The encoding
productions (PD8 - PD11) are the same. However, the
decoding productions (PD2 - PD5) are responsive to
REPEAT rather than to (PROBE). To make them identical
would require another level of indirectness--one that
might be expected perhaps in the early stages of performance (when the subject, in effect, must interpret

```
00100   PS.MS2: (PD1 PD1.1 PD2 PD3 PD4 PD5 PD8 PD9 PD10 PD11 PD13)
00200   ;
00300   PD1: (REPEAT AND (ELM) ABS AND (SET) ABS --> (OLD **))
00400   PD1.1: ((ELM X1) AND REPEAT --> (OLD **) (RESPONSE X1) RESPOND)
00500   PD2: ((SET X1 X2 X3 X4) AND REPEAT --> (OLD **) X4 X3 X2 X1)
00600   PD3: ((SET X1 X2 X3) AND REPEAT --> (OLD **) X3 X2 X1)
00700   PD4: ((SET X1 X2) AND REPEAT --> (OLD **) X2 X1)
00800   PD5: ((SET X1) AND REPEAT --> (OLD **) X1)
00900   PD8: (X1 == (ELM) AND X2 == (ELM) AND READY -->
01000      (OLD **) (NTC (ELM)) (OLD **) (SET X2 X1))
01100   PD9: (X1 == (ELM) AND (SET X2 X3 X4) AND READY -->
01200      (OLD **) (NTC (SET)) (OLD **) (SET X2 X3 X4 X1))
01300   PD10: (X1 == (ELM) AND (SET X2 X3) AND READY -->
01400      (OLD **) (NTC (SET)) (OLD **) (SET X2 X3 X1))
01500   PD11: (X1 == (ELM) AND (SET X2) AND READY -->
01600      (OLD **) (NTC (SET)) (OLD **) (SET X2 X1))
01700   PD13: (ANY --> ATTEND)
```

Fig. 21. PS.MS2: PS for memory span, with encoding.

the signal in terms of a common meaning--to decode),
but would presumably be adapted out with practice.
Finally, PD1, which recognizes the end of the task, is
responsive to different features in the two tasks.
Figure 22 shows a run of PS.MS2 on a three element
sequence, which can be seen to perform appropriately.

Let us summarize. Substantively, we have found
that the encoding hypothesis is not only consistent
with behavior in another distinct task, but provides
an appropriate solution to a difficulty (the ordering)
that arises from the application of a naive formulation.
We showed, however, that it was not the only way to
overcome the difficulty. Some of the alternatives,
despite our disparagement, clearly represent alternatives to be considered further. We indicated some
other tasks in which they appear to operate. Nevertheless, the encoding hypothesis comes through appearing substantially less *ad hoc*.

Methodologically, we say that it was relatively
easy to move to a new task and to construct a theory
that had substantial contact with the initial one.
With a little care one could insist that exactly the
same theory (i.e., the same total production system)
be able to perform both tasks. To be sure, some of
the productions will be unique to each task. Indeed,
they must be if the unique aspects of a task are to
be represented.

In seeking support for the decoding hypothesis in
the phenomenon of response order we have taken the
structure of the STM to be fixed. As we observed
earlier, it is the last-in first-out character of the
STM that creates this problem and makes it a fundamental
one. Alternatively, the solution might lie in changing
the structure of the underlying system. One can certainly construct STM models that have a first-in first-
out character and thus make the response order identical
to input order. However, such systems must ultimately
have other problems. For the underlying empirical reality is that humans appear to behave in positive time
order (first-in first-out) in the short run and in
inverse time order (last-in first-out) in the long run.

```
00100    STIMULUS: (READY (ELM A) (ELM B) (ELM C) REPEAT)
00200
00300    PS.MS2 START!
00400    0.  STM: (JUNK NIL NIL NIL NIL NIL NIL)
00500    PD13 TRUE
00600    0.  ACTION- ATTEND
00700    ATTEND TO: READY
00800    1.  ACTION- READY
00900    2.  STM: (READY JUNK NIL NIL NIL NIL NIL)
01000    PD13 TRUE
01100    2.  ACTION- ATTEND
01200    ATTEND TO: (ELM A)
01300    3.  ACTION- (ELM A)
01400    4.  STM: ((ELM A) READY JUNK NIL NIL NIL NIL)
01500    PD13 TRUE
01600    4.  ACTION- ATTEND
01700    ATTEND TO: (ELM B)
01800    5.  ACTION- (ELM B)
01900    6.  STM: ((ELM B) (ELM A) READY JUNK NIL NIL NIL)
02000    PD8 TRUE
02100    6.  ACTION- (OLD **)
02200    7.  ACTION- (NTC (ELM))
02300    8.  ACTION- (OLD **)
02400    9.  ACTION- (SET X2 X1)
02500    10. STM: ((SET (ELM A) (ELM B)) (OLD (ELM A)) (OLD (ELM B)) READY JUNK NIL NIL)
02600    PD13 TRUE
02700    10. ACTION- ATTEND
02800    ATTEND TO: (ELM C)
02900    11. ACTION- (ELM C)
03000    12. STM: ((ELM C) (SET (ELM A) (ELM B)) (OLD (ELM A)) (OLD (ELM B)) READY JUNK NIL)
03100    PD10 TRUE
03200    12. ACTION- (OLD **)
03300    13. ACTION- (NTC (SET))
03400    14. ACTION- (OLD **)
03500    15. ACTION- (SET X2 X3 X1)
03600    16. STM: ((SET (ELM A) (ELM B) (ELM C)) (OLD (SET (ELM A) (ELM B))) (OLD (ELM C))
03650            READY (OLD (ELM A)) (OLD (ELM B)) JUNK)
03700    PD13 TRUE
03800    16. ACTION- ATTEND
03900    ATTEND TO: REPEAT
04000    17. ACTION- REPEAT
04100    18. STM: (REPEAT (SET (ELM A) (ELM B) (ELM C)) (OLD (SET (ELM A) (ELM B)))
04150           (OLD (ELM C)) READY (OLD (ELM A)) (OLD (ELM B)))
04200    PD3 TRUE
04300    18. ACTION- (OLD **)
04400    19. ACTION- X3
04500    20. ACTION- X2
04600    21. ACTION- X1
04700    22. STM: ((ELM A) (ELM B) (ELM C) (OLD (SET (ELM A) (ELM B) (ELM C)))
04750            REPEAT (OLD (SET (ELM A) (ELM B))) (OLD (ELM C)))
04800    PD1.1 TRUE
04900    22. ACTION- (OLD **)
05000    23. ACTION- (RESPONSE X1)
05100    24. ACTION- RESPOND
05200    25. ACTION- (NTC (RESPONSE ANY))
```

Fig. 22. Run of PS.MS2.

```
05300   26. ACTION- (SAY ANY)
05400
05500   ********** A
05600
05700   27. ACTION- (OLD **)
05800   28. STM: ((OLD (RESPONSE A)) (OLD (ELM A)) REPEAT (ELM B) (ELM C)
05850        (OLD (SET (ELM A) (ELM B) (ELM C))) (OLD (SET (ELM A) (ELM B))))
05900   PD1.1 TRUE
06000   28. ACTION- (OLD **)
06100   29. ACTION- (RESPONSE X1)
06200   30. ACTION- RESPOND
06300   31. ACTION- (NTC (RESPONSE ANY))
06400   32. ACTION- (SAY ANY)
06500
06600   ********** B
06700
06800   33. ACTION- (OLD **)
06900   34. STM: ((OLD (RESPONSE B)) (OLD (ELM B)) REPEAT (OLD (RESPONSE A))
06950        (OLD (ELM A)) (ELM C) (OLD (SET (ELM A) (ELM B) (ELM C))))
07000   PD1.1 TRUE
07100   34. ACTION- (OLD **)
07200   35. ACTION- (RESPONSE X1)
07300   36. ACTION- RESPOND
07400   37. ACTION- (NTC (RESPONSE ANY))
07500   38. ACTION- (SAY ANY)
07600
07700   ********** C
07800
07900   39. ACTION- (OLD **)
08000   40. STM: ((OLD (RESPONSE C)) (OLD (ELM C)) REPEAT (OLD (RESPONSE B))
08050        (OLD (ELM B)) (OLD (RESPONSE A)) (OLD (ELM A)))
08100   PD1 TRUE
08200   40. ACTION- (OLD **)
08300   41. STM: ((OLD REPEAT) (OLD (RESPONSE C)) (OLD (ELM C)) (OLD (RESPONSE B))
08350        (OLD (ELM B)) (OLD (RESPONSE A)) (OLD (ELM A)))
08400   PD13 TRUE
08500   41. ACTION- ATTEND
08600   END: NO PD TRUE
```

Fig. 22 (continued).

Thus, there is a reversal at some stage (from primacy
to recency, if you like to think of it that way) and
the structure of the system must account for both
aspects.

Applications of the Theory

We have now developed a theory of the simple
Sternberg binary classification task that has modest
standing. It should be possible to apply it to the
experiments discussed in this symposium that make use
of similar task situations. To do this properly requires that we extend the theory to these variant
situations, much as we did to the memory span task,

keeping as much communality with the original situation
as possible. However, there is a limit to an intro-
ductory paper and to go into the results of Posner
(Chapter 2) and Hayes (Chapter 4) in detail exceeds
those limits. Thus, we must be content with a cursory
examination of a few aspects. Methodologically, we
can make a virtue of this restriction, since it provides the opportunity to apply the theory in a qualitative way, thereby illustrating how such applications
might go.

Perceptual Enhancement

The brief discussion in Posner's paper on the
phenomenological experience of perceptual enhancement
of the successful item in a Neisser paradigm offers a
simple example. He observes that Cavanagh and Chase
(1971) found that in a Sternberg task with two probes
(one positive, one negative) the positive one only was
enhanced. Posner's argument was that this controverted
the use of the enhancement as an indicator of the
boundary between pre-attentive and attentive processes,
since much attentive processing (i.e., the search) went
on prior to the enhancement and did so for both probes.
The present model offers a somewhat different
characterization. Presenting two probes rather than
one has no effect on the linear-time component, which
is the decoding time. It might have an effect on the
intercept if the two probes are themselves encoded in
some way, or enter STM serially. One and only one of
the probes evokes the positive production (PD6). The
other probe simply does not evoke anything. Thus a
single decoding operates for both probes.[14]
Examination of the production system puts the

---

[14]The actual slopes are somewhat higher than the
usual 35 ms. This complicates the interpretation. It
suggests (as only one among several alternatives) that
some subjects may have processed each probe separately
and that the data represent a mixture of methods.

enhancement effect on PD6, which is to say on the multiple occurrence of a variable in the matching. This offers a clue about how one might explore the details of the match processes. However, the present model does not offer a clear interpretation of pre-attentive versus attentive processes. First of all, the model does not include a perceptual component so that one can determine whether the match is or is not part of the same apparatus that carries out perception. No matter how one determines the latter question, the match (the selection of the next production), and hence the enhancement, is involved intimately with whatever can be called attentive processes.[15]

Having gone this far, it is tempting to state a hypothesis about the locus of conscious experience. It is not to be associated with the content of any memory, not even of STM which defines in an operational sense what the subject is momentarily aware of, i.e., to what he can respond to in the next tens of milli-seconds. Rather, phenomenal consciousness is to be associated with the *act* of matching, and its content is given by the set of STM items extracted by the matched condition. Thus, it is an ephemeral fleeting thing that never stays quite put and never seems to have clearly defined edges (the never-step-into-the-same-river-twice phenomenon). It seems like an inter-esting hypothesis. That the hypothesis can be stated in such a precise form is attributable to having a detailed model of the control structure.

Recency Effects

Posner's paper discusses several Sternberg-like tasks in detail. A prominent feature of his data is

---

[15]The diffuseness of this discussion only shows that each theory puts its own classification on phenomena and one cannot easily discuss one in terms of the other (attentive versus pre-attentive derive from a certain rough model of the total machinery).

the non-linear relation to positive set size. This
leads him to plot all of his graphs against the
logarithm of set size, since this tends to linearize
the curves somewhat. This decision of how to display
the data makes me uncomfortable, I confess, since it
seems not to be theoretically motivated. In fact it
serves to obscure, rather than clarify the explanation
Posner provides in passing. He notes that the effect
may be a recency effect on the first item, namely, that
subjects respond more quickly to sets of size one than
to larger sets. If this is so, then the curves should
be linear for set sizes greater than one. However, all
the data are limited to three sizes, 1, 2 and 4, and
thus no direct empirical test of this is possible.

This recency phenomenon appears to be not unknown
elsewhere in the literature on the Sternberg task and
seems to be associated with dynamic presentation--
defining the set just prior to test--with a relatively
short delay between set definition and probe. Posner's
experiments fit this format, since they run from set
to probe continuously (at half second pacing) and
without warning.

An explanation is not far to seek within the
present theory, consisting of both the production
system framework and the decoding hypothesis. With
set size of one the system delays encoding until the
second element arrives. If instead the probe arrives,
then there is no decoding step; rather, the system
simply responds. In fact, if one runs the full range
of set sizes one finds the recency effect. From the
formula given earlier, which expresses the correct
linear growth,[16] one gets:

$$T(1) = 3*T.\text{evoke} + 6*T.\text{action} + 1*T.\text{action}$$

$$= 3*T.\text{evoke} + 7*T.\text{action}$$

-----

[16] In deriving that formula we simply did not reflect
the special circumstances of the special case. A careful enough analysis would have revealed it, of course,
and perhaps the perspicacious reader in deriving it
independently detected the flaw.

The measured value is:

$$T(1)' = 2*T.evoke + 5*T.action$$

This provides a difference of T.evoke + 2*T.action, which is something in excess of 70 ms, taking the 35 ms figure for T.action. This is somewhat high for the measured values, which run 40 - 60 ms. As with the discrepancy on the response bias, we do not know whether or not to be disturbed by the approximate fit. Basically, the ambiguity of interpretation arises because the experimental numbers are averages over trials and over subjects. This means they are undoubtedly generated by mixtures.of strategies to some unknown extent.

Posner's Figure 2 shows a strong serial position effect for a set size of four. This is a recency effect in which the last item (the fourth) is processed about 50 ms faster than the other three, which are reasonably constant. Our theory as it stands does not handle this, since it produces the recency phenomenon only for sets of one. We can extend it to the new situation, however, if we assume that the subject can react to the last element directly, even though he has also encoded it. The size of the effect indicates that this happens sometimes, but not always, so that the data would be a mixture of two ways of doing the task. If this is the explanation, we should also find recency effects for the other set sizes.

In general terms, such an explanation is consistent with the nature of production systems. There is no reason why the responding production (PD6) should not pick up the data of the unencoded element directly. In fact the ability to short circuit a longer process and to mix methods would seem to be a major point in favor of production systems, providing a detailed explanation for variety and lability of behavior. However, as our experience on the several production systems should indicate, it may not be trivial to construct the production system to get the recency result. We may find that it works just as well on all members of the set, if we fix it up to work on the most recent.

Whereas recency seems consistent with the unreliability
assumption of STM, so that the subject might trust the
most recent one but not the older ones, the system may
not be able to tell the two situations apart. We
mention these potential difficulties to indicate the
gap between having the right sort of theory and having
it deliver the right predictions in detail.

Continuous Sternberg Experiment

Enough work has been done with the Sternberg paradigm to accumulate a number of experiments whose interpretation appears to pose extreme difficulties. One of
these is an experiment by Sternberg and Scarborough
(1969). Unfortunately it has not been replicated nor
extended, but it is still worth attempting an explanation in terms of the present theory.

Briefly, a subject was given a fixed positive set.
Then he was tested with 20 probes in sequence. Exactly
one probe was positive or none was. The time between
probes was 70 ms, so the entire set of 20 probes went
by in under 1.5 seconds. The subject was to react to
the positive probe in the usual way. The result: the
reaction time was identical to that in the basic task,
being a linear function measured from the time of the
probe, with a slope of about 35 ms and an intercept of
about 350 ms.

This result is extremely difficult for search
theories to deal with. Sternberg and Scarborough erect
an *ad hoc* pipeline processing system with stages for
each probe. The present theory produces the essential
result on the assumption that the probes trigger the
decoding of the set, thus filling STM with both probes
and elements. Due to the unreliability of STM, if a
hit gets made, the set is decoded again to confirm the
hit.

Figure 23 gives a production system, PS.CST1, for
the continuous Sternberg task. It differs somewhat,
as it must, from PS.ST7, the production system for the
basic task. We have kept the names of productions the
same, so that the correspondence is evident. Mostly,

511

```
00100   PS.CST1: (PD1 PD1.1 PD2 PD3 PD4 PD5 PD6 PD12 PD13)
00200   ;
00300   PD1: ((MARK) AND (OLD (RESPONSE)) --> (OLD **))
00400   PD1.1: ((PROBE <DIGIT>) AND (ELM <DIGIT>) AND (RESPONSE) ABS -->
00500         (MARK **) (RESPONSE YES) POSITIVE.SET)
00600   PD2: ((SET X1 X2 X3 X4) AND (PROBE) --> (OLD **) X4 X3 X2 X1)
00700   PD3: ((SET X1 X2 X3) AND (PROBE) --> (OLD **) X3 X2 X1)
00800   PD4: ((SET X1 X2) AND (PROBE) --> (OLD **) X2 X1)
00900   PD5: ((SET X1) AND (PROBE) --> (OLD **) X1)
01000   PD6: ((MARK (PROBE <DIGIT>)) AND (ELM <DIGIT>) --> RESPOND)
01100   PD12: (READY AND (SET) ABS (OLD (SET)) ABS --> POSITIVE.SET)
01200   PD13: (ANY --> WAIT)
```

Fig. 23. PS.CST1: PS for continuous Sternberg task.

productions drop out. Since the subject has the set
in LTM, no encoding productions are needed (though they
could have been left in the system). Instead, PD12 is
modified to put the positive set into STM, either on
the ready signal or whenever there is an indication
that some elements might be lost from STM. The cues
to this are there not being any set in STM, either
undecoded--(SET) ABS--or decoded--(OLD (SET)) ABS.[17]
Thus, the system dumps sets into STM at every indication, so to speak, in an attempt to avoid losing some
elements of the positive set from STM.

Decoding of a set takes place whenever there is a
set in STM to be decoded and a probe to initiate it.
Since there is a continuous stream of probes (once they
start), decoding takes place immediately (and produces
small refractory periods). The task itself dictates
the removal of the negative response production (PD7),
since the test is only for presence. (Actually, the
production system could have been expanded to say NO
at the end of the sequence.) The positive response
production (PD6) is modified to only sense an identical
probe and set element with a marked probe (with MARK).
The key production is PD1.1, which responds to an

———————————

[17]The vigilant reader will notice an error in the
figure, namely the AND missing between two condition
elements of PD12. The interpreter does not in fact
require the AND. Thus it behaved correctly, so that
the error was not noticed until later.

```
00100   POSITIVE.SET: (SET (ELM 4) (ELM A))
00200
00300   PS.CST1 START!
00400   0.  STM: (JUNK NIL NIL NIL NIL NIL NIL NIL NIL NIL NIL)
00500   PD13 TRUE
00600   0.  ACTION- WAIT
00700       INPUT FORCED STIMULUS (IF ANY) = READY
00800   1.  STM: (READY WAIT JUNK NIL NIL NIL NIL NIL NIL NIL NIL)
00900   PD12 TRUE
01000   1.  ACTION- POSITIVE.SET
01100   2.  STM: (POSITIVE.SET READY WAIT JUNK NIL NIL NIL NIL NIL NIL NIL)
01200   PD13 TRUE
01300   2.  ACTION- WAIT
01400   3.  STM: (WAIT POSITIVE.SET READY WAIT JUNK NIL NIL NIL NIL NIL NIL)
01500   PD13 TRUE
01600   3.  ACTION- WAIT
01700       INPUT FORCED STIMULUS (IF ANY) = (PROBE 1)
01800   4.  STM: ((PROBE 1) WAIT WAIT POSITIVE.SET READY WAIT JUNK NIL NIL NIL NIL)
01900   PD4 TRUE
02000   4.  ACTION- (OLD **)
02100   5.  ACTION- X2
02200       INPUT FORCED STIMULUS (IF ANY) = (PROBE 2)
02300   6.  ACTION- X1
02400   7.  STM: ((ELM 4) (PROBE 2) (ELM A) (OLD POSITIVE.SET) (PROBE 1)
02450           WAIT WAIT READY WAIT JUNK NIL)
02500   PD13 TRUE
02600   7.  ACTION- WAIT
02700       INPUT FORCED STIMULUS (IF ANY) = (PROBE 3)
02800   8.  STM: ((PROBE 3) WAIT (ELM 4) (PROBE 2) (ELM A) (OLD POSITIVE.SET) (PROBE 1)
02850           WAIT WAIT READY WAIT)
02900   PD13 TRUE
03000   8.  ACTION- WAIT
03100   9.  STM: (WAIT (PROBE 3) WAIT (ELM 4) (PROBE 2) (ELM A) (OLD POSITIVE.SET) (PROBE 1)
03150           WAIT WAIT READY)
03200   PD13 TRUE
03300   9.  ACTION- WAIT
03400       INPUT FORCED STIMULUS (IF ANY) = (PROBE 4)
03500   10.  STM: ((PROBE 4) WAIT WAIT (PROBE 3) WAIT (ELM 4) (PROBE 2) (ELM A)
03550           (OLD POSITIVE.SET) (PROBE 1) WAIT)
03600   PD1.1 TRUE
03700   10.  ACTION- (MARK **)
03800   11.  ACTION- (RESPONSE YES)
03900       INPUT FORCED STIMULUS (IF ANY) = (PROBE 5)
04000   12.  ACTION- POSITIVE.SET
04100   13.  STM: (POSITIVE.SET (PROBE 5) (RESPONSE YES) (MARK (PROBE 4)) (ELM 4)
04150           WAIT WAIT (PROBE 3) WAIT (PROBE 2) (ELM A))
04200   PD4 TRUE
04300   13.  ACTION- (OLD **)
04400       INPUT FORCED STIMULUS (IF ANY) = (PROBE 6)
04500   14.  ACTION- X2
04600   15.  ACTION- X1
04700       INPUT FORCED STIMULUS (IF ANY) = (PROBE 7)
04800   16.  STM: ((PROBE 7) (ELM 4) (ELM A) (PROBE 6) (OLD POSITIVE.SET) (PROBE 5)
04850           (RESPONSE YES) (MARK (PROBE 4)) (ELM 4) WAIT WAIT)
04900   PD6 TRUE
05000   16.  ACTION- RESPOND
05100   17.  ACTION- (NTC (RESPONSE ANY))
05200   18.  ACTION- (SAY ANY)
05300
05400   **********  YES
```

Fig. 24. Run of PS.CST1.

513

identical probe and set element by marking the probe
and reinitializing the positive set. This realizes
the checking assumption.

Figure 24 shows a run of PS.CST1 with a two element
set, consisting of (ELM 4), to be matched to the probe,
and (ELM A), the irrelevant one. The executive for the
run was modified so that it came to the console on
almost every other action. At 35 ms per action, this
approximated a 70 ms interstimulus duration. The
experimenter forced an element into STM at each of
these times, starting with READY and then, after a
slight wait, a sequence of probes. Examination of the
run shows that it reacts to (PROBE 4) appropriately,
marking it, going through another decode and responding
YES, despite the fact that other probes are being
entered throughout.

The system deals with the main effect in an
appropriate way. It would appear to have a slightly
higher intercept, which was not found in the experiment.
However, this is an uncertain measure, since the absolute value of the intercept is always contaminated.
Also, a somewhat higher error rate might be expected,
due to the chances of missing the match with PD1.1 if
the probe arrives and STM has just lost the key set
element. However, experimentally the error rate
remained low. It is possible that the scheme of PS.CST1
is in fact relatively reliable, but it requires more
exploration than has been done.

A Difficult Experiment

The impression should not be that the theory is
unchallenged. The total set of Sternberg-like experiments is too diverse for that. For instance, the
theory appears to have great difficulty with another
experiment reported by Sternberg (1970). The positive
set (digits) is stored in LTM and its transmission into
STM is held in abeyance by an auxiliary STM task of
remembering a set of letters. Sometimes the subject
gets a probe digit to classify as in the positive set
or not. Sometimes he gets a signal to repeat the letter

set, which helps to assure that he attends to the
letter set prior to the signal. The result is a slope
of about twice that of the normal paradigm (which was
run as a control)--namely, 80 ms versus 40. The inter
cept is also higher by about 100 ms in the experiment&
situation.

Sternberg interprets the higher slope as being du
to the time to transmit the positive set from LTM to
STM, which is a close analog of the decoding hypothesi
The difficulty for the present theory is that, if this
is a decoding, then the slope should be exactly the
same as in the control case, since both have involved
one act of decoding. Alternative interpretations are
always possible, but none has occurred that comes close
to resolving this experimental result.

Conclusion

Let us sum up what we have done in this paper.
(1) We introduced the notion of a control structure.
(2) We introduced a general class of systems--
production systems--that could serve as models of the
human control system. (3) We developed in detail a
specific production system--PSG--which incorporated
assumptions about the structure of the human information processor. (4) We exercised the theory on the
basic Sternberg binary classification experiment, which
led to an additional psychological assumption--the
decoding hypothesis. (5) We pursued in lesser detail
some other applications--the memory span and some
aspects of the experiments in Posner's paper.

Our intent throughout has been jointly substantive
and methodological and we have mixed the two thoroughly.
In the remainder of the conclusion we will attempt to
sort out the main points and issues.

Production Systems as Theories

Production systems offer an explanation of human
behavior at the information processing level (Newell &
Simon, 1972). They are only one of many forms of programming system that can be used to describe behavior

515

in information processing terms. As we have seen in
PSG, the production system itself has become the car-
rier of the basic psychological assumptions--the system
architecture of PSG is taken to be the system architecture of the human information processing system.
In this respect these systems represent an evolution
beyond programming language systems, such as LISP, IPL,
SNOBOL (and even more, ALGOL and FORTRAN). In these
earlier systems the programming language was an essentially neutral affair, designed for the user to write
his specific systems. In production systems, as represented by PSG, any particular set of productions
represents a possible momentary performance organization
of a human subject.

The evolution to a theory-laden programming language, to use a term of Pylyshyn, appears to me a
major advance. By the same coin, however, the language
is not neutral, so that variations in the psychological
theory imply variations in the programming system. A
moment's reflection will show how wide is the potential
variation in system architecture. The STM can be run
according to many disciplines: last-in first-out, as
now; first-in first-out, which preserves order; random
replacement in a fixed set of addressable cells; a cir-
culating loop, which provides another form of rehearsal,
etc. The matching rules can be varied: no multiple
variables in the condition; only single levels in the
condition (not nested expressions); no recognition of
absence; etc. The operations can be varied: a decoding
operation that simply dumps the contents into STM,
rather than the encoding operation as now; etc. The
selection of productions can be varied: more than one
satisfied production producing a psychologically meaningful conflict state; evocation of a production leading
to an automatic refractory state that inhibits re-
evocation immediately; etc. The timing model can be
varied: parallel processing in the action sequence;
matching time dependent on the elements in the satisfied condition.

Listing many alternatives emphasizes that PSG is
only one member of the class of psychologically relevant

production systems. Despite this variety, production
systems as a class incorporate some psychological
assumptions that seem highly plausible. One is the
recognize-act cycle of activity in which the human
continually recognizes some features in the situation
and acts accordingly. Another is making the locus of
the condition correspond to those aspects of the situation that the subject is momentarily aware of, and
the identification of this as the relevant short term
memory. Yet another, though it applies to a somewhat
narrower class of systems, is the incorporation of
encoding into all STM processing, not simply as an
added mechanism.

The structure of production system models, as
we have described them here, are seriously deficient
in several respects. They do not model the perceptual
component, including the various buffer memories and
the control interface between perceptual structures
and the contents of STM (see Newell, 1972). They do
not model LTM, especially the acquisition of new information. We took the contents of LTM as consisting of
productions, but never defined the way new productions
were to be created. They do not model the motor apparatus, including the control interface to the contents
of STM and the actions of productions. These missing
aspects cripple the model with respect to many phenomena, though there is no reason why the model should not
be extended appropriately.

Completeness

Production systems, like other programming systems
and mathematical theories, are complete in the sense
of producing theoretical consequences that are deduc-
tions from the theory. We are interested also in completeness of another sort. Is the theory complete for
the phenomena of interest? Does it provide a vehicle
of sufficient richness and scope to model what appears
to need modeling? Production system models, like other
so-called simulation models, seem to have this completeness. This is often expressed by saying that they perform what they model. Thus PS.ST7 not only is a theory

517

of binary classification; it can *do* binary classification. As long as the interest of the psychologist
remains focussed on the performance of the task, including its behavioral details, a production theory claims
theoretical coverage (though of course it can be dead
wrong in its predictions).

It is useful to compare this situation with some
of the other techniques we currently use for describing
our processing theories. As commented upon in the
companion paper (Newell, this volume, Chapter 6), the
theoretical structure of work on the immediate processor has been dominated by the classification of
mechanisms. We have serial versus parallel, exhaustive
versus self-terminating, attentive versus preattentive,
and so on. Such terms hold low-level generalizations
resulting from the experimental studies. Suppose
PS.ST7 were the actual mechanism. Is the human, then,
a serial or a parallel system? It appears to be parallel on selecting productions, serial on executing
micro-sequences of actions, parallel on examining STM,
serial on the order of that parallel examination as
revealed by shielding of one STM element by another.
Is its search exhaustive or self-terminating? Within
a given task there are production systems of each type.
Slightly more complex systems would yield strategies
that mix the type of search conditionally within a given
trial. Is something pre-attentive or attentive? We
found it hard to ascertain that as well. The point is
not that a given system does not give rise to classifications. The present system has sharp distinctions,
e.g., between the use of STM and of the variable memory,
or between sequences of actions and the evocation of a
sequence of recognitions on STM. The point is that the
existing classifications don't seem to help much in
describing more complete systems.

Flow diagrams have become a primary vehicle for
expressing theories of processing, and they represent
a substantial advance on the simple classification of
mechanisms. There is an example in the paper by Cooper
and Shepard (Chapter 3) in the present symposium, which
summarizes well a processing structure that might give
rise to their experimental results.

What is the relationship between production systems and flow diagrams as they are used in the psychological literature? The flow diagram provides a precise model of control flow--of what follows what.[18] It provides a frame within which informal specification of operations can be made (the little descriptive phrases that go in the boxes). It does not provide any way of disciplining the structures so built up. As noted, the operations themselves are informal. Sometimes, as in some of the diagrams in Sternberg (1970), the boxes appear so elementary as to be well-defined (e.g., a comparator, a match register, etc.), but in fact the flow diagram still remains informal.

More important from the present view, there is no discipline on the control structure. There are neither primitives of control, nor ways of determining that additional apparatus or processing must occur to effect control. The effect of this is to make the flow diagram unique to each task. It must of course be unique in some way since the tasks are different. But there is then no way to assert when two different flow diagrams represent the same processing mechanism.

The production system, on the other hand, provides a complete set of primitives and determines what auxiliary control processing is necessary to perform a task. This comparison between tasks is possible. This is not a peculiar property of production systems, of course, but is true of any programming system. Writing programs in SNOBOL or FORTRAN would do as well, methodologically, except that their underlying structure does not mirror reasonable psychological assumptions about the human system architecture.

The virtue of the flow diagram is that it expresses clearly the independence and ordering of stages derived experimentally by careful design (e.g., Sternberg, 1969). Flow diagrams, by their very incompleteness, do not

---

[18]Besides flow diagrams, which show control flow, block diagrams, which show data flow, are also used. The remarks of this section apply equally well to both.

over-commit their user to more than what the data say.
Thus they are good for summarizing experimental data,
at the same time that they are weak for constructing
theory.

The Problem of Methods

Variability over subjects comes in large part from
the variation in the methods (strategy, program, ...)
they use for a task. This is conjectural, of course,
but much evidence supports it. A major contribution
of a detailed theory of control is to make possible
the proper posing of the question of what method a
subject used for a given task. It does this by providing the space of all methods (based on the constants
of system architecture and the primitive operations)
for a subject. Thus, the problem of discovering the
method takes the form of a programming problem. As we
illustrated, there are often many solutions, i.e., many
production systems that perform the task, but these
can be generated and analysed, and scientific reasons
found for selecting one over another within the limited
set. This is a quite different situation than currently,
where anything seems possible in discussing what might
go in a subject's performance.

This formulation of the problem of methods comes
not just from the use of a precise language (e.g., a
simulation language). It comes from the identification
of the space of all programs defined by the system with
the space of all programs feasible for the subject.

A theory of control is more important to analyzing
methods than just another aspect of the total system
necessary to complete specification. Much of what goes
on in information processing is control. Almost every
operation in a large complex program does nothing except
arrange things so something else can do something. This
appears to hold for both humans and computers. For
instance, Dansereau (1969) found it to be true of humans
doing mental multiplication (e.g., 36 x 152). The times
for the additions and multiplications--the productive
part of the process, so to speak--played a small role

compared to the times for fixation, operand positioning,
etc. The same is certainly true of the theory as developed in this paper. The decoding hypothesis is in fact
a form of the same magicians trick, in which the actions
that take time are not the apparently productive part
(the iterated test for identity), but a preparatory
piece of housekeeping. In short, methods are mostly
control, so that any theory of methods must operate
within an explicit theory of control.

The Problem of Scope

How to construct theories that range over a wide
diversity of tasks is a major issue for psychology.
To do so would seem to require a theory that was
specific about those aspects of structure and content
that in fact were used in common in diverse tasks. A
detailed theory of the control structure would seem
to offer this, since it specifies the common architecture and the boundaries within which a task-specific
method can be sought.

The evidence we have presented that production
systems will indeed make a major contribution to this
issue is still meager. In this paper we applied the
theory only to a couple of tasks. The original production system was applied to a puzzle, a much vaster
task than any discussed here, and there are some other
applications in Newell (1972). The PSG production
system by Klahr (Chapter 11) in this volume provides
one more example.

All these efforts provide evidence only about half
the issue. They show that it is relatively easy to
construct a theory in a new task environment that is
responsive to the empirical issues in that environment.
One obtains, as well, strong comparability. For
instance, Klahr's counting production system can be
examined in conjunction with the Sternberg one here.
In an important sense they are the same system, since
they both use PSG and therefore make the same assumptions about underlying structure. However, the constants of the time model differ. Klahr also uses

521

replacement operators--(X ==> Y) replaces the symbol X in an element with the symbol Y--whereas the model here uses only the encode operator, (**). This leads to a quite different style of programming. Some of his conditions are very long and raise questions about whether constraints should exist on the size or complexity of conditions.

This collection of production systems does not constitute a coherent theory for the set of tasks involved. To do so, they must be melded together into a single production system that performs all the tasks, corresponding to the total organization of a single human. Such a production system will have productions that are unique to each task. But ic must face scrutiny about using disparate mechanisms for common operations. It must also handle the instructional problem, since something in the environment must select out the performance relevant to the task at hand. The interaction of the instructions with the task performance program is as much central to control as the internal part of the performance program. It is predictable that a full fledged theory of task instruction will be required.

I stress the creation of a single production system to represent the unified performance on a set of tasks. This seems to me the only way to validate a theory of control. We saw in the discussion of the basic Sternberg paradigm that many degrees of freedom were available, though they showed up as alternatives in method, rather than freedom of parameter settings. This arises primarily because the datum taken from a single trial is so small (i.e., overall reaction time) compared to the complexity of the system that generates it. To compensate, behavior in many disparate tasks must be obtained, so that finally the mechanisms and methods being used become uniquely identified. My own personal estimate is that a model of the control structure should claim to handle some dozens of diverse experiments before it is a genuine contender. The present theory, though promising, still has a ways to go.

It should be noted in passing that the theory
refers to individual performance with a specific
method. Thus all forms of aggregation raise the spectre
of averaging over disparate methods, hence producing
mixed estimates. Thus one is driven towards collecting
and reporting data only on individual subjects, and
even there not averaging disparate performances.

The Prospects for this Particular Theory

As noted, the present theory is only nascent. A
few words might be said about its prospects. Missing
from the model as it stands is a theory of error. The
theory makes only time predictions. Errors are indeed
possible in the system, due to incorrect programs and
to limited STM. Both of these sources are important
in some task environments. Neither of them appears
to provide the errors that occur, say, in a Sternberg
paradigm. The current theory has implicit in it a
model of error, but whether it will work out is not yet
clear. It is worth stating because it transforms the
theory in an interesting way.

Take STM as having indefinite length but being
sufficiently unreliable so that there is an increasing
probability of an element disappearing entirely.
Whether this is decay with time, with activity or what
not is secondary. The fate of each element is somewhat
independent so that early ones can disappear before later ones. This is the primary error source, from which
error propagates to all tasks according to the strategy
with which the subject operates. Such a strengthening
of the unreliability assumption will reinforce the
encoding hypothesis, so that all tasks must be dealt
with by encoding. The role of STM becomes one of holding a few items after decoding (dumping into STM) to be
picked up quickly by coupled productions, and of holding
a few items strung out prior to encoding into a new
chunk. Thus the short term capacity is not the length
(or expected length) of STM, but is composed from the
size of codes and the space for their decoding. For
example, a short term capacity of seven might occur via

a chunk of three and four, with the STM holding four items reliably enough to get them decoded and emitted. Thus, no memory structure exists in the system that has a capacity of seven. In particular the STM would appear to be misnamed.

As we have already mentioned, the theory is missing perceptual mechanisms, effector mechanisms and a good theory of LTM acquisition. All of these are serious. The question of how to acquire new productions seems to me the most serious of all. In part this is because we know it to be a hard problem, whereas the others appear to be simply aspects that have not received their share of attention.

All existing theory is delightfully vague on the mechanism of LTM acquisition. It is tied somehow to amount of residence in STM, measured either by time or by rehearsals. But what is stored is left unspecified. Proposing to create a new production makes clear that decisions (by the system) must be made about both conditions and actions. The condition is essentially the access path. The action is essentially the content, though it consists of both passive content (elements to STM) and active content (operators). Since there is good, though indirect, evidence that humans do not have voluntary control of the acquisition process (i.e., operators for constructing productions, which can be part of actions), there must be some more automatic process for learning. Its structure is a puzzle.

The fate of the decoding hypothesis is extremely uncertain. The appeal of an indirect non-obvious explanation of a major regularity in behavior must be resisted. There are an immense number of studies whose interpretation seem straightforward in terms of linear search. Until the decoding hypothesis is shown to be compatible with many more of these than the present paper has considered, the hypothesis should be taken as a strictly secondary challenger. However, the emphasis that it gives to the processes of coding and decoding seems certainly on the right track.

References

Bell, C. G., & Newell, A. *Computer structures: Readings and examples*. New York: McGraw Hill, 1971.

Cavanagh, J. P., & Chase, W. G. The equivalence of target and nontarget processing in visual search. *Perception & Psychophysics*, 1971, 9, 493-495.

Crowder, R. G., & Morton, J. Precategorical acoustic storage (PAS). *Perception & Psychophysics*, 1969, 5, 365-373.

Dansereau, D. An information processing model of mental multiplication. Unpublished Doctoral Dissertation, Carnegie-Mellon University, 1969.

Johnson, N. F. The role of chunking and organization in the process of recall. In G. H. Bower (Ed.), *The psychology of learning and motivation*, Vol. 4, New York: Academic Press, 1970.

McLean, R. S., & Gregg, L. W. Effects of induced chunking on temporal aspects of serial recitation. *Journal of Experimental Psychology*, 1967, 74, 455-459.

Miller, G. A. The magical number seven, plus or minus two: some limits on our capacity for processing information. *Psychological Review*, 1956, 63, 81-97.

Newell, A. A theoretical exploration of mechanisms for coding the stimulus. In A. W. Melton & E. Martin (Eds.), *Coding processes in human memory*. Washington D. C.: Winston, 1972.

Newell, A., McCracken, D., Robertson, G., & Freeman, P. The kernel approach to building software systems. *Computer Science Research Review*, Carnegie-Mellon University, 1971.

Newell, A., & Simon, H. A. *Human problem solving*. Englewood Cliffs, N. J.: Prentice-Hall, 1972.

Sperling, G. The information available in brief visual presentations. *Psychological Monographs*, 1960, 74, Whole No. 11.

Sternberg, S. The discovery of processing stages: Extensions of Donders method. *Acta Psychologica*, 1969, 30, 276-315.

Sternberg, S. Mental scanning: mental processes
revealed by reaction time experiments. In J. S.
Antrobus (Ed.), *Cognition and affect*. Boston:
Little Brown, 1970.
Sternberg, S., & Scarborough, D. L. Parallel testing
of stimuli in visual search. Visual information
processing and control of motor activity, *Proceed-
ings of the international symposium*, Bulgarian
Academy of Sciences, Sofia, July 1969.
Waugh, N. C, & Norman, D. A. Primary memory.
Psychological Review, 1965, 72, 89-104.

Acknowledgments

This research was supported in part by Public
Health Service Research Grant MH-07722 from the
National Institute of Mental Health and in part by the
Advanced Research Projects Agency of the Office of the
Secretary of Defense (F4620-70-C-0107) which is monitor-
ed by the Air Force Office of Scientific Research.

A PRODUCTION SYSTEM FOR COUNTING, SUBITIZING AND ADDING[1]

David Klahr

Carnegie-Mellon University

This paper describes an explicit model of the process of quantification that was described in the previous chapter. The general model states that quantification of n items takes place via subitizing for $n \leq 4$ and via subitizing and addition for $n > 4$. The latter process is what is conventionally called counting. Although the previously presented model enabled us to utilize empirical results to estimate the processing time for each subprocess, it did not provide any detailed explanation of the operation of those processes, nor did it allow us to predict the effects of variations in the way that small clusters of stimuli might be grouped. The model is stated in the form of a *production system*, a relatively new formalism for describing process models. Before presenting the model, we will give a brief introduction to production systems.

---

[1]This paper presents a detailed description of production systems; there are several background papers that are required to fully understand the methodology and the particular substantive problems to which it is applied. For the general theoretical orientation, see Newell and Simon (1972); for the details of production systems and the rules of a production system interpreter, see Newell (1972). For the problems of cognitive development involving quantitative comparison, see Klahr and Wallace (1972); for quantitative processes data and theory, see Klahr (1972), and Klahr and Wallace (1973).

Production Systems: A Theory
and Language for Process Models

A new form for describing information processing
models of cognition has recently been proposed and
successfully applied to a modest range of complex
problem solving activities (Newell, 1966; Newell &
Simon, 1972). The models form a collection of independent rules, called *productions*, that form a production system. The rules are stated in the form of a
condition and an action: C→A. The condition refers
to the symbols in short-term memory (STM) that represent goals and knowledge elements existing in the
system's *knowledge state*; the action consists of transformations on STM including the generation, interruption
and satisfaction of goals, modification of existing
elements, and addition of new ones. A production
system obeys simple operating rules.

  i. The productions are considered in sequence,
     starting with the first.
 ii. Each condition is compared with the current
     state of knowledge in the system, as repre-
     sented by the symbols in STM. If *all* of
     the elements in a condition can be matched
     with elements (in any order) in STM, then
     the condition is satisfied.
iii. If a condition is not satisfied, the next
     production rule in the ordered list of
     production rules is considered.
 iv. If a condition is satisfied, the actions to
     the right of the arrow are taken. Then the
     production system is reentered from the top
     (Step i).
  v. When a condition is satisfied, all those
     STM elements that were matched are moved to
     the front of STM. This provides a form
     of automatic rehearsal.
 vi. Actions can change the state of goals,
     replace elements, apply operators, or add
     elements to STM.

vii. The STM is a stack in which a new element appears at the top pushing all else in the stack down one position. Since STM is limited in size, elements may be lost.

These rules operate within the framework of a theory of human problem solving extensively described by Newell and Simon (1972), and briefly summarized by Newell (1972):

"Structurally, the subject is an information processing system (IPS) consisting of a processor containing a short-term memory which has access to a long-term memory (LTM). The processor also has access to the external environment, which may be viewed as an external memory (EM)....

"All action of the system takes place via the execution of elementary processes, which take their operands in STM. The only information available upon which to base behavior is that in STM; other information (either in LTM or EM) must be brought into STM before it can effect behavior. At this level the system is serial in nature: only one elementary information process is executed at a time and has available to it the contents of STM as produced by prior elementary processes. Seriality here does not imply seriality either of perception or of accessing in LTM."

This general model and the verbal rules listed above have been precisely specified in a special programming language created by Newell (1972) called PSG (for Production System, version G). Production systems written in PSG can be run on the PSG interpreter in a time sharing mode under user (i.e., model-builder) control. The user can observe the sequential consequences of his model, and provide inputs for as yet unspecified subprocesses.

529

The example to be presented in this section is
intended not as a psychological model, but rather as a
demonstration of some of the features of PSG *qua* programming language. Figure 1a shows a production system
that represents the hammering of a nail into a board,
and Fig. 1b shows a trace of the system as it is
executed.

First, some PSG conventions. Everything to the
right of a semi-colon is ignored: Line 100 is merely a
title. The last line (1000) contains information used
by the loading routines, and is not part of the model,
per se. Everything else is in the form of a label,
followed by a colon, followed by some sort of structure enclosed in parentheses. The first four of these
structures (lines 200-500) are production rules. They
consist of a condition written as a conjunction of
elements, an arrow (→), and a series of actions. The
details of these productions differ, but they are all
of this same general form. We will return to the meaning of their particulars when we describe their execution. Line 600 contains a special structure, named
LOOK, which requests input from the terminal. That is,
LOOK represents a part of the model that has not yet
been programmed, and whose operation must therefore be
"simulated" by the model builder. When LOOK is evoked
as an action, the model builder must decide what information to give it before the system can continue to
function. Line 700 contains the information that the
system needs to get started: when PSG initializes the
interpretation of a production system, it inserts
TOP.GOAL into the top of STM. The structure named
BUILD (line 800) determines the sequence in which the
productions will be considered: thus, P4 will be tried
first, then P1, etc. Finally, the size of STM is
determined by the number of NILs (empty slots) allo-
cated to it.

Now for the dynamic behavior of the system
(Fig. 1b). Everything in lower case letters is typed
by the model builder, everything in upper case is typed
out by the system. The command *build start!* initializes the production system interpreter: STM is cleared
to all NILs, the count of actions is set to zero, the

(a)

```
00100    ,DEMO OF PSG USING SIMPLE EXAMPLE
00200    P1:((GOAL * JOIN) AND (UP HAMMER) AND (NAIL UP) --> (UP ===> DOWN))
00300    P2:((GOAL * JOIN) AND (DOWN HAMMER) --> (DOWN ===> UP) LOOK)
00400    P3:((GOAL * JOIN) --> (DOWN HAMMER))
00500    P4:((GOAL * JOIN) AND (NAIL FLUSH) -->(* ==> +))
00600    LOOK:(OPR CALL)
00700    TOP.GOAL:(GOAL * JOIN)
00800    BUILD:(P4 P1 P2 P3)
00900    STM:(NIL NIL NIL)
01000    ("BUILD LOADED. DO BUILD START!") RETURN.TO.TTY!
```

(b)

```
*build start!
0.  STM:  ((GOAL * JOIN) NIL NIL)
P3 TRUE
1.  STM:  ((DOWN HAMMER) (GOAL * JOIN) NIL)
P2 TRUE
      (GOAL * JOIN)
      ()
      OUTPUT FOR LOOK = *(nail up)
*|z
,z
4.  STM:  ((NAIL UP) (GOAL * JOIN) (UP HAMMER))
P1 TRUE
5.  STM:  ((GOAL * JOIN) (DOWN HAMMER) (NAIL UP))
P2 TRUE
      (GOAL * JOIN)
      ()
      OUTPUT FOR LOOK = **(nail up)
*|z
,z
8.  STM:  ((NAIL UP) (GOAL * JOIN) (UP HAMMER))
P1 TRUE
9.  STM:  ((GOAL * JOIN) (DOWN HAMMER) (NAIL UP))
P2 TRUE
      (GOAL * JOIN)
      ()
      OUTPUT FOR LOOK = **(nail flush)
*|z
,z
12.  STM:  ((NAIL FLUSH) (GOAL * JOIN) (UP HAMMER))
P4 TRUE
13.  STM:  ((GOAL * JOIN) (NAIL FLUSH) (UP HAMMER))
END: NO PD TRUE
```

Fig. 1. A Simple Production System (a) and
its Trace (b).

structure named TOP.GOAL is put into STM, and a scan
of the list of productions in BUILD commences. The
first production to be considered is P1. It scans STM
for the three elements: (GOAL * JOIN), (UP HAMMER),
and (NAIL UP). Only the first of these is currently
in STM, so P4 is not satisfied. Next P1 looks for the
two elements in its condition, and fails. P2 also
fails; and finally P3 finds a match between its condition and the elements in STM. Since P3's condition
is satisfied, the actions associated with it are taken.
In this case the action consists of simply adding a new
element (DOWN HAMMER) to the "front" of STM, and pushing
everything else in STM down one "notch." The current
state of STM is printed out in Fig. 1b after "1." (to
indicate that one action has been taken since the system
started).

After a production has "fired," i.e., after its
condition has been matched and its associated actions
have been taken, the production system is re-entered
at the top. Thus, after P3 has completed its actions,
the sequence of productions, as listed in BUILD, is
tested sequentially once again. P4 and P1 fail again,
but this time P2 is satisfied. The two actions in P2
are (DOWN===>UP) and LOOK. The first of these is an
action that modifies an element already in STM: the
second element in STM is scanned for DOWN, and it is
changed to UP. The action LOOK is, as described above,
a call upon the terminal for the output of an as yet
unprogrammed routine that is supposed to determine
whether the nail is up or flush. At this point, the
the modeler decided that it was still up, entered
(nail up), and returned control to the system. The
state of STM after 4 actions is now printed out. The
same basic control cycle is repeated with the determination of which production will fire being entirely
dependent upon the contents of STM. Further explanations of the details of PSG will be given in the
following description of the quantification model.

The entire production system, listed in Fig. 2,
consists of three subsystems: a subitizing system, an
addition system, and a control system (the counting

system) for initiating subitizing and/or addition as appropriate. The subitizing production system will be described first as an independent entity, followed by addition, and finally the integrated system will be described, and its behavior compared with the empirical results of the previous chapter.

Subitizing

The subitizing subsystem, PSUBIT, is contained in lines 5100-7200 of Fig. 2, and a trace of the system running on a display of 3 elements is shown in Fig. 3. The productions serve three general functions: the PDT's are part of a template matching system, PSTMP: the PDB's correspond roughly to the earlier notion of doing "nexts" on a list of stored quantitative symbols; and the PDS's provide the control for initiating and terminating the subitizing process.

Initialization and Termination

PSUBIT can function either in the context of a goal of counting or directly as an explicit subitizer. In the former case, the elements to be encoded will have already entered STM; otherwise, PSUBIT must deal "directly" with its environment. PDS4 and PDS1 determine which condition obtains and then one of them does the appropriate initialization, adding two symbols to STM in either case. Similarly, PDS2 and PDS3 detect a satisfied (+) subitizing goal and either "say" the result or reactivate the superordinate COUNT goal. So much for starting and stopping; now let us look at the central dynamics of PSUBIT.

General Logic

Subitizing is viewed as a combination of template matching and a sequential transfer from LTM to STM of both template "pieces" and number names. The highest priority productions in PSUBIT are those in PSTMP: they seek a one-to-one match between stimulus elements

```
00100   ,COUNT.AL1
00200   , PRODUCTION SYSTEM FOR COUNTING VIA SUBITIZING AND ADDITION.
00300   , COMPOSITE OF FILES: COUNT.A02, ADD.A01 AND SUB.E02.
00400   ,
00500   ;
00600   <TE>:(CLASS TSA ELM)
00700   <QS>:(CLASS SUB SUM QS)
00800   <Q1>:(CLASS <QS>)
00900   <Q2>:(CLASS <QS>)
01000   <SAY>:(VAR)
01100   X0:(VAR)
01200   X1:(VAR)
01300   X2:(VAR)
01400   <NUM>:(CLASS 1 2 3 4 5 6 7 8 9 0)
01500   ,
01600   ,ADDITION PRODUCTION SYSTEM. ***************************
01700   PDAA0:((<Q2> 0) AND (<Q1> X0) AND (GOAL * ADD) -->
01800     (<Q2> ==>  OLD <Q2>)(<Q1> ===> SUM)(* ====> +))
01900   PDAA1:((<Q2> 1) AND (<Q1> X0) AND (GOAL * ADD) -->  (<Q2> 1 ==> NEW <Q2> 2))
02000   PDAA2:((<Q2> 2) AND (<Q1> X0) AND (GOAL * ADD) -->  (<Q2> 2 ==> NEW <Q2> 3))
02100   PDAA3:(( <Q2> 3) AND (<Q1> X0) AND (GOAL * ADD) -->  (<Q2> 3 ==> NEW <Q2> 4))
02200   PDAA4:((<Q2> 4) AND (<Q1> X0) AND (GOAL * ADD) -->  (<Q2> 4 ==> NEW <Q2> 5))
02300   PDAA5:((<Q2> 5) AND (<Q1> X0) AND (GOAL * ADD) -->  (<Q2> 5 ==> NEW <Q2> 6))
02400   PDAA6:((<Q2> 6) AND (<Q1> X0) AND (GOAL * ADD) -->  (<Q2> 6 ==> NEW <Q2> 7))
02500   PDAA7:((<Q2> 7) AND (<Q1> X0) AND (GOAL * ADD) -->  (<Q2> 7 ==> NEW <Q2> 8))
02600   PDAA8:((<Q2> 8) AND (<Q1> X0) AND (GOAL * ADD) -->  (<Q2> 8 ==> NEW <Q2> 9))
02700   PDAA9:((<Q2> 9) AND (<Q1> X0) AND (GOAL * ADD) -->  (<Q2> 8 ==> NEW <Q2> 10))
02800   PSA:(PDAA9 PDAA8 PDAA7 PDAA6 PDAA5 PDAA4 PDAA3 PDAA2 PDAA1)
02900   ,
03000   PDAB4:((<Q2> 4) AND (NEW <Q1>) AND (GOAL * ADD) --> (4 ==> 3)
03100     (NEW ===> ))
03200   PDAB3:((<Q2> 3) AND (NEW <Q1>) AND (GOAL * ADD) --> (3 ==> 2)
03300     (NEW ===> ))
03400   PDAB2:((<Q2> 2) AND (NEW <Q1>) AND (GOAL * ADD) --> (2 ==> 1)
03500     (NEW ===> ))
03600   PDAB1:((<Q2> 1) AND (NEW <Q1>) AND (GOAL * ADD) --> (1 ==> 0)
03700     (NEW ===> ))
03800   PSB:(PDAB4 PDAB3 PDAB2 PDAB1 )
03900   ,
04000   PSADD:(PDA1 PDAA0 PSB PSA PDA2)
04100   ,
04200   PDA1:((<NUM>) --> (<NUM> ==> QS <NUM>))
04300   PDA2:((GOAL + ADD) AND (SUM) --> (SUM ===> SAID SUM) SAY)
04400   ,
04500   ,
04600   , MARK TSA'S AND ELM'S UNTILL ALL MARKED
04700   PDM1:((GOAL * MARK) AND (<TE>) --> (<TE> ===> OLD <TE>))
04800   PDM2:((GOAL * MARK) AND (<TE>) ABS --> (* ==> +))
04900   PSM:(PDM1 PDM2)
05000   ,
05100   ;SUBITIZING PRODUCTION SYSTEM. ***************************
05200   PDT1:((GOAL * SUBIT) AND (ELM) AND (TSA) AND (<TE>) ABS --> (* ==> +))
05300   PDT2:((GOAL * SUBIT) AND (ELM) AND (TSA) AND (ELM) AND (TSA) AND (<TE>) ABS --> (* ==> +))
05400   PDT3:((GOAL * SUBIT) AND (ELM) AND (TSA) AND (ELM) AND (TSA) AND (ELM) AND (TSA) AND (<TE>) ABS --> (* ==> +))
05500   PDT4:((GOAL * SUBIT) AND (ELM) AND (TSA) AND (ELM) AND (TSA) AND(ELM) AND  (TSA) AND (ELM) AND (TSA) AND (<TE>) A
        BS --> (* ==> +))
05600   PSTMP:(PDT4 PDT3 PDT2 PDT1)
05700   ,
05800   PDS1:((GOAL * SUBIT) --> NOTICE (SUB 1)(TSA ))
05900   PDS2:((GOAL *) ABS AND (GOAL + SUBIT) AND (SUB) -->
06000     (SUB ===> SAID SUB) SAY)
06100   PDS3:((GOAL *) ABS AND (GOAL + SUBIT) AND (GOAL % COUNT) --> (% ===> *))
06200   PDS4:((GOAL * SUBIT) AND (GOAL % COUNT) --> (SUB 1)(TSA ))
06300   ,
06400   PDB2:((GOAL * SUBIT) AND (SUB 1) --> (1 ===> 2)(TSA))
06500   PDB3:((GOAL * SUBIT) AND (SUB 2) --> (2 ===> 3)(TSA))
06600   PDB4:((GOAL * SUBIT) AND (SUB 3) --> (3 ===> 4)(TSA))
06700   ,
06800   PSNB:(PDB2 PDB3 PDB4 )
06900   ,
07000   PSUBIT:(PSTMP PDS3 PDS2 PSNB PDS4  PDS1)
07100   ,
07200   SAY:(ACTION (NTC (SAID <QS> <SAY>)) (OPR <SAY> PRVL))
07300   ,
07400   ,COUNTING PRODUCTION SYSTEM. ***************************
07500   PDC1:((GOAL * COUNT) AND (<Q1> X1) AND (<Q2> X2)
07600     -->(GOAL * ADD))
07700   PDC2:((GOAL * COUNT) AND (<QS>) AND (END) --> (* ==> +) (<QS> ===> SAID <QS>) SAY )
07800   PDC3:((GOAL * COUNT) AND (<QS>) AND (<TE>) --> (GOAL * MARK))
07900   PDC4:((GOAL * COUNT) AND (<QS>) --> NOTICE (GOAL * SUBIT))
08000   PDC5:(( GOAL * COUNT) --> (SUM 0) NOTICE (GOAL * SUBIT))
08100   ,
08200   PSC:(PDC1 PDC2 PDC3 PDC4 PDC5)
08300   ,
08400   PDG1:((GOAL *) AND (GOAL *) --> (* ===> %))
08500   PDG2:((GOAL *) ABS AND (GOAL %) --> (% ==> *))
08600   ,
08700   PSCOUNT:(PDG1 PSM PSC PSUBIT PDG2 PSADD)
08800   ,
08900   NOTICE:(OPR CALL); INPUT ELMS : (ELM 1)(ELM 2) ... (END).
09000   TOP.GOAL:(GOAL * COUNT)
09100   STM:(NIL NIL NIL NIL NIL NIL NIL NIL NIL NIL NIL NIL NIL NIL)
09200   ("COUNT.AL1 LOADED.  DO PSCOUNT START! ") RETURN.TO.TTY!
```

Fig. 2. Production System for Subitizing, Adding, and Counting.

```
.run dsk psgasc
W09 RESTARTING
*top.goal:(goal * subit)
*psubit start!
0.  STM: ((GOAL * SUBIT) NIL NIL NIL NIL NIL NIL NIL NIL NIL NIL NiL NIL NIL)
PDS1 TRUE
        (GOAL * SUBIT)
        ()
        OUTPUT FOR NOTICE = *(elm 1)(elm 2)(elm 3)
*|z
,z
6.  STM: ((TSA) (SUB 1) (ELM 3) (ELM 2) (ELM 1) (GOAL * SUBIT) NIL NIL NIL NIL NIL NIL NIL NIL)
PDB2 TRUE
8.  STM: ((TSA) (GOAL * SUBIT) (SUB 2) (TSA) (ELM 3) (ELM 2) (ELM 1) NIL NIL NIL NIL NIL NIL NIL)
PDB3 TRUE
10.  STM: ((TSA) (GOAL * SUBIT) (SUB 3) (TSA) (TSA) (ELM 3) (ELM 2) (ELM 1) NIL NIL NIL NIL NIL NIL)
PDT3 TRUE
11.  STM: ((GOAL + SUBIT) (ELM 3) (TSA) (ELM 2) (TSA) (ELM 1) (TSA) (SUB 3) NIL NIL NIL NIL NIL NIL)
PDS2 TRUE
<SAY>: 3
15.  STM: ((SAID SUB 3) (GOAL + SUBIT) (ELM 3) (TSA) (ELM 2) (TSA) (ELM 1) (TSA) NIL NIL NIL NIL NIL NIL)
END: NO PD TRUE
**
```

Fig. 3. Trace of Subitizing Subsystem, PSUBIT, on a 3-Element Display.

from the environment (ELM's) and template pieces retrieved from LTM (TSA's). As soon as one of the conditions in the PDT's is satisfied, the subitizing goal is changed from active to satisfied.

Template pieces are symbols representing tolerance space atoms (TSA's), the elementary unit of "countable-ness" (Klahr and Wallace, 1973). Somewhere in the system, there must be a class of symbols that repre-sents what "countable" things are. Although the TSA's are defined as primitives, the decision about what things in the environment will be considered as unitary objects is dependent upon such things as goal of the quantification attempt, the discriminability and saliency of cues, and the current state of the system. In our experiments, there is no ambiguity about what constitutes a countable element: they are the dots in the display. And the entire subitization process can be viewed as an attempt to match these stimuli with the elementary symbols.

Note that the PSNB productions implicitly tie cardinality and ordinality together, since the failure to match n items is followed by the addition of a $single$ additional TSA and the change of the quantitative symbol from n to $n+1$. Other variants of quantification (see Klahr, 1972) do not include this assumption.

Quantitative symbols correspond to templates of appropriate size, but the entire template must be loaded
into STM for each match. Such models are necessary to
account for certain developmental data about the onset
of cardinality prior to ordinality.

Dynamics

   The general flow of PSUBIT is:

a. NOTICE the stimulus. This is a call upon the
   terminal for input of the entire stimulus as a
   set of independent elements. (The elements are
   numbered for illustrative purposes only; note
   that no productions use these numerical values.)
b. Transfer the name of the first possible response
   (SUB 1) and a single piece of the template (TSA)
   from LTM to STM.
c. If there are as many (TSA's) as (ELM's), then
   satisfy the SUBIT goal and "say" the name of
   the current response.
d. Otherwise, modify the response name to its next
   value and add another template piece to STM.

Figure 3 shows a trace of this general scheme on a
3-element display.
   In the range $1 \leq n \leq 4$, PSUBIT takes 3 actions
per item. The actions are: the input of an additional
ELM, the addition of an extra TSA, and the modification
of a response symbol. One may equate this to the 40
msec. slope for subitizing reported earlier, by assuming that these actions take an average 15 msec. each,
and that no other activity in the interpretation of
the production system contributed appreciably to the
time. The most important specific assumption is that
all conditions are tested in parallel: the sequential
nature of both the testing of conditions and the STM
"scan" for a particular condition is to be viewed as
a serial simulation of a parallel process. (On this
issue see Newell, 1972.) Notice that this is quite a
different view of contemporary STM scanning models,

and a PS(G) model of typical STM experiments (Newell, this volume) suggests an interpretation that bears little resemblance to the well-known flow chart models (e.g., Sternberg, 1967).

Addition

The addition subsystem, PSADD, consists of lines 1600-4300 in Fig. 2, plus some of the class variables defined in lines 600-1400. A trace of PSADD is shown in Fig. 4. The logic of addition (say x + y) is to add the smaller number to the larger by incrementing the max of (x,y) while decrementing the min. As soon as the min reaches zero, the max is taken as the sum (PDAAO).

PSADD consists of a relatively large set of "addition rules;" however, it runs quite efficiently. It adds nothing to STM, working entirely with the initial three elements that evoke it, and it has a slope of 3 actions per min (x,y). In this case we would like to posit a correspondence between these 3 actions and the 20 msec. slope for addition reported by Groen and Parkman (1972). Of course, this would be discrepant with the 15 msec. per action assumption we made for subitizing, so at present the fit is unsatisfactory. Furthermore, we have finessed the

```
   run dsk psgasc
W09 RESTARTING
*stm:((goal * add)(3)(1) nil)
*psadd ps!
0.  STM: ((GOAL * ADD) (3) (1) NIL)
PDA1 TRUE
1.  STM: ((QS 3) (GOAL * ADD) (1) NIL)
PDA1 TRUE
2.  STM: ((QS 1) (QS 3) (GOAL * ADD) NIL)
PDAA3 TRUE
3.  STM: ((NEW QS 4) (QS 1) (GOAL * ADD) NIL)
PDAB1 TRUE
5.  STM: ((QS 0) (QS 4) (GOAL * ADD) NIL)
PDAA0 TRUE
8.  STM: ((OLD QS 0) (SUM 4) (GOAL + ADD) NIL)
PDA2 TRUE
<SAY>: 4
12.  STM: ((SAID SUM 4) (GOAL + ADD) (OLD QS 0) NIL)
END: NO PD TRUE
*
```

Fig. 4. Trace of Addition Subsystem, PSADD, on (3) + (1).

difficult issue of the determination of max (x,y) by
utilizing the order of the productions. Since the
serial nature of production system interpretation is
usually taken as a necessary evil with no psychological
import, the current procedure for finding the max should
be viewed as an aspect of incompleteness in this model.

Counting

General Description

The model for counting, described in the previous
chapter (1), consists of several subprocesses.

"The first one segments the stimulus into a
subgroup.... The next process is subitizing.
The groups are presumed to be within the
subitizing range and once noticed, they are
subitized. Next, the result from subitizing
is added to a running total. Finally, the
group is marked.... If there are more objects
to be accounted for, the process is repeated."

PSCOUNT contains the productions that follow this
general scheme for quantification. There are four
central productions, PDC1, PDC3, PDC4, and PDC5 (Fig. 2,
lines 7500–8000), that introduce goals for addition,
subitizing or marking, and one production, PDC2,
terminates activity and says the final result.
PDC1 detects two quantitative symbols, (<QS>),
and a COUNT goal, and adds an ADD goal to STM. The
goal manipulation productions PDG1 and PDG2 (lines 8400
–8500) handle the goal stack that is distributed in STM.
As soon as the active goals ADD and COUNT are detected
by PDG1 (the top priority production), COUNT is changed
from active to interrupted, and the system functions as
if PSADD had been "called" as a subroutine. (The
capability to execute an entire production system as
an action is available in PS(G), but it is not used
here. Although we have mentioned "subsystems" in
PSCOUNT, there is no hierarchical organization: it is
one long string of 36 production rules.)

538

PDC2 tests for a single quantitative symbol (in this case the final result) as well as a signal (END) that the most recent scan of the environment, NOTICE, exhausted the display. Having detected this case, it marks the count goal as satisfied, marks the quantitative symbol, and says it.

If a single <QS> and an ELM or a TSA (<TE>) are detected, then PSCOUNT must prepare for additional environmental input. The input will add the next batch of ELM's to STM and then seek a perfect match with a series of TSA's. If any residual <TE>'s are in STM at this point, they must be marked so that they do not interfere with the next subitizing attempt. Thus, PDC3 introduces the MARK goal. This activates PSM (lines 4700-4900) until all the TSA's and ELM's in STM have been marked OLD.

PDC4 and PDC5 generate the calls on NOTICE and insert the subitizing goal. On the first pass, PDC5 fires, initializing the SUM to 0; on all subsequent passes PDC4 fires. NOTICE (as simulated by the theorist) produces a series of from one to four ELM's and with the final such string, a termination indicator (END). The behavior of PSCOUNT varies with assumptions about how the stimulus is segmented by NOTICE, and these effects will be discussed in a subsequent section.

Traces of PSCOUNT

A trace of PSCOUNT on a 2-element display is listed in Fig. 5.[2] The first production to be satisfied is PDC5, which initializes the sum and generates the call for NOTICE. The assumption here is that the entire

---

[2]For illustrative purposes, STM has been limited to 10 elements in this example. The maximum size necessary for all the cases in Table I was 14. Increasing STM to the size required for these larger problems does not affect performance on the smaller problems, i.e., they do not depend upon the loss of information from STM.

display is input to STM in a single "glance." After
COUNT is interrupted (7.), the subitizing sequence is
fired, producing a quantitative symbol (SUB 2) and a
reactivated COUNT (13.). This result is added to the
(SUM 0) symbol (14. -18.) and finally the system says
the result. Note that since the (END) element entered
on the first glance, no marking was necessary, and the
addition was a bit superfluous. As long as the entire
display enters on the first glance, the only variance
in the number of actions in PSCOUNT comes from PSUBIT,
i.e., it is 3 actions per element (see below).

Figure 6 shows PSCOUNT operating in a situation
where a 5-element display is segmented into glances of
4 elements and 2 elements. The trace can be viewed as
a series of episodes: noticing and subitizing the
first group (0. -18.), adding the result to the total
(19. -24.), marking the old <TE>'s (25. -33.), seeking additional input and subitizing it (34. -46.),
adding that result to the total thus far (47. -57.)
and producing the final output.

```
pscount start!
0.   STM: ((GOAL * COUNT) NIL NIL NIL NIL NIL NIL NIL NIL NIL)
PDC5 TRUE
     (SUM 0)
     ()
     OUTPUT FOR NOTICE = *(elm 1)(elm 2)(end)
*|z
,z
6.   STM: ((GOAL * SUBIT) (END) (ELM 2) (ELM 1) (SUM 0) (GOAL * COUNT) NIL NIL NIL NIL)
PDG1 TRUE
7.   STM: ((GOAL * SUBIT) (GOAL % COUNT) (END) (ELM 2) (ELM 1) (SUM 0) NIL NIL NIL NIL)
PDS4 TRUE
9.   STM: ((TSA) (SUB 1) (GOAL * SUBIT) (GOAL % COUNT) (END) (ELM 2) (ELM 1) (SUM 0) NIL NIL)
PDB2 TRUE
11.  STM: ((TSA) (GOAL * SUBIT) (SUB 2) (TSA) (GOAL % COUNT) (END) (ELM 2) (ELM 1) (SUM 0) NIL)
PDT2 TRUE
12.  STM: ((GOAL + SUBIT) (ELM 2) (TSA) (ELM 1) (TSA) (SUB 2) (GOAL % COUNT) (END) (SUM 0) NIL)
PDS3 TRUE
13.  STM: ((GOAL + SUBIT) (GOAL * COUNT) (ELM 2) (TSA) (ELM 1) (TSA) (SUB 2) (END) (SUM 0) NIL)
PDC1 TRUE
14.  STM: ((GOAL * ADD) (GOAL * COUNT) (SUB 2) (SUM 0) (GOAL + SUBIT) (ELM 2) (TSA) (ELM 1) (TSA) (END))
PDG1 TRUE
15.  STM: ((GOAL * ADD) (GOAL % COUNT) (SUB 2) (SUM 0) (GOAL + SUBIT) (ELM 2) (TSA) (ELM 1) (TSA) (END))
PDAA0 TRUE
18.  STM: ((OLD SUM 0) (SUM 2) (GOAL + ADD) (GOAL % COUNT) (GOAL + SUBIT) (ELM 2) (TSA) (ELM 1) (TSA) (END))
PDS3 TRUE
19.  STM: ((GOAL + SUBIT) (GOAL * COUNT) (OLD SUM 0) (SUM 2) (GOAL + ADD) (ELM 2) (TSA) (ELM 1) (TSA) (END))
PDC2 TRUE
<SAY>: 2
24.  STM: ((SAID SUM 2) (GOAL + COUNT) (END) (GOAL + SUBIT) (OLD SUM 0) (GOAL + ADD) (ELM 2) (TSA) (ELM 1) (TSA))
```

Fig. 5. Trace of PSCOUNT on a 2-Element Display
Quantified in a Single NOTICE.

Summary of Behavior of PSCOUNT

PSCOUNT was run under several different segmentation strategies, listed in Table I. In all cases the maximum size of any glance was 4 elements. Three segmentation strategies were used. Strategy A encodes as much of the remaining stimulus as possible (i.e., less than 5) on each glance; Strategy B encodes only

```
0.  STM: ((GOAL * COUNT) NIL NIL NIL NIL NIL NIL NIL NIL NIL NIL NIL)
PDC5 TRUE
      (SUM 0)
      ()
      OUTPUT FOR NOTICE = *(elm 1)(elm 2)(elm 3)(elm 4)
*|z
7.  STM: ((GOAL * SUBIT) (ELM 4) (ELM 3) (ELM 2) (ELM 1) (SUM 0) (GOAL * COUNT) NIL NIL NIL NIL NIL)
PDG1 TRUE
8.  STM: ((GOAL * SUBIT) (GOAL % COUNT) (ELM 4) (ELM 3) (ELM 2) (ELM 1) (SUM 0) NIL NIL NIL NIL NIL)
PDS4 TRUE
10.  STM: ((TSA) (SUB 1) (GOAL * SUBIT) (GOAL % COUNT) (ELM 4) (ELM 3) (ELM 2) (ELM 1) (SUM 0) NIL NIL NIL)
PDB2 TRUE
12.  STM: ((TSA) (GOAL * SUBIT) (SUB 2) (TSA) (GOAL % COUNT) (ELM 4) (ELM 3) (ELM 2) (ELM 1) (SUM 0) NIL NIL)
PDB3 TRUE
14.  STM: ((TSA) (GOAL * SUBIT) (SUB 3) (TSA) (TSA) (GOAL % COUNT) (ELM 4) (ELM 3) (ELM 2) (ELM 1) (SUM 0) NIL)
PDB4 TRUE
16.  STM: ((TSA) (GOAL * SUBIT) (SUB 4) (TSA) (TSA) (TSA) (GOAL % COUNT) (ELM 4) (ELM 3) (ELM 2) (ELM 1) (SUM 0))
PDT4 TRUE
17.  STM: ((GOAL + SUBIT) (ELM 4) (TSA) (ELM 3) (TSA) (ELM 2) (TSA) (ELM 1) (TSA) (SUB 4) (GOAL % COUNT) (SUM 0))
PDS3 TRUE
18.  STM: ((GOAL + SUBIT) (GOAL * COUNT) (ELM 4) (TSA) (ELM 3) (TSA) (ELM 2) (TSA) (ELM 1) (TSA) (SUB 4) (SUM 0))
PDC1 TRUE
19.  STM: ((GOAL * ADD) (GOAL + COUNT) (SUB 4) (SUM 0) (GOAL + SUBIT) (ELM 4) (TSA) (ELM 3) (TSA) (ELM 2) (TSA) (ELM 1))
PDG1 TRUE
20.  STM: ((GOAL * ADD) (GOAL % COUNT) (SUB 4) (SUM 0) (GOAL + SUBIT) (ELM 4) (TSA) (ELM 3) (TSA) (ELM 2) (TSA) (ELM 1))
PDAA0 TRUE
23.  STM: ((OLD SUM 0) (SUM 4) (GOAL + ADD) (GOAL % COUNT) (GOAL + SUBIT) (ELM 4) (TSA) (ELM 3) (TSA) (ELM 2) (TSA) (ELM 1
))
PDS3 TRUE
24.  STM: ((GOAL + SUBIT) (GOAL * COUNT) (OLD SUM 0) (SUM 4) (GOAL + ADD) (ELM 4) (TSA) (ELM 3) (TSA) (ELM 2) (TSA) (ELM 1
))
PDC3 TRUE
25.  STM: ((GOAL * MARK) (GOAL * COUNT) (SUM 4) (ELM 4) (GOAL + SUBIT) (OLD SUM 0) (GOAL + ADD) (TSA) (ELM 3) (TSA) (ELM 2
) (TSA))
PDG1 TRUE
26.  STM: ((GOAL * MARK) (GOAL % COUNT) (SUM 4) (ELM 4) (GOAL + SUBIT) (OLD SUM 0) (GOAL + ADD) (TSA) (ELM 3) (TSA) (ELM 2
) (TSA))
PDM1 TRUE
27.  STM: ((GOAL * MARK) (OLD ELM 4) (GOAL % COUNT) (SUM 4) (GOAL + SUBIT) (OLD SUM 0) (GOAL + ADD) (TSA) (ELM 3) (TSA) (E
LM 2) (TSA))
PDM1 TRUE
28.  STM: ((GOAL * MARK) (OLD TSA) (OLD ELM 4) (GOAL % COUNT) (SUM 4) (GOAL + SUBIT) (OLD SUM 0) (GOAL + ADD) (ELM 3) (TSA
) (ELM 2) (TSA))
PDM1 TRUE
29.  STM: ((GOAL * MARK) (OLD ELM 3) (OLD TSA) (OLD ELM 4) (GOAL % COUNT) (SUM 4) (GOAL + SUBIT) (OLD SUM 0) (GOAL + ADD)
(TSA) (ELM 2) (TSA))
PDM1 TRUE
30.  STM: ((GOAL * MARK) (OLD TSA) (OLD ELM 3) (OLD TSA) (OLD ELM 4) (GOAL % COUNT) (SUM 4) (GOAL + SUBIT) (OLD SUM 0) (GO
AL + ADD) (ELM 2) (TSA))
PDM1 TRUE
31.  STM: ((GOAL * MARK) (OLD ELM 2) (OLD TSA) (OLD ELM 3) (OLD TSA) (OLD ELM 4) (GOAL % COUNT) (SUM 4) (GOAL + SUBIT) (OL
D SUM 0) (GOAL + ADD) (TSA))
PDM1 TRUE
32.  STM: ((GOAL * MARK) (OLD TSA) (OLD ELM 2) (OLD TSA) (OLD ELM 3) (OLD TSA) (OLD ELM 4) (GOAL % COUNT) (SUM 4) (GOAL +
SUBIT) (OLD SUM 0) (GOAL + ADD))
PDM2 TRUE
33.  STM: ((GOAL * MARK) (OLD TSA) (OLD ELM 2) (OLD TSA) (OLD ELM 3) (OLD TSA) (OLD ELM 4) (GOAL % COUNT) (SUM 4) (GOAL +
SUBIT) (OLD SUM 0) (GOAL + ADD))
PDS3 TRUE
34.  STM: ((GOAL + SUBIT) (GOAL * COUNT) (GOAL + MARK) (OLD TSA) (OLD ELM 2) (OLD TSA) (OLD ELM 3) (OLD TSA) (OLD ELM 4) (
SUM 4) (OLD SUM 0) (GOAL + ADD))
PDC4 TRUE
      (GOAL * COUNT)
      (<QS> SUM)
      OUTPUT FOR NOTICE = **(elm 5)(elm 6)(end)
```

Fig. 6. Trace of PSCOUNT on a 5-Element Display Quantified in Two NOTICE's (4 + 1).

```
39. STM: ((GOAL * SUBIT) (END) (ELM 6) (ELM 5) (GOAL * COUNT) (SUM 4) (GOAL + SUBIT) (GOAL + MARK) (OLD TSA) (OLD ELM 2)
    OLD TSA) (OLD ELM 3))
PDG1 TRUE
40. STM: ((GOAL + SUBIT) (GOAL % COUNT) (END) (ELM 6) (ELM 5) (SUM 4) (GOAL + SUBIT) (GOAL + MARK) (OLD TSA) (OLD ELM 2)
    (OLD TSA) (OLD ELM 3))
PDS4 TRUE
42. STM: ((TSA) (SUB 1) (GOAL * SUBIT) (GOAL % COUNT) (END) (ELM 6) (ELM 5) (SUM 4) (GOAL + SUBIT) (GOAL + MARK) (OLD TSA
    ) (OLD ELM 2))
PDB2 TRUE
44. STM: ((TSA) (GOAL * SUBIT) (SUB 2) (TSA) (GOAL % COUNT) (END) (ELM 6) (ELM 5) (SUM 4) (GOAL + SUBIT) (GOAL + MARK) (O
    LD TSA))
PDT2 TRUE
45. STM: ((GOAL + SUBIT) (ELM 6) (TSA) (ELM 5) (TSA) (SUB 2) (GOAL % COUNT) (END) (SUM 4) (GOAL + SUBIT) (GOAL + MARK) (O
    LD TSA))
PDS3 TRUE
46. STM: ((GOAL + SUBIT) (GOAL * COUNT) (ELM 6) (TSA) (ELM 5) (TSA) (SUB 2) (END) (SUM 4) (GOAL + SUBIT) (GOAL + MARK) (O
    LD TSA))
PDC1 TRUE
47. STM: ((GOAL * ADD) (GOAL * COUNT) (SUB 2) (SUM 4) (GOAL + SUBIT) (ELM 6) (TSA) (ELM 5) (TSA) (END) (GOAL + SUBIT) (GO
    AL + MARK))
PDG1 TRUE
48. STM: ((GOAL * ADD) (GOAL % COUNT) (SUB 2) (SUM 4) (GOAL + SUBIT) (ELM 6) (TSA) (ELM 5) (TSA) (END) (GOAL + SUBIT) (GO
    AL + MARK))
PDAA4 TRUE
49. STM: ((NEW SUM 5) (SUB 2) (GOAL * ADD) (GOAL % COUNT) (GOAL + SUBIT) (ELM 6) (TSA) (ELM 5) (TSA) (END) (GOAL + SUBIT)
    (GOAL + MARK))
PDAB2 TRUE
51. STM: ((SUB 1) (SUM 5) (GOAL * ADD) (GOAL % COUNT) (GOAL + SUBIT) (ELM 6) (TSA) (ELM 5) (TSA) (END) (GOAL + SUBIT) (GO
    AL + MARK))
PDAA5 TRUE
52. STM: ((NEW SUM 6) (SUB 1) (GOAL * ADD) (GOAL % COUNT) (GOAL + SUBIT) (ELM 6) (TSA) (ELM 5) (TSA) (END) (GOAL + SUBIT)
    (GOAL + MARK))
PDAB1 TRUE
54. STM: ((SUB 0) (SUM 6) (GOAL * ADD) (GOAL % COUNT) (GOAL + SUBIT) (ELM 6) (TSA) (ELM 5) (TSA) (END) (GOAL + SUBIT) (GO
    AL + MARK))
PDAA0 TRUE
57. STM: ((OLD SUB 0) (SUM 6) (GOAL * ADD) (GOAL % COUNT) (GOAL + SUBIT) (ELM 6) (TSA) (ELM 5) (TSA) (END) (GOAL + SUBIT)
    (GOAL + MARK))
PDS3 TRUE
58. STM: ((GOAL + SUBIT) (GOAL * COUNT) (OLD SUB 0) (SUM 6) (GOAL + ADD) (ELM 6) (TSA) (ELM 5) (TSA) (END) (GOAL + SUBIT)
    (GOAL + MARK))
PDC2 TRUE
<SAY>: 6
63. STM: ((SAID SUM 6) (GOAL + COUNT) (END) (GOAL + SUBIT) (OLD SUB 0) (GOAL + ADD) (ELM 6) (TSA) (ELM 5) (TSA) (GOAL + S
UBIT) (GOAL + MARK))
```

Fig. 6 (continued).

a single new item at a glance; Strategy C uses A below
5 and B for 5 and above. Curves for the number of
actions as a function of n and strategy are plotted
in Fig. 7. The slope ratio for one-at-a-time quantification (Strategy B) vs. subitizing (Strategy A) is 3/23,
roughly equivalent to the subitizing/counting slope
ratios reported earlier. The curve for Strategy C also
has the second order (slope) discontinuity commonly
found in this experimental situation, while the Strategy A curve displays the first order discontinuity that
is suggested by the figures of the previous chapter
(see Figs. 4 and 6).

542

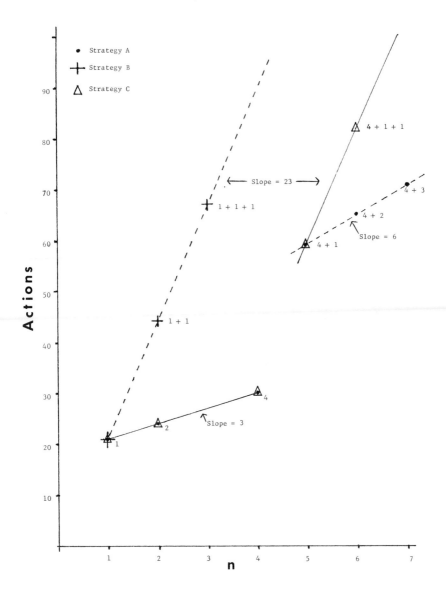

Fig. 7. Number of Actions Taken by PSCOUNT as a Function of n and Strategy.

TABLE I

NUMBER OF ACTIONS FOR DIFFERENT SEGMENTATION
STRATEGIES FOR n ITEMS.

Segmentation Strategy	n	Notices			Actions
		1st	2nd	3rd	
A,B	1	1			21
A	2	2			24
B	2	1	1		44
B	3	1	1	1	67
A	4	4			30
A,C	5	4	1		59
A	6	4	2		65
C	6	4	1	1	82
A	7	4	3		71

Conclusion

We now have a precise and detailed model that can
coordinate subitizing and adding in a way that is fairly
true to the empirical data. At the same time the model
is identical in basic structure to a general theory of
the human information processor (Newell, 1972). Thus,
it avoids the *ad hoc* nature of the "Flow Chart" models
presented in our earlier chapter. However, as is
always the case with information processing models,
PSCOUNT raises questions more difficult than those
initially posed.

One problem is that we have introduced an undefined
but crucial operator: NOTICE. It must determine what

aspects of the stimulus constitute legitimate items to be quantified; it must attend to them in some sequence, and it must decide when all have been accounted for. There are several possibilites for providing NOTICE with the appropriate context in the form of a tag on the last (but nonterminal) element in each scan. However, provision of attention directing information has proven to be a non-trivial matter in other process models (Simon & Barenfeld, 1969), and its inclusion here is a problem yet to be solved.

Another question raised by PSCOUNT concerns the value of R, the point of slope discontinuity. Although the model provides a plausible mechanism for *what* leads to the slope change (e.g., marking and addition), it is silent on *why* there is an upper limit. R could take on any value with the inclusion of additional PDT's, PDB's, and PDAB's and an increase in STM. However, if the template matching productions are interpreted as a PS(G) approximation to visual images of dot configurations, then some plausible reasons for the low upper limit of subitizing come to mind. For example, the "true" templates stored in LTM might consist of all unique geometrical configurations of n dots. For $n=1$ or 2, there is 1; for $n=3$, there are 2 (triangle and line); for $n=4$, there are 4 (line, triangle, quadrilateral, star). For $n=5$, the possible configurations abruptly get quite numerous. The increase in complexity as a function of n for these "visual" templates is much more rapid than the linear increase necessitated by simply adding new productions and enlarging STM.

These speculations have ontogenetic implications which we are exploring in our current experiments with children's quantification processes. They also suggest further experiments with adults. However, this short paper is not the place to do more than raise the questions. Only the continued interaction between theory building and data collection can resolve them. We have attempted to indicate in this paper that models of this form, because of their increased precision, improve our ability both to account for existing empirical facts and to efficiently search for additional ones.

References

Groen, G. J., & Parkman, J. M.   A chronometric analysis of simple addition. *Psychological Review*, 1972, 79, 329–343.

Klahr, D.   Production systems for quantification. Unpublished working paper, Graduate School of Industrial Administration, Carnegie-Mellon University, 1972.

Klahr, D., & Wallace, J. G.   Class inclusion processes. In S. Farnham-Diggory (Ed.), *Information processing in children*. New York: Academic Press, 1972.

Klahr, D., & Wallace, J. G.   The role of quantification operators in the development of conservation of quantity. *Cognitive Psychology*, 1973, in press.

Newell, A.   On the representation of problems. *Computer science research review*, 1966, 18–33.   Pittsburgh: Carnegie Institute of Technology.

Newell, A.   A theoretical exploration of mechanisms for coding the stimulus. In A. W. Melton & E. Martin (Eds.), *Coding processes in human memory*. Washington, D. C.:   Winston & Sons, 1972.

Newell, A., & Simon, H. A.   *Human problem solving*. Englewood Cliffs, N. J.:   Prentice-Hall, 1972.

Simon, H. A., & Barenfeld, M.   Information processing analysis of perceptual processes in problem solving. *Psychological Review*, 1969, 76, 473–483.

Sternberg, S.   Retrieval of contextual information from memory. *Psychonomic Science*, 1967, 8, 55–56.

Acknowledgments

This is a part of a larger research program in collaboration with J. G. Wallace.   I have been greatly assisted in this effort by Allen Newell.   He has generously contributed to my understanding of the details of the use of PSG and the general style of this (rather difficult) form of "programming."   These programs were run on the PDP-10 at C-MU's Computer Science Department.

AUTHOR INDEX

Numbers in italics refer to the pages on which the complete references are listed.

A

Abelson, R. P., 112, *173*
Adams, J. A., 62, *67*
Alekhine, A., 216, *279*
Armstrong, D. M., 76, *173*
Arnheim, R., 35, *67*
Atkinson, R. C., 297, *306, 313, 380*
Atkinson, R. L., 313, *380*
Attneave, F., 64, *67,* 126, *173*
Audley, R. J., 342, 344, 345, *378*
Averbach, E., 7, 22, *32*

B

Baddeley, A. D., 195, *213*
Ball, W. W. R., 179, *212*
Barclay, J. R., 385, 428, *435,* 453, *458*
Barenfeld, M., 245, 249, *281,* 545, *546*
Bartlett, F. C., 35, *67,* 76, *173*
Baylor, G. W., 270, 273, *279*
Beaver, W. S., 62, *73*
Beckwith, M., 7, 9, 24, *32*
Begg, I., 408, *434*
Bell, C. G., 466, *525*
Beller, H. K., 45, *67*
Bem, S. L., 334, *378*
Benson, B., 64, *67*
Berkeley, G., 62, *67*
Bierwisch, M., 336, *378,* 442, *458*
Blecker, D., 114, *173*
Blumenthal, A. L., 421, *435*
Bobrow, S. A., 432, *435*
Bogen, J. E., 79, *173*
Boies, S. J., 38, 54, 56, *68, 71,* 81, 82, *174,* 202, 204, 206, *213*
Boucher, J., 446, *458*
Bourne, L., 35, *68*
Bower, G. H., 36, *68, 173,* 402, 432, *435*

B (continued)

Brand, J., 39, *68*
Bransford, J. D., 385, 386, 391, 393, 408, 410, 428, *435, 436,* 453, *458*
Briggs, G. E., 53, 59, *72,* 199, *213*
Broadbent, D. E., 301, *306, 307*
Brooks, L. R., 35, *68,* 79, *173,* 179, *212,* 278, *279*
Bruchon, M., 62, *68*
Brune, K. H., 179, *212*
Bruner, J. S., 36, *68*
Burrows, D., 45, *68*
Byrnes, D. L., 289, *308*

C

Calfee, R. C., 199, *212*
Carpenter, P. A., 312, 319, 320, 323, 326, 327, 341, 357, *378, 380,* 446, *459*
Carter, B., 195, *213*
Carter-Sobell, L., 416, *437*
Cavanagh, J. P., 41, *68,* 271, *279,* 507, *525*
Chafe, W. L., 452, *458*
Chase, W. G., 21, *32,* 41, *68,* 105, 137, *173,* 199, *212,* 215, 218, 247, 248, 273, 274, *279,* 296, *307,* 312, 319, 320, 327, 329, 331, *379,* 433, *435,* 441, 457, *458,* 502, *525*
Chen, S. S., 76, *174*
Chi, M. T. H., 9, 20, *32*
Chipman, S., 77, 87, 141, *175,* 179, *213*
Chomsky, N., 383, *435*
Clark, E. V., 377, *379, 380*
Clark, H. H., 37, 105, 137, *173,* 272, 273, 274, *279,* 296, *307,* 312, 316, 319, 320, 327, 328, 329, 331, 335, 336, 337, 341, 357, 366, 377, *379,* 433, *435,* 441, 457, *458*
Cleary, J., 408, *436*
Clifton, C., 53, 59, *69,* 199, *212*

Cohen, G., 46, *68,* 195, *212*
Coles, L. S., 273, *280*
Collins, A. M., 35, *68,* 433, *435, 436*
Coltheart, M., 38, *68*
Connolly, K., 63, 65, *68, 70*
Conrad, C., 36, 37, 46, *71*
Conrad, R., 52, *69*
Crowder, R. G., 467, *525*
Cruse, D., 53, 59, *69,* 199, *212*

D

Danks, J. H., 36, *69*
Dansereau, D., 304, *307, 520, 525*
Dantzig, T., 177, *212*
de Groot, A., 215, 238, *280,* 304, *307*
Dement, W. C., 76, *173*
DeSoto, C. B., 37, *69,* 271, *280*
Doll, T. J., 410
Donaldson, W., 451, *459*
Dooling, D. J., 401, 433, *436*

E

Egeth, H., 114, *173*
Eichelman, W. H., 45, 53, *69, 71,* 81, 82, *174,* 202, 204, 206, *213*
Eisenberg, K., 334, *380,* 424, *436*
Elias, M. F., 57, *69*
Ellis, S. H., 21, *32,* 345, *379*
Ells, J. G., 62, *70*
Ernest, C. H., 61, *70*

F

Feigenbaum, E. A., 247, *280*
Feng, C., 85, *175,* 180, *213*
Fillmore, C. J., 387, 392, 423, *436*
Fishman, J. A., 439, *458*
Flavell, J. H., 31, *33*
Flores d'Arcais, G. B., 341, 348, *380*
Francis, W., 342, *380*
Franks, J. J., 385, 428, *435,* 453, *458*
Frase, L. T., 453, *458*
Freeman, P., 469, *525*

Freijda, N., 35, *69*
Freud, S., 76, *173*
Frost, N. H., 52, *69,* 305, *307*
Furth, H. G., 67, *69*
Fusella, V., 78, *174,* 278, *280*

G

Galton, F., 35, *69*
Gardner, J. T., 38, *72*
Garner, W. R., 7, 8, 9, *34,* 275, *280*
Gazzaniga, M. S., 79, *173,* 195, *212*
Gibson, E. J., 38, 39, 40, *69*
Gibson, J. J., 442, *458*
Gilmartin, K., 244, *281,* 300, *308*
Glucksburg, S., 36, *69*
Goetz, E. T., 62, *67*
Goodnow, J. J., 63, 64, *70*
Gordon, P. E., 77, *174*
Gould, J., 20, *33*
Green, B. F., 305, *307*
Greenberg, J. H., 336, 353, *380*
Greenfield, P. M., *68*
Gregg, L. W., 24, *34,* 502, *525*
Groen, G. J., 26, 28, *33, 34,* 537, *546*

H

Hadamard, J., 178, *212*
Hall, C. S., 76, *173*
Handel, S., 37, *69,* 271, *280*
Harris, C. S., 62, *72*
Hay, L., 62, *68*
Heimer, W., 126, *174*
Herman, L. M., 62, *71*
Higgins, E. T., 441, *458*
Hilgard, E. R., 313, *380*
Hubel, D. H., 292, *307*
Hunt, E., 305, *307,* 444, *458*
Huttenlocher, J., 37, *70,* 334, *380,* 424, *436,* 441, *458*
Hyde, T. S., 432, *436*

I

Inhelder, B., 36, 62, *71*

J

Jenkins, J. J., 432, *436, 437,* 443, *458*
Jenson, E. M., 7, 8, 9, 23, *33*
Jevons, W. S., 5, *33*
Johnsen, A. M., 53, 59, *72,* 199, *212*
Johnson, E. S., 301, *307*
Johnson, M. K., 386, 391, 393, 408, 410, *435, 436*
Johnson, N. F., 467, *525*
Johnston, C. D., 432, *437*
Jones, B., 63, 65, *68, 70*
Just, M. A., 312, 319, 320, 323, 326, 327, 341, 357, *378, 380,* 446, *459*

K

Katz, J. J., 428, *437*
Kaufman, E. L., 5, 7, 8, 30, *33*
Keele, S. W., 35, 38, 62, 63, *70, 71*
Kinsbourne, M., 57, *69, 79, 174*
Kintsch, W., 273, 274, *280,* 387, *437*
Klahr, D., 3, 4, 9, 31, *33,* 303, *307,* 527, 535, *546*
Klatzky, R. L., 195, 196, *212, 377, 380*
Klima, E. S., 323, *380*
Koffka, K., 76, *174*
Köhler, W., 76, *174*
Kohlers, P., 88, *174*
Konick, A. F., 62, *71*
Konorski, J., 60, *70*
Krueger, L., 39, *70*
Kucera, H., 342, *380*

L

Laabs, G. J., 62, 63, *70*
Lachman, R., 401, *436*
Landauer, T., 24, *33*
Langendoen, D. T., 392, 423, *436*
Lapinsky, S., 410
Lasker, E., 262, *280*
Ledlow, A., 195, *213*
Levy, J., 79, *175*
Lewis, J., 36, 37, 46, *71*
Light, L. L., 416, *437*
Lively, B., 45, *70*
London, M., 37, *69,* 271, *280*

Lord, M. W., 5, 7, 8, 30, *33*
Lunneborg, C., 305, *307*

M

Macken, M., 377, *380*
Mandler, G., 403, *437*
Marin, J., 444, *458*
Marks, D. F., 345, *380*
Marks, L. E., 404, *437*
Marshall, P. H., 62, *67*
McCracken, D., 469, *525*
McLean, R. S., 502, *525*
Metzler, J., 60, *72,* 85, 89, 95, 121, 140, 143, 163, *175, 213*
Millar, S., 63, 65, *70*
Miller, G. A., 217, *280,* 402, 404, *437,* 466, *525*
Mitchell, R. F., 195, 199, *213*
Morton. J., 467, *525*

N

Neisser, U., 36, 37, 39, *70*
Newell, A., 31, 32, *33, 34,* 35, *70,* 212, *213,* 250, 269, 273, 275, *280,* 293, 300, 301, 304, 305, *307, 308,* 465, 466, 469, 470, 471, 515, 517, 521, *525,* 527, 528, 529, 536, 544, *546*
Nielson, G. D., 52, *72*
Norman, D. A., 35, *70,* 449, *459,* 466, *526*
Nyberg, S., 408, *436*

O

Oliver, R. R., *68*
Olshavsky, R. W., 24, *34*
Olson, D. R., 405, *437,* 440, *459*
Olson, R. K., 126, *173*
Osgood, C. E., 446, *458*
Osler, S., 396, 416, *438*

P

Paivio, A., 36, 61, 67, *70,* 76, *174,* 402, 408, *434, 437*

Parkinson, S. R., 52, *71*, 195, *213*
Parkman, J. M., 26, 28, *33, 34,* 339, *381,*
    537, *546*
Pascual-Leone, J., 32, *34*
Peoples, D. R., 20, *33*
Pepper, R. L., 62, *71*
Perkins, D. N., 88, *174*
Phillips, W. A., 195, *213*
Piaget, J., 3, *34,* 36, 62, *71*
Posner, M. I., 35, 36, 37, 38, 46, 54, 60, 62,
    63, 64, *72,* 81, 82, *174,* 179, 195, 199,
    202, 204, *213*
Postal, P. M., 428, *437*
Potts, G., 391, *437*

Q

Quillian, M. R., 35, *68,* 273, *280,* 433, *435,*
    436

R

Radojcic, M., 265, *280*
Rawlings, E. I., 76, *174*
Rawlings, I. L., 76, *174*
Reese, E. P., 7, 8, 9, 23, *33*
Reese, T. W., 5, 7, 8, 9, 23, 30, *33*
Reinfeld, F., 223, 241, 242, 244, *280*
Reitman, W., 3, *34*
Restle, F., 7, 9, 24, *32*
Richardson, A., 75, *174*
Robertson, G., 469, *525*
Rock, I., 62, *72,* 126, *174*
Rogers, M., 58, *72*
Rollins, H., 105, 137, *173,* 318, 319, 327,
    381, 444, *459*
Rossman, E., *71*
Rundell, O. H., 62, *73*

S

Sachs, J., 424, 428, *437*
Saltzman, I. J., 7, 8, 9, *34*
Sanford, B. J., 45, *70*
Scarborough, Ð. L., 511, *526*
Schlosberg, H., 7, 9, *34*
Scurrah, M. J., 304, *308*
Segal, S. J., 77, 78, *174,* 278, *280*

Shagan, J., 63, *72*
Shaughnessy, E., 105, 138, *175,* 318, 319,
    327, *381,* 444, *459*
Shepard, R. N., 60, *72,* 77, 79, 84, 85, 87,
    88, 89, 90, 95, 104, 121, 123, 140, 141,
    143, 163, *174, 175,* 178, 180, *213*
Shiffrin, R. M., 38, *72,* 297, *306*
Simon, H. A., 32, *34,* 35, *70,* 211, *213,* 215,
    218, 244, 245, 247, 248, 249, 250, 269,
    273, 275, *279, 280, 281,* 293, 300, 301,
    304, *308,* 457, *459,* 465, 515, *525,* 527,
    528, 529, 545, *546*
Skemp, R. R., 177, *213*
Slobin, D. I., 424, *437,* 455, *459*
Smart, J. J. C., 76, *175*
Smith, E. E., 52, *72*
Snyder, C. R. R., 36, 60, 61, *72*
Soloman, S., 386, *436*
Spence, M. T., 62, *73*
Sperling, G. A., 37, *72,* 270, 277, *281,* 467,
    525
Sperry, R. W., 79, *173, 175*
Stark, L., 292, *308*
Stelmach, G. E., 62, *72*
Sternberg, S., 21, *34,* 41, *72,* 271, *281,* 472,
    496, 511, 514, 519, *525, 526,* 537, *546*
Stone, P., 444, *458*
Strauss, S., 334, *380,* 424, *436*
Swanson, J. M., 53, 59, *72,* 195, 199, *213*
Syer, H. W., 179, *214*

T

Taylor, R. L., *71,* 81, 82, *174,* 202, 204,
    206, *213*
Thompson, D. M., 416, *438*
Trabasso, T., 105, 137, *173,* 318, 319, 327,
    381, 433, *438,* 444, 446, 454, 457, *459*
Tukey, J. W., 112, *173*
Tulving, E., 396, 402, 416, *438,* 451, *459*
Turnbull, E., 39, *72*
Tversky, B., 52, 57, *72,* 202, 206, *214*

V

Van de Castle, R. L., 76, *173*
Volkman, J., 5, 7, 8, 30, *33*
Von Szeliski, 5, 23, *34*

W

Wagner, D. A., 304, *308*
Wald, J., 454, *459*
Wallace, C. P., 342, 344, 345, *378*
Wallace, J. G., 3, 4, 9, 31, *33,* 303, *307,*
  527, 535, *546*
Warren, R., 36, 38, 59, *72, 73*
Wattenbarger, B., 42, 51, *73*
Waugh, N., 466, *526*
Weiner, S. L., 334, *380,* 424, *436*
Weisberg, R. W., 36, *69*
Wertheimer, M., 25, *34*
West, L. J., 76, *175*
Whorf, B. L., 35, 67, *73,* 440, *459*

Wickelgren, W. A., 78, *175*
Wiesel, T. N., 292, *307*
Williams, H. L., 62, *73*
Williams, T. G., 273, *281*
Wilson, M., 62, *72*
Wingfield, A., 289, *308*
Winikoff, A., 270, *281*
Winograd, T., 305, *308*
Woodworth, R. W., 7, 9, *34*

Y

Yilk, M. D., 76, *174*
Yonas, A., 39, 40, *69*

SUBJECT INDEX

A

Addition
 in enumeration, 24, 25, 27-29
 implicit rate of, 26, 28, 29
 production system model of, 537-545
 short-term memory scanning model of, 29
Active memory, *see* Short-term memory
Apprehension, *see* Subitizing

C

Class inclusion, 3, 4
Code
 coordination, 46-50
 kinesthetic, 62-66
 motor, 35
 multiple, 43-46
 retention of visual and kinesthetic, 63-65
 rivalry of visual and name, 52-54
 verbal, 35
 visual, 35, 62-66
Cognitive development, 3, 31
Comparatives, 314, 335-340, 442
 brighter-darker, 342-345
 longer-shorter, 345-350
Congruity effect, 342-345, 371
Conservation
 of quantity, 4
 of transitivity, 4
Control structure, 297-298, 301-302, 464-465
Conversion strategies, 446-447
Comprehension
 and context, 415-416, 449
 and images, 453
 and knowledge acquisition, 429-433
 and linguistic inferences, 384-392, 422-427, 450-453

 of consequences of input events, 388-389
 of instruments to carry out acts, 386-388
 of relations between two events, 389-392
 of spatial relations, 384-386
 and prior knowledge, 392-414, 422-424, 439-441, 448-453
 of familiar contexts, 400-402, 407-408
 of irrelevant contexts, 409-414
 of novel contexts, 392-400, 406-407
 of relations between two events, 403-405
 and subsequent context (recomprehension), 416-420
Counting, 5, 7, 23-29, 527, 538-545
 in children, 24, 28
 implicit rate of, 15-23, 26-29
 points, 185-186
 production system model of, 538-545

D

Decoding hypothesis, 484-492, 496-506
Dichotic listening, 289-290

E

Elementary Perceiver and Memorizer
 (EPAM), of chess positions, 244-252
Encoding, 37-42
Estimation, 5, 8, 29-31
Eye movements
 of chess patterns, 245
 and sentence-picture verifications, 326
 and subitizing, 19-20, 295

G

Generation
  attention demands of, 57-60
  of auditory images, 54-57, 81-82
  and perception, 60-61
  of visual images, 54-57, 58-59, 81-82,
    181-183, 202-207
Grouping
  in enumeration, 24, 27
  Gestalt principles of, 25

I

Iconic memory, *see* Short-term visual store
Imagery
  and perception, 60
  and language comprehension, 453
Information processing models, 300-305
  of chess perception, 244-252
  of mental rotation, 134-139
  of quantification, 20-31
  of sentence-picture verifications, 455-457
Item recognition task, *see* Short-term
    memory scanning

K

Knight's tour, 265-267

L

Language
  and cognition, 35, 434, 439-441, 454-457
  and perception, 311-317, 328-329,
    335-342, 349-354, 357, 360-361,
    364-367, 370, 372, 374-378, 383-384,
    434, 439-448, 454-457
Laterality, of physical vs name matches,
    194-202
Linguistic relativity hypothesis, *see*
    Whorfian hypothesis
Locatives, 314, 328-335, 447
  above-below, 312, 314, 329-335
  and perception of the 3-dimensional world,
    328-329, 335, 341
Long-term memory
  of chess games, 258-261

of chess patterns, 244-258
and language comprehension, 428-449
of PSG, 467-468

M

Marking, 336-342, 351, 357, 359, 364, 369,
    377, 441-442; *see also* Locatives and
    Comparatives
  scanning model of, 339-341
Mental images, *see also* Visual images
  experimental paradigms for investigating,
    77-85
    mental transformations, 82-85
    selective interference, 77-80
    selective reduction of reaction times,
      80-82
  nature versus function of, 76-77
Mental multiplication, 304
Mental rotation
  information processing model of, 134-139
  of letters, 109, 121-125, 128-133,
    149-156, 168, 207-209
  of three-dimensional objects, 61, 85-92,
    109, 121-125
Method of loci, 421-422
Min model, *see* Addition, implicit rate of
Mind's eye, in chess, 269, 270, 271-272,
    275-278

N

Negation, 314, 317-328
  absent-present, 319-322, 327
  few-many, 322-326, 446-447
  of a picture code, 319-322
  role in picture coding, 327-328

P

Perceptual structures, *see* Propositional
    structures
Precategorical acoustic storage (PAS), 467
Primary memory, 466
Production system
  of addition, 537-545
  of chess perception, 250-251, 269

of counting, 538-545
of memory span, 499-506
PSG (version G), 465-471, 529-533
  buffer memory of, 477-478
  long-term memory of, 467-468
  reaction time model of, 478-481,
    492-493
of short-term memory scanning, 472-496
of subitizing, 533-545
Production systems, 32, 301-302, 463-465,
  528-533
  completeness of, 517-520
  as psychological theories, 515-524
  and subject methods, 520-521
Propositional structures, 273-275, 312

Q

Quantification
  models for, 20-31, 533-545
  operators, 3, 4-9, 303-304
Quantitative symbols, 4, 29
  in long-term memory, 20, 24, 29
  in short-term memory, 20

R

Recency, and serial position, 44
Reference point, see Locatives and
  Comparatives
Rehearsal and translation, 51-61

S

Search, in chess, 215-217, 269-271
Secondary memory, 466
Sentence-picture verifications, 311-378,
  454-457
Short-term memory
  capacity, 14
    in chess, 217, 245-252
    developmental changes in 31-32
  for chess moves, 261-264
  for chess patterns, 215-240
  of PSG, 466-467, 499-504
  recognition vs recall, 52-53
  scanning, 14, 20, 23, 29, 41, 42-51,
    472-473

context recognition, 21
continuous, 511-514
decoding hypothesis of, 484-492,
  496-506
item recognition, 21
production system model of, 472-496
recency effects in, 508-511
and serial position, 21, 44
Short-term visual store, 277, 467
Size transformation, of letters, 209-210
Spatial adjectives, 350-376
  height vs depth: tall-short and deep-
    shallow, 352-364, 444-445, 448
  size vs height and width: large-small,
    tall-short, and wide-narrow, 364-376
Spatial propositions, see locatives
Sternberg task, see Short-term memory
  scanning
Stimulus vs response organization, of chess
  patterns, 240-244
Subitizing, 5, 20-23, 25, 27, 527, 533-545
  confidence judgments, 8
  and eye movements, 19-20, 295
  latency procedure, 8
  production system model of, 533-545
  range, R, 8, 15-23
  slope, B, 8, 15-23, 26
  threshold procedure, 7, 22

V

Visual image, see also Mental images
  combined with sensory image, 181-183,
    189-194, 211, 276
  generation of, 54-57, 58-59, 62-66, 81-82,
    181-183, 202-207
  as mnemonic devices in arithmetic,
    183-185, 211
  and response modality, 79-80
  and signal detection, 77-78
  in thought, 35
Visual search, 39-42
  pre-attentive processes in,
    41, 507-508

W

Whorfian hypothesis, 67, 439

Northern Michigan University

3 1854 001 713 489

EZNO
BF455 S94 1972
Visual information processing; proceedin